Great Books,
Honors Programs,
and Hidden Origins

STUDIES IN THE HISTORY OF EDUCATION
Edward R. Beauchamp, Series Editor

EDUCATIONAL PHILOSOPHY
A History from the Ancient World to Modern America
by Edward J. Power

SCHOOL AND SOCIETY IN VICTORIAN BRITAIN
Joseph Payne and the New World of Education
by Richard Aldrich

DISCIPLINE, MORAL REGULATION, AND SCHOOLING
A Social History
edited by Kate Rousmaniere, Kari Dehli, and Ning de Coninck-Smith

JAPANESE AMERICANS AND CULTURAL CONTINUITY
Maintaining Language and Heritage
by Toyotomi Morimoto

RADICAL HEROES
Gramsci, Freire, and the Politics of Adult Education
by Diana Coben

WOMEN'S EDUCATION IN EARLY MODERN EUROPE
A History, 1500–1800
edited by Barbara J. Whitehead

ESSAYS IN TWENTIETH-CENTURY SOUTHERN EDUCATION
Exceptionalism and Its Limits
edited by Wayne J. Urban

GIRLS' SCHOOLING DURING THE PROGRESSIVE ERA
From Female Scholar to Domesticated Citizen
by Karen Graves

COMMON, DELINQUENT, AND SPECIAL
The Institutional Shape of Special Education
by John Richardson

GENDER, RACE, AND THE NATIONAL EDUCATION ASSOCIATION
Professionalism and Its Permutations
by Wayne J. Urban

TRANSITIONS IN AMERICAN EDUCATION
A Social History of Teaching
by Donald H. Parkerson and Jo Ann Parkerson

WHEREVER I GO I WILL ALWAYS BE A LOYAL AMERICAN
Schooling Seattle's Japanese Americans during World War II
by Yoon K. Pak

CHARTERED SCHOOLS
Two Hundred Years of Independent Academies in the United States, 1727–1925
edited by Nancy Beadie and Kim Tolley

CHILDREN OF THE MILL
Schooling and Society in Gary, Indiana, 1906–1960
by Ronald D. Cohen

ANTI-SEMITISM AND SCHOOLING UNDER THE THIRD REICH
by Gregory Paul Wegner

THE SCIENCE EDUCATION OF AMERICAN GIRLS
A Historical Perspective
by Kim Tolley

GREAT BOOKS, HONORS PROGRAMS, AND HIDDEN ORIGINS
The Virginia Plan and the University of Virginia in the Liberal Arts Movement
by William N. Haarlow

Great Books, Honors Programs, and Hidden Origins
The Virginia Plan and the University of Virginia in the Liberal Arts Movement

William N. Haarlow

ROUTLEDGEFALMER
NEW YORK AND LONDON

Published in 2003 by
RoutledgeFalmer
29 West 35th Street
New York, NY 10001
www.routledge-ny.com

Published in Great Britain by
RoutledgeFalmer
11 New Fetter Lane
London EC4P 4EE
www.routledgefalmer.com

Copyright © 2003 by Taylor & Francis Books, Inc.

RoutledgeFalmer is an imprint of the Taylor & Francis Group.
Printed in the United States of America on acid-free paper.

All rights reserved. No part of this book may be reprinted or reproduced or utilized in any form or by any electronic, mechanical, or other means, now known or hereafter invented, including photocopying and recording, or in any information storage or retrieval system, without permission in writing from the publishers.

10 9 8 7 6 5 4 3 2 1

Library of Congress Cataloging-in-Publication Data

Haarlow, William Noble.
  Great books, honors programs, and hidden origins : the Virginia Plan and the University of Virginia in the liberal arts movement / William Noble Haarlow.
    p. cm. — (Studies in the history of education)
  Includes bibliographical references and index.
  ISBN 0-415-93509-1
  1. University of Virginia—Curricula—History. 2. Education, Humanistic—Curricula—History. 3. Universities and colleges—Curricula—United States—History. I. Title. II. Studies in the history of education (RoutledgeFalmer (Firm))

LD5672.H33 2003
378.755'481—dc21

2003046555

Series Preface

The RoutledgeFalmer Studies in the History of Education series includes not only volumes on the history of American and Western education, but also on the history of the development of education in non-Western societies. A major goal of this series is to provide new interpretations of educational history that are based on the best recent scholarship; each volume will provide an original analysis and interpretation of the topic under consideration. A wide variety of methodological approaches from the traditional to the innovative are used. In addition, this series especially welcomes studies that focus not only on schools but also on education as defined by Harvard historian Bernard Bailyn: "the transmission of culture across generations."

The major criteria for inclusion are (a) a manuscript of the highest quality and (b) a topic of importance to understanding the field. The editor is open to readers' suggestions and looks forward to a long-term dialogue with them on the future direction of the series.

Edward R. Beauchamp

Dedicated to my mother, Lynne R. Haarlow,
and the memory of my father, A. W. Haarlow III

Contents

Acknowledgments		ix
Introduction	Virginia, Columbia, Chicago, St. John's, and the Liberal Arts Movement	1
Chapter 1	Before the Virginia Plan	15
Chapter 2	The University of Virginia and the Creation of the Virginia Plan	41
Chapter 3	The Virginia Plan and Its Reception at Virginia	69
Chapter 4	Developments at Virginia, Chicago, and St. John's	101
Chapter 5	Great Plans, Modest Accomplishments	135
Chapter 6	The Virginia Plan at Virginia	171
Conclusion	An Unfinished Story	197
Sources		203
Notes		205
Bibliography		243
Index		247

Acknowledgments

The core of this book was originally my dissertation. Additional interviews, archival research, and revisions have ameliorated the work, but my first debt is to the faculty of the Center for the Study of Higher Education at the University of Virginia. I am foremost grateful to my advisor, Jennings L. Wagoner, Jr., who provided unwavering encouragement, knowledge, and insight during my graduate years and since. Dr. Wagoner has taught me much of what it means to be an historian, and how to be an exemplary teacher, mentor, colleague, and friend. Working with Dr. Wagoner has been, and continues to be, a privilege and honor in the best Jeffersonian senses of these words. Drs. Annette Gibbs, Jay Chronister, and Alton Taylor all provided support, encouragement, and direction. Dean David Breneman generously gave his time and resources during my time as his intern and later when he served on my doctoral committee. Sam Kellams provided initial direction and insight on this study while Brian Pusser rose to the occasion of a late committee appointment with voluminous editing and undaunted energy. Peter Onuf, chairman emeritus of the History Department, likewise served on my doctoral committee with patience, insight, and good humor.

I am indebted to the individuals I was fortunate enough to interview in Charlottesville, Chicago, New York, and Washington, D. C. Their recollections and insight aided in piecing together this history and made it come alive. In Charlottesville, Samuel A. (Pete) Anderson, II, architect for the University of Virginia; Staige D. Blackford, editor of the *Virginia Quarterly Review* at the University of Virginia; and George B. Thomas, professor of philosophy emeritus at the University of Virginia, were all students of Stringfellow Barr at Virginia in the early 1950s. Their recollections of Barr and his great books classes were helpful in pulling together the specifics of that time. In particular, Thomas provided invaluable insight into the Virginia Plan as he was one of a handful of students to take both parts of the Virginia Plan curriculum. Thomas also later served as the director of the Honors Program as a Virginia professor. Thomas's colleague, philosophy professor John Marshall, provided ample details on the philosophy honors program, having served as its director for multiple years. I was fortunate to be able to talk with the two official University of Virginia Historians, both now emeritus: Charles E. (Chick) Moran and psychology professor Raymond C. Bice. Moran offered insight into Barr from several perspectives: first as Barr's student at Virginia in the 1930s, later as a relative of Barr's by marriage, and finally as the first official University of Virginia Historian. Bice followed Moran in the historian position. In addition to his knowledge of Virginia history, Bice's service in the late 1940s and early 1950s on the Lower Division Committee responsible for implementing the full Virginia Plan proved very helpful. Classics professor emeritus Arthur F. Stocker offered valuable insight into Virginia culture in the 1950s and the faculty perspectives at that time. L. Harvey Poe, Jr. was a student of Scott Buchanan's at Virginia in the 1930s and a tutor at St. John's College in the 1940s. His past acquaintance with Barr and Buchanan and continuing interest in the great books and their place at Virginia was most enlightening.

I received important help from scholars outside the University of Virginia. Warden Alan Ryan of New College, Oxford University was helpful in providing details of the English tutorial system both in the past and present. Sidney Hyman, senior fellow at the Great Books Foundation in Chicago, provided lively recollections of his experience as a student in Hutchins' and Adler's great books honors course at the University of Chicago in the 1930s and the great books movement over the course of the twentieth century. Professor Carol Rigolot, Executive Director of the Princeton University Council of the Humanities, read the dissertation and provided thoughtful insights. I wish also to acknowledge with sincere gratitude the multiple meetings, telephone conversations, and critical correspondence with Charles A. Nelson and Chauncey G. Olinger, Jr. Nelson served as Barr's intern at St. John's in the mid-1940s. He is Visitor Emeritus and former chairman of the Board of Visitors and Governors of St. John's College, and a biographer of Barr and Buchanan. Nelson provided great insight and practical assistance in my work. His knowledge of and passion for the great books is matched by Chauncey G. Olinger, Jr.'s knowledge of and passion for the honors tutorial system at Virginia. As a student of Barr's at Virginia in the 1950s and a graduate of the Virginia honors program in philosophy, Olinger has aided me with guidance, documentation, and an appreciation for the promise of the Virginia Plan. Their help with my research has been invaluable.

I am grateful to the archivists in Special Collections at Alderman Library at the University of Virginia, in Special Collections at Regenstein Library at the University of Chicago, and Special Collections at Greenfield Library at St. John's College. In particular I wish to acknowledge the assistance of Lisa Richmond, Library Director, St. John's College. Given the wealth of archival material at St. John's, her continuing assistance was greatly appreciated. Also, R. J. Rockefeller at the Maryland State Archives and the archivists at the Wisconsin State Archives made my time in Annapolis and Madison both directed and productive. Travel for archival research and interviews was aided by financial assistance from a Curry School of Education Dissertation Research Award and a Gibbs Research and Publication Award.

My time at Mr. Jefferson's University was greatly enriched by my fellow doctoral students—especially Gene Crume, Chris Foley, Don Hasseltine, Sam Miller, Steve Titus, and Ben Boggs. They provided comic relief, frank appraisal, commentary and, most important, steadfast friendship. Earlier encouragement and insight came from professors Carol Rigolot, James Ward Smith, John F. Wilson, and the Rev. Frederick H. Borsch at Princeton University. Thanks also to the following professors at the University of Chicago: Philip Jackson, John MacAloon, Martin Marty, and especially Barry Karl, who encouraged me to follow an academic career.

Finally, I wish to thank my family, particularly my parents; they have always been my first teachers. To my son Bill, I say thank you for reminding me of the most important things in life. To my wife Laurel, I can say with true gratitude that I hope you know how much your love and unending support mean to me and to everything that I do.

Chicago, Illinois
April 2003

Introduction
Virginia, Columbia, Chicago, St. John's, and the Liberal Arts Movement

"The Virginia Plan deserves to be where people can inspect it."
—Stringfellow Barr

Toward the end of the 1930s, with the Depression continuing at home and the possibility of war threatening from abroad, Walter Lippmann saw a ray of hope in the "Great Books" program that had recently been inaugurated at St. John's College in Annapolis, Maryland. Lippmann praised the return to the classics at St. John's as holding out promise that the principles that had guided the Founding Fathers at the time of the nation's birth might once again be revived. He was encouraged that at St. John's and a scattering of other institutions of higher education a rebirth of traditional liberal learning was underway. During the dark winter of 1938 Lippmann proclaimed in the pages of the *New York Herald Tribune* that:

> ... in this country and abroad there are men who see that the onset of barbarism must be met not only by programs of rearmament, but by another revival of learning. It is the fact, moreover, that after tentative beginnings in several of the American universities, Columbia, Virginia, and Chicago, a revival is actually begun—is not merely desired, talked about, and projected, but is in operation with teachers and students and a carefully planned course of study.... I venture to believe that... in the future men will point to St. John's College and say that there was the seed-bed of the American Renaissance.[1]

Of the institutions acknowledged by Lippmann, the twentieth-century role of the University of Virginia in the revival of "traditional" liberal arts undergraduate education is the least studied and the least well understood. In contrast, Columbia, Chicago, and St. John's have gained notoriety for their liberal education programs. Indeed, as noted below, numerous writers and historians have addressed the importance of these schools and their significance in the liberal arts movement: a reform effort that, from the 1930s through the 1950s, rejected the didactic lecture and the pervasive electivism in American collegiate education. Instead the leaders of the liberal arts movement argued in favor of a curricular philosophy that, to varying degrees at different institutions, promoted a more prescribed curriculum based on the study of the great books of the western canon and a pedagogy that emphasized honors seminar and tutorial work conducted in a dialectical manner.[2]

Columbia University was the first institution of higher learning in the country to offer a liberal arts great books course: John Erskine's "General Honors" course which began in 1920. Since the late 1930s Columbia has required its undergraduates to take two great books courses: Literature Humanities and Contemporary Civilization. These "Western civilization" surveys have been at the center of Columbia's well-known core curriculum for decades; indeed, David Denby's 1996 account of these courses in *Great Books: My Adventures with Homer, Rousseau, Woolf, and Other Indestructible Writers of the Western World,* was a national bestseller. The Literature Humanities course, which debuted in the 1937–38 academic year, is "devoted to a standard selection of European literary masterpieces." Similarly, Contemporary Civilization, which began in 1919 as a topical survey of the social sciences, evolved to offer "a selection of philosophical and social-theory masterpieces."[3] In addition to Denby's popular account, the institutional history of Columbia's core curriculum has received scholarly attention from Justus Buchler, Daniel Bell, Lionel Trilling, Gerald Graff, and Timothy Cross.[4]

Another leading institution, the University of Chicago, has held an imposing position in American higher education since its founding in 1892. Chicago calls itself "the teacher of teachers" and boasts the most Nobel Prize winners of any school in the world. William Rainey Harper, Robert Maynard Hutchins, the Manhattan Project, the undergraduate "common core" curriculum, the "Chicago schools" of economics, jurisprudence, and sociology—all of these have contributed to Chicago's distinctive place in American higher education. Modifications to the common core, instituted in the autumn of 1999, raised a storm of controversy among some nationally known academicians who were concerned that the core, with its emphasis on Western classics, would be watered down. The controversy not only made professional publications, but also the front page of the *New York Times*. In addition to this topical attention, numerous scholarly and autobiographical accounts of Chicago's role in liberal arts education have been written by Michael Harris, Robert Hutchins, Mortimer Adler, Harry Ashemore, Milton Mayer, William McNeill, Mary Ann Dzuback, and others.[5]

Though less prestigious and far from mainstream, St. John's College has likewise distinguished itself in academia with its prescribed curriculum based entirely on the liberal arts and the Western canon. Proudly distancing itself from the dominant philosophies of higher education, St. John's represents an unconventional approach to higher education. First implemented in the 1937–38 academic year (the same year as Columbia's Literature Humanities course), St. John's "New Program," a four-year-all-required curriculum based on the great books, continues today at the college's campuses in Annapolis, Maryland and Santa Fe, New Mexico. Harris Wofford, Charles Nelson, Richard

Miller, and J. Winfree Smith have all written about the creation and evolution of the great books curriculum at St. John's.[6]

The influence of Columbia, Chicago, and St. John's in the promotion of "traditional" conceptions of liberal learning is well documented. These institutions, or at least individuals associated with them, advanced a philosophy of education that was centered on twentieth-century reconstructions of the traditional liberal arts that had their origin in the thought of classical antiquity and the Middle Ages. This philosophy of education was often manifest in the promotion of the great books as the primary material, and seminar dialectical discussion as the pedagogical means, thought most appropriate for collegiate education.

But what about the role of the University of Virginia? There have been revolutionary curricular innovations and reforms at Virginia since its founding in 1819 by Thomas Jefferson. Yet the developments initiated at Virginia in the 1930s are especially significant, albeit under-appreciated, in terms of the twentieth-century curricular history of American higher education. This book argues that the University of Virginia and its 1935 "Virginia Plan" for curricular reform are integral to the liberal arts movement that challenged and reshaped American curricula in the 1930s, 40s, and 50s and which continues to inform curricular debates today. Drawing on earlier efforts at Columbia and Chicago, part of the Virginia Plan, described in Appendix A to the Plan, expanded the Western canon and its influence first by making mathematical and scientific classics integral to the study of great books and then, via Virginia professors Stringfellow Barr and Scott Buchanan, by taking this augmented philosophy back to Chicago, St. John's, and other institutions. By adopting the second part of the Virginia Plan, explicated as Appendix B to the Plan, the University of Virginia, under the leadership of professor Robert Gooch, also introduced honors "Oxbridge"-style tutorial work to American public higher education. In short, Virginia played a significant and formative role in the liberal arts movement.

In spite of these unique contributions, the University of Virginia's significance in the liberal arts movement is not widely understood today. For example, in *Orators and Philosophers: A History of the Idea of Liberal Education*, historian Bruce Kimball asserted that in accounts of liberal education, "the big names are always noted—Aydelotte, Meiklejohn, Hutchins; Chicago, Columbia, Harvard . . . ."[7] Likewise, historians John Brubacher and Willis Rudy in their book *Higher Education in Transition: A History of American Colleges and Universities*, wrote that the great books curriculum was "spawned at Columbia, encouraged at Chicago, and actually put into operation at St. John's College in Maryland."[8] As far as they go, these accounts include necessary but also insufficient information, for absent from these accounts are Barr, Buchanan, Gooch, and the University of Virginia. Yet Virginia's twentieth-century curricular reform history makes clear that more attention should be paid to its place in that movement.

Contemporaneous accounts certainly suggest that such inclusion is warranted. Indeed, Walter Lippmann was not the only national figure who had no association with Virginia to acknowledge the role of the University of Virginia in the promotion of liberal learning at that time. In 1944 Frank Aydelotte, the director of the Institute for Advanced Study at Princeton and former president of Swarthmore College, wrote that "honors plans are in operation in a number of our stronger state institutions and . . . two at least, Virginia and Ohio, have taken positions of leadership in the movement." Aydelotte argued further that, "If the faculty of the University of Virginia builds upon the foundations which have been so well laid, the result will be an outstanding example of the possibility of the adaptation of the honors idea to the conditions of a state university."[9] Even newspaper articles of the time acknowledged Virginia's role. A 1946 article on the St. John's great books curriculum noted the well-known program was "organized on the basis of research and planning that was done over a period of years at the University of Virginia and the University of Chicago."[10]

Like the broader historical accounts mentioned above, even more specialized and relatively accurate accounts do not reflect the events or significance argued by Aydelotte. For example, Charles Nelson's edited compendium *Stringfellow Barr: A Centennial Appreciation of His Life and Work*, included The Virginia Plan with Appendix A (the great books scheme), but not Appendix B (the honors tutorial scheme). Yet together these components comprised the entire Virginia Plan which was offered, as its authors argued, "as an integral whole."[11] St. John's chronicler, J. Winfree Smith, acknowledged the honors scheme in his history titled *A Search for the Liberal College: The Beginning of the St. John's Program*, but noted only that the great books scheme proposed in Appendix A was not implemented in Charlottesville during the 1930s when the Virginia Plan was produced. He failed to record that the honors scheme proposed in Appendix B of the Plan was adopted with slight modification at Virginia in 1937.[12] Even the most accurate prior description of the entire Virginia Plan, found in Amy Kass' dissertation *Radical Conservatives for Liberal Education*, included only one sentence on the fate of the two schemes at Virginia in which she noted that the university decided "to accept the last two years of the plan [Appendix B]—providing tutorial work for the better students—and to shelve the general education plan [Appendix A] for the first two years."[13] In light of Virginia's adoption of the honors program in 1937 and Aydelotte's enthusiasm for it seven years later, the relative neglect of the honors tutorial program by later chroniclers inappropriately minimizes its place in the Virginia Plan and in the larger liberal arts movement.

In addition to assembling the full history and import of this curricular reform effort, this study also argues that greater examination of the University of Virginia is warranted because it is more typical of American higher education's interaction with the liberal arts movement than are the other formative institutions: Columbia, Chicago, and St. John's. Specifically, Virginia did not completely reformulate its undergraduate curriculum as was done at St. John's and Chicago in the 1930s and 1940s. Nor did Virginia even go as far as setting up core courses in Western civilization required of all undergraduates as was done at Columbia. Rather, Virginia engaged in substantial conversations with other institutions regarding undergraduate curricular reforms; undertook extensive self-study as manifest by the numerous committees and reports created to study liberal arts education at the university; and ultimately made curricular changes in 1937 and 1951 for a relatively small number of "honors" students. In summary, the University of Virginia, although unique because of its leadership in both its expansion of the great books corpus and its introduction of honors tutorial work in American public higher education, was nevertheless far less radical, and hence more typical of universities across the nation, in terms of the curricular innovations adopted during the height of the liberal arts movement.

Finally, in addition to the arguments that the University of Virginia made formative and unique contributions to the liberal arts movement—and was at the same time more representative than other formative higher education institutions engaged with that movement—the case will be made that the current historical literature contains insufficient formulations to explain fully various institutional reactions to the liberal arts movement, and thus its place in curricular history. For example, in his classic work, *The American College and University*, historian Frederick Rudolph dismissed the great books philosophy attributed to Hutchins, Barr, and Buchanan by stating that "a return to ancient Rome and Greece was not an idea that recommended itself to most educators and observers."[14] Yet it is an oversimplification to suggest that the Virginia Plan was adopted or not solely on the merits, or demerits, of its curricular philosophy; Rudolph's summation is only part of the story, faculty self-interest also played a role. In his 1998 book *As If Learning Mattered*, Rutgers University English professor Richard Miller, drawing on sociologist Pierre Bourdieu, argued that:

> ... Bourdieu's analysis points to the impossibility of radically reforming any highly developed educational system, since that system will, of necessity, be predominantly inhabited by individuals who have profited from that system, who are invested in that system, and whose felt sense of distinction has been established and certified by that system.[15]

Miller's thesis is a useful addition to Rudolph's, but Miller's thesis is also insufficient because of what it omits. Arguments that privilege self-interest factors over philosophical considerations equally miss the point that the truth is more complex than presented in either of these theories singularly or in combination. Both philosophical and self-interest factors played significant and demonstrable roles in the history of the Virginia Plan specifically and in curricular reform generally. But they must be combined with a third group of considerations, namely, institutional factors, before these historical events can be fully understood.

The importance of institutional factors, such as the role of Depression-era finances, is supported by archival evidence. For example, in a 1936 letter to University of Virginia President John Newcomb, the members of the Committee on Honors Courses who authored the Virginia Plan wrote:

> After being advised by the president that he was unable, at the present time, to finance such a plan for the more gifted first and second year students as that outlined in [the great books plan] of this committee's former report, the Committee on Honors Courses desires to recommend the consideration of the plan for third year and final honors set forth in [the honors tutorial plan] of that report. . . . We confidently hope that some means may be found in the near future to put this plan into execution.[16]

Institutional factors such as this have been largely ignored in the historical literature on the liberal arts movement's place in American higher education. This study will address this historiographic omission, arguing that by themselves the theories offered by Rudolph and Miller are important, but they are also incomplete. Only when combined with institutional factors do these theories account for all of the archival evidence. To privilege one type at the expense of the others, as has been done in the previous literature, is to do a disservice to the evidence and distort a legitimate interpretation of this curricular reform movement.

Some Definitions

At this point some definitions of subjects and terms need to be provided. The subject of this book—to a degree the liberal arts movement but essentially the formative and heretofore underappreciated place of the Virginia Plan and the University of Virginia within that movement—needs to be delimited for several reasons. First, as noted earlier in this introduction, the roles and histories of Virginia's sister institutions in the movement have already been discussed. Although relevant corrections and historical context will be provided throughout, this study will not recount history already well documented in the existing literature.

Second, terms such as the liberal arts, the liberal arts movement, general education and liberal education, great books, and honors programs, have been used varyingly over time. Historian Laurence Veysey, for example, argues that in the twentieth century "the liberal arts curriculum" increasingly has been redefined "away from the genteel tradition and toward identification with critical intellect and creativity."[17] This sort of fluidity in the definitions of terms has made certain aspects of American curricular history confusing and consequently greater clarity is desirable. Below are brief definitions for some of the primary concepts discussed in the book. These terms and their contexts will be discussed more fully in the following chapters.

The Liberal Arts and the Liberal Arts Movement

In her 1973 doctoral dissertation titled *Radical Conservatives for Liberal Education*, Amy Apfel Kass argued that the liberal arts movement was "an attempt on the part of a few men to completely transform education by reviving and reconstructing the traditional liberal arts." These academicians thought of themselves as "liberal artists."[18] Writing in 1943 Columbia professor and "liberal artist" Mark Van Doren argued that the liberal arts "are specific arts, clearly distinguished from other arts and performing necessary human functions."[19] What are they by name? Van Doren offered a classical definition:

> Tradition, grounded in more than two millenniums of intellectual history, calls them grammar, rhetoric, and logic; arithmetic, music, geometry, and astronomy.... The liberal arts are seven, but a division occurs between the first three, which Latin Europe called the *trivium* and the last four, which it called the *quadrivium*.[20]

Mortimer Adler later wrote that the *trivium* (grammar, rhetoric, and logic) "taught the arts of reading and writing, of listening and speaking, and of sound thinking." The *quadrivium* (arithmetic, geometry, astronomy, and music ["not audible music," wrote Adler, "but music conceived as a mathematical science"]) "taught the arts of observation, calculation, and measurement, how to apprehend the quantitative aspect of things."[21]

As will be seen, the liberal artists believed that collegiate education in America had lost its way, but because of their rediscovery and reconstruction of the traditional liberal arts, the liberal artists believed they had found a way by which higher education might be saved, namely, by the study and practice of the liberal arts. Kass elaborated that:

> ... Mortimer Adler, Scott Buchanan, and Richard McKeon provided the original impetus and major insight behind the Liberal Arts Movement; Robert Hutchins was its organizer and leader; Hutchins and Stringfellow Barr were its principal spokesmen. Mark Van Doren and Alexander Meiklejohn played important but less central roles.[22]

While the subject and importance of the liberal arts movement will be developed later, one purpose here is to establish that, in the context of the liberal arts movement, the "liberal arts" are the seven traditional liberal arts of the *trivium* and *quadrivium*.

Also, this book concurs with Kass' definition of the liberal arts movement in terms of the individuals involved, and by extension, their era of activity in the academy. Other aspects of her argument will be challenged in the following chapters, but for the purposes of this study, the liberal arts movement, in concert with Kass, is defined as the efforts of the above individuals, along with Virginia professor Robert Gooch, to reform the American collegiate curriculum along the lines of the traditional liberal arts. This movement lasted from the mid–1930s, when the liberal artists first articulated their curricular ideas in comprehensive ways, up through the mid-1950s, by which time the liberal artists had desisted from their attempt to remake their respective institutions and higher education in general. This cessation of direct institutional activity by the original group of liberal artists is important, for although direct manifestations of the movement continued to exist after the 1950s, and to varying degrees still exist at Columbia, Chicago, St. John's, and Virginia, it marks the end of the liberal arts movement. By definition then, the liberal arts movement should not be understood as encompassing any and all attempts since World War I, successful or not, to implement great books courses of study, or honors programs, or core courses in Western civilization, not to mention the many general and liberal education reforms that have occurred in American higher education throughout the twentieth century. Some of these attempts, such as Columbia's War Issues Course, and Alexander Meiklejohn's Experimental College at Wisconsin-Madison, transpired before the liberal arts movement came into its own, and others followed it. But these various attempts were made by other individuals at other times for reasons both similar and dissimilar from those argued by Hutchins, Barr, Buchanan, and the other "liberal artists" between 1934 and 1954. Some of these other efforts either precipitated the liberal arts movement, are related to it, such as the Program of Liberal Studies at the University of Notre Dame, or are descended from it, but they are not, strictly speaking, part of the movement.[23] The philosophy and parameters of the liberal arts movement are elucidated by looking more closely at other terms, starting with general and liberal education.

General and Liberal Education

In their 1981 Carnegie Foundation essay, *A Quest for Common Learning*, Ernest Boyer and Arthur Levine wrote that the purpose and proprietorship of the academic major and electives are easily asserted; however, "though general education can be defined as the breadth component of a college education, any agreement beyond that quickly fades." As evidence they argue:

> A. S. Packard, the Bowdoin College professor who popularized the term, viewed [general education] as a prerequisite for specialized study. Alexander Meiklejohn, father of the "survey course" and creator of the University of Wisconsin's acclaimed experimental college, considered general education to be precisely the opposite: an antidote to specialization! John Dewey thought of general education as "an integrative experience underlying the unity of knowledge." But A. Lawrence Lowell, the

Harvard president who promoted distribution requirements, described it as the sum total of "a number of general courses in wholly unrelated areas." In 1947, the Presidential Commission on Higher Education defined general education as education for public participation. Yet John Stuart Mill, years before, claimed it to be education for a satisfying private life. The famed Harvard Report of 1945, *General Education in a Free Society*, called it plainly and simply "liberal education." But Daniel Bell, in his book on general education, said just as positively that liberal education and general education are by no means synonymous.[24]

Boyer and Levine's examples demonstrate the general confusion about general and liberal education and their differences, assuming there are any in the first place. Those who have seen the two as synonymous avoid making distinctions. However, those who believe there is a difference between general and liberal education must distinguish them from each other. In 1966 Columbia professor Daniel Bell argued that general education had three broad aims: "to provide a common learning; to give the student a comprehensive understanding of the Western tradition; [and] to combat intellectual fragmentation with interdisciplinary courses."[25] On the other hand, Bell argued that liberal education could be defined through six purposes: "To overcome intellectual provincialism; to appreciate the centrality of method; to gain an awareness of history; to show how ideas relate to social structures; to understand the way values infuse all inquiry; [and] to demonstrate the civilizing role of the humanities."[26]

Bell belonged to a group noted by historian Christopher Lucas, who argued that:

> Interestingly, in the 1940s and 1950s, some writers attempted to introduce a sharp distinction between "liberal" and "general" education, the suggestion being that the former consisted of a fixed body of traditional liberal-arts disciplines, and the latter any course of study exhibiting breadth or diversity. This usage was decidedly at odds with earlier practice in the 1920s and 1930s, when the two terms were used interchangeably and almost synonymously. As always, writers harbored great expectations about what liberal-general education might accomplish, but were forever in disagreement over structure and substance.[27]

Others did not make such distinctions. Historians John Brubacher and Willis Rudy argued that, while there was a "close similarity" between general and liberal education, general education "was not so much a synonym for liberal education as it was a way of organizing it." They also offered that, as "a facet" of liberal education, general education developed two characteristics: "On the one side it faced the great proliferation of subjects and tried to determine what everyone ought to know, regardless of departmental organization. On the other it tried to interrelate subjects into some meaningful whole."[28]

With their emphasis on essential knowledge and skills and their belief in the unity of knowledge, the liberal artists who formulated the liberal arts movement would certainly agree with the necessity of these two characteristics, but they did not argue for "general education," but rather for "liberal education."

These contentions notwithstanding, in the literature on higher education, general education reform or revival usually refers to a "traditional" model of general education, that is, an effort to combat "those academic bugaboos vocationalism, over-specialization, and the elective curriculum."[29] Although other curricular models, such as the progressive and the technocratic, also found expression in general education, *historically* general education, as described by Boyer and Levine, Bell, Brubacher, Rudy, and others, is a "traditionalist" or "restorationist" endeavor aimed at promoting liberal education.

The general/liberal dilemma will not be resolved here. Instead, for clarity and except where otherwise noted, "general education" and "liberal education," in concert with the literature, are understood in this study in the traditional senses noted above. At the same time, it is acknowledged that these terms are interwoven, used differently by different writers, and have changed meaning over time. As noted earlier, this book argues that the liberal arts movement was a distinct curricular reform movement. It makes no such claims of relative precision for "liberal" or "general" education.

General/Liberal Education and the Liberal Arts Movement

While the distinctions between general and liberal education are obviously contested, the relation of the three general education movements (referred to as revivals by Boyer and Levine) to the liberal arts movement is instructive for understanding both the influence and limits of the liberal arts movement. As will be seen in Chapter 1, the events at Columbia following World War I precipitated both the first general education movement and the liberal arts movement. Yet by the mid-1930s, when the liberal arts movement was coming into its own, particularly with the drafting of the Virginia Plan at Charlottesville (part of which served as the model for St. John's), the first general education movement had fallen victim to the vocational necessities of the Depression era. Boyer and Levine noted, for example, that ". . . the 'Great Books' curriculum at St. John's in Maryland [was] produced [in 1937] when interest in general education was on the decline at many institutions."[30]

World War II precipitated a general education revival, and a further blurring of terms. Kimball noted:

> One other argument continuing after World War II [was] the recommending of general education. As these recommendations gained strength after the war, there emerged more and more clearly a standard plan of undergraduate studies resembling that of Columbia University: general education in the three areas of humanities, social sciences, and

natural sciences in the first two years, and a major or concentration in the last two years. The college of the University of Chicago was also influential through its brief abstention from prescribing a major, a reluctance based on "the notion that a liberal education should constitute a single whole." Nor was Columbia insensitive to this outlook, viewing its Contemporary Civilization and Humanities course as the unifying aspect of its undergraduate program. By 1960, a selective nationwide study found only St. John's College in Annapolis rejecting the distribution and concentration format.[31]

Clearly, Kimball is conflating general and liberal education since he uses "general education" to describe the Columbia program, includes "liberal education" to describe Chicago's program, and concludes that St. John's remained distinct from the dominant academic model.

While the second general education movement that followed World War II was eventually supplanted by the technocratic concerns raised by Sputnik, the curricular manifestations of the liberal arts movement, which had faded as a generative force in the curriculum by the mid-1950s, generally were maintained until the Vietnam Era. Indeed, even though Columbia, Chicago, and St. John's all retain the spirit, if not always the courses themselves, that resulted from the movement, it took the curricular upheavals of the late 1960s and early 1970s to direct the focus of higher education away from the great books, honors programs, and "western civ" promoted by the liberal arts movement. The periods of general education reform postulated by Boyer and Levine, by contrast, were from 1918–1930, 1943–1955, and 1971–1981 (the last of which was a reaction to the Vietnam era upheavals). While the liberal arts movement and the general education movements share some common features, it is clear that these are not one in the same. Rather they are better understood as roughly parallel movements that shared a common ancestry, that waxed and waned, and in the case of general education, cycled in and out of influence.

The Great Books

The "great books" philosophy of education will be developed more fully later in this study as it was integral to the liberal arts movement. For the current purpose, the following defining ideas of the philosophy are briefly noted. Lists of great books have existed since classical antiquity. The Roman orator and educator, Quintilian, assembled a list of orators and historians "whose books should be studied."[32] But as embodied as a distinct means to liberal education, the great books philosophy was first manifest in John Erskine's 1920 General Honors course at Columbia.[33] Fully elaborated, however, to include not only literary and humanistic but also mathematical and scientific works, this philosophy was first manifest in the 1935 Virginia Plan which eventually reached its greatest expression in the great books curriculum of St. John's College.

Essentially the great books philosophy, argued most succinctly by Robert Hutchins in his 1954 book, *Great Books: The Foundation of a Liberal Education*, contends that: "The West needs to recapture and reemphasize and bring to bear upon its present problems the wisdom that lies in the words of its greatest thinkers and in the discussion that they have carried on." When one engages in this "Great Conversation," the liberal artists contended, one will see that: "These books shed some light on all our basic problems . . . . These books show the origins of many of our most serious difficulties. The spirit they represent and the habit of mind they teach are more necessary today than ever before."[34] Hutchins argued these qualities are found in classic works:

> Great books are great because of their excellence of construction and composition, immediate intelligibility on the aesthetic level, increasing intelligibility with deeper reading and analysis, leading to maximum depth and maximum range of significance with more than one level of meaning and truth.[35]

In other words, said Hutchins, "a classic is a book that is contemporary in every age" and hence essential to education in every age.[36]

Honors Programs

Like great books, honors tutorial work was central to the Virginia Plan. As will be discussed later, honors programs have taken different forms since their introduction at Swarthmore College in the 1920s. At some institutions honors programs have consisted of a set of prescribed courses; in other cases they have been completely elective in their requirements. What they all have in common is an elite notion that the brightest students will benefit from a curricular program different from that available to the average college student. The honors program embodied in the Virginia Plan, not coincidentally proposed by three Rhodes Scholars (Barr, Buchanan, and Gooch), was based on the English tutorial method of instruction found at Oxford and Cambridge.[37]

Honors programs and great books programs and courses existed before the Virginia Plan and continue to exist. Although ones implemented since the Virginia Plan have the Plan as part of their provenance, great books courses today, save at St. John's and to a degree at Chicago, are not descended directly from the Plan, although they are arguably informed by the Plan and its philosophy. For example, Allan Bloom's 1988 call in *The Closing of the American Mind* for a return to the great books model of collegiate education is indebted to the liberal arts movement, but also removed from it by virtue of being promoted at a different time by a different historical actor for both old and new reasons. Similarly, while the honors program implemented at Virginia in 1937 still exists in two departments at Virginia, it remains unusual with its traditional emphasis (not always followed by participating departments) on one-on-one tutoring.

As will be discussed later, most other honors programs have often rejected one-on-one tutoring for financial and sometimes pedagogical reasons.

Synopsis

In summary, although the liberal arts movement was related to the general education movements it was also different from them, even though the movements shared many ideas and goals in common. Likewise, the liberal arts movement was not synonymous with great books courses nor the honors program movement, although its different manifestations at Columbia, Chicago, St. John's, and Virginia always incorporated one or both of these related elements at their core. Last, because of their changing definition over time, the liberal arts movement is not synonymous with "the liberal arts" or "liberal education." Instead this book treats the liberal arts movement as a distinct event in twentieth-century American curricular history that had a beginning and an end. It was formulated and led by Mortimer Adler, Stringfellow Barr, Scott Buchanan, Robert Gooch, Robert Hutchins, Mark Van Doren and, to a lesser extent, by Alexander Meiklejohn, and Richard McKeon. The liberal arts movement had precedents in the first general education movement after World War I; it came into its own in the 1930s, especially at Virginia, Columbia, Chicago, and St. John's; ebbed and flowed during the 1940s and 50s; and ultimately succumbed to the politics of Sputnik and the Vietnam era.

The following chapters present a history of the Virginia Plan: its origins, manifestations, and legacy, all found at the University of Virginia and elsewhere, and in the larger story of American twentieth-century curricular history. In addressing a neglected yet clearly formative and thus important topic in the history of the collegiate curriculum in the twentieth century, this study ameliorates the historical literature on the liberal arts movement and sheds light on the alchemy of how and why academic innovation succeeds or fails. These considerations raise this study from being local to universal. Ultimately then, this book endeavors to more fully interpret the past and also inform contemporary understandings of problems inherent in curriculum formulation and implementation.

In an interview late in his life, nationally-known educator Stringfellow Barr asserted that: "The Virginia Plan deserves to be where people can inspect it."[38] This book endeavors to promote greater familiarity with an important development in American higher education in the twentieth century. To paraphrase Robert Maynard Hutchins, educators at America's colleges and universities should know what they are teaching and why. As an "integral whole," the Virginia Plan was a significant and enduring answer to that charge.

CHAPTER 1
Before the Virginia Plan

"It is impossible to think clearly about the curriculum of the American college or university without some sense of its past."
—Clark Kerr

At the opposite end of the Lawn from the Rotunda at the University of Virginia stands Old Cabell Hall. Completed in 1898 under the auspices of the eminent architect Stanford White, Cabell Hall closed off the open end of Thomas Jefferson's Academical Village and, in doing so, not only eliminated the prospect of the hills south of Charlottesville but also flipped the intended entry to the university from the south end to the north end of the Lawn. More than Jefferson's physical design, however, had been dramatically altered at the university by the close of the nineteenth century. Virginia's curriculum and the philosophy behind it had changed substantially during the 1800s. To understand these changes and how they precipitated the 1935 Virginia Plan, one must first place the University of Virginia in the larger context of American higher education history.

This chapter briefly discusses the evolution of certain aspects of American higher education from the founding of Harvard College in 1636 up to the 1935 Virginia Plan. Although primary emphasis is placed on curricular developments and philosophies during this three-hundred-year period, attention is also given to the place of the student in American colleges and universities, as the two are closely related topics. Indeed, both the curriculum and what is today referred to as "student life" were central to the philosophy of undergraduate education articulated in the Virginia Plan. While this chapter highlights significant historical points, influences, ideas, actors, and developments of this evolution, it is not intended to be exhaustive. Instead, it initially presents background for, and themes central to, the history of higher education relevant to the creation of the Virginia Plan.

The focus of the historical overview then shifts to the pre-Virginia Plan manifestations of the general education and liberal arts movements at Columbia University and the University of Chicago. Because accounts of the origins of general education at Columbia and Chicago have been told elsewhere by numerous capable historians, these overviews are relatively brief, intending not to be comprehensive institutional histories, but rather to provide a context in which to place the Virginia Plan.

The Curriculum and the Student in American Higher Education

The evolution of curriculum and college student development in American higher education is a long and telling story. Long because although the American history of curriculum and student development ostensibly starts with the founding of Harvard in 1636, its foundations are linked directly to the medieval university of the European High Middle Ages and stretch even further back to classical antiquity through what historian Bruce Kimball calls the oratorical and philosophical traditions of liberal education.[1] The evolution of curriculum and student development in America is likewise telling because the forms they have taken over time in terms of their manifestations, pedagogical and theoretical assumptions, content, structure, and requirements say a great deal about the contemporaneous society. Understanding this history is essential if one is to grasp the significance of the Virginia Plan and the liberal arts movement.

There are four related and essential themes fundamental to any understanding of the college curriculum and student in America that are particularly germane to the Virginia Plan. First, since the beginning of its history in the seventeenth century, there has been a recurring fear of declension in American higher education. As a result, this concern has played a continuing role in approaches to the curriculum and the student. Second, there has been an ongoing debate about what constitutes a good college education, that is, what are its proper goals. Third, there has been a related battle between election and prescription, or more broadly, between freedom and restriction in the curriculum. Fourth, there has been an ongoing argument about whether higher education should groom a leadership elite, or emphasize the democratizing effects of mass education. As will be seen in the following historical overview, these four themes are fundamental to any understanding of the evolution of the curriculum and the student in American institutions of higher education in general, and to the formulation and implementation of the Virginia Plan in specific.

The Colonial College

Nine young men made up the first cohort of graduates in America, the Harvard Class of 1642.[2] These first American bachelors of arts were inheritors of the "Oxbridge" academic tradition of England, yet they were also products of very colonial American concerns. Of course they did not think of themselves as "Americans," but as Englishmen. Nevertheless, the colonists of Massachusetts Bay believed with great urgency that education was essential to the survival of their community in a way perhaps not envisioned in Europe, for in America the future of civilization was not to be taken for granted. The barbarism of the wilderness was literally all around them, and it threatened to overwhelm their holy compact at any time. Education was thus deemed essential to the very survival of the Puritan endeavor. Literate ministers were necessary not just because of the Protestant emphasis on reading the Word, but also because the small colony was responsible for providing its own Puritan clergy. Civilization was literally only one generation deep, so the younger generation had to be prepared to persevere and prosper. As conceived by the colonists, self-reliance was required, but only possible with higher education.

The Puritan concern about declension is a perennial concern in the story of the curriculum in America and the American student, a concern which has both indicted and motivated higher education and which continues literally up through the present day. The lurking danger has taken different forms over time: the Old Deluder, the wilderness, threatened English liberties, an uneducated republican citizenry, irrelevance, vocationalism, the elective system—the list goes on, up through contemporary concerns about declining morality, political correctness, and scholastic standards.

The early curriculum of the colonial colleges was thoroughly classical and prescribed. Emphasis was on the three Aristotelian philosophies: natural, moral, and mental (that is, physics, ethics, and metaphysics), ancient languages (Greek, Latin, and Hebrew), and especially divinity. These subjects were largely taught via the seven liberal arts as codified in the early Middle Ages: the *trivium* (logic, grammar, and rhetoric) and the *quadrivium* (arithmetic, geometry, astronomy, and music).[3] In sum the colonial curriculum was part medieval with its scholastic concerns, part Renaissance with its interest in producing a governing class and gentlemanly refined culture, and part Reformation with its dedication to Protestant Christianity.[4]

Over the course of the eighteenth century, the original classical course of study was enlarged to include Enlightenment thought and subjects, including "more mathematics, greater specialization in the natural sciences, the study of literature and history, and a more prominent role for moral philosophy."[5] Moral philosophy, which developed as the capstone course for collegiate education, was broadly a course in ethics that "was wonderfully reassuring in its insistence on the unity of knowledge and the benevolence of God."[6] Although the colonial college curriculum was expanded, the trend could not continue unchecked. The introduction of *belles lettres*, modern languages, history, and especially the sciences increasingly crowded the classical curriculum so that by the early nineteenth century important choices had to be made. The antebellum college would be forced to deal with this inevitable eventuality.

During the seventeenth and eighteenth centuries it was believed that the classical course of study promoted morality and character because of its difficult content and the academic rigor required to master it. Although colonial educators believed that academic knowledge was important for students, their primary concern was the development of character and piety, whether they were training ministers or secular leaders. Accordingly, colonial schools invoked a strict discipline for students.

The schools also served *in loco parentis*, that is, as parental surrogates for students. With both their severe theology and their acute consciousness that the place of their civilization in the new world was tenuous, it is not surprising that a form of *in loco parentis* would be employed by colonial colleges, especially considering the relative youth of the college students in those years. Starting from the beginning of American higher education, reaching an apogee in the Antebellum era and then slowly declining, *in loco parentis* arguably existed up through the 1960s. The nature of that relationship changed over this long span of time, but the essential assumption that schools should in some form proscriptively direct student development—via rules or appeals to conscience, and manifested in characteristics such as compulsory chapel—was the modus operandi for most of the history of American higher education.

The second essential theme noted in the beginning of this chapter, the debate over the aims of higher education—between liberal/general education and practical/vocational education—came into sharper focus starting in the mid-nineteenth century, but can be linked to the ancient debates between the Sophists and Socrates in Greece during the fifth century B.C. Frederick Rudolph argues:

> An exclusively cultural or nonutilitarian education is a concept contrary to experience. As Christopher Jenks and David Riesman put it, "The question has always been how an institution mixed the academic with the vocational, not whether it did so." And the question has also been how much value society attached to the academic, the cultural, and supposedly nonutilitarian.[7]

The colonial college placed itself above this liberal/practical distinction. Trades would be mastered through apprenticeship, outside of formal higher education, while "classical erudition was believed to afford the sure guide for those destined to conduct the affairs of state and church." Moreover, "Shared in common by all academicians, whatever their sectarian persuasion, was the presumption that classical learning was essential for success in the various learned professions of law, medicine, or theology."[8] These views would find a renewed voice in the twentieth-century liberal arts movement.

The Antebellum College
The antebellum college curriculum maintained a focus on the classical course of study, but, continuing the practice started in the eighteenth century, it also increasingly supplemented the traditional course with modern languages, mathematics, and more science. To cover these subjects, "parallel" or "partial" courses of study that often led to a B.S. degree were also introduced. These alternatives to the classical B.A. program gave students a choice between a classical and an arguably more practical course of study.[9] In spite of these curricular additions, antebellum higher education curriculum is usually exemplified by the famous *Yale Report of 1828* which claimed: "The two great points to be gained in intellectual culture, are the discipline and the furniture of the mind;

expanding its powers, and storing it with knowledge. The former of these is, perhaps, the more important of the two."[10] As for the arguments that collegiate education should have greater orientation toward the practical concerns of the business and professional realms, the Report responded that, "our object is not to teach that which is peculiar to any one of the professions; but to lay the foundation which is common to them all."[11] In short, the mission of the liberal arts college was "to serve as a custodian of high culture; to nurture and preserve the legacy of the past; to foster a paideia, or 'common learning,' capable of enlarging and enriching people's lives; and to impart the knowledge, skills, and sensibilities foundational to the arts of living themselves."[12]

Although the Yale Report is often portrayed as a deeply conservative document, arresting the progress of higher education in America for decades, more recently this view has been challenged. Recent interpretation has suggested that the Yale Report was actually innovative in an important way. Instead of trying to cover the entirety of knowledge in a universal curriculum, as additions to the curriculum in the eighteenth century were designed to do, the Yale Report, acknowledging that such coverage was no longer possible, held that "the purpose of a college education was to train all the faculties of the human mind, rather than to teach all branches of knowledge." In short, emphasis was being shifted from the furniture to the discipline of the mind.[13]

Whether or not the Yale Report represents innovation, there is little question that collegiate education too often remained a grim affair as an example from Princeton in 1846 demonstrates.

> When word reached [Princeton Vice President John] Maclean that Professor [Evert M.] Topping was teaching Greek literature rather than the Greek language, he at once called him to account. Topping replied that he used literature as a means to an end, in order to interest the students in their work. After years of futile attempt in the familiar method of teaching, in which he was often interrupted "by groans and other wilful (sic) noises," he began to intersperse the translation and parsing with such comments on the passages as had attracted his own attention. The effect was immediate. From being notoriously unruly and apathetic, the students became docile and studious. "We must succeed, it seems to me, by interesting the understanding of the students," he concluded, "by rousing a manly interest of thought and then turning them back upon themselves." That this was rank heresy we conclude from the fact that a few days later Topping's resignation was accepted by the trustees.[14]

Cognizant of the content and pedagogy commonly employed in American colleges, Franklin, Jefferson, Jacksonians, and others criticized the classical curriculum to varying degrees as being insufficient if not irrelevant to the needs of the young Republic. Their criticisms notwithstanding, the spirit and content of the Yale Report largely encapsulates the stance taken by the colleges up through the Civil War.

It would be incorrect to assume, however, that there were no modifications to the classical curriculum during the Antebellum era. During the first decades of the 1800s, students, as they had always done, used ancient passages to study the classical languages. Generally they did not read classical texts in full. Instead, textbooks such as the *Graeca Majora* were used to study the learned classical languages. These textbooks were compilations of extracts, not classical works in their entirety. In short, "it was not classical literature, poetry, drama, archaeology, antiquities, biography, or history that occupied college boys in the classical classroom, but language."[15] This had been true since the founding of Harvard in 1636 and at its predecessors, Oxford and Cambridge. However, during the humanist revolution that occurred roughly between 1820 and 1860, a new philosophy of education emerged, one which sought to promote a virtuous citizenry, not just classical erudition. It was believed that the study of the classical world as a whole, and not just classical grammar and language, would help preserve the young American Republic from declension. Coinciding with the Greek Revival that developed after 1820, the college curriculum saw "the tragedies of Sophocles, Euripides, and Aeschylus; the comedies of Aristophanes; the orations of Demosthenes; the *Illiad* and *Odyssey* of Homer; and the dialogues of Plato all appear with increasing frequency after 1830 next to Cicero, Horace, Livy, and Tacitus."[16]

This is an important point, for when the liberal artists of the twentieth century argued that their philosophy of education, based in part on the great books, was a re-introduction of what had always been the basis of Western education, they were only partly correct. True, classical texts were used before the rise of the research university in the latter half of the nineteenth century, but it would be incorrect to assume that American college students had generally followed something akin to a great books course of study. The liberal artists were on firmer ground when they sought precedence for their philosophy of education in the Antebellum era, rather than the Republican era of the late eighteenth century, or earlier.

Women's Education and Curricular Innovation

Female higher education in the Antebellum era was similar in numerous respects to male education at the time, but it also introduced for the first time some of the subjects that would later be found in most colleges and universities. Women's colleges taught Latin and sometimes Greek; foreign languages, with an emphasis on French; mathematics; and science, which demonstrated God's designs. They also pioneered the study of the fine arts, particularly music and art, which along with embroidery, dance, and conversation, made up the "ornamental" subjects in the curriculum. Like the male antebellum colleges, female colleges gradually introduced parallel courses of study; young ladies chose between a classical course and an English course. Yet the notion of "separate spheres," of different societal roles for men and women, meant that questions of vocational training for women did not emerge, especially in the South. Higher education for antebellum Southern women was a mark of gentility and status. Although higher education also served this role in male education, vocational considerations were not a concern when it came to educating Southern women because antebellum ladies invariably took up their prescribed domestic roles in the home, whether they enjoyed the benefits of higher education or not.[17]

Antebellum Student Life

In loco parentis continued as the dominant paradigm, as student development and student life for men and women in the antebellum college was strictly regimented. Compulsory chapel, common dining, classes, and scheduled study hours were designed not only to build character and impart knowledge, but also to reduce mischief and other bad behavior bred by idle time. However, the result was a continuance of disciplinary problems, student riots, and general resentment on the part of students. Because American faculty members remained in charge of student discipline, they were sometimes unable to develop mentoring relationships with the students. This fact was different from the experience of students at Oxford and Cambridge where, starting in the eighteenth century, disciplinary responsibility increasingly fell to deans, proctors, and beadles. As a result, the Oxbridge dons were freed from these responsibilities and "the English colleges found it easy to liberalize their instructional procedures by developing the individual tutorial system."[18] This system eventually became a model for educators who sought a reformation of American higher education in the twentieth century.

Rise of the University

In the years following the Civil War, the old college curriculum was sharply challenged by the rise of the land-grant institutions, the German research model university, and the introduction of the elective curriculum, which historian Frederick Rudolph calls "one of the most creative, and also one of the most destructive developments of the post-Civil War years."[19] The practical and service-oriented nature of higher education associated with the land-grant institutions was made financially possible by the Morrill Acts of 1862 and 1890. The pure and applied research and professional emphases of the newly founded and expanded universities, inspired by German higher education ideals and fueled by philanthropic largess as well as increased public funding, likewise greatly broadened the curriculum. Both the land-grant institutions and the newly emerging research universities were made socially acceptable by a society increasingly impressed by claims made for practicality, service, and research in higher education. These changes eventually broadened the appeal of higher education in an American society that, throughout much of the nineteenth century, had not considered higher education to be of practical value. The later 1800s are thus particularly important to the third theme put forth in the introduction to this chapter: prescription versus election.

Although the elective system had first appeared at Jefferson's University of Virginia in the 1820s—a fact that would play a role in debates concerning the Virginia Plan—the practice there was a half-century ahead of its time. It was not until the 1870s, under the leadership of Harvard president Charles W. Eliot, that election began to gain widespread acceptance, even though calls for it had been made by various reformers for decades. In 1872 Eliot wrote: "With regard to the college proper, the one thing we are doing at Cambridge is the introduction of a true University freedom of studies under the name of the 'elective system.' . . . I believe that Harvard is doing a great service to American education by leading the way in this reform. All other issues are comparatively unimportant."[20] Rudolph wrote: "The rationale that Eliot offered for the elective system rested on a combination of desire, necessity, principle, and preference." Preference and desire were found in Eliot's belief that: "A young man could learn to discipline himself . . . only if he were released from external controls and only if he were interested enough in some goal to see the worth of self-discipline."[21] As for necessity, election "gave vitality to the American college at a time when its remoteness from society threatened the whole structure of American higher education with disaster." And finally, as for principle, "Jefferson, Jackson, and Lincoln had already expressed on the level of democratic belief what Eliot was now saying should be an operative principle in higher education."[22] Eliot was not alone responsible for the adoption of the elective system, but he was the most influential spokesman for it.

Once election did arrive, it spread quickly, becoming the dominant curricular paradigm by the beginning of the twentieth century. Many of the subjects in the old classical curriculum remained, but the widespread prescription and discipline codified in the Yale Report did not survive. It will be recalled that the Yale Report shifted the primary emphasis of a collegiate education from the furniture—the content—of the curriculum to the discipline—the mental training—of the mind. While the authors of the Report believed that the classical subjects were superior in their ability to encourage mental discipline, by the last quarter of the nineteenth century, with the disciplinary argument in decline, the Yale Report's argument was used, ironically, to reject the prescribed curriculum. Regardless of whether or not classical subjects promoted mental discipline, as the mental discipline argument was increasingly rejected as antiquated, so was the inherent primacy of the classical curriculum.

In spite of the decline of the disciplinary argument, initially many educators believed the changes at Harvard were preposterous and that they would destroy American higher education. The specter of declension had appeared once more. James McCosh, the president of Princeton, was one of the most prominent academics to raise his voice against electivism. He and others argued that electivism assumed a maturity on the part of students which they did not possess, that students would avoid essential subjects not to their liking and, and in the process, that students would lose the unity of knowledge that the college had always sought to provide.[23] As will be seen, these various arguments against electivism later found voice in the proponents of "liberal culture," general education, and in the arguments of the liberal artists who fostered the liberal arts movement.

The detractors notwithstanding, arguments ranging from student interest, motivation, and even rights, to practicality and applicability all enabled the elective system to take hold. The transformation of the curriculum was a fundamental one. In *The Emergence of the American University*, Laurence Veysey writes that:

> When the disciplinary outlook finally died, its passing reflected an important shift in American thought. . . . The collapse of mental discipline marked one of the last of the long series of declensions from seventeenth-century Puritanism. American society, which had always tended toward increasing blandness of conviction, took a further notable step in this direction during the last fifteen years or so of the nineteenth century.[24]

As noted earlier, the debate between prescription and election is fundamental to an understanding of the evolution of the curriculum in America. This debate has been going on since the time of Jefferson, and it continues today as manifest by the prevalence of distribution requirements at many schools and more prescribed core curricula at still others. Nevertheless, the revolution initiated by Eliot shifted dominance for the first time in American curricular history from prescription to election, a dominance which election has maintained ever since. This fundamental shift likewise "led step by step over time to the practice of instituting academic 'majors' and 'minor' study concentrations, the development of academic departments devoted exclusively to one or another specific discipline, and a marked specialization of scholarship within academe."[25] By 1900 many of the features familiar to higher education today had appeared, features inconceivable without the shift from prescription to election.

Although increasingly supplanted in the curriculum, "discipline" remained a guiding force in the development and life of the student—at least as far as the schools were concerned. Although under increasing attack, the *in loco parentis* stance remained during the latter half of the nineteenth century, a stance according to historian George Marsden, "associated with some old-time Calvinist vigilance."[26] Indeed, "the price of retaining the *in-loco-parentis* stance of the old-time college seemed to be that of preserving the old-time campus disorders as well." Nevertheless, there was some accommodation of student interests. When James McCosh arrived as President of the College of New Jersey in

1868, for example, he was not "a Puritan like Jonathan Edwards in his attitude toward students":

> Rather, as in other matters, he mixed the new with the old, attempting to retain the essential principles, while looking for whatever was good, or at least a matter of indifference, in modernity . . . , for instance, he immediately endorsed building a gymnasium and in good British fashion encouraged collegiate sports. When he heard that students were gathering at a local billiard hall, he ordered three billiard tables for the gymnasium.[27]

As it had since colonial times, the religious condition of the students remained a concern and a priority. As McCosh put it: "No student passes through our College without his being addressed from time to time, in the most loving manner, as to the state of his soul."[28]

The rise of faculty advisers and student counseling, first appearing at Johns Hopkins in 1877 and Harvard in 1889 respectively, was a formal recognition that "[institutional] size and the elective curriculum required some closer attention to undergraduate guidance than was possible with an increasingly professionally oriented faculty."[29] Though paternalism remained the guiding principle toward students, some of the focus did change. Interest in utility, particularly as manifest in philosophies such as the "Wisconsin Idea" with its emphasis on service, did allow students more latitude in their pursuits. The relative place of service and research relative to liberal learning remained, as it does today, in contention. Many argued that liberal culture, not utility or vocationalism, ought to be at the heart of the academic program, regardless of institutional type. This contention, and the related claim that liberal education was as "practical" as research or vocational training, if indeed not more so, would gain adherents in the next era of evolution in American higher education.

Insights from Black and Women's Education

The evolution of African-American higher education is a poignant example of the evolution of the curriculum that speaks directly to the themes noted at the beginning of the chapter. During the Antebellum era, collegiate education for blacks was practically nonexistent. Black higher education really started after the Civil War and it provides one of the clearest examples of the liberal-vocational dichotomy, especially in the competing philosophies promoted by Booker T. Washington and W. E. B. DuBois. Essentially, Washington argued that collegiate education for blacks ought to be of a vocational nature. He believed blacks would be best served by practical training that would help them to succeed in the real world of work. Study in the classical subjects of the liberal arts might serve an ornamental purpose, but would do little to advance blacks in American society. DuBois, on the other hand, believed passionately that an education in the liberal arts, at least for "the talented tenth," would produce men who were roundly educated to care for more than monetary success and, more important, who would lead the elevation of the black race in America.[30]

DuBois argued that vocational education would ensure second-class status for blacks and therefore he rejected Washington's accommodationism. His claims point to the fourth essential theme associated with the evolution of the curriculum and the student: elite versus mass notions of higher education. Charges of an ulterior or hidden curriculum, sometimes made one hundred years later, but also of concern at the time, asserted that proponents of black education were most interested in producing a compliant workforce that would serve the needs of white agriculture and industry. Particularly strident were revisionist charges that, starting after the Civil War and for long thereafter, black education was geared not for citizenship or even for vocational servitude, but for the preservation of a caste system, an assertion of white class hegemony over blacks. That more philanthropic money went to support vocational training than for liberal arts instruction was taken as proof of the revisionist claim; altruistic motivations were dismissed as disingenuous.[31] Historically black colleges and universities offered both liberal and vocational education for blacks throughout the twentieth century, but the opportunities afforded African Americans did not begin to approach those of whites until white majority institutions began opening their doors to minorities in significant numbers in the 1960s and 1970s.

The focus of women's education shifted in terms of geography and curriculum in the latter half of the nineteenth century. Although arguably more prominent in the South and Midwest during the antebellum period, after the war women's collegiate education made its strides in the North. By that time, women's education in the South had been devastated by the war and social proscriptions against educating women in the North had relaxed. Although antebellum Southern education for women had been based on the idea of "separate spheres"—that women were to be educated differently than men and for different purposes—women's education in the North was more varied in its philosophies. Even as female collegians pursued courses of study fairly comparable to those in male institutions, many women at the women's colleges supported activism, service, and ultimately professionalism.[32] Through involvement with suffrage, social service and later social phenomena like flapperdom, women's education became a progressive force in collegiate and national life. At the same time, it chaffed against and eventually helped overturn the old morality symbolized by parietals. Like black education, women's collegiate education made significant strides before the wave of coeducation in the 1960s and 1970s made women's education a pervasive part of American higher education.

Reaction, Liberal Culture, and General Education

Although the principle of election was the norm by the turn of the century, there was increasing concern that electivism had been taken too far, that students' courses of study had a lack of coherence and intellectual integration. More worrisome was the presumed lack of liberal learning, that learning which " 'liberated' the learner from ignorance, provincialism, and philistinism" and acquainted one with a broader common culture.[33] As put by historians Brubacher and Rudy:

> The elective system . . . had made an earnest attempt to make the curriculum more meaningful to the undergraduate by allowing him to choose studies for their intrinsic rather than their disciplinary value. But even this gain was offset by a concomitant loss. It won interest but it lost integration. . . . the elective principle resulted in a fragmentation of the curriculum. With the atomization of the course of study it became possible for students to turn in their credits as if they were clipping so many coupons to get a degree. The whole system was symptomatic of an intellectual agnosticism about any over-all unity or design. Nor did requirements of concentration or distribution, where in force, produce it, since even here individual courses were taught without much conscious attention to their interrelation.[34]

The result was an interest in preserving and promoting liberal culture. The liberal culture believed produced by liberal learning was an amalgamation of "an aesthetic, a moral and a tacit social code" and it gained support in academia because although "the idea of a shared 'culture' or *paideia* had been too narrowly circumscribed in the classical conception of liberal learning . . . the social and personal needs it sought to satisfy were real."[35] Liberal culture stressed values, aesthetics, taste, and appreciation. Its advocates—Abbott Lawrence Lowell at Harvard, Andrew Fleming West at Princeton, George E. Woodberry at Columbia and many others, usually from the older eastern schools, strongly favored the gentlemanly and humane tradition of English education over what they perceived as the soulless fact-driven Germanic research model.[36]

Notably, the philosophy of liberal culture "was unwilling to bring science within its understanding or under its influence."[37] Its advocates sought breadth of knowledge in art, literature, history, and philosophy.[38] This point is most important for, as will be seen, the creators of the liberal arts movement shared the belief with those who espoused the philosophy of liberal culture that the literary and humane traditions were critical to liberal education. However, starting with the 1935 Virginia Plan, the liberal arts movement also argued an equal place for mathematics and science alongside the humanities. The liberal arts movement thus had some roots in the development of liberal culture in the late nineteenth century, but by virtue of its advocacy for mathematics and science, was also independent of the liberal culture movement.

Liberal culture was also elitist and was "associated with the rights, privileges, and responsibilities of a limited class."[39] As a philosophy, argued Rudolph, liberal culture "did not intend to be democratic, for it clearly was an open and honest assertion of superiority."[40] Here again, interesting contrasts with the later liberal arts movement can be drawn. As will be discussed more fully in the following chapters, the first manifestations of the liberal arts movement at Columbia, Chicago, and Virginia were all of an elite variety. These schools all developed "honors courses" designed for select students. However, advocates of, and institutions associated with, the liberal arts movement generally came to see the liberal arts as critical to the education of all college students, and thereby instituted courses required of all students at Chicago, Columbia, and St. John's. Yet Virginia largely maintained an elite Jeffersonian conception of work in the liberal arts and thus shared a similarity with the liberal culture philosophy that other institutions affected by the liberal arts movement eventually shed.

When one takes in the totality of American colleges and universities in the late nineteenth century, it becomes clear that there were several efforts to ensure the place of "liberal culture" in the curriculum.[41] One solution to balance election and prescription, still widely employed today, but of questionable results in the promotion of liberal learning, was to institute concentration and distribution requirements. Requirements provided a theoretically compelling synthesis because they provided for both breadth and depth in the college course of study. A second approach, discussed later, was the introduction in the 1910s and 1920s of honors work. A third approach, variously known as general education, general studies or general culture, proposed an even more integrated approach. Frederick Rudolph writes: "The general education movement, from its beginnings at Columbia in 1919 to the celebrated Harvard report on the subject in 1945, was an attempt to capture some of the sense of a continuing intellectual and spiritual heritage that had fallen victim to the elective principle." In short, it "proposed to restore some balance, to revitalize the aristocratic ideal of the liberal arts as the passport to learning."[42] As noted in the introduction, the general education movement also sowed the seeds of the liberal arts movement which gave rise to the Virginia Plan in 1935.

The first general education reform movement, started by John Dewey and Alexander Meiklejohn in the early 1900s, gained momentum around the time of World War I and was eventually slowed by vocational concerns raised by the Great Depression, although the related liberal arts movement started in the 1930s and continued through the 1950s.[43] These curricular reform movements were direct reactions to the perceived dominance of illiberal education—a commonly-held view. Indeed, writing in the 1970s, Frederick Rudolph echoed Robert Maynard Hutchins' assertions from the 1930s by positing that,

"If in the nineteenth century the curriculum defined the market for higher learning, in the twentieth the market defined the curriculum."[44]

There were many sometimes contradictory goals and values associated with the general education movement. As would be seen throughout the twentieth century, the devil was in the details. Some proposals were progressive, others traditional, but they generally took aim at vocationalism, overspecialization, and election.[45] In the end, argued Ernest Boyer and Arthur Levine, "Perhaps the central contradiction in the general education rhetoric of the 1920s was between the demand that higher education adapt to the complexities of the modern world, and equally the insistent call to recapture the idealism and cultural unity of the prewar era."[46] Rudolph argued that those who ventured into the general education realm "were trying to retrieve for the curriculum a function that had sustained it since the Middle Ages: the cultivation and transmission of the intellectual and philosophical inheritance of the Western world as an instrument of man's understanding of himself."[47] As will be seen, even more than the first general education movement of the post-World War I era, Rudolph's analysis speaks to the goals of the liberal arts movement.

The Shifting Locus and Decline of In Loco Parentis

Just as academic reforms were reshaping higher education, so too were there changes in student culture. The spread of literary societies, fraternities, and organized athletics along with other student activities all contributed to the rise of the "extracurriculum." By 1900 administrators "expected administrative changes and extracurricular activities to solve the problem of undergraduate character development." This period marks a significant divergence between the curriculum and student development—a decision which many in higher education would later come to regard with ambivalence. It would not be until the 1990s that convergence would begin to bring the curriculum and student development closer again. An example of this divergence, according to historian Julie Reuben, was the rise of "student life," which "replaced the classroom and the chapel as the locus of the moral mission of the university."[48] Specifically, "[institutions] hired special administrators to handle 'student life,' instituted programs for student advising, hired special faculty for undergraduate teaching, and created new activities such as "freshmen orientation." The overall effect of these administrative and extracurricular developments was to lessen "the expectation that faculty should provide moral guidance and [to create] an institutional separation between morality and knowledge."[49]

Most important, argued Reuben, "by settling on group cohesiveness as the best source of moral influence, university officials came to equate morality with morale."

> Student-service professionals would never have the power to define moral norms that the president and faculty of the classical college had

exercised. They devoted themselves to facilitating social bonds among students. They discovered that imposing their own standards of behavior risked alienating students from campus-sponsored social life. Regulating extracurricular activities meant reaching a compromise between the demands of morale and those of morality. The subsequent history of fraternities and athletics indicates that morale often won.[50]

This separation of morality and knowledge which occurred after the turn of the twentieth century has, at best, created ambiguity about morality, rights and responsibilities, and student life in the academy, both in the past and in the current day. The result has been that there are no broadly accepted standards for evaluating moral claims that might be made in an effort to teach students how to live in a proper and civil manner, particularly when such claims bump up against personal freedoms.[51] As will be discussed in the following chapters, the reforms proposed in the Virginia Plan and its manifestations directly interacted, not only with the curriculum, but also with various aspects of student life, including dormitory living, fraternities, and collegiate athletics in its attempt to unify the disparate experiences that characterized collegiate life by the 1930s.

Before the Virginia Plan: General Education at Columbia

Beginnings in Morningside Heights

Although older than the nation, much of Columbia's renown has come from its twentieth-century curricular innovations. In his essay on Columbia, Justus Buchler remarked that "the year 1919 can be justly regarded as marking the actual birth of the new Columbia College" because of the introduction of its famous general education courses.[52] Daniel Bell argued:

> What is important here is that the new Columbia College was dedicated firmly to the tradition of the liberal arts rather than to professionalism; that it sought for social diversity in its student body; and that unlike some later schools [read Chicago and St. John's] it was committed to no doctrinal philosophy of education other than exposing the student to major intellectual ideas and expanding his imagination. It is the combination of these three elements that gave general education at Columbia its distinctive stamp.[53]

From its founding in 1754 as King's College, Columbia College (as it was renamed in 1784), was the sixth of the colonial colleges and, like the others, for many years it offered a strictly classical curriculum.[54] Indeed, an 1876 account by professor John Burgess noted that Columbia was "a small old-fashioned college, or rather school, for teaching Latin, Greek, and mathematics, and a little metaphysics, and a very little natural science."[55]

As was the case at many of its peer institutions, successive decades brought electivism and an emphasis on graduate research to Columbia. Then, in 1920, John Erskine began offering a General Honors course in which students read and discussed one classic of Western literature a week.[56] According to Kass, "Erskine was primarily motivated by the desire to make up for the lack of acquaintance with the best literature that he noticed among the undergraduates in his classes. In addition, he thought that such a course would be useful to the students later on in life by providing a common groundwork for discussion and argument."[57] Bell argues further that, "The intention in reading the 'great books' was to inculcate in the student a humanistic rather than a professional orientation; to force him to confront a great work directly, rather than treat it with the awe reserved for a classic; and, in the contemporary jargon, 'to acculturate' a student whose background and upbringing had excluded him from the 'great traditions.' "[58] As will be seen in Chapter 2, all of the forgoing reasons, plus some additional ones, served as rationale for the proposals put forth in the Virginia Plan.

The impetus for Erskine's course also came from two other sources. One was the desire to integrate the burgeoning knowledge produced by the German research model increasingly employed in America. An earlier response was the course set up during Alexander Meiklejohn's presidency at Amherst College in 1910 titled "Social and Economic Institutions." It was designed to "unify" or "integrate" the social sciences.[59] The other source was World War I. The United States government asked Columbia to set up a "War Issues" course that would educate young American men in their democratic heritage. Additionally, the faculty soon proposed a course devoted to "Peace Issues." The two "issues" courses resulted in an interdisciplinary course titled "Contemporary Civilization" which drew on disciplines such as economics, history, philosophy, and politics. First offered in the autumn of 1919, it was required of all freshmen.[60]

Unlike the Contemporary Civilization course, or "C.C." as it was known, Erskine's course was not required. In fact, it was open only to those students interested in an extra course; this was thought of as "honors" work, hence the name of the course, "General Honors."[61] Erskine believed that the course should be a requirement, but initially there was significant faculty opposition to the course, and approval was only secured when the course was made optional. Many faculty members, some of whom had spent their entire careers studying a particular author or work, rejected the notion that any good would come of undergraduates reading a classic a week. The result, they feared, would be butchery or, at best, dilettantism. Many also claimed that the youth had no interest in reading masterpieces. Erskine countered that every book had to be read for the first time at some point, and that acquaintance was far different from mastery. It shows the profound effect that the great books movement had on American higher education in the twentieth century to reflect on the fact that, according to Mark Van Doren, who at the time was a young instructor in Columbia's English Department, many professors believed it was better for students to read a textbook about the classics than to read the classics themselves.[62] Once implemented, and as would be the case with similar courses at Chicago and Virginia, Erskine's great books course proved tremendously popular with students—so much so that it had to meet in sections.[63] In light of earlier faculty opposition it is ironic that, when Columbia's Literature Humanities course was instituted in 1937 for all undergraduates, it drew heavily on Erskine's course.[64]

In the following passage Bell provides a succinct summary of the development of general education at Columbia and the courses in which that education was manifest.

> The tradition of the liberal arts at Columbia was embodied in the idea of three broad courses—Contemporary Civilization, the Humanities, and the Sciences—which would be required of all students. These courses evolved slowly. Contemporary Civilization, at the start a one-year course, in 1929 became a two-year sequence, the first year dealing primarily with the intellectual traditions and institutional development of Western society, and the second year, with changing emphases, focusing on contemporary socioeconomic problems. The two-year Humanities sequence (the first year was initiated in 1937, the second in 1947) concentrated in the first year on the masterpieces of literature and philosophy, from Homer to the nineteenth century, and in the second year on the masterpieces of music and the plastic arts. Though in principle the College was committed to a parallel organization in the Sciences (successive committees called for a 'specially constructed and well-integrated two-year course in the natural sciences' and courses 'to stress inclusive organizing principles of the sciences rather than special techniques for mastering specialized subject matters'), institutional and staffing difficulties confounded the various efforts to create such general education science courses. From 1934 to 1941, a two-year course, Science A and B, was offered as an option to the specialized science courses, but this ended during the war. Since World War II the Science requirement has remained simply two years of any science courses, a requirement that can be fulfilled by any selective combination of two one-year or one two-year course, in any of a half-dozen fields.[65]

Although changes have been made to them over time, the C.C. and Humanities courses are still required of all Columbia undergraduates and still adhere to the intention of familiarizing students with the Western tradition and its civilization.

Before the Virginia Plan: General Education at Chicago

Developments at Chicago

More than the events at Columbia, which gave birth to the general education movement, the events at the University of Chicago, starting with the reorganization of its undergraduate college in the 1930s, served to make the reaction against electivism a national issue. Boyer and Levine argue that:

> The most hotly debated experiment of the [first general education revival] was "the College" at the University of Chicago. The person whose name is inextricably linked with this venture is, of course, Robert Hutchins. In reality the college was a series of experiments. It was launched before Hutchins arrived and continued not only after he retired, but even after the initial wave of general interest had long faded. The College at Chicago was a radical approach to general education, embodying, in varying degree, great books, interdisciplinary courses, early college admission, comprehensive examinations, and a four-year fully-required course of study. The prestige of the University of Chicago and the charisma of Robert Hutchins caught the nation's imagination. Parts of the Chicago program were replicated in experimental colleges, honors colleges, and schools across the country. St. John's College is a direct descendant of the Chicago plan.[66]

Here again is evidence that the literature relating to the liberal arts movement is incomplete and sometimes confused, for while what transpired at St. John's was certainly related to the reforms—ones both adopted and rejected—at Chicago, the "New Program" at St. John's was first and foremost a descendant of the Virginia Plan, which came to St. John's via Chicago.[67]

By not conflating the two programs, Daniel Bell does a better job than Boyer and Levine in describing the connection. In 1966 Bell argued that:

> Over the past twenty-five years the College of the University of Chicago has undergone the most thoroughgoing experiment in general education of any college in the United States. Many confusions about the purposes and curriculum of the Chicago College have arisen because of a loose identification of its curriculum with that of St. John's College of Annapolis or with the Great Books program, which has been conducted in the university extension. Actually, the Chicago experiment resembled neither of these. Nor was the college completely the embodiment of the ideas of Robert M. Hutchins, the genie of the university. Though the general conception of the "Chicago plan" was outlined by President Hutchins in his 1936 Yale lectures (published as *The Higher Learning in America*), the character of the college was developed by its successive deans, Aaron J. Brumbaugh, Clarence Faust, and F. Champion Ward, and its curriculum by the college faculty; and the detailed program, in fact,

was somewhat removed from Hutchins' ideas, most of which were embodied, rather, in the curriculum of St. John's.[68]

The history of curricular development at Chicago is convoluted, a "tangle" as Bell put it. How did this come about? Reform of the undergraduate college at Chicago started before the arrival of Hutchins on the Midway in 1929. From its founding in 1892, the university split undergraduate education into two parts. The first two years were called the Academic College (later changed to the Junior College) and, according to Chicago's first president, William Rainey Harper, "the work of the first two years partakes largely of the Academic character. The regulations must still be strict. The scope of election is limited." Reflecting the vestiges of the classical curriculum, from 1892 until 1905, Latin was prescribed in the Junior College, being understood as "the foundation of the curriculum and essential to a liberal education." However, at the urging of faculty members in the sciences, starting in 1905 students pursuing the bachelor of science degree could elect to take a modern language in place of Latin.[69]

The last two years of undergraduate work, first known as the University College and later the Senior College, were preparatory for graduate study. According to Harper's initial 1891 notes:

> The close of the second year marks the beginning of a new period. . . . The student begins to specialize and in many cases may to advantage select subjects which will bear directly or indirectly upon the work of his chosen calling. . . . The student gradually changes from the College atmosphere to that of the University. Different motives entice him to work.[70]

In 1923 a commission on the Future of the Colleges was appointed by President Ernest DeWitt Burton. The commission emphasized the centrality of "general education," which it defined as: "the attainment of independence in thinking in which civilized societies of the past and of the present have done and are doing their thinking; . . . independence in appreciation of the fine arts, and the absorption of the fine arts into the individual's life; . . . independence in moral living."[71]

To achieve these ends, it was proposed that all undergraduate education be reorganized into an administrative unit known as "The College." Also, the credit system would be abolished, replaced with a number of comprehensive examinations that an undergraduate could take at any time. A student who successfully passed these exams could theoretically receive his bachelor's degree after only one year of residence.[72] Coupled with later reforms, the possibility that young students could receive their bachelor's degree in less than the four years common at other institutions eventually contributed to the undoing of the most radical undergraduate reform at Chicago, but this was not to happen until the 1950s. Nevertheless, it is worth noting that, as had happened at Jefferson's University of Virginia more than a hundred years prior, the most radical and idiosyncratic elements of the curriculum and administrative organization—which were integral to the reforms from their inception—ultimately had to be revised to be more commensurate with the standard practices of other institutions.

When Robert Maynard Hutchins came to the Quadrangles of the University of Chicago in 1929, he was one of the youngest presidents ever to lead a major research university in America. Only thirty years old, he had been Dean of the Yale Law School before accepting the invitation to come to Hyde Park. Soon after arriving on the Midway, Hutchins promised to bring renewed vitality to the institution that had burst so brightly into the educational establishment in the 1890s under the guiding hand of Harper, only to languish subsequently under the direction of more patrician presidents in the 1910s and 1920s.

Hutchins' tenure as President and later Chancellor of Chicago lasted more than two decades, from 1929 to 1951. In *Hutchins' University*, Chicago historian William McNeill argues that Hutchins did more to shape the institution than any of the presidents before or since, save perhaps Harper. For just as Harper went about establishing the University of Chicago as something "bran splinter new," so too did Hutchins create a new philosophy of undergraduate education at Chicago that continues to influence curricula. McNeill argues that Hutchins' philosophy came directly out of Hutchins' own life long search for metaphysical and moral truth. Like many academics of the time, Hutchins came from a strong Protestant background. Son of a Presbyterian minister who worked at Oberlin and was later president of Berea College, Hutchins in many ways embodied the Protestant ethic throughout his life. His family's Eastern and Puritan background, combined with the social connections he made at Yale as an undergraduate, assured him of a place in the WASP Establishment. Yale and his stint in the service during World War I also introduced him to the martini, tobacco, and ensured that ". . . his speech henceforth would be sprinkled with the mild profanity customary in masculine precincts."[73] His slip from orthodoxy was also manifest in his gradual abandonment of Calvinist religion as a source of truth.

As a student at Yale Law School Hutchins had flirted with the law as a path to truth and justice, but quickly came to believe that the law had little to do with either of the realms. Of law schools, Hutchins later wrote, "Jurisprudence, which should be central in any law curriculum, is studied by few and like legal history is regarded as a peripheral or ornamental subject."[74] Ultimately he came to believe that truth could be found by delving into the great classical texts of the Western cultural tradition. In accordance with this growing conviction, the Chicago College was to have "general—that is, liberal-arts—education as its primary objective."[75]

Much of Hutchins' increasing confidence in the veracity of this path found its promulgation in the thoughts of his friend and fellow faculty member, Mortimer Adler. McNeill argues that Adler, even more than Hutchins, was the true radical influence at the university. Adler "was interested only in the pages of the Great Books, and, in particular, in the pages of Aristotle and St. Thomas Aquinas's *Summa Theologica*."[76]

Before establishing the role that Thomist Aristotelianism played in the educational philosophies of Adler and Hutchins—a role that led to the pejorative charge by their critics that the liberal artists were engaged in "neo-medievalism"—a brief examination of the *Summa* and its historical context is useful. Writing in 1945, Bertrand Russell recorded that:

> [Medieval Christian philosophy] which hitherto had been Augustinian and therefore largely Platonic, was enriched by new elements due to contact with Constantinople and the Mohammedans. Aristotle, during the thirteenth century, came to be known fairly completely in the West, and, by the influence of Albertus Magnus and Thomas Aquinas, was established in the minds of the learned as the supreme authority after Scripture and the Church. Down to the present day, he has retained this position among Catholic philosophers.[77]

What philosophical contributions did Albertus Magnus [Albert the Great] (1193–1280) and his pupil Thomas Aquinas (1225 or 1226–1274) make that were so revolutionary? Historian Edward Peters argued that:

> Albert's greatest efforts were directed at assimilating the body of Aristotle's natural philosophy [which emphasized dialectic, i.e., logic] into a plan of Christian learning without conflicting with revelation and dogma. To do so, Albert distinguished between two spheres of knowledge. Theology, he said, dealt with supernatural things and was reached by faith; philosophy dealt with natural things and was reached by reason. Albert argued that these two kinds of knowledge and two ways of knowing were not incompatible, for they lead to the same faith and the same truth.... Albert attempted to create a system of natural philosophy that could be tested by reason and experience and proved by purely rational means without dependence upon revelation or theology. By sharpening the distinction between theology and philosophy, Albert, heavily influenced by Aristotle, created one sphere in which reason could claim legitimate authority.[78]

Although Albert was formative in Aquinas's development, it took Aquinas, and his superior knowledge of Aristotle, whom he called "The Philosopher," to establish scholasticism in its highest form. Russell offered that:

> Even if every one of his doctrines were mistaken, the *Summa* would remain an imposing intellectual edifice. When Aquinas wishes to refute some doctrine, he states it first, often with great force, and almost always with an attempt at fairness. The sharpness and clarity with which he distinguishes arguments derived from reason and arguments derived from revelation are admirable. He knows Aristotle well, and understands him thoroughly, which cannot be said of an earlier Catholic philosopher.[79]

These Aristotelian philosophical developments of the High Middle Ages were significant, Peters argues, because: "They helped to challenge the Platonic-Augustinian tradition of thought that neglected material reality and focused upon invisible forms and ideas in the mind of God that were more 'real' than their crude and imperfect earthly copies. The new [Aristotelian] studies argued instead for the regularity, coherence, and intelligibility of material creation."[80] Whereas Plato had argued that only philosophers had the gift of leaving the cave and understanding the world of Truth and Forms, Aristotle argued that the truth was revealed in the sensible world, where universals, not Forms, were reality.

Aquinas wrote his *Summa Theologica* as a ". . . vast compendium of both philosophy and theology, the monument to Aristotelianism in its Christian form."[81] In it, Aquinas deals with numerous "first questions," including: the existence of God, the soul, evil, ethics, man's ultimate happiness, free will, first causes, and so on.[82] In 1879 Pope Leo XIII codified the *Summa* as the official philosophy of the Roman Catholic Church. Because of this enduring official status, Russell argues that "Saint Thomas, therefore, is not only of historical interest, but is a living influence, like Plato, Aristotle, Kant, and Hegel—more, in fact, than the latter two."[83]

Adler's interest in Aquinas was hardly pre-ordained, and in some sense ironic. Adler was a nonobservant Jew and his promotion of Thomist Aristotelianism was dumbfounding to a largely Protestant faculty. His "espousal of Aristotelian philosophy, and his agile defense of the version of Aristotelianism set forth in the bulky pages of Aquinas's *Summa Theologica*, seemed perverse and, indeed, incredible to almost everyone he encountered at Chicago." In fact, in university circles at that time, the *Summa* was widely dismissed "as mere lumber from Europe's medieval attic."[84] Yet Aquinas appealed to Adler because:

> Aquinas's scholastic method of introducing every question with objections to his views, then spelling out the truth in crisp, logical form before refuting the initial objections with the same clear logic fitted Adler's habit of mind perfectly. Here he found reasoned answers to the most important questions a man could ask, as well as armor against a vast array of objections to the answers St. Thomas found convincing.[85]

It is unclear, however, whether Adler's formidable intellect was the genesis of Hutchins' belief "that the core of a liberal arts education ought to rest in firsthand acquaintance with the books that had shaped Western literary culture...." This proposition, argues McNeill, "... seemed completely convincing to Hutchins even before he made his own acquaintance with a suitable selection of such books through his classroom partnership with Adler."[86] Similarly, Hutchins' friend and biographer Harry Ashmore notes that "... employing the liberal arts as the basis for general education [was] an acknowledged inheritance from William Rainey Harper, as was Hutchins' insistence that specialized research and training be confined to the graduate and professional schools of the University."[87] However, Ashmore also argues that Hutchins "had no firm ideas about the content of undergraduate education, except that it should be different from the miscellaneous elective courses he had endured at Yale."[88] During this early time in Hutchins' tenure, Adler argued strenuously that "the classics of Western civilization, beginning with the ancient Greeks, . . . could provide 'the whole of a liberal education or certainly the core of it.'" In fact, Adler told Hutchins, after his assessment of what Hutchins had learned at Yale, that he would be a "wholly uneducated man" if he did not take a crash course in the classics."[89] Hutchins' curricular philosophy may not have been solely influenced by Adler, and indeed Hutchins never claimed that it was, but there is no doubt that Adler was a primary influence in Hutchins' beliefs about liberal education.

By Hutchins' appointment to the presidency in 1929 the College proposals first conceived during Burton's tenure were well-formulated and with Hutchins' support a revised undergraduate curriculum, known as the "New Plan," was developed. Year-long interdisciplinary courses in the humanities, natural sciences, and social sciences were instituted. Under the New Plan, once these and additional departmental requirements were completed, and competency was assured by success on the comprehensive exams that included English composition and foreign language, a student was awarded the bachelor's degree. These developments not only served to focus increased attention on the undergraduate experience at Chicago, but they helped resolve a tension that had existed since the institution's founding when John D. Rockefeller's desire for a vital college, with a focus on teaching, was overshadowed by William Rainey Harper's unceasing promotion of a world-class university devoted to research.[90] Additional changes to the undergraduate college would be made in the late 1930s and in the 1940s. However, one further development of significance needs to be noted here.

Although Chicago did not adopt a curriculum based on the great books as was done later at St. John's, it does, as Bell has noted, carry that association. There are three reasons for this: one, the New Plan interdisciplinary courses all employed many classics of the Western tradition in their syllabi; two, the ill-fated University of Chicago Committee on the Liberal Arts, which was formed in 1936 with Adler, Barr, Buchanan, and others as members, advocated a curriculum based on the Virginia Plan great books scheme; and three, Hutchins and Adler played formative roles in the great books movement, which took several manifestations, including a great books course for undergraduates (and later for law students), a great books extension program for adult education, and the development of the Great Books Foundation, which influenced *Encyclopedia Britannica* and its *Great Books of the Western World* series.

The sole development mentioned above to precede the Virginia Plan was the great books course co-taught by Hutchins and Adler starting in 1930. This course, titled simply "General Honors 110," used essentially the same reading list that Erskine had employed for his General Honors course at Columbia, which, it will be recalled, Adler had taken as an undergraduate.[91] Because Adler was disdainful of the practice of employing textbooks when original readings were available, the course used only primary sources. Hutchins agreed: "If the student should know about Cicero, Milton, Galileo, or Adam Smith, why should he not read what they wrote? Ordinarily what he knows about them he learns from texts which must at best be second-hand versions of their thought."[92]

Eighty freshmen applied to be in the new General Honors 101 course; after interviewing them, Adler selected twenty to participate. The class met once a week for two hours around a large oval table to discuss the week's book. Accounts suggest that Adler played "the heavy," pushing the students to clarify their thoughts, while Hutchins, who himself had only recently read most of the classics under Adler's tutelage in preparation for the course, usually played a softer, nurturing role.[93] One student at the time, Sidney Hyman, recalls that the class was very serious, with little laughter at first. Students were required by Adler to stick to the text at hand; the class was not a college bull session. Indeed Adler was often miserable until a student had an epiphany, at which point the students felt heroic. Hutchins, by contrast, was relatively lighthearted and witty. In addition to guiding students he made common cause with them. In class Hutchins quipped lines including, "If appointed Pope I'd want to be called Blasphemous I" and "The Faculty aren't very good, but the President and the students are wonderful." The real benefit of the course, according to Hyman, was that the students came to appreciate that ideas mattered and that "although we had only a half-baked understanding of these ideas, at least we were aware that these books were out there."[94] The course took two years to complete. At the end of each year, outside examiners such as Scott Buchanan of Virginia and Richard McKeon of Columbia would conduct oral examinations. When the course ended, some of the students successfully petitioned the University to extend the course for two more years so that the students could reread the books.[95]

Of the great books impetus, former dean of the University of Chicago Humanities Division Robert Streeter notes that:

Hutchins's advocacy of study programs based upon the classic texts, which came to be known as the Great Books, challenged conventional compartmentation in the academy. The works were chosen as noble illuminations of persistent human problems, from the writings of philosophers, artists, and scientists. A major presupposition underlying the study of these major works, whether undertaken in school and college or among adult groups, was that the discussion these books stimulated led to a more mature understanding of present-day issues, while at the same time sharpening the students' skills as readers and thinkers.[96]

It is interesting to note that while the faculty generally reacted negatively to Hutchins' perceived circumvention of faculty prerogatives and to the doctrinaire Adler, the great books course was wildly popular with the students and it took the campus by storm.[97] The immense popularity of the great books course would later be replicated in Chicago's extension program. The same scenario would be found some twenty years later at Virginia when Barr, likewise subject to withering attacks from some faculty members, taught a great books seminar which was extremely popular with the students, so much so that it too received a successful student petition for continuance. The Virginia scenario will be treated in detail in Chapter 6.

Conclusion

The developments at Columbia and Chicago show that, after halting moves toward reclamation of a curricular middle ground as attempted by the earlier proponents of liberal culture, the general education movement gave further impetus to those who sought amelioration of the elective system's worst results. Rudolph wrote that:

> The general education movement, as the effort to define and enforce a common curriculum has been called, began as a response to the sense of bewilderment with which many students faced the freedom of the elective course of study. It received clarification during and after World War I, when a consciousness of western values and national problems found expression in courses designed to orient students to their cultural inheritance and their responsibilities as citizens.[98]

This fear, that cultural inheritance and civic responsibilities were being lost, was not new. Rather it was a twentieth-century manifestation of the fear of declension. As noted earlier, many of the Calvinist Puritans who founded Harvard were Oxbridge men who understood the necessity of an educated ministry. They feared their city on a hill might be lost to the barbarism of the wilderness lest they ensured the production, in the New World, of ministers to safeguard and promote the Word. While seventeenth-century divines feared the power of the Old Deluder and the wilderness, their eighteenth-century counterparts saw declension in the adoption of Restorationist culture by Boston's elite and the increasing Yankee quest for mammon. Likewise, preservation of cultural inheritance and promotion of civic responsibilities were deemed critical by Jefferson to the success of the republican experiment, if the tenuous rescue of English liberties by the American Revolution was not to be lost. It is to Jefferson and his University that this book now turns.

CHAPTER 2

The University of Virginia and the Creation of the Virginia Plan

"We wish to establish . . . a university on a plan so broad and liberal and modern"
—Thomas Jefferson

The University of Virginia

Mr. Jefferson's University

The institutional history of Virginia requires additional consideration. The early history of the University of Virginia, which is well known, offers a unique window on some of the most significant curricular developments in American educational history. Unlike the colonial colleges and even the earlier state universities, from its founding the University of Virginia was distinctive. Jefferson's placement of the Rotunda, for example, with its library containing the best of classical and enlightenment thought, rather than a chapel at the center of the academic grounds made physical this original and symbolic change.

Yet Jefferson's Enlightenment philosophy extended far beyond the architecture of the university. Like others of his generation, Jefferson was anxious that the liberties secured in the Revolution be nurtured and preserved, for history had shown that the republic was a most fragile political form. A natural aristocracy of leaders, one based on merit as opposed to an artificial one based on the accidents of birth, was needed to prevent the young country from declining into ignorance and tyranny. "Those persons whom nature hath endowed with genius and virtue," Jefferson wrote, "should be rendered, by liberal education, worthy to receive, and able to guard the sacred deposit of the rights and liberties of their fellow citizens, and that they should be called to the charge without regard to wealth, birth, or other accidental condition or circumstance."[1]

Jefferson's proposal for a pyramidal—and elitist—structure of public education in Virginia from elementary education up to a capstone university was not realized during his lifetime, save for the university. Of it, Jefferson had written: "We wish to establish . . . a university on a plan so broad and liberal and *modern* as to be worth patronizing with the public support, and be a temptation to the youth of other states to come and drink of the cup of knowledge, and fraternize with us."[2] These conditions were achieved, albeit largely for Southern young men of "artificial" aristocratic lineage.[3] When the University of Virginia opened for classes in 1825, Jefferson's curriculum was primarily elective in approach and broad in content.

41

Letting the student choose what courses to take—the elective system—was a radical idea and Virginia was the sole institution in the country to employ electivism as the modus operandi; other colleges had prescribed curricula. In 1823 Jefferson wrote to Harvard tutor George Ticknor that:

> I am not fully informed of the practices of Harvard, but there is one principle we shall certainly vary, although it has been copied, I believe by nearly every college and academy in the United States, that is, the holding of the students all to one prescribed course of reading, and disallowing exclusive application to those branches only which are to qualify them for the particular vocation to which they are destined. We shall, on the contrary, allow them uncontrolled choice in the lectures they shall choose to attend, and require elementary qualifications only and sufficient age.[4]

While far beyond what was offered at other institutions, election was nevertheless qualified. The University of Virginia *Catalogue, 1832–33* stated that: "Every student is free to attend the schools of his choice, and no other than he chooses; provided, that if under the age of twenty-one, he shall attend at least three professors . . . ."[5] While students were allowed to choose which school or schools in the University they wished to attend, their choices ended at that point. "Once a student had chosen his field of specialization, no electives were permitted *within* a school; there the course leading to the degree was entirely prescribed. Students not interested in securing a degree, however, were free to take whatever courses they wished. This was essentially a 'parallel' course scheme, combined with provision for 'partial' courses for special students."[6] Finally, the *Enactments by Rector and Visitors of the University of Virginia* [1825] reflected that Jefferson was a dedicated student of the classics and believed them integral to liberal education. These original Enactments provided that only upon passing an examination in the Latin language could one receive a diploma from the University.[7]

Qualified election was not the only significant change made in Charlottesville. Traditional degrees, such as the *Artium Baccalaurei* were not awarded; instead graduates received a diploma from one or more of the eight schools at the university. Such novelty could not last. As later happened with the "Hutchins College" at the University of Chicago, the University of Virginia was forced by necessity to largely abandon its idiosyncrasies and adopt more conventional academic policies.[8] Nevertheless, Virginia was recognized as establishing electivism in American higher education. Significantly, Harvard President Charles Eliot, who, starting in the 1870s finally won a permanent and indeed dominant place for electivism in American higher education, credited Jefferson as the progenitor of the elective system in America although Virginia was apparently not the first school to employ a form of the elective system.[9] In a report to the Virginia General Assembly in 1845, Professor

William B. Rogers wrote that, "Many years before the establishment of the University of Virginia an election of studies was allowed at the College of William and Mary."[10] While Williamsburg witnessed limited election in its curriculum, Charlottesville was nevertheless the first to see electivism made central in its philosophy of higher education.

Within the eight "schools" Jefferson established at the university, both classical and contemporary subjects were offered. Bruce listed them as follows:

I.—Ancient Languages: Latin, Greek, and Hebrew; and there were to be taught in the same school in addition, *belles-lettres*, rhetoric, ancient history, and ancient geography; II.—Modern Languages: French, Italian, Spanish, German, and English in its Anglo-Saxon form, while modern history and modern geography were also to be included in the same course; III.—Mathematics in all its branches, to which was to be appended military and civil architecture; IV.—Natural Philosophy: the laws and properties of bodies in general, such as mechanics, statics, hydrostatics, hydraulics, pneumatics, acoustics, and optics; and the science of astronomy was also to be attached to this chair; V.—Natural History: the sciences of botany, mineralogy, zoology, chemistry, geology, and rural economy; VI.—Anatomy and Medicine: the sciences of anatomy and surgery, the history of the progress and the theories of medicine, physiology, pathology, *materia medica*, and pharmacy; VII.—Moral Philosophy: the science of the mind, general grammar, and ethics; and VIII.—Law: common and statute law, chancery law, federal law, civil and mercantile law, law of nature and nations, and the principles of government and political science.[11]

One will remember from the discussion of the Yale Report of 1828 that advocates of collegiate education during the colonial and antebellum periods believed that the prescribed classical course of study prepared one for life, and thus by definition, one's vocation. As noted above, Jefferson believed that to be educated, men of necessity needed to be familiar with the classic works of Western civilization. The crafters of the Virginia Plan more than one hundred years later would draw on this fact in support of their curriculum centered in part on the great books. The validity of their claim will be treated in the next chapter. For now, suffice it to say that in consideration of his emphasis on election and a broad curriculum that included the classics, historians of American higher education rightfully acknowledge Thomas Jefferson's bold and farsighted educational vision, the "hobby of his old age."

What Became of Jefferson's University

The radical quality of Jefferson's innovations at his university had long faded by the twentieth century. The historical literature bears out that Virginia's notoriety has traditionally derived from its early nineteenth-century innovations, not its twentieth-century ones. One reason is that in terms of its structure and educational philosophy, other universities had come to look more like Virginia with the spread of electivism in the postbellum era, and Virginia had come to look much like other universities with a standardized curriculum and standard degrees. That Virginia had not maintained its unique character is not surprising. The lack of preparation and maturity possessed by many students, for example, made Jefferson's desire to offer only university-level instruction essentially impossible. From the start the University had served as much as an academy as it had a college, not to mention a university. Jefferson wrote to W. B. Giles in December 1825:

> We were obliged to receive last year shameful Latinists in the classical school of the University, such as we will certainly refuse as soon as we can get from better schools a sufficient number of the properly instructed to form a class. We must get rid of the Connecticut tutor.[12]

It seems unlikely that nineteenth-century Virginia was ever able to rid itself of "shameful Latinists" since Latin was required for the B.A. degree until World War II. In 1892 President Henry Shepherd of the College of Charleston recalled that:

> During my own student life at the University of Virginia I cannot recall, in my course of instruction in Latin, a single shadowy reminiscence of aesthetic hint, critical suggestion, culture flavor, or stylistics inspiration. It was a mournful and plaintive round of local relations and prepositions, . . . the distinction between *sic* and *ita, ergo* and *igitur*. . . . Nothing, save my early home environment and my own instinct, preserved me from chaos and disintegration. I survived the ordeal of my university training by a species of literary transcendentalism.[13]

By the early 1900s, the University of Virginia was quite similar to other colleges and universities. Jefferson's vision had been significantly remodeled, not only with the academic and degree alterations mentioned earlier, and the symbolic changes that came with the reconstruction of the Rotunda after the disastrous fire of 1895, but also with the decision, quite contrary to Jefferson's vision, to install a president as the leader of the university. Edwin A. Alderman, who was president of Tulane and previously of the University of North Carolina, was named the first president of the University of Virginia in 1904. It would be Alderman who first undertook the goal of restoring real distinction to the university. Two future authors of the Virginia Plan—Robert Gooch and Stringfellow Barr—were undergraduates during Alderman's tenure and it is to them, and their friend Scott Buchanan, that this study now turns.

Gooch, Buchanan, and Barr

Robert Kent Gooch was born on September 26, 1893 in Roanoke, Virginia. As an undergraduate at Virginia, Gooch was the quarterback of the football team and was very popular with his classmates. Gooch also excelled in the classroom and he was a member of Omicron Delta Kappa and the Raven Society, the University's two oldest honor societies. After receiving his B.A. and M.A. from Virginia in 1914 and 1915 respectively, he proceeded to Oxford as a Rhodes Scholar. Lord Annan noted that "Before the war, Oxford was a private liberal arts university with an exceptionally privileged social-class composition and ethos."[14] This elite environment made a profound imprint on Gooch and, as will be seen, informed his educational beliefs for his entire career.

Gooch's time at Oxford was interrupted by World War I, after which he spent a short time working for the Burrough's Adding Machine Company. Out of boredom he returned to England to finish his work at Oxford from which he earned a B.A. in 1920, and as a non-resident, an M.A. in 1922, and a Ph.D. in 1924. After three years of teaching at William and Mary, Gooch returned to Charlottesville in 1924 where he became a faculty member in the Political Science department.[15] An Anglophile, Gooch inherited a love of academic ritual at Oxford, which he subsequently sought to uphold at the University of Virginia. In 1932 he succeeded Armistead Dobie as the grand marshal of all academic functions at the university, a post he held until his retirement in 1964.[16]

Born on March 17, 1895 in Washington, as a young boy Scott Milross Buchanan moved with his family to Jeffersonville, Vermont. He attended Amherst College during Alexander Meiklejohn's tenure, and after graduating in 1916, taught Greek at Amherst for a year. After serving in the Navy during World War I, Buchanan attended Balliol College, Oxford for two years as a Rhodes Scholar where he read philosophy. He received his Ph.D. in philosophy from Harvard in 1925 and then until 1929 was Assistant Director of the People's Institute in New York where he worked with Mark Van Doren, Richard McKeon, and John Erskine's former student, Mortimer Adler, who was offering programs of study in western civilization to interested adults as part of the Institute's educational programs.[17]

The Institute had been in existence for three decades when Buchanan joined in 1925 and it was in this environment that Buchanan first began to formulate his philosophy of education.[18] Long discussions on a host of topics, including ethics, philosophy, science, history, literature, and epistemology often followed formal lectures at the Institute. After immersing himself in this environment for a few years Buchanan "began to see some form in the chaos and to make some judgments." In addition to agreeing to accept Adler's advice to use the Columbia Honors Course in Great Books for Institute seminars being held at the Public Library, Buchanan decided that he should teach two subjects that seemed to be missing in the minds of Institute students. The first was mathematics, "ignorance of which was proving a real barrier to communication and understanding." The second was "poetry or poetics, the free use of the imagination as an auxiliary to abstract doctrine." Why these two? Buchanan stated that:

> Much to my surprise, I found that mathematics and poetry run parallel patterns, such that one illuminates the other and sometimes, though not always, they can be understood together when they are unintelligible apart. Ordinary language attests to the connection, as when one counts numbers and recounts a story, or when geometrical figures are compared with figures of speech, or when in Greek the word for ratio is *analogon*, or when physiological functions can be expressed in mathematical functions. . . . The symbolic elements of poetry are words, and the corresponding elements of mathematics are ratios. It is rather easy to pass from these symbolic elements to the aspects of reality which they designate. Words stand for qualities; ratios stand for relations. Qualities in relation can be built by *ratio-cination* into the structure of poetry and mathematics, into the worlds that tragedies and comedies comprehend. But clear as such a conclusion can be made, it floats like a nebula in space, or like a cloud in the wind. It begs for context and substantiation. The elements seem to be fictions.[19]

Buchanan's increasing understanding of the relations between poetry and mathematics was augmented by insight from another Institute colleague, Richard McKeon. Like Adler, McKeon was on the faculty of Columbia University and also a regular fixture at the People's Institute. McKeon had studied medieval philosophy at the Sorbonne and when Buchanan published *Poetry and Mathematics* in 1929 McKeon provided the book's context. Many years later Buchanan wrote that:

> [McKeon] insisted that I had stumbled into a rediscovery of the seven liberal arts, the *trivium*—grammar, rhetoric, and logic—and the *quadrivium*—arithmetic, geometry, music, and astronomy. He further insisted that we three ought to proceed with a revision of the traditional forms and a reconstruction of them for the sake of the order and articulation they could bring to the contemporary college and university. We also speculated on the possibility of making a modern *trivium* and *quadrivium* the basis of a curriculum for a People's University. . . .[20]

The desire, because of its hoped-for-utility, to understand contemporary knowledge within the historical framework of the seven liberal arts of the *trivium* and *quadrivium*, became a guiding goal for Buchanan, Adler, and later others including Mark Van Doren, Robert Hutchins, and Stringfellow Barr. Buchanan described the beginning of this effort in the later 1920s as follows:

> The first year Adler, McKeon, and I gave a series of lectures at Cooper Union on the traditional structure of a university, using the forms of the traditional European universities and filling them with the content of modern learning. For the sake of clarity we kept the old terminology, po-

etry divided into grammar, rhetoric, and logic; mathematics divided into arithmetic, geometry, music, and astronomy.[21]

The decision on the part of Buchanan, Adler, and the others to keep the historical terminology of the seven liberal arts would prove to be pivotal to the future of their endeavors. Even though Buchanan and the others claimed that they were interested in applying the old terms to modern knowledge and research because of the clarity they would hopefully provide in their effort, their detractors saw not clarity but instead a reactionary scholasticism implicit in the use of the historical terminology of the *trivium* and *quadrivium*. By the 1940s these vying contentions commanded national attention, especially within the academy.

These debates will be treated in subsequent chapters; for now it is important to understand how this historical conceptualization of the liberal arts was applied by Buchanan and his colleagues. Buchanan's own words nicely summarize his understanding of the relation between contemporary knowledge and traditional terminology:

> Modern mathematical content fits into the traditional forms pretty much as [follows]. . . figures, numbers, ratios and proportions, equations and functions, correspond to the *quadrivium*. The poetic content is well revised to fit the *trivium*: grammar, rhetoric, and logic. These seven liberal arts, the two divisions paralleling each other, form the trunk of the tree of knowledge. The three-branched top of the tree divides into the traditional professional subject matters, medicine, law, and theology.[22]

This conceptualization of knowledge provided these budding "liberal artists" not only with an understanding of the relation of various branches of contemporary knowledge but also with a powerful pedagogical tool, namely, the study of the great books of the Western canon. Again, in Buchanan's own words:

> Our study of the formal liberal arts began to throw light on the [great] books. A great book is the product of the liberal arts; the authors are liberal artists, masters of the arts. The great books improve the mind because they induce the formal habits of learning in the reader and discussant. The aim of the liberal arts is insight, understanding, imagination, and finally the transformation of the student into his own teacher and the teacher of others. The result of liberal education is lifelong learning and teaching. The social fruit of the tree of knowledge is an intellectual culture. The rediscovery of the liberal arts could be the much-needed beginning of the reconstruction of education in this country.[23]

Buchanan's years at the People's Institute thus proved to be formative for they strongly influenced the intellectual and career paths that he would subsequently follow over the course of his life. At the end of the 1920s the People's Institute group scattered. Buchanan joined the philosophy faculty at the University of Virginia in 1929 where he and his old friend from Oxford, Stringfellow Barr, initiated a true educational collaboration that waxed and waned for the next forty years.[24]

Frank Stringfellow Barr was born on January 15, 1897, in Suffolk, Virginia. When he was ten, his mother, Ida Stringfellow, and his father, William Alexander Barr, who was the Episcopal minister of the church in Suffolk, moved the family to Lynchburg, Virginia, and later to New Orleans, where his father was the dean of the Episcopal Cathedral. Early in childhood Barr became known by the nickname "Winkie" which he and those close to him used throughout his life.[25] After one year at Tulane University, which he did not enjoy, Barr decided to transfer to the University of Virginia, where, in counsel remarkably similar to what Buchanan would later advocate for undergraduates, Barr was told by his father to take math, Latin, and Greek, and whatever else he took did not matter, because he had "no faith" in what the colleges were teaching.[26]

Barr excelled once he was in Charlottesville. The college curriculum at Virginia in the 1910s featured a conventional mix of requisite classical languages and a series of distribution requirements.[27] Barr did very well in his courses and ironically, given his professional career as an historian, Barr never took a course in history.[28] Of Richard Dabney, one of the history professors with whom Barr would later be a colleague, Barr said: "I loved Richard Heath Dabney, he was a wonderful old boy, but what he would say about history didn't interest me at all."[29] Barr also served on the yearbook—*Corks and Curls*—and was a member of Alpha Tau Omega. In 1916 Barr earned his B.A. degree in English. The following year he was inducted into the Raven Society and received his M.A., both in May 1917.[30] In spite of his successes, Barr would recall many years later that he had no mentor while he was a student at Virginia. This differed from Buchanan, "who'd been in [Amherst] College with Meiklejohn and a personal friend of Meiklejohn's and had in a funny sense been tutored by Meiklejohn." Barr said, "I had no comparable adventure with a lecturer that I could name."[31]

After a stint in the Army Medical Corps during World War I, Barr left for Balliol College, Oxford where he studied as a Rhodes Scholar from 1919 to 1921. It was at Oxford that he met Scott Buchanan who became his lifelong friend and colleague. At Oxford, Barr quickly became disillusioned with his course in literature. At the same time he became fascinated with the depth of Buchanan's intellect and it was Buchanan who suggested Barr read history for the duration of his time at Balliol. He did, and after Oxford, Barr also studied at the Universities of Paris, where he earned a diploma, and at Ghent. It was also at this time that he married Gladys Baldwin, known to her friends as "Oak."

After time in Paris and a stint as a tutor in Asheville, North Carolina, Barr endeavored to return to Charlottesville. In planning a trip to Virginia in the spring of 1924, Barr wrote to Edwin A. Alderman, President of the University:

> Aside from the pleasure of greeting you, I am of course anxious to know whether the History department is to undergo the expansion you spoke of. This may sound like a very gracelessly direct bid: it is precisely that. An offer of a berth in that Department at Virginia would receive my weightiest consideration when I form my next year's plans. At each successive return to America from Europe I have been more convinced that I wished to cast my lot with the State, and if possible with the University, of Virginia.[32]

Barr returned to the University of Virginia in 1924 to teach in the School of History. As an assistant professor, he was one of three faculty members; Dumas Malone was the associate professor and Richard Heath Dabney was a full professor.[33] Barr taught modern European history, a position he held for the next dozen years: three as an assistant professor, three as an associate professor, and six as a full professor starting in 1930 at the age of thirty-three, "to the fury of some of the faculty, because I was too young for a full professorship."[34] In addition to teaching during the 1924–1936 period that he was at the University of Virginia, Barr served as the business manager of the *Virginia Quarterly Review*, and then from 1930 until 1934, as editor.[35] Barr remained on the history faculty until 1936, when he left with Buchanan for the University of Chicago.[36]

Three Professorial Styles

Although Barr and Gooch shared numerous traits in common—former student leaders, Rhodes Scholars, and a shared love of the University of Virginia to name a few—the two men were at opposite extremes of the professorial image. Barr, who was very popular with the students and widely regarded as one of the best lecturers at the University, was rumpled, "tweedy," academic, and outspoken. He had "fabulous flaming red hair" and wore a "knickered flannel suit."[37] He was eloquent and a good "front man," but his lecturing style was regarded by some as cheap theater. Nevertheless, in the 1930s Barr loved the University and its sons loved him.

Robert Gooch, by contrast, was handsome, elegant, fastidious, and politically savvy. Particularly striking was the artificial British accent which Gooch used after his return from England, and which he continued to affect for the rest of his life.[38] One student from the 1930s, Charles Moran, recalled that

Gooch was widely thought of as a very good teacher and that his argumentative style was appropriate to his interests in government and law.[39] A student of Gooch's in the 1950s, Staige Blackford, likewise respected him, but also thought his government and foreign affairs class was dull, and that Gooch "was one of the worst teachers I ever had."[40] While not as captivating as Barr, Gooch was highly regarded. When he retired in 1964, accolades named Gooch "the living symbol of the university," "the students' professor," and "the Virginia man's Virginia man."[41]

Scott Buchanan, by contrast, was often described in more contemplative and reserved terms, sometimes as melancholic, but also as a man who had an incredibly sharp mind that made a distinct impression on people. J. Winfree Smith, who took Buchanan's course on metaphysics at Virginia in the early 1930s recalled that Buchanan had an "extra-ordinary ability as a teacher. To some extent this depended on personal qualities very hard to define, such seemingly accidental things as intonation of the voice or a penetrating look. Sometimes it depended on a flair for startling paradoxes, sometimes on deliberate avoidance of the conventional."[42] Another student of Buchanan's during the 1935–1936 academic year, L. Harvey Poe, Jr., recalled that Buchanan's classes were more like discussion sessions than lectures. Buchanan would promote discussion by asking questions and then avoid intruding too much into the discussion, except to continue it on a productive course. Buchanan believed that one could not make another person learn. Rather, one knew that learning had occurred when a student exclaimed "I see!" Another pedagogical distinction was that Buchanan gave only essay exams to his students.[43] In spite of their differences in character all three men pushed relentlessly for the common goal of intellectual rigor and excellence.

Continuing Academic Atrophy

Jefferson had wanted his institution to be a true university and not a *de facto* academy as he believed the other American institutions of higher education were during his time. As noted earlier, the necessity of engaging "shameful Latinists" and the "Connecticut tutor" at the start of the university's history had belied Jefferson's hope. One hundred years later many believed Jefferson's hope had yet to be realized. A critical article in *College Topics*, the student newspaper, stated the university had "such a serene detachment from what is commonly considered the chief purpose of a university." What the university did have was an air "of gentlemanly aloofness, of elaborate negligence in a beautiful setting. But from the machinery of education proper, not a whir."[44]

In 1922 the requirements for the B.A. were revised, but new requirements alone did not assure either rigorous classes or student achievement.[45] In 1931 Gooch attacked the university's undergraduate program, comparing it to a "kindergarten or grammar school."[46] Some idea of the approach students took to their classes is seen in the recollections of Charles Moran, who was a student in Barr's 1931 world history course. Moran contends that Barr was *more* demanding than most professors because Barr actually enforced certain classroom rules—rules which illustrate the seriousness, or lack thereof, with which many Virginia students took their course work. For example, Barr did not allow students to read newspapers in class if the students could not keep the papers from rustling. Also, no sleeping was allowed to the point of snoring. This latter injunction could be a real problem, especially around the time of "Easters," the main social event of the Spring, when the students would often be "half-crocked" in class. Those students who actually worked in class were rewarded. For example, Barr conferred the William Cabell Reeves Fellowship in History on Moran, meaning Moran graded student papers and received much welcome financial assistance during the early years of the Depression.[47]

The "Special Honors" System

One step made toward increasing the academic quality of the university was the creation of a system of "Special Honors" that predated the honors proposals made in the 1935 Virginia Plan. The original provisions for Special Honors at Virginia were introduced by the Academic Faculty for the 1924–1925 academic year. They were designed for students "who possess greater ability and application than the average." In order to motivate the better students, and to give them "authoritative recognition of unusual ability and high achievement," the Special Honors system established Intermediate and Final Honors. Intermediate Honors were awarded to students who had no failures and a grade point average of 85 percent or more in all of their underclassmen courses. Those students who wished to be candidates for Final Honors had to apply to the new Special Committee on Honors at the end of their second year of classes and be accepted by the committee. Final Honors were awarded by the committee solely on the basis of a given student's performance on an oral or written special comprehensive exam administered at the end of their collegiate course work. Although their four-year course work record was not taken into account in the determination of Final Honors, upperclassmen candidates for Final Honors were not excused from classes in their last two years—an important point that would be revised in the 1935 Virginia Plan. Though small, the Special Honors system established in the 1920s was the first manifestation of honors work at the University of Virginia.[48]

Barr's Developing Convictions

Stringfellow Barr would be one of the members of the committee which revised the honors requirements and it is instructive to consider his educational thinking during the time that he was a member of the Virginia faculty. During his years as a history professor at Virginia in the 1920s and 1930s, Barr was somewhat influenced by the German historian Oswald Spengler, who proposed in his monumental *Decline of the West*, published as two volumes in

1918 and 1923, that all civilizations are deterministically organic; that is, that they go through an inalterable process of birth, bloom, and ultimately, decay. Barr recalled that "I did fall for it when . . . volume I . . . first came out. . . . I lectured on [Spengler], because I couldn't lecture on what I should have lectured on 'cause I'd been lying on my belly reading Spengler in a panic." Barr later rejected Spengler's deterministic view of history, claiming that "Spengler was too dramatic for my taste really."[49] However, educational declension remained a dominant theme in Barr's view of the world. He never wavered from his conviction that the liberal arts had been displaced by the spread of the elective system that had come, unfortunately in Barr's opinion, to dominate American higher education.

Barr's tenure at the University of Virginia was seminal. Although Buchanan recorded that he and Barr "had spent long hours in talk about the plight of American education when we were both Rhodes Scholars at Oxford," it was during their time in Charlottesville that Barr first became interested in reforming undergraduate education by reestablishing the liberal arts as the foundation of the undergraduate curriculum.[50] Barr recorded that:

> My teaching had been in large lecture courses, but I got up a section of the course and read great historical works with them—Herodotus, Thucydides, Plutarch. I began to see why Scott was hipped on these great books. I'd read some of these books before, of course, some of them partly in Greek, but I didn't really get the point of any of them. I suppose one never does, it's all relative—but certainly I didn't. Slowly Scott got me to understand why they had such extraordinary effects or had had for him and Adler and McKeon. . . .[51]

One student who was chosen by Barr for this special discussion section in the autumn of 1935 was L. Harvey Poe, Jr. Poe recalled that while the regular students in Barr's history class read from a textbook and took a true-false final examination (for which Buchanan chided Barr), a small group of better students, hand-picked by Barr, read primary works and discussed them seminar style: an intellectually exciting and likewise unusual occurrence at Virginia.[52] This evolutionary change in the way Barr thought about education eventually led to his desire, shared by Buchanan, Gooch, and others to attempt the reformation of collegiate education at the University of Virginia.

The Appeal of Curricular Reform

During an interview late in life, Stringfellow Barr was asked to recount the events leading up to the creation of the Virginia Plan in 1934 and 1935. He replied: "It's an incoherent story but events were incoherent." Barr then explained that, although Virginia "had a system under which [a student] could get honors," the program was perceived as being poorly formulated.[53] In September 1934 Barr had accepted the appointment by the University's new president, John Lloyd Newcomb, to serve on a committee with Chairman Robert Gooch, Scott Buchanan, and others to study Virginia's honors program and come up with a better plan that would enable the University to "do more than it does now for the more favored college student."[54]

Barr, Gooch, and Buchanan had all been critical of contemporary undergraduate education before official committee work on the Virginia Plan got underway in 1934. Although each had in his own way been interested in curricular reform for some time, the formation of this committee marked the formal beginning of the somewhat incoherent story of Barr, Buchanan, Gooch, and their "Virginia Plan" as it played out at various times at the University of Virginia, the University of Chicago, and St. John's College over the next thirty years.

To appreciate the situation faced by Barr, Buchanan, Gooch and the other committee members who created the Virginia Plan, one must be reminded that, in spite of its vaunted beginnings a century earlier, the University of Virginia was not perceived as being academically distinguished during the early decades of the twentieth century. For the first seventy-five years of its existence, the University's internal governance had been by committee. Thomas Jefferson had not provided for the office of president, preferring instead to establish the Board of Visitors as the legal and external authority for university affairs and leaving routine institutional governance in the hands of a faculty committee with a rotating chairmanship. In 1904 this system was finally abolished and while the first president, Edwin A. Alderman, and his successor John L. Newcomb, had done much to bring the University out of the doldrums, the institution's position vis-a-vis the leading American universities was less than enviable.

The unremarkable academic quality of the University of Virginia in the 1920s had persisted into the 1930s. A 1937 *Life Magazine* issue devoted to the American University "as one of the basic institutions of our present-day cultural heritage" highlighted Virginia's non-academic reputation:[55]

> Aside from a common eccentricity in not calling a campus a campus, Virginia and Harvard are not at all alike. Thomas Jefferson, who founded the University in 1819, wrote that while "nearly every college and academy in the United States" was copying Harvard in prescribing rigid courses, he wanted the Virginia student to "come and listen to whatever he thinks may improve the condition of his mind." Virginia still sticks to this broadly gentlemanly attitude which does not breed or encourage scholars. Harvard's attitude is just the reverse. . . . There is very little of the "collegiate" about Virginia. Its students try to be cosmopolite gentlemen and they are indisputably among the ablest college drinkers in the country. Except for its Law School, Virginia does not enjoy top rank as an educational institute. Good Virginians and F.F.V.'s

invariably attend the University unless they have serious educational aims. Then they go north. At Virginia, in the lovely town of Charlottesville, the student can spend a few surpassingly pleasant years among gentlemen, getting what has been called the "finest training for convivial and mannerly social intercourse to be found anywhere in the world."[56]

This impression of the social aspect of the university was supported editorially by the student newspaper, *College Topics*, which stated that the University of Virginia, Princeton, and Williams are "generally recognized as the 'country club' colleges of America.... And well may it be said, for the students of these three take more pains in dress, and the etiquette of play than the students of any other colleges in the country. But does this detract from the specifications of a gentleman? It definitely does not." As for studies, *College Topics* declared that Virginia "stands neither highest nor lowest."[57] To the extent that this was a common perception of the university's academic stature, President Newcomb's interest in improving standards seems warranted.[58]

It would be incorrect to assume that Virginia had no academic standing during this time. In a 1935 article Stringfellow Barr wrote that:

Because of its origins and its early conditions, the University of Virginia has the distinctive character so often found in Europe and so rarely found in America.... It is a singular fact that as late as the present century it was possible to speak merely of "the University" in any Southern state and still be widely understood, and this even after numerous institutions had grown up throughout the South that would eventually make it necessary to specify the full title.[59]

Non-Virginians also held respect for Mr. Jefferson's University. Frank Aydelotte, the former president of Swarthmore College, referred to the University of Virginia as one "of our stronger state institutions."[60] Nevertheless, academic quality, or the perceived lack thereof, became a motivating concern that permeated university policy in the mid-1930s.

President Newcomb was interested in improving undergraduate instruction at all levels. In 1935, the B.A. requirements were revised for the second time since World War I.[61] While all students might benefit from the new requirements, Newcomb believed the "more able student" deserved even better. It was against this backdrop that Newcomb reached out to Gooch and through him to Barr and Buchanan to develop a better honors program to challenge Virginia's most able students. Barr and Buchanan's mid-1930s collaboration in Charlottesville, which became so integral to the liberal arts movement, thus began in part as an attempt to respond to Newcomb's concern for the better students. However, the result of the committee's work—the Virginia Plan—

had roots that ran much deeper than the committee's work in Charlottesville in 1934 and 1935.

Propaedeutic Experiences at Oxford

Barr and Buchanan's conversations with Gooch, Newcomb, and others at Virginia built upon earlier, albeit less directed, discussions that Barr and Buchanan had had while at Oxford, and on their subsequent experiences, especially Buchanan's time with Adler at the People's Institute in New York in the 1920s. Of their first discussions in England, Buchanan wrote that: "[Barr] and I had spent long hours in talk about the plight of American education when we were both Rhodes Scholars at Oxford, he from Virginia and I from Massachusetts."[62]

At Oxford, Buchanan had been exposed to the famous arts courses that comprised the honors school known colloquially as "Greats" or "Ancient Greats." Of this course of study Daniel Bell noted that:

> The *Literae Humaniores*, or "Greats," which in one sense is the inspirer of the general education ideal, is not simply a reading of classical authors for the sake of learning about a tradition. "Greats" is itself a specialization and training in the way to read texts, in order to produce a distinctive mind. As two Oxford dons characterize the course, perhaps a bit smugly, "The effect of *Literae Humaniores* on its students is to develop thought and speech and a keen and critical intellect. It is deficient in providing knowledge of the modern world, and history and economics will remain a closed book unless the student, as often indeed happens, makes himself well informed by his own efforts and intelligent general reading. But it is said to produce men who are unrivaled as expositors and judges of any situation or set of facts placed before them."[63]

Former Swarthmore president and Rhodes Scholar Frank Aydelotte wrote in 1944 that in terms of intellectual discipline, Greats had for over a century, "stood first in the entire university world." He also argued that while "its preeminent value is commonly attributed to the superiority of the Greek and Latin classics as training for the mind and to the severity of the standard which has prevailed in this School" it could be maintained that Greats "owes as much of its value to its breadth as to its content." This contention argued Aydelotte, explained why the other significant honors school at Oxford was the "Modern Greats." Established at the end of World War I, "Modern Greats" was an honors school of Philosophy, Politics, and Economics. Aydelotte concluded that "the success of Modern Greats seems to me to prove the soundness of the theory on which it was organized. . . ."[64] In other words, Aydelotte believed that the Greats courses at Oxford demonstrated how disciplined independent tutorial work using the best ancient and modern material, all in preparation for the final honors examinations, was the preeminent form of education for better students.[65]

Mortimer Adler recorded that Buchanan, who was very interested in the great books approach to education by the time he arrived at the University of Virginia in 1929, "regarded the 'great books course' as a characteristically American extension of the 'ancient greats' and 'modern greats' that, in his day at Oxford, were the main undergraduate programs."[66] Together, Buchanan and Adler had promoted the great books philosophy during their work together at the People's Institute in New York in the 1920s. By 1929, which Buchanan described as "the year of dispersal for our idea of the liberal arts," Buchanan and Adler were ready to try their ideas at other institutions. Adler went to the University of Chicago and Buchanan to the University of Virginia. Buchanan later wrote that these "new soils . . . proved both energizing and hostile" to their ideas about liberal arts education.[67]

Buchanan and Charlottesville

Upon arrival at the University of Virginia in 1929, Buchanan took up a position as associate professor of philosophy.[68] Virginia had an interesting assortment of rich personalities on its faculty at that time; Barr and Buchanan should have been right at home. As Barr put it:

> They were a little eccentric, if you like, a little more like Oxford actually, in teaching and in what they thought life was about. Scott [Buchanan] was, I think, genuinely intrigued by Charlottesville. He considered it a foreign country and acted accordingly and was kind of terribly amused by it.[69]

Yet perhaps because of his Congregational New England background, Buchanan never really took to Virginia, and he quickly became despondent at what he perceived to be a dearth of intellectual life at the University.[70] There were a few bright spots, especially his renewed friendship with Barr, but to Buchanan academic declension was everywhere:

> Stringfellow Barr and I quickly picked up our conversations where we had left off [at Oxford,] and the University of Virginia was a fertile field for participant observation as well as speculation. The college of the University was being squeezed, exploited, and reduced to the size and functions of a secondary preparatory school for the graduate schools, which in turn were losing their professional statuses and becoming handmaidens to the going concerns of science, technology, and business. The superficial symptoms of the disease appeared as worries about the better undergraduate students who were not getting liberal arts training commensurate with their powers. It was reported that an *ad hoc* Honors Course for the better students had been chosen by only two and a half

students per year, one of those statistical monstrosities of computerized dean's offices. President Alderman set up a committee to study the problem and make recommendations. Barr and I were members.[71]

Notwithstanding his renewed association with Barr, within months of his arrival in Charlottesville Buchanan despairingly contacted Adler, who had recently been brought to Hyde Park by Robert Hutchins, himself only a few months into his tenure as the president of the University of Chicago. Buchanan wrote, "We are just beginning the second lap of what is an old course, and it feels like wholesale disillusionment. Faculty, students, landscape, accent, housekeeping, even leisure, all are flat and unprofitable."[72] At Adler's urging, Buchanan started a correspondence with Hutchins in February, 1930. Buchanan wanted a position at Chicago and after an initial letter of introduction, Buchanan wrote a second letter to Hutchins in which he stated that:

> ... for reasons which I confess I don't completely understand the discomforts here in Charlottesville seem to be more acute.... It seems that my interest in Chicago is a comment on Virginia, and that my presence here is taken to be the only hope for philosophy in Virginia. I fail to understand this but have to accept it as a fact with all the attendant discomforts. I can assure you that in a small university town they are many.[73]

While claiming that he did not want to rush matters, Buchanan concluded that, "... I want to do all I can to ease the silly but nonetheless real misery here."[74]

It is not particularly clear why Buchanan chose Virginia, other than because he had an offer to do so and that he would be with his old friend Stringfellow Barr. To Hutchins he wrote:

> On account of various incidents in my moderately wide experience with universities I have for some time assumed that very little if anything of importance could be done with them; they should be born (sic) with fortitude and humor. Hence my decision to come here [to Charlottesville] where there is as little of a university as there can be and still provide a living for its members.[75]

Most likely, Buchanan's best option in 1929 was to go to Charlottesville. Many years later, Buchanan recorded that: "... my own sense that the enterprises the People's Institute had fostered should be carried on elsewhere; the idea of a people's university might well be reintroduced to the conventional university. I therefore accepted an invitation to join the philosophy department at the University of Virginia."[76]

Regardless of the reasons for his unhappiness, Buchanan did meet Hutchins in Chicago in March of 1930, ostensibly to discuss Buchanan's options. Although employment decisions were "postponed," Buchanan was quite pleased with the visit, particularly with their discussion on "a revaluation of values in academic scholarship." Once back in Charlottesville, Buchanan wrote to Hutchins:

> I do not mean popularisation of this knowledge by this revaluation but rather a shift of emphasis and effort away from fact-finding research to a critical search for "clear and distinct" ideas, as our gang [Adler, Buchanan, McKeon] calls them. The best example of what I mean is what Mortimer is doing in law and psychology. This and what little else I have seen of it, particularly in England, have been done under the university-community conditions that you would like to see at Chicago, but they have always seemed to involve "sweating" and underpaying the teacher and researcher. I think it a sound scheme, and money may be able to solve the difficulties. I hope it does. . . .
>
> I have to-day been telling my best friend here about the project for [Adler's proposed] School of Philosophical Studies. At the end of the conversation [Barr] said that this Chicago business, especially my trip, was the most exciting thing that had happened to him in years; I had led up to the Philosophical Studies as a climax. I told him about them in terms of the lectures on Scientific Apologetics that Mortimer and I have been giving in New York, how they had involved saying things about science that no scientist would say, and things about religion that no theologian would say, and finally forcing a formal statement of both that would completely re-organise all subject matters on a basis similar to the medieval *Summa's*. I went on to say that such a statement would turn all academic political argument into a discussion of intellectual subject matters. I apparently got quite eloquent; I repeat it for your amusement. I seem to be more serious than I supposed about this; I believe the success of your whole scheme depends on the results of this, and the doing of it will be most exciting for whoever does it. It would be like the rediscovery of the classics leading to the renaissance in Europe.[77]

With a clear hope in continuing their Chicago-Virginia discussions, Buchanan concluded: "Let me remind you that the Jeffersonian architecture and a very seductive countryside are waiting for you to come and see them; with them also I and my friend, Barr, who 'belongs'."[78]

Buchanan also wanted to bring Richard McKeon, then at Columbia, and Mortimer Adler, then at Chicago, to Charlottesville and he suggested to them that he would ask the chairman of the Philosophy Department, Albert Balz, to invite them to the University. Once there, they could work together on their liberal arts philosophy.[79] Such considerations, however, were soon postponed. Buchanan spent the 1931–32 academic year at Cambridge University researching the mathematician George Boole. From this work, Buchanan published a small book, entitled *Symbolic Distance*: "In which the bridge between the poetry of the *trivium* and the mathematics of the *quadrivium* was presented as a theory of measurement and fiction." Buchanan believed that "it would be through some such understanding that the modern liberal arts and sciences could bring together the modern literatures and sciences into intelligible and teaching order."[80]

When his time in England was drawing to a close, Buchanan wrote to Adler, "When I go back, I shall install the liberal arts in the school of philosophy or in a new honors school. Will you come to Virginia?"[81] Although they remained at Chicago and Columbia, Adler and McKeon both visited Virginia several times during Buchanan's years there as professor (1929–1936), sometimes to give formal lectures and always to continue their philosophical discussions.[82] Adler likewise wanted Buchanan and Barr to come to Chicago. In June 1931 they went to Chicago to act as external examiners for the great books seminar led by Adler and Hutchins. There they engaged each student in the seminar in a half-hour oral examination.[83]

President Newcomb and Curricular Reform

Upon his return from Cambridge in 1932, Buchanan reengaged the nascent discussion of curricular reform in Charlottesville:

> When I returned from England, the battles of the liberal arts at Chicago and Virginia had grown to sieges and campaigns. At Chicago there were hardy recruits to the new investigations and construction that Adler was leading.... The emphasis at Chicago was on the subject matters of literature and the humanities, including philosophy. I decided that I would balance this emphasis by attending courses in mathematics and physics taught by friends who were sympathetic to my questions. We kept the two universities in communication by exchanging lecturers who dealt mainly with the technical doctrines of symbols in logic and in mathematics, a kind of counter-doctrine to the growing movements of semantics, logical positivism, and pragmatism.[84]

Buchanan also continued his teaching in the philosophy department. Barr recorded that, "Buchanan taught only small classes and he taught these in the Socratic manner that had exerted such curious power at Balliol. He became something of a legend among students, although few of them knew him."[85]

A significant event at Virginia during this period was the death of Edwin Anderson Alderman, the first president of the university, in April 1931. John Lloyd Newcomb, who had been Alderman's assistant since 1926, was appointed acting president by the Board of Visitors. One of the candidates for the office was Barr, but in October 1933 the Board, after a long and drawn out consideration of other candidates, finally decided to appoint Newcomb as president.[86]

As noted at the beginning of this chapter, Newcomb believed improvements in the curriculum were necessary, no doubt out of a sincere desire to promote academic quality at the university. But Newcomb was not predisposed to consider radical changes in the curriculum. Virginius Dabney, in his history of the University of Virginia, recorded that the Student Senate passed a resolution supporting Newcomb as Alderman's successor because Newcomb, said the Senate, would not "wish to foist on Virginia any experimental schemes or ultramodern theories of education." Dabney argued that: "[Newcomb] was a man who could be counted on not to 'rock the boat;' his views were well known. Most members of the faculty were conservative, in contrast to many professors in later years, and they preferred a man who would move ahead in the old grooves to one who might go 'wenching after strange gods.'"[87]

In spite of Newcomb's disposition, Buchanan had promising discussions with him about possible curricular reforms for the better students. In March 1934, six months before President Newcomb actually appointed the committee that eventually drafted the Virginia Plan, Buchanan wrote Adler in Chicago that Newcomb was "very interested in my plan for general honors."[88] Buchanan's "plan" at this point was still in the formative stages. It would not be set to paper until the honors committee created by Newcomb several months later eventually included it as one of the two schemes in the Virginia Plan.

Buchanan, however, was also upset because Newcomb, perhaps true to his disposition, had expressed reservations to Barr about Buchanan's nascent plans. As Buchanan understood Newcomb, the problem was that "the requirements I had made in mathematics would scare the good students away and wreck the whole scheme. You see [Newcomb] objects to the quadrivium being an important part of the Liberal Arts, too. He must be an Aristotelian, but he didn't dare tell me."[89] Barr recalled that:

> ... after Newcomb got in, Scott [Buchanan] was more and more unhappy ... with the state of the School of Philosophy. ... and he talked with Bob Gooch and me, and. ... I don't know who succeeded. ... I think Bobby probably succeeded in getting Newcomb to appoint that committee [on Honors Courses], and appointed him chairman."[90]

Thus it was most likely Buchanan who first prompted Newcomb to consider changes in the existing honors program at Virginia and it was probably Robert Gooch who actually precipitated action by the president.

In short, Newcomb's decision to appoint a committee to consider curricular reform in September 1934 did not initiate the 1930s discussions regarding liberal education at Virginia; Barr, Buchanan, and Gooch had been discussing the issues for some time.[91] But the creation of the Gooch Committee, officially known as the Committee on Honors Courses, and which drafted the Virginia Plan, was a milestone event, not only at the University of Virginia, but in the liberal arts movement overall. As noted in Chapter 1, Erskine's great books course at Columbia and Hutchins and Adler's great books course at Chicago preceded the 1935 Virginia Plan. In crafting their curricular proposal, the members of the Virginia Committee on Honors Courses drew on these courses, the existing Special Honors program at Virginia, and their own experiences. The committee members ameliorated these precursors and packaged them into an integrated whole, which they called the "Virginia Plan." As will be seen, the Virginia Plan informed, and thus in a very real sense made possible, the curricular revolutions which followed at Chicago in the later 1930s and the 1940s, at St. John's in 1937, and the less radical curricular innovations at the University of Virginia, which likewise started in 1937.

Newcomb Appoints the "Gooch" Committee on Honors Courses
In his September 15, 1934 letter to Robert Gooch, President Newcomb stated that:

> I am very anxious to have a committee of the faculty study the whole question of Honors Courses in the University of Virginia. While the American State University must in my judgment never lose sight of the necessary training for the average student, I think the University of Virginia should do more than it does now for the more favored college student.... In any event, I should like to have the benefit of the judgment of a representative committee of our faculty on the whole subject of Honors Courses in the University.[92]

Gooch, who because of the discussions that he, Barr, and Buchanan had already had with Newcomb on the subject of honors work, was probably fully aware that such a letter was coming. Gooch replied to Newcomb that he was appreciative of Newcomb's confidence in him, that he was pleased with "the representative character of the members you [Newcomb] have chosen," and of his "desire and hope that the work of the committee shall be serious, intelligent, and fruitful."[93]

No longer merely a topic of discussion on Grounds, the creation of the Committee on Honors Courses meant that formal work on what became the Virginia Plan had begun. Although the Committee had six members, the three Rhodes Scholars—Barr, Buchanan, and Gooch—dominated its work and wrote its recommendations. Of Gooch's Honors Committee, Barr recalled that "we worked like hell. We met once every week or fortnight or something for a lot of months."[94]

Buchanan, Gooch, and Their Competing Proposals
The committee worked with several different ideas. All members agreed that the "Special Honors" program, which had been in existence at Virginia since 1924, was not working and needed to be overhauled. But the committee members found it difficult to agree on much else at first. Scott Buchanan wanted a whole new approach to honors work. He proposed the establishment of an

honors college within the regular College of Arts and Sciences. The honors students in this new college would be exempt from the regular curricular requirements and course work. Instead they would be required to take a completely prescribed program of study that utilized seminars, lectures, and the great books of the Western tradition to teach the liberal arts. Unlike the existing great books courses at Columbia and Chicago, Buchanan proposed that the Virginia program would include mathematical and scientific classics in addition to the great literary works. Buchanan also proposed that the students in the honors program would take a special laboratory class in which they would reproduce the momentous experiments of Western science, starting with those of the ancient Greeks. Final comprehensive examinations, both written and oral, would be administered at the end of the course, and "be given with as much dignity and severity as the group can stand."[95]

Robert Gooch, on the other hand, was particularly interested in establishing "Oxbridge"-style tutorial work for honors students. In Gooch's conception of honors work, which was very similar in substance to what he had experienced as a Rhodes Scholar at Oxford, the select students would have a workload in excess of that required of the average student, but also be exempt from all regular and departmental course requirements. Honors students would have weekly meetings with their tutors, write papers or conduct experiments, and at the end of their work, take oral and written final comprehensive exams on whatever subject they had been "reading," to use the Oxford parlance. This honors work, overseen by the Committee on Honors Courses, would take place within the existing structure of the academic departments of the College of Arts and Sciences and thus was more compatible with the last two years of conventional college work when students had an academic major.

Because Gooch's proposal lent itself better to the upperclass years, and Buchanan's proposal, with its emphasis on breadth, seemed especially relevant to the underclass years, the committee members eventually conceived of their overall plan as encompassing both proposals, but such a consensus did not come easily. Barr later recalled that Gooch, "unfortunately" in Barr's opinion, was political, that is, Gooch believed that "you mustn't do this because you would offend the sociologist, you mustn't do that because, and so on."[96] Yet because of his more accommodating stance, Gooch believed his proposal would work within the existing structure of the college far better than Buchanan's proposal. Gooch's interest in compromise—his willingness to design an honors program that could work within the status quo without too much disruption—would also increase the chance of the committee's eventual proposal actually being adopted by the faculty. Buchanan however, as Barr recalled, took a position at "just the extreme opposite" of Gooch. Buchanan wanted no accommodation with the status quo if the status quo was not worth preserving. Buchanan wanted first to figure out "what we must do" and only afterward was Buchanan willing to "talk about compromises. . . ." As Barr put it,

Buchanan was of the opinion that the committee should "find out what it is you've got to compromise, is it worth doing [?]"[97]

The Committee's work continued into 1935. Both Gooch and Buchanan continued to develop their proposals. In a statement on the "Special Honors" program that had existed at Virginia since 1924, Gooch stated: "The question why work in Final Honors at the University of Virginia has not been a success seems to me clearly to be a leading question, inasmuch as it implies that Final Honors work really exists. I consider this contrary to fact." Gooch felt the crux of the problem resulted from the fact that special honors upperclassmen had course requirements in their major department. As Gooch put it: "I see no reason for believing that a system in which the attempt is made to have the same student do some Honors work and some non-Honors work can possibly succeed."[98] Accordingly, Gooch was steadfast in his opinion that honors tutorial work, at least in the upperclass years, should prohibit any required course work. As Barr later stated, Gooch ". . . had been a Rhodes Scholar and was very much an advocate of the freedom that the Oxford undergraduate has for study on his own."[99]

Buchanan, however, was not particularly enthusiastic about the upperclassman "Oxbridge"-style tutorial plan promoted by Gooch. Barr recollected: "Of course, Scott [Buchanan] would say, '[Upperclassmen] aren't ready for a specialty. They've got no education and they're not getting it at present.'"[100] Instead, Buchanan believed that his great books scheme would introduce the students to the liberal arts in a way that had been lost in the fragmented world of the research university and its compartmentalized academic disciplines.[101] Only a program that endeavored to use all of the liberal arts of the *trivium* and *quadrivium* could make clear the unity of knowledge sought by the liberal artists. Buchanan wrote:

> The educational principle underlying the [great books] scheme might be called the principle of mutually implicated abilities and mutually supporting disciplines. The principle can be stated as follows: balanced training in two or more mutually implicated abilities increases the disciplinary effect in each ability over and above the results of any specialized training in single abilities. . . . It follows from this principle that the omission of a supporting discipline will tend to vitiate and nullify the effects of any given discipline. This result may be regretted but accepted as inevitable in the case of second-rate minds and those who come to college in order to earn a living or climb a professional ladder; it cannot be accepted without protest for the best minds. It is on this ground that this scheme has insisted on the wholeness and balance in the well-rounded humane disciplines of both ancient and modern classics, and has chosen to subordinate the present emphasis on free choice and intensive specialization, which already have their places in secondary education and

the graduate schools. The width and difficulty of the course demands, therefore, the ability to balance and integrate disciplines and subject-matters. Facilitation is sought in the mutual intelligibilities and interdependencies of the classics, rather than in the evanescent and specious trainings that we now hypocritically expect in our students. It seems that this course in principle demands no more than the equipment of the average student, and that therefore the determination of modes of selection of the better students can be left to the exigencies of administrative policy as this is dictated by circumstances.[102]

Clearly, Buchanan's scheme was promoting first and foremost a particular educational philosophy—one which supported the idea of the unity of knowledge and which argued that apprehending that unity had to precede any specialized study.

With its proposed college within the college, Buchanan's honors scheme was far more ambitious than Gooch's and this made it more difficult for Buchanan to get other committee members, and later the college faculty, to accept his proposals. While some committee members probably never really understood what Buchanan was arguing, he did make enough headway that the committee began to envision using both schemes together. Many years later Barr stated that, in the course of the committee's deliberations, what Buchanan had really come up with was "a kind of minute St. John's operation" while Gooch "really wanted to imitate Oxford."[103]

As the deliberations of the Committee on Honors Courses wore on, Buchanan continued to refine his proposal and the book list that went with it. The specifics of Gooch's scheme also needed further consideration. One or more of the committee members produced a document titled "Tentative Suggestions to Serve as Possible Basis of Discussion" to continue moving the process along. The "Tentative Suggestions" were a set of procedural proposals designed to make Gooch's scheme more specific. In the document it was noted that the committee's overall work was based on two assumptions. The first was that since they constituted the Committee on Honors Courses ("the Gooch Committee"), they understood their charge to be the creation of an honors program. Accordingly, "there must be a certain number of specially selected students" for such a program. They were not attempting to reform the entire college. Rather, they had adhered to President Newcomb's letter that had established the committee in September 1934 in which he had said, as the "Tentative Suggestions" noted: "I think the University of Virginia should do more than it does now for the more favored college student."[104] That being said, in the document the author or authors suggested that: "The expression 'Honors' might perhaps well be abolished. It seems to serve no indispensable purpose and is perhaps in some conflict with American traditional terminology." Instead, "An institution called 'The President's List,' analagous (sic) to the various Deans' Lists, might well be established. On this list would be students chosen toward the end of their second year (and possibly third) from among distinguished students who have completed all their required work."[105]

The second assumption noted in the document was that: "There should be established a central University authority, representative of the University in its corporate and impersonal aspect. This authority would in general be responsible for establishing and maintaining standards for students on the President's List. It might be called 'The President's List Authority' (P.L.A.)."[106]

With these two broad assumptions in mind, the author or authors of the "Tentative Suggestions" document proceeded to outline some specifics regarding the students named to the proposed President's List. Students on the President's List were to have the following privileges:

(1) To become candidates for the Bachelor's Degree with the President's Diploma. (If successful, they might receive their degrees at Finals from the Rector of the Board of Visitors upon presentation by the President of the University.)
(2) To be exempt from courses of the regular curriculum.
(3) To attend any classes of the regular curriculum without obligation to take quizzes, examinations, et cetera. (In any case, no class grades would determine in any way a candidate's final standing.)
(4) To pursue with relative independence a program of studies approved by the P.L.A.
(5) To receive direction and assistance in their studies adequate to their individual cases, as arranged by the P.L.A.
(6) To possess membership in the Colonnade Club.
(7) To have at their disposal properly equipped, quiet quarters.

Likewise, the President's List Authority was to have the following powers and duties:

(1) To establish the President's List.
(2) To arrange for the formulation of programs of study, with bibliography, syllabus, et cetera.
(3) To approve programs which guarantee study at least equal in quantity to that of programs for the last two years under the regular curriculum and which offer the possibility of doing work of a quality warranting award of the Degree with the President's Diploma.
(4) To arrange satisfactory direction and instruction for students on the President's List.
(5) To make regulations concerning residence for students on the President's List.

(6) To arrange final written and oral examinations for determining the degree of success with which students on the President's List have completed their studies.
(7) To recommend recipients of the Degree with the President's Diploma.
(8) To recommend students on the President's List as recipients of the ordinary Degree.
(9) To recommend the removal of students from the President's List and to determine the credit to which such students should be entitled in the regular curriculum.[107]

With these further considerations laid out, the overall Virginia Plan began for the first time to take concrete form. Although he had initially been skeptical of Buchanan's proposal, Barr eventually came to see considerable merit in the plans submitted by both Buchanan and Gooch. In a paper submitted to his fellow committee members, Barr stated that "each [proposal] seems to me infinitely preferable to what is now being done here as Honors Work." Because of this, Barr wrote to the other committee members that:

> I therefore urge the recommendation by this committee of both plans, to be used at different stages of college work. I shall continue to urge this unless somebody can submit a third plan that is better, or can convince me that Buchanan's and Gooch's plans cannot exist together in the same college, or that one would indisputably work better than the other.[108]

Barr believed that both schemes held promise and that it was not clear which would yield better results. He was interested in Buchanan's scheme because its statement of "mutually implicated abilities" was a statement of the unity of knowledge, "without which any general education becomes a farce." Barr thought the Buchanan's concern about Gooch's scheme—that it would inevitably lead to premature specialization—was legitimate. However, he also believed that: "Gooch's scheme recommends itself as being far superior to our present Honors Work, and as capable of being better still if the student had first passed through the discipline Buchanan has outlined."[109]

Eventually the members of the Committee on Honors were unanimously agreed. They would recommend Buchanan and Gooch's schemes as two complimentary parts of a whole: the "Virginia Plan." During the first two years of college, honors students would follow Buchanan's honors great books scheme, and in the last two years, Gooch's honors tutorial scheme. Barr anticipated a difficult fight with the faculty, but also believed that "the Committee will waste its time if it seeks for a scheme against which no objections can be raised." Indeed, the only way to avoid objections, said Barr, was to create a scheme "that did not merit objections." But Barr took comfort in his belief that "President

[Newcomb] appears to me ready to finance any scheme we can persuade him is worth it."[110]

The end result of the committee's work—the Virginia Plan—was an honors program unique in American higher education. The Virginia Plan (also sometimes called the "Virginia Report") called for prescribed great books seminars for select underclassmen and "Oxbridge"-style honors tutorials for select upperclassmen. Barr later recalled of the committee's work that:

> what came up, the Virginia Report, was a kind of first esquisse of what happened at Annapolis. It was the nearest to it of anything I know. It's true that [the] Columbia University Colloquium in the 'twenties had a good deal of St. Johnsish stuff in it, but the big contribution that Buchanan made was insisting on mathematics and science. . . . So we met a long time, six or eight of us, and came up with the Virginia Report. . . .[111]

CHAPTER 3

The Virginia Plan and Its Reception at Virginia

"St. John's For Two Years, Oxford For Two"
—Stringfellow Barr

The Virginia Plan

The Report of Gooch's Committee on Honors Courses

The Virginia Plan consisted of three sections. The first was an overview and condemnation of American collegiate education. The second section—the first half of the proposed remedy—was the underclassmen great books scheme.[1] The third section—the other half of the proposed remedy—was an amelioration of the upperclassmen Final Honors special program which already existed in a weaker form at Virginia. Barr recalled:

> The "Virginia Report" that emerged consisted of three parts. The first, which I wrote, was an acid assessment of the intellectual bankruptcy of the liberal arts in American "liberal arts" education. The second part, which Buchanan wrote, provided an all-required course that drew on the experiences of both the Columbia Colloquium and the adult seminars of the People's Institute. But the reading list differed drastically from that of the Colloquium. About half the books were mathematical or scientific. The list reflected the title of his *Poetry and Mathematics* and the connection between these two modes of thought and expression; between the medieval trivium and quadrivium that he and Adler and McKeon had argued about in the days of his seminars for the People's Institute; between, if you like, what C. P. Snow would many years later call *The Two Cultures*. The third part of the Virginia Report, written by R. K. Gooch, another former Rhodes Scholar, provided for a continuation and improvement of independent reading in the third and fourth years under a volunteer tutor of sorts.[2]

Late in his life, Barr stated: "I think . . . things like the Virginia Plan, you can't write in a sentence or two and then maybe a footnote—see Appendix Two, or something and have all those as part of the documentation." Instead Barr argued that "the Virginia Plan deserves to be where people can inspect it."[3] The Virginia Plan follows below in its entirety as it was originally submitted to President John Newcomb in November, 1935.

REPORT OF THE COMMITTEE ON HONORS COURSES
TO THE PRESIDENT OF THE UNIVERSITY

In a letter dated September 15, 1934, the president appointed a committee consisting of R. K. Gooch, Chairman, J. J. Luck, A. F. Benton, Scott Buchanan, F. S. Barr, and G. O. Ferguson, ex officio, who were to give their judgment "on the whole subject of honors courses in the University." In that letter, the President also wrote: "I think the University of Virginia should do more than it does now for the more favored college student." The committee has met almost weekly for a period of nearly six months and now wishes to lay before the president the conclusions it has reached.

It has seemed wise to the committee to ask itself first what is wrong with the present system that it should be considered inadequate for the better type of undergraduate. The committee offers the following diagnosis, which it believes will be recognizable to many who teach and to many who learn. College education has gotten itself into a vicious circle. The professor recognizes that neither the lectures he gives nor the text books he assigns for study are worthy of his ablest students. But the professor feels that, in view of the apparent difficulty with which most of his students learn what is now assigned to them, no real improvement is possible without much better human material to work with. However, given the financial crisis in our educational institutions, there seems little chance of excluding from admission to the college, or of sending home after they have shown deficiencies, the very undergraduates whose presence now drags down college courses. The able student, on his part feels—and is very vocal in expressing that feeling—that many of the lectures now given are not worth listening to and that the textbooks assigned are not worthy of his serious study. In his more charitable moods he recognizes that, given the present student body, its lack of sound preparation for work on a college level and its lack of any real seriousness of purpose, the professor is not much to blame. Observing this low morale on the part of both professor and student alike, the publishers have done their best to supply increasingly "easy" texts, more and more derivative, oblique, and irrelevant to the real subject at hand. The self-respecting professor has consoled himself with research, justifying his lectures as a means of subsidizing such research. Or he has found consolation in graduate courses, in which "real work" may be attempted, if only because the graduate student has professional and largely economic reasons for cooperating. The able undergraduate has turned to the university's "sideshows," that is to athletics and other "activities," in an effort to find an interest and even to secure discipline which he despairs of finding in the classroom. Or he undertakes serious reading of his own, perhaps with a group of his fellow students, perhaps with the friendly if casual advice of a professor. He comes to look on the strictly curricular exercises of the university as interruptions that must be borne patiently but which he quite sees through, which he knows his professor sees through, and which he knows his professor knows the student sees through. Under such conditions, professor and student come to substitute social courtesy and mutual tolerance for the rigors of intellectual cooperation.

The above diagnosis is purposely stated in black terms. Obviously it cannot apply to all professors, to all able students, or to all undergraduate courses in equal degree. But the committee believes that it does portray a nemesis which threatens every college course given under present conditions. In these circumstances the committee is convinced that some measure of segregation for the able student is imperative if he is to be freed from the inappropriate devices of mass education. Such segregation may obviously be achieved by either of two methods. On the one hand, the abler undergraduate may be freed during his last two years from the routine of courses, quizzes, and term examinations, and allowed to master a subject under the general supervision of one of the Schools in the College. On the other hand, a small group of picked students might be enrolled in a "college within a college" and the best curriculum the faculty can devise might be provided to them.

The committee on honors courses proposes two definite schemes, designed respectively to apply these two methods. It recommends that these two schemes be considered as supplementary to each other. Appendix A of this report outlines one of these schemes, to be applied to the first two years of college residence. It provides a basic general education, to be secured in a college within the college. Appendix B outlines the other, to be applied during the last two years of college when the student can best be freed from course requirements in order to master the field of his choice.

The committee is convinced that the first two years of the regular curriculum are not themselves likely, under present social and economic conditions, to supply the unusual student with the opportunities which he deserves. It proposes, therefore, that a small group of such students should be furnished with a college within the college and the best possible conditions for securing a liberal education. It proposes that a small corps of instructors be assigned to this group and freed of all other academic duties.

The committee assumes that with "good" instructors and "good" students the best possible subject matter ought to be provided, a subject matter which assures the student a liberal education and general culture. It is the committee's considered judgment, based on long discussion, that the subject matter of a liberal education at this level consists of a selected list of the greatest classics of our cultural tradition, from the Greeks to the moderns; and that these classics should be the highest achievements, on the one hand, in languages and literature, and, on the other, in mathematics and the sciences. Such classics should be read in their entirety and the maximum possible understanding achieved. The goal to be aimed at would be the comprehension of the main elements of Occidental thought. The scheme recognizes that such classics have stood the test of time, as permanently significant embodiments of our cultural inheritance. It recognizes that to live in our civilization at all requires some understanding of them, although that understanding under the present system is meagre, erroneous, and circuitous in origin. It assumes that the matters treated in these books ought therefore to be faced, and that they ought to be faced, not indirectly through "written-down" textbooks, but directly, through the books themselves, books which have been recognized generation after generation as containing the clearest and most forceful statements available, of just such matters. It assumes that a properly disciplined study of such books would therefore be a more formative and more liberalizing discipline and therefore a sounder basis for third and fourth-year college work—or indeed for wise living—than any curriculum under the present system. The committee feels that this scheme of studying our literary and mathematical classics is indeed "radical" in the etymological sense of that word, but that it is also the most conservative, most direct and most safe solution of a problem that has been dealt with long enough in ways that were "progressive," indirect and dangerous. The committee knows of no better method than this one of furnishing a student with a liberal education, and believes that the inherent practical difficulties in the scheme are exciting problems that face any college. Although reading courses have been used to supplement the regular course curriculum at both Columbia and Chicago, the scheme as a whole, as outlined in Appendix A is to the best of the committee's knowledge basically different from any discipline applied in our times; but the committee feels that this is a challenge and not a condemnation.

It follows that if the scheme in Appendix A with its choice of books, is adopted, then the subject matter may be allowed, so to speak, to dictate the choice of both instructors and students. This is theoretically what happens in college today, where men capable of teaching the required students are engaged as professors and where students capable and desirous of engaging in such studies are enrolled. Clearly, in this case, the instructors must be men interested in guiding first-rate students in securing a liberal education under favorable conditions. They must be prepared, for the time being, to subordinate their "professional" ambitions and their status as specialists to the real purpose and function of the group they are teaching. Similarly, the most relevant test of a student's probable fitness to pursue such studies for his first two college years would be his desire to do so; although the instructor should certainly be empowered to pick the apparently best applicants by the use of whatever standards or tests seemed applicable.

The committee feels that it is absolutely essential to the scheme of general honors outlined in Appendix A that both the literary and the mathematical sides be included, since both sides are integral to the cultural whole which the course is intended to pass on and to the equipment for effective thinking which the course aims to supply. It feels, moreover, that our college students are intellectually too immature to be allowed to blackball whole segments of a liberal education in the name of special interests; and that when they are allowed to do so, vocational specialization replaces automatically the goal of a liberal education. The committee feels that the two aspects of occidental thought are mutually implicated, and that this mutual implication is regularly recognized. It is recognized every time an "orientation course" is launched, in an effort to patch up a system that is based on second-rate and derivative subject matters.

During the last two years of college the exceptional student should be freed from routine course requirements, under the provisions outlined in Appendix B. These provisions are, of course, only a development of the existing honors arrangements including improvements which the committee regards as basic and essential. Whatever detailed steps may be necessitated may be left largely to the individual School to work out in cooperation with some central authority. Such provisions would certainly, in the hands of a good School, substitute a relatively thorough mastery of one field of knowledge for course-smatterings. They would place responsibility for learning more definitely than it now is, on the student himself, where it belongs. It is imperative, however, that the individual School, in setting up its program of honors work, bear in mind that the objective in view is a liberal education and not a species of premature graduate work.

It is presumably clear from the forgoing consideration that these two schemes are recommended as an integral whole, calculated on the one hand to lay sound foundations for a developed understanding of our intellectual traditions, and on the other to permit the student to follow in his maturer years his special bent. Nevertheless, in view of the fact that Appendix A calls for only twenty students, and in view of the fact that several times that number are capable of profiting by greater opportunities than they are now furnished, the committee recommends that students who, in the eyes of competent authority, are qualified to spend their last two years under the provisions of Appendix B, be allowed to do so, whether or not they have undergone the discipline outlined in Appendix A.

R. K. Gooch, Chairman
March 1935

Attached: Appendix A,
Appendix B.

APPENDIX A
The Proposed Course in General Honors

This course has been devised to bring whatever is known of the European tradition of liberal education to bear on the education of the best minds in the

University of Virginia. It is, therefore, in order to quote Aristotle on the ends and means of education. He says that the aim of liberal education is the production of the intellectual virtues, and that they are five in number, as follows:

1. <u>Art</u>, which is the state of a capacity to make changeable things, involving a true course of reasoning.
2. <u>Practical Wisdom</u>, which is a true and reasoned state of the capacity to act with regard to human goods, involving opinions.
3. <u>Scientific Knowledge</u>, which is the state of the capacity to demonstrate by induction and syllogism, involving knowledge of the eternal and the necessary.
4. <u>Intuitive Reason</u>, which is the state of a capacity to grasp first principles.
5. <u>Philosophical Wisdom</u>, which is intuitive reason and scientific knowledge of things highest by nature.

The means invented by the Greeks, and used and improved during the following twenty centuries are the Liberal Arts. These are seven in number and divided into two groups, called respectively the trivium and the quadrivium, as follows:

Trivium

<u>Grammar</u>, the art and science of concrete things as they are used in mediums of expression.

<u>Rhetoric</u>, the art and science of applying such notations to things both concrete and abstract for practical and theoretical ends.

<u>Logic</u>, the art and science of discovering and applying abstract forms.

Quadrivium

<u>Arithmetic and Geometry</u>, the mathematical arts and sciences that correspond to grammar in the trivium.

<u>Music</u>, the art and science that deals with applied mathematics in all the natural sciences.

<u>Astronomy</u>, the art and science that deals with proportions, propositions, and proofs, including mathematical logic.

It has been the aim in the construction of this scheme to detect the principles in this formulation of liberal education and to find the best subject-matter that is available for passing on the tradition. These materials have been found in their highest form in the literary and scientific classics of Europe. Some of these classics are clear and effective expositions of the principles of the liberal arts; all of them are products of the practice of the liberal arts; all of them are fine exemplary materials for analysis and practice, and many are outstanding models for imitation. They are crystallizations of the experience of the race, reminiscent of the past, clarifying for any present time, and they project the unchanging problems on the future. They are eminently formative studies.

It will be noted that the division of the liberal arts dictates a division in the subject-matter along the lines of language and literature on the one hand and of mathematics and science on the other. This division will appear in the scheme that follows, and the parts are understood as complementary parts of a single disciplinary whole.

Program of Instruction

All instruction will be based on the reading, analysis, interpretation, criticism, imitation, and discussion of the books in the following list:

1. Expository for Language and Literature
   Plato: *Cratylus, Republic, Sophist*
   Aristotle: *Organon, Poetics*
   Horace: *Ars Poetica*
   Augustine: *De Musica*
   Bonaventura: *The Reduction of the Arts to Theology*
   Thomas: *Summa Theologica*, Part I
   Locke: *Essay Concerning Human Understanding*
   Hume: *Treatise of Human Nature*
   Kant: *Critique of Pure Reason*
   Goethe: *Dichtung und Wahrheit*
   Coleridge: *Biographia Literaria*

2. Expository for Mathematics and Science
   Plato: *Timaeus*
   Euclid: *Elements*
   Apollonius: *Conics*
   Galileo: *Two New Sciences*
   Descartes: *Geometrie*
   Newton: *Principia*
   Leibniz: Mathematical papers
   Gauss: Mathematical papers
   Galois et al: Group Theory
   Boole: *Laws of Thought*
   Cantor: *Tansfinite Numbers*
   Poincare: *Science and Hypothesis*
   Hilbert: *Foundations of Geometry*

3. Exemplary Models in Language and Literature
   Homer: *Iliad* and *Odyssey*
   Aeschylus: *Oresteia*
   Herodotus: *History*
   Thucydides: *History of the Peloponnesian Wars*
   Aristophanes: *Frogs, Clouds, Birds*
   Plutarch: *Lives* (selected)
   Dante: *Divine Comedy*
   Francis Bacon: *Novum Organum*
   Montaigne: *Essays*
   Cervantes: *Don Quixote*
   Shakespeare: *Hamlet, King Lear*
   Milton: *Paradise Lost*
   Fielding: *Tom Jones*
   Calvin: *Institutes*
   Rousseau: *Social Contract*
   Adam Smith: *Wealth of Nations*
   Gibbon: *Decline and Fall of the Roman Empire*
   Marx: *Capital*
   Flaubert: *Madame Bovary*
   Dostoevski: *Crime and Punishment*
   Tolstoi: *War and Peace*
   James: *Principles of Psychology*

4. Exemplary Models in Mathematics and Science
   Nicomachus: *Introduction to Arithmetic*
   Aristarchus: *On the Sizes and Distances of the Sun and Moon*
   Galen: *On the Natural Faculties*
   Ptolemy: *Almagest*
   Copernicus: *De Revolutionibus*
   Kepler: *Epitome of Astronomy*
   Lavoisier: *Elements de Chimie*
   Dalton: *A New System of Chemical Philosophy*
   Darwin: *Origin of Species*
   Barnard: *Introduction to Experimental Medicine*
   Faraday: *Experimental Researches in Electricity*
   Joule: Scientific Papers
   Maxwell: *Treatise on Electricity and Magnetism*
   Peacock: *Algebra*
   Hamilton: *Quaternions*
   Riemann: *The Hypothesis of Geometry*
   Lobachevski: *Theory of Parallels*
   Veblen & Young: *Projective Geometry*

5. Materials for Analysis and Practice

Literature:	Science:
Old Testament	Hippocrates
Sophocles	Lucretius
Euripides	Archimedes
Lucian	Leonardo
Virgil	Harvey
Cicero	Gilbert
Ovid	Boyle
Marcus Aurelius	Clifford
Plotinus	Ostwald
New Testament	Galton
Volsunga Saga	Mendel
Song of Roland	
Chaucer	
Machiavelli	
Erasmus	
More	
Rabelais	
Grotius	
Corneille	
Molière	
Spinoza	
Racine	
Swift	
Voltaire	
Malthus	
Hegel	
Schopenhauer	
Balzac	
Zola	
Thackeray	
Dickens	
Ibsen	

Machinery of Instruction
1. Meetings of the whole class. All members of the class will meet once a week for discussion of reading with two instructors in charge. The instruction will consist of all the pedagogical devices used at present, ranging from textual criticism to open discussion of opinion.
2. Formal lectures. These lectures will be formal expositions of current topics in the liberal arts as they may arise in the reading. They will be based on the expository texts, and in the course of the two years will

complete an exposition of all the liberal arts both in their historical settings and in their contemporary applications. Such lectures will be given to all the students at least once a week.
3. Tutorials. Since tutorials offer the maximum versatility in teaching, they will be held for various purposes. Perhaps the most important tutorial instruction will be given in the more difficult stages of languages and mathematics, where formal drill and supervised practice are necessary. They would also be held for detailed criticism and discussion of papers written by the students. These tutorials are for the individuals or groups as needs dictate.
4. Laboratory. A laboratory will be established and equipped for the performance of the crucial experiments in the history of science, for the practice of the arts of measurement and experimentation, and the illustration of scientific theory.

Staff of Instruction
The major staff of instruction will be at least four in number, and they should be distributed in their training and major interests in such a way that the subject matters in this course may be covered by the combined competence of the group. This is particularly important with respect to languages and mathematics proper. There should be assistants to the instructors.

Students
The students will be selected by the instructors in the course from those applying on entrance to the college. Selection will be made on the basis of:
1. General intelligence and ability, as shown by previous records in secondary schools.
2. Judgment of the variety of complementary abilities and interests to make an efficient working group.
3. Not over twenty students should be chosen in the first year.

Rooms and Equipment
The arrangement of rooms and equipment should be understood as functional parts of the instruction. Special rooms should be provided for this course, as follows:
1. Rooms for reading with a special library at hand.
2. A laboratory.
3. Facilities for common living, including a common dining room for the students.

Degree Requirements
The requirements for satisfactorily passing the two years work in the honors course are as follows:

1. Reading knowledge, competence in grammar, and evidence of actual work in the course done in two languages, one ancient and one modern, at the end of the first year.
2. Working knowledge of mathematics through the calculus at the end of the second year.
3. Passing of a comprehensive examination on the subject matter of the course at the end of the second year.

Final degree requirements are left for determination of the regular college authorities.

APPENDIX B
Third Year and Final Honors

An arrangement shall be made whereby "the more favored college student" shall, during the latter half of the usual four year course, be enabled to pursue their studies in their chosen field of concentration on a firmer basis and on a higher plane than less gifted students. These honors students shall be afforded unlimited opportunity, under proper guidance, to master thoroughly their specially chosen subject. In order for their opportunity to be unlimited, they shall be at liberty, though of course under no compulsion, to claim exemption from course requirements. In this way they will avoid the danger of being penalized for pushing things to their end, where the course is not organized on the assumption that they will be so pushed, or for seeking understanding of the interrelationships among several aspects of a chosen subject, where those aspects are treated in uncoordinated courses. The freedom of opportunity for such honor students shall be matched by a correspondingly extensive ability of guidance. Elementary justice suggests that honor students shall have special access to the best teaching talent which the University affords.

The catalogue shall indicate to gifted students the availability to them of special opportunity in some such terms as the following:

Degrees with Honors

A student who is recommended by an academic School and accepted by the Dean of the College, acting on the advice of such body as he may designate, may become a candidate for a Degree with Honors.

Degrees with Honors shall consist of degrees awarded (a) with Third Year Honors (b) with Final Honors.

A student who has been accepted as a candidate for a Degree with Honors shall register as such when the programme of courses in his field of concentration is arranged with the official adviser of the School in question.

A candidate for a Degree with Honors is exempted from the usual requirements of class attendance in all courses in his field of concentration. He is likewise exempted from the usual examinations in all courses in his field of concentration which his Major School may include in comprehensive examinations at the end of his third year and his final year respectively.

Final comprehensive examinations for a Degree with Honors demand a rigid compliance with particularly exacting standards of scholarship. In the event that performance in the examination is not of sufficiently high quality for a Degree with Honors to be conferred, the School in charge may recommend that credit be granted towards the Degree without honors.

Comment

1. In order that opportunity for especially gifted students shall not, through inertia implicit in the status quo remain almost wholly theoretical, the Dean of the College will undoubtedly do well to act, in connection with honor students, on the advice of a specially chosen body, representative of the University in its corporate and impersonal aspect. Upon this body will in general rest responsibility for making real the opportunity offered to honor students. Thus, this body, in cooperation with the various Academic Schools, shall assume responsibility for establishing and maintaining the highest standards possible, to the end that only the very gifted student shall be considered worthy of pursuing honors work and that only honors work worthy of the very gifted student shall be offered to him.

2. The distinction between Third Year Honors and Final Honors is made with a view to offering special opportunity to very gifted students who remain only three years in the College. Among twenty-nine of the most recent recipients of Intermediate Honors who, out of a total of thirty-seven, replied to a questionnaire addressed to them by the Honors Committee, eighteen (or 62 per cent) were ineligible to undertake honors work, as at present instituted, because they were not to remain four years in the College.[4]

"St. John's For Two Years, Oxford For Two"

The Committee on Honors Courses had completed its first task. Of the committee's work Barr said: "the Virginia Plan put in a miniature St. John's program for the first and second year . . . You didn't do any elective system stuff. . . . In effect you went Oxonian in the third and fourth years and went to St. John's, which was unborn, in the first two. St. John's for two years, Oxford for two. . . . And it was a good statement."[5]

It was noted earlier that, as the committee's discussions progressed, both Buchanan and Gooch had believed that their respective philosophies belonged at the core of the recommendations to be proposed to Newcomb. Although the two corrective schemes were unanimously recommended "as an integral whole" and were "to be considered supplementary to each other," Buchanan and Gooch remained partial to the schemes they had each proposed.[6] Buchanan's recollections of the committee's work, for example, demonstrated his partiality to the great books program. As he later put it:

> By 1935 the Virginia Committee on honors had argued itself to a unanimous report which went far beyond the original assignment. Instead of recommending special work for selected students in the last two undergraduate years of the college, we proposed that a curriculum be offered to a few students in their first two years. This curriculum would be based on a hundred great books, the original list for the Columbia honors students reduced to half-length and supplemented by great books in science, Euclid, Ptolemy, Copernicus, Kepler, Galileo, Newton, Fourier, Clerk-Maxwell, and Claude Bernard. There would be tutorials in languages and mathematics, and laboratories in which the great crucial experiments would be repeated. The central piece in the curriculum would be seminars for discussion of the great books themselves.[7]

In this instance, Buchanan's recollections are somewhat problematic. They give the impression that Gooch's scheme for the upper-class years was dropped. As has been seen in the Virginia Plan itself, this is not true, rather, the existing Special Honors program for the final two years of college work was modified and strengthened from its pre-Virginia Plan form.

As will be seen, Buchanan's and Gooch's preferences would continually manifest themselves throughout their respective careers. Many years later Barr recalled how Buchanan's and Gooch's predilections, and his own, had played into the crafting of the Virginia Plan:

> Columbia and the People's Institute, and of course some Oxford stuff, because Bobby [Gooch] had already done the last two years. . . . Well, that part didn't interest Scott [Buchanan] so much, he wasn't as romantic about Oxford as Bobby, or . . . or, I guess, as I. He was maybe a little Scottish about Oxford: while Balliol College was a Scottish foundation, it had gone pretty English in the seven hundred years since.[8]

Barr saw value in both schemes, but Barr, as demonstrated by this recollection and by his career choices over the next thirty years, favored the new great books scheme over Gooch's improved honors tutorial scheme. Indeed, the great books scheme was the part of the Virginia Plan that Barr and Buchanan carried first to the University of Chicago in 1936 and subsequently to St. John's College in Annapolis in 1937, where they expanded it to encompass all four undergraduate years.[9]

This sequence of events also suggests why the honors tutorial part of the Virginia Plan has been essentially ignored by accounts of the liberal arts movement. When Barr and Buchanan left Charlottesville for Chicago in 1936 they left behind the tutorial program as well, and later chroniclers have done the same. J. Winfree Smith's 1983 history, *A Search for the Liberal College*, contains only two paragraphs on the tutorial part of the Virginia Plan, which is understandable considering that the book is ostensibly about the beginning of the St. John's Program, and the one-on-one tutorial program was not brought to Annapolis. Amy Apfel Kass' unpublished 1973 doctoral dissertation, *Radical Conservatives for Liberal Education*, supplies only one paragraph on the honors tutorial part of the Virginia Plan out of 350 pages on the liberal arts movement. Charles A. Nelson's 1997 edited volume, *Stringfellow Barr: A Centennial Appreciation of His Life and Work*, reprints the Virginia Plan in its entirety, except for Appendix B—the honors tutorial scheme—which is not included at all. In short, half of the Virginia Plan's proposed curriculum has been neglected.

To be fair, in works primarily focused on St. John's, it is not surprising that the honors tutorial part of the Virginia Plan has received scant attention, for it was the great books philosophy of education, not the "Oxbridge" tutorial, which figured most prominently in the curricular program at St. John's. Yet Kass' work on the liberal arts movement is problematic for another reason. She argued that her account "describes and analyzes the circumstances and problems that prompted the Liberal Arts Movement, the ideas and ideals that informed it, and the various efforts that were made to develop and institutionalize it."[10] Kass correctly asserted that, "The plan for the first two years [survived] the administrative shelving at the University of Virginia. In a more fully worked out form, it eventually became the core of the 'New Program' at St. John's College...."[11] Yet Kass neglected discussion of the last two years of the Plan, which as noted above, received one paragraph of explanation from her. If the tutorial plan is not to be considered part of the liberal arts movement, then her work is effectively a study of the great books movement, with emphasis on certain key individuals and their associated institutions. However, if the liberal arts movement, at least at Virginia, is a composite of the great books movement and the honors program movement—a logical assumption given that the two programs were unanimously proposed as supplementary and as "an integral whole" in the Virginia Plan—then both need to be given proper consideration. Even if one were to argue that these distinctions are merely matters of semantics, it is clear that the new honors tutorial program at Virginia, like the "New Program" at St. John's, was ultimately the result of the Virginia Plan submitted by Gooch's Committee on Honors Courses in 1935. Indeed, as will be seen, Barr believed that their later reforms at St. John's were influenced in part by the Oxbridge model. In short, if the liberal arts movement is to include the Oxbridge-style reforms (and the historical evidence unequivocally suggests that it must), then a more capacious definition of the liberal arts movement is required than the one offered by Kass. This definition must encompass both the place of the great books and the honors tutorial with its emphasis on final comprehensive examinations.

This more inclusive definition also makes more pertinent the fact that the Oxbridge tutorial plan crafted and adopted at Virginia remains a neglected topic in the history of curricular reform. This omission is peculiar given the place of Oxford and Cambridge in the history of higher education, the renown of their tutorial system, and the presence during the twentieth century of thousands of Rhodes Scholars in America who experienced the tutorial system in England. All of these facts argue that a program implemented in America, one which was based in part on the tutorial model and all its attendant history, is important.

The Elite Quality of the Virginia Plan

Another important point to be noted about the Virginia Plan was its elitist Jeffersonian quality. In spite of Buchanan's later recollection to the contrary, the Virginia Plan gave no indication that it was intended for everyone. Instead it indicated just the opposite. Of Appendix A—the great books scheme—of the Virginia Plan, Buchanan wrote in 1962 that "We hoped that this recommendation would start a few students on their own self-education, and that the curriculum would finally be accepted by the whole college."[12] While the committee, or individual members, may have hoped the curriculum would eventually be accepted by the whole college, the Plan, as presented to Newcomb and the faculty, was explicitly for a small group of elite students.

The culture of the University of Virginia in the 1930s was certainly what one could call aristocratic and this culture was conducive to a program for selected, academically advanced students. For example, Barr's colleague in the History Department, Richard Heath Dabney, wrote that "Jefferson was right, . . . The unfit should be weeded out, for their own good as well as that of the public. . . . The best brains in the state should have the best training available, but mediocre and stupid persons should be positively discouraged from entering college and positively prevented from getting degrees."[13] In a similar vein, *College Topics*, the college newspaper, wrote an open letter to the governor of Virginia, James Price, asking him to make the university "a retreat for the intellectual aristocracy. . . ."[14] Whether or not the Gooch committee envisioned that its Plan might eventually be extended to the entire college, as Buchanan later claimed, is unclear, but there is no mention of such an intention in the Plan itself. The radical makeover of the college that would have been required in terms of faculty commitments alone suggests the remote possibility of such a complete collegiate conversion.

The Committee and Plan A—The Great Books Scheme for Underclassmen
"A Scheme for a Course in General Honors"

In November 1935 the Virginia Plan, which had taken more than a year to create, was completed and unanimously submitted by Gooch's committee to President Newcomb. Many years later, long after they had established their great books program at St. John's, Barr recollected that: ". . . Newcomb didn't like [the introduction to the Plan], he thought it was very offensive."[15] But Newcomb was intrigued by the Plan's prescriptions. Once Newcomb had read the Virginia Plan it was split into its two schemes for presentation to the Committee on Academic Legislation for faculty consideration. The members of Gooch's Honors Committee decided first to attempt adoption of Buchanan's honors great books scheme for underclassmen laid out in Appendix A of their Virginia Plan. Once the faculty had made a decision on that scheme, then they would present Gooch's upper-class scheme for the new honors tutorial program laid out in Appendix B of the Virginia Plan.

Perhaps because of Newcomb's initial negative reaction to Barr's introduction to their report, the members of Gooch's committee believed it necessary to re-phrase the introduction and Appendix A before submitting it for faculty consideration. Accordingly, a new preamble and a restatement of Appendix A, collectively titled "A Scheme for a Course in General Honors," was drafted to argue the case for the plan in Appendix A—the great books scheme for gifted underclassmen. As best as they could, given its radical proposal for setting up an honors college within the regular college, the committee members clearly crafted "A Scheme for a Course in General Honors" for maximum acceptance by the Virginia faculty. Because he was the primary author of Appendix A, Buchanan most likely oversaw this restatement.

"A Scheme for a Course in General Honors" opened with a preamble that repeated Barr's acerbic critique of collegiate education, but which avoided the complete condemnation of collegiate education found in the initial version of the Virginia Plan submitted to Newcomb. This time the Virginia Plan authors noted that some benefits had accrued from the adoption of electivism: "By means of the free elective system we have been able to absorb the natural sciences and useful arts in our academic system and consequently to increase the range of our services to a democratic industrial society." However, they also quickly noted that electivism had created two major problems: "First, we no longer know what the few essential subject-matters are that go to make up the best education. Secondly, we are not providing the techniques and disciplines without which the best geniuses go away undeveloped and unsatisfied." The committee members believed their Virginia Plan was a good way to start correcting the situation. They argued that "this plan is devised to meet these two problems and to provide a method by which we may put ourselves on the way to working out a solution."[16]

The Committee's new preamble also made appeals to Jefferson, arguing that the Virginia Plan would revive his educational philosophy at his University. That Jefferson had introduced electivism to American higher education was ignored, thereby implicitly arguing that Jefferson would have never approved of the alleged perversions that electivism had undergone between the first and last quarters of the nineteenth century. Apparently, the circumscribed electivism that Jefferson had advocated as a way to free the university from the low level of education enforced at other colleges had evolved, according to the Virginia Plan authors, into a radical electivism that declared all subjects as equal, and perhaps more important, none as essential. It will be recalled that Jefferson did not promote total electivism. During Jefferson's tenure as Rector of the University of Virginia, a student was free to choose in which school or schools he would study, but once in a school, he had to follow the prescribed course of study for that school. Jefferson had also believed that all university students should be familiar with their classical heritage and his belief was manifest in the Board of Visitors requirement that all diploma recipients be able to pass an examination in Latin.

With this knowledge in mind, the Virginia Plan authors stated that their plan had:

> been developed from two main sources: 1) a study of the curricula of medieval universities which laid down the framework within which all European and American education worked until the middle of the nineteenth century; and 2) a study of recent experiments in the administration and teaching of honors courses in American colleges and universities. It has been the aim to extract the principle from the practice in each case and to find the conditions necessary for its application in the University of Virginia. It is assumed that this is the wise way to combine tradition and innovation.[17]

Regarding the first problem noted by them—that of the curriculum—the authors argued that: "The curriculum of the medieval university, preceding the professional schools of theology, medicine and law, consisted of the Seven Liberal Arts, grouped in two divisions, the Trivium and the Quadrivium." The committee members stated that the trivium "consisted of grammar, rhetoric, and dialectic, the three disciplines that study language, literature, and their ideal subject matters, including what Mr. Jefferson called ideology, and what we moderns call civilization and culture." Likewise, the quadrivium "consisted of Arithmetic, music (measurement by the application of number to things), geometry, and astronomy (the measurement by the application of geometry to moving bodies). It is these last arts from which our natural sciences have grown and in terms of which they are still to be made intelligible." Having stated these points, the committee members proceeded to argue that: "A glance at the original plans of Mr. Jefferson for the curriculum of this university will show the same framework; it had not been forgotten in his time." To bolster their case, a list describing "the original Jeffersonian curriculum" was attached to the document.[18]

The committee members then discussed how their proposed curriculum, informed by these earlier guides, might be applied to honors work for the better students: "The working hypothesis in such a course of study is that languages and mathematics contain the formative factors and instruments for the development of the human mind and keep thought alive in any subject-matter. The applicability of these disciplines and techniques in any subject-matter is prima facie evidence of their educational powers." Even though these disciplines and techniques "are still tacitly recognised (sic) in our present curricula," the problem, as the committee members saw it, was that "they are increasingly ignored in our actual administration and teaching." Buchanan and the others argued that:

> This is partly due to the fact that with large numbers of students it is impossible to prevent these disciplines from becoming rote and ritual, and partly due to the fact that it is only the best minds that can profit in the more obvious ways from these studies even under the best conditions. In spite of the present attempt to provide ideal conditions for students of special ability in the honors courses of American colleges, these studies have everywhere been displaced by President Eliot's elective system, and they have been relegated to an antiquarian status because of the supposed modern necessity for specialisation (sic).[19]

The answer to these problems was "the reapplication of the seven liberal arts to the best products of human thought as we have them in the recognised classics of the European and American tradition by selected students and instructors." If Virginia adopted these changes for its best students, then the authors believed that the university "would meet some of the problems of our present educational depression."[20] Having made its re-packaged case in the preamble, the rest of "A Scheme for a Course in General Honors," then re-stated with only minor modifications the content and pedagogy proposed in the original Appendix A to the Virginia Plan.

The "Supplement" to "A Scheme for a Course in General Honors"

In spite of its slightly expanded reading list, its grudging acknowledgment of some benefits arising from the elective system, and its institutional appeals to Jefferson's original curricular intentions for the university, it soon became clear that the Virginia Plan great books scheme advocated by Buchanan and his fellow committee members in the "Scheme for a Course in General Honors" faced several difficulties. It was noted in the introduction to this book that the claim that the curricular reforms advocated by Barr, Buchanan, Hutchins, Adler, and other "liberal artists" were rejected, as historian Frederick Rudolph put it, "because a return to ancient Greece and Rome did not recommend itself to most professors." Archival evidence relevant to the Virginia Plan's fate at Virginia suggests that Rudolph's conclusion is too glib and limited to explain adequately the reasons given for not supporting the great books scheme first presented in Appendix A of the Virginia Plan and in the re-packaged "Scheme for a Course in General Honors."

The initial concerns about the great books scheme are lost, but are nevertheless known because the authors of the Virginia Plan responded in writing to the objections that had been raised by some of the Virginia faculty. To be sure, "return to old-fashioned and outmoded cultural studies," a variant of the objection later noted by Rudolph, was one of the reasons listed why some Virginia faculty opposed the scheme, but it was only one of nine reasons noted in the Committee's response titled: "Supplement to a Scheme for a Course in General Honors." The other eight reasons reflected, not curricular concerns, but rather concerns relating to either personal interests or institutional factors.

In their supplement Buchanan and the other authors of the Virginia Plan great books scheme argued that: "An appropriate and effective elucidation of this scheme would come only from reading the books in the reading list. In place of this a few comments can be made on the questions that have been explicitly raised." Regarding the choice of students, the committee members noted the objection that: "There is the generally accepted opinion that a required fixed curriculum does not take account of individual differences in ability. For these and similar reasons it is presumed that students would not and probably should not choose to enter upon a course that demands as much as this one does." Regarding faculty approval they noted that: "It seems that on account of settled habits and customs in present educational procedure that the faculty would not approve of a quasi-separate honors school that would devote itself to general education." The reasons included the following:

(1) The duplication of present courses
(2) Expense
(3) Irresponsibility of staff to present schools
(4) Loss of better students from present classes
(5) Loss of prestige of present curriculum and staff
(6) Return to old-fashioned and outmoded cultural studies
(7) Omission of pet subjects
(8) Doubt of the abilities of both students and instructors to do thorough work in such a wide and difficult course of studies within the practicable time limits
(9) The establishment of a new degree[21]

In terms of the choice of students, the Virginia Plan authors replied that, while the details were "open to discussion," clearly "the 'best minds' are those that have the ability and preparation to read the hundred greatest books in the

European or Occidental tradition with a certain minimum of understanding and appreciation." Furthermore, "It should be recalled in this connection that none of these books was written as a textbook for technical or esoteric specialization. Their styles present only the difficulties of intellectual clarity, and mathematical or literary elegance." Thus, regarding the choice of students, "the minimum of required ability would be average rationality and the required formal preparation might well consist of elementary reading, writing, and arithmetic."

The authors continued by responding to the problem of faculty approval. They suggested that:

> Most of the difficulties of getting faculty approval of any scheme will arise from a general funk and a consequent set of fears that evidence a loss of effective standards and convictions in our present educational practice. Faculties at present progressively un-educate themselves, and compensate by praising themselves for their heroic renunciation of the intellectual life in behalf of teaching. Students imitate them in behalf of graduation. This course was devised to meet this situation. Its proposal and discussion by the faculty might restore enough morale to eliminate the nine objections listed above as shamefully irrelevant.[22]

The Virginia Plan authors believed that the forgoing faculty concerns were not particularly significant. They did, however, believe that the elective principle was "a serious objection directed against the underlying principle in this [honors great books] scheme." As they paraphrased the argument:

> It is held that the individual student has a moral right of free choice which should be allowed for at every step in his educational career. Modern progressive education has derived from this the psychological principle that learning is effective only if the interest of the individual student is enlisted and held. These principles seem to conflict with the principles of discipline as they are applied in morale and education. There are two revered solutions of the dilemma: one says that internal freedom comes only through self-imposed disciplines, the other that external freedom comes only through intelligently imposed disciplines. This scheme seems to satisfy both these demands in the large.[23]

Finally, the authors proposed that the objections might be better met by giving an idea of what the great books scheme would look like in operation. Under the Virginia Plan, "A modernized trivium and quadrivium would make mathematics and literature the basic formal disciplines." The trivium component would be manifest as follows:

> The study of grammar would consist in the study of at least two linguistic grammars on the background of a universal grammar, and the appli-

cation of these to the reading of texts and the writings of essays in these languages. Rhetoric would consist of the study of literary forms, including the analysis of lyric and epic poetry, the essay, dialogue, drama, history, and scientific exposition. Logic would consist of the study of formal syllogistic logic and the structures of scientific systems as given in Aristotle's *Organon*, and other relevant writings in philosophy. Reading and writing would be practiced to illustrate these formal studies, mostly by way of imitating literary styles and analytical methods.

The quadrivium component would be manifest as follows:

Mathematics would be studied in three parts corresponding to the divisions of the trivium. Arithmetic, geometry and algebra would be studied as mathematical grammars in the same fashion that languages are studied, with exercises to illustrate the formal principles. These would be taught from the higher standpoint as given in projective geometry or number theory. Mathematical rhetoric would consist of the devices, both symbolic and instrumental, by which mathematics is applied. This would include such separate sciences as analytic geometry, trigonometry, and calculus, and a special laboratory, where standard types of measurement used in the various sciences would be practiced as leading to the great historical crucial experiments, which would also be performed with the original instruments and materials. Mathematical logic consists of the formal analysis of proportions, equations, propositions, and proofs used in the other branches of mathematics and the sciences.[24]

The day-to-day operation of the great books honors program would consist of lectures, weekly seminar meetings, and tutorial sessions. The Virginia Plan authors proposed that: "The trivium and quadrivium would be presented in lectures and practiced, as indicated, to parallel the reading"; that "all members of the Honors school would attend the lectures, and the weekly meetings to discuss the reading of the books"; that "the schedule of readings would be made up to keep the subject-matter in step with the lectures"; and that "these are the required exercises for all members of the school." Additionally, "there would be special groups and tutorial hours for individuals in which the interests, tastes, and special abilities of the individual students would be allowed free exercise with any subject-matter that they might choose. These might or might not be within the lines of the set curriculum."[25]

Decision Time
The conversations that followed this stage of the debate unfortunately are lost, save one anonymous faculty member's written response to the Committee's

proposals. In it he made several points. First, that "the proposals of the Committee are . . . , in spirit at least, pointed in a direction which I approve." Second, that a solution must be found to three distinct problems: "(i) the selection of the honors students, (ii) the instruction of those selected, and (iii) the testing of their achievement." While "of these three the Committee has seen fit to regard the second as central," the author contended that the other two problems, which were procedural and not curricular, were just as, if not more, significant than the question of instruction. Ultimately, this faculty member argued that the determination of "honors" should not be made until a student reached graduation. Taking the great books program as an underclassman should not entitle that student to "honors," until his work during the last two years had proven to be highly superior. In short this faculty member questioned, not the curriculum of the Committee's proposal, but rather the procedural issue of when "honors" would be determined.[26]

President Newcomb's response to the great books scheme likewise indicated that factors other than the proposed curriculum may have been more important to its reception. Newcomb may well have been intimidated by the great books scheme, or never entirely certain as to what implementation of the scheme would ultimately mean for the rest of the faculty and the college, but there was another critical factor: university finances. When asked years later about Newcomb's response to the proposal, Barr replied:

> I think we could have counted on the students being excited, and I think we could have staffed it. But Newcomb felt he couldn't finance it. . . . I don't know whether Newcomb would have done it if there had been money, I never knew. I think it frightened him a little bit. . . . I still think it was the way to go at it; just a small group of undergraduates, and let them choose this instead of the ordinary curriculum. And I think it would have demonstrated its value so sensationally that it . . . you could have expanded it. And I think Charlottesville would have been a pretty swell place to do it.[27]

None of these recollections suggest that the proposed great books curriculum for honors underclassmen was itself the primary reason for the rejection of Buchanan's great books scheme. Indeed, as will be seen, later evidence from the 1940s and 1950s demonstrated the continuing appeal of the great books plan at Virginia.

The Importance of Financial Constraints
What does figure prominently in the recollections of the people involved is the role of the university's finances. While other factors may have played into the fate of the Virginia Plan at Virginia, there is little doubt that the ability, or lack thereof, to finance the underclassman great books scheme was critical to

its failure to win adoption by the university faculty in 1936. The anonymous faculty member quoted above stated that "the more grandiose scheme for the first two years (the great books scheme) was admittedly impracticable unless a considerable sum of money could be found to finance it."[28] Indeed, the university's financial health was critical enough during this time that it is a testament to the strength of the committee's proposals that they were considered at all.

To be sure, Newcomb may have been wary of the great books scheme and its call for an honors college within the college. He may have pled lack of funds as a convenient excuse to prevent adoption of the honors great books scheme for underclassmen. But, Newcomb's *possible* reservations cannot be known with certainty. What can be ascertained is the dire financial condition in which the university found itself during the Great Depression of the 1930s. Indeed, there can be little doubt that the horrible economic environment quickly figured into the reception given to the committee's Virginia Plan proposals. Because of the Depression, the General Assembly in Richmond decreed a 10 percent across-the-board cut in appropriations to the university in the 1932–33 academic year. Then, within Newcomb's first year as president (1933–34), an additional 10 percent cut was enacted, and some allowances were even more drastically cut; "austerity was the rule throughout the university."[29] The Gooch Committee's Virginia Plan thus came out during a time of true economic hardship for the university and Newcomb's apparent claim that the great books scheme in Appendix A of the Virginia Plan could not be financed seems most plausible given the university's financial condition.

A more detailed look at the university's finances during this period is instructive. For the academic year 1929–1930, the time of the initial stock market crash, the university had a total income of $1,583,269. For the next several years the university's total income fell as the Depression deepened. By the 1933–1934 academic year the university's total income amounted to only $1,229,866; a decline of almost twenty-five percent. The state appropriation, which made up a significant portion of the university's total income, likewise fell from $452,747 in 1930–1931 to $329,850 in 1933–1934. After this time the university's overall finances slowly recovered, although it was not until the 1937–1938 academic year that the university's total income returned to its 1929–1930 level. Also, although total income started to recover after 1934, the year that Newcomb appointed Gooch's Committee on Honors Courses, the state appropriations continued to suffer. From 1933–1934 to 1934–1935 the state appropriation rose from $329,850 to $384,664. However, it fell slightly in 1935–1936 to $382,621 and then plummeted in 1936–1937, the second downturn during the Depression, to $302,974. This decline in state appropriations occurred at the very time that the university was considering Buchanan's great books scheme from the Virginia Plan.[30]

The question of how to pay for the underclassmen scheme was critical to the scheme's demise at the University of Virginia. At a time when the university had cut faculty salaries by twenty percent, it was untenable for the university to allocate almost one-tenth of its annual state appropriation to a new curricular program for honors students. Years later Buchanan pointed directly to the problem of funding when he recalled that:

> We had asked for what has later come to be called a pilot plant. It would take money to make it the model that would be imitated, $30,000 annually for thirty students, six instructors, and separate living and study arrangements. By this time President Alderman, who had originally appointed the committee, had died, and Acting President Newcomb did not want to seem to overreach his temporary powers by undertaking such a radical departure from the conventional elective system in undergraduate education. The committee's recommendations were put on the shelf for lack of money.[31]

Buchanan's recollection that the committee's underclassman recommendation was put on the shelf for lack of money is corroborated by Barr's recollections. In a 1972 interview, Barr stated that:

> Newcomb just said, you know, "There's a depression on, and there's no hope of getting money for this kind of thing." I don't think he knew what we wanted to do, and I think if he'd had the kind of interest in it that several of us had, I think he'd have found some money. But it was tight, it was tight. But my God, I think I'd have loved the job of selling one of the DuPonts on that, because given Jefferson and DuPont and that business, you could say, "This would be the kind of leadership that Jefferson would care about." So . . . it fell by the way.[32]

Clearly both men believed that money was the primary obstacle to implementation of Buchanan's great books scheme, and as will be seen, it was this scheme for underclassmen, not the entire Virginia Plan, that was tabled for lack of funds.

Newcomb's lack of willingness to find additional funding for the great books scheme may have also played a role in its difficulties. Barr later opined that:

> [Newcomb] just said [the money] couldn't be found. Well, I think this is highly unlikely. [Buchanan] always said of the University of Virginia, all the foundations in New York were baffled by the University of Virginia because its origins and early history was such that it should by now be really one of *the* Universities, and it just wasn't. . . . The University was sort of just being elegant and sitting back.[33]

Barr believed that Newcomb could have done more to secure funding. A letter from Newcomb to Dr. Frederick Keppel, the president of the Carnegie Foundation, suggests that Newcomb's efforts to get outside funding were perhaps half-hearted. In his letter, Newcomb asked Keppel to review the Virginia Plan and "give me the benefit of your reaction." Newcomb also noted that he was going to be in New York and would "appreciate an opportunity of seeing you for a few moments during my visit."[34] Via Western Union, Keppel replied that, because of prior commitments, he would not be able to make any specific engagement, but hoped Newcomb would drop in. Whether Newcomb met with Keppel or with any other foundation is unknown, but not likely, as there is no extant correspondence of such a nature. Coincidentally, Keppel suggested to Newcomb that, "You ought certainly to see President Aydelotte in New York next week. He is the authority on Honors Courses."[35] As will be seen, it was Aydelotte who, in 1944, praised Virginia's honors tutorial program as holding great promise, particularly if the great books part of the Virginia Plan could be implemented in Charlottesville.

The possibility that Newcomb never pursued foundation-funding vigorously is supported by a final recollection from Barr. In the years following his departure from Charlottesville for Chicago and then Annapolis, Barr occasionally returned to the University of Virginia. On one such occasion Barr, Newcomb, and Chicago department store magnate Marshall Field were at a university reception. Field had previously promised Barr fifty thousand dollars for his work in Annapolis. Barr recollected that:

> We started in the house to cocktails . . . somebody said, "Newk, here you and Winkie are, and here's one of the wealthiest men in the country, so why don't you do business?" And [Newcomb] says, "Huh uh, there's no hope of that, is there, Winkie?" And I went on in and as I passed Marshall, Marshall said, "Let me know when you want me to mail that fifty thousand." Newk couldn't hear him, but it was rather typical of him. I felt like saying, "Now, that's what I mean, Newk, we could have done that thing. But if you're going to say, "Well, where the hell is the money coming from?" it ain't coming, Buddy, it ain't coming. First you've got to understand what it is, so you can talk about it understandingly, and he didn't know what it was, poor devil. He was a nice guy, nice guy, but he never knew the price of eggs.[36]

Whatever Newcomb's possible shortcomings as perceived by Barr and Buchanan, he must nevertheless be credited with providing the official impetus for the Virginia Plan in 1934 and, as a result, for all that ultimately would come of it.

The Committee and Plan B—
The Honors Tutorial Scheme for Upperclassmen
"Third Year and Final Honors"

By early spring of 1936 it was clear that Buchanan's great books scheme for first- and second-year men would not be implemented. Newcomb sent a short letter to mathematics department chairman John Jennings "Pot" Luck, temporary chairman of the Committee on Honors Courses, in Gooch's absence. Newcomb wrote:

> It now appears certain that we shall have to abandon the Committee's proposal for the first two years of honors work. I think your Committee should meet as early as you can for the purpose of reporting the second section [Appendix B] of the Committee's report to the Committee on Academic Legislation in order that we may get this matter settled and, if possible, settled during the current session.[37]

Luck, writing on behalf of the members of the Committee on Honors Courses, subsequently submitted the following statement to the Committee on Academic Legislation:

> After being advised by the president that he was unable, at the present time, to finance such a plan for the more gifted first and second year students as that outlined in Appendix A [the great books scheme] of this committee's former report, the Committee on Honors Courses desires to recommend the consideration of the plan for third year and final honors set forth in Appendix B [the honors tutorial scheme] of that report. To the comments included in that appendix we have added a comment 3. The committee is still of the opinion that the most important part of its recommendation is included in Appendix A. We confidently hope that some means may be found in the near future to put this plan into execution.[38]

The Committee on Honors Courses re-submitted the Virginia Plan scheme for honors tutorial work—"Appendix B: Third Year and Final Honors"—but the Committee on Academic Legislation decided, perhaps in part because there were questions regarding of what an honors tutorial program in a given department would actually consist, to postpone consideration of the plan until the fall of 1936.

As noted earlier, Virginia had a system of "Special Honors" that existed prior to the Virginia Plan. The primary difference between the old Special Honors provisions and Gooch's new honors tutorial program outlined in the Virginia Plan was that the new program prohibited any and all course requirements in the third and fourth undergraduate years. Although this difference might appear insignificant, this exemption was regarded as very important, both to its supporters and its detractors.[39] The new Virginia Plan program also proposed to install a permanent Committee on Honors Courses (also referred to as the Committee on Degrees with Honors) to oversee the program in the various participating departments.[40]

From the extant documents, it is clear that the faculty's reaction to Gooch's scheme for honors tutorial work was generally favorable, although particular points were contested. One professor wrote:

> I am sympathetic with the report of the special committee. However, I find the report too negative. It appears to me to rest too largely upon a somewhat despairing reaction to existing conditions. In consequence, the recommendations of Appendix B suffer from generality. The situation requires primarily an effort to improve existing conditions. Even admitting the critical contentions of Appendix A, improvement can be found by a better utilization of existing resources. If a barrage of textbooks intervenes between the student and classical sources, that barrage can be diminished, if not removed. If the lecture system is over-extended and abused, something could be done to reform the system. More specifically, I am sympathetic with the general point of view of Appendix B, which, I understand is alone to be considered at the present time. The suggestions I would offer are not inconsistent with Appendix B, but rather seek to correct its generality.[41]

The author went on to say that he was not sure that all course requirements ought to be waived, for, "just as we assume intelligence on the part of the gifted student, so we must assume intelligence on the part of the faculty of the school, and the expression of this intelligence in the organization of the school's courses." As a result, "I would urge that a sound, scholarly course of lectures is an indispensable part of the guidance of the gifted student." Additionally, "the gifted student in his third and fourth years, however, excellently trained, is still intellectually immature, and the lack of any course requirements may mean the lack of important guiding and solidifying frame-work." In closing this faculty member argued that honors students, except in exceptional circumstances, should be required to take up to three prescribed courses of a fundamental nature; that, in addition to their individual tutors, each department should have an official adviser to honors students; and that the University should consider requiring a thesis of all honors students.[42]

Another faculty member, chemistry professor Allan T. Gwathmey, submitted his opinion that, "It seems to me that the average student can obtain an A.B. Degree at the University with very little work and with practically no intellectual interests." As a result, Gwathmey noted that he would be in favor of a special system of study for honors students. He wrote:

> Assuming that the necessary faculty were available, I thoroughly endorse any system whereby good students would have the opportunity to carry on independent study at their convenience. It would benefit both the students and faculty concerned. Massachusetts Institute of Technology has been carrying out something of this nature for several years and it

has been considered successful. The general plan ... of beginning the honors school in the junior year seems to me to be satisfactory. I do not think that grades should be the sole criterion for eligibility to the school. Also, I am rather opposed to a member of this school graduating with any particular honors but this is a rather minor point.[43]

Some of these concerns were addressed by Gooch's Committee on Honors Courses, which submitted recommended changes to the proposed college regulations to be listed in the 1937–1938 *University of Virginia Record*. In response to the question of course attendance, the committee proposed that, "questions of residence and attendance on lectures are determined by the Dean of the College, acting on the advice of the University Committee on Final Honors."[44] Regarding the issue of student selection, which had also been raised in conjunction with the earlier consideration of Buchanan's scheme in Appendix A, the committee recommended several criteria. In addition to superior work in all courses in the first two years of college—for which a student would receive Intermediate Honors—the student was to submit a plan: "to pursue a programme of studies which has been formulated in such a way as (a) to be quantitatively equivalent to at least ten courses, (b) to offer the possibility of work of Honors quality, and (c) to be otherwise acceptable to the University Committee on Final Honors."[45]

These new provisions were supplemented with departmental honors program outlines drafted for eventual consideration by the Committee on Honors Courses. The question of what honors work in a given department might consist was answered first by the political science and philosophy departments.[46] Appropriately, Professor Gooch was the first to draft "the kind of thing 'programme of studies' means to me." Composed in October 1936, when the Virginia Plan honors tutorial program (Appendix B) was still under consideration by the faculty, Gooch noted of his "programme of studies" that "I sat down and wrote this off with almost no preparation or reflection." Moreover, "I mention this (a) because I think the difficulty of formulating a programme is much overestimated and (b) because I am sure that I could have done better with more time and, more especially, in collaboration with my colleagues in the School of Political Science."[47] In this document titled *Candidates for Final Honors Programme of Studies in Political Science*, Gooch proposed five divisions, some of which had multiple subjects. They were:

I. Government and Politics of the United States
   (a) Structure and Function of Government in the United States
   (b) State and Local Government in the United States
   (c) Party Politics in the United States
II. Government and Politics of Europe
   (a) Parliamentary Government and Modern Dictatorships
   (b) History of Modern Political Thought

      (c) Contemporary Political Theory
III. International Law and Relations
IV. Constitutional History
      (a) English Constitutional History
      (b) American Constitutional History and History of American Political Thought
      (c) European History
V. Additional Subjects
      (a) Economics
      (b) Sociology
      (c) Philosophy
      (d) History[48]

Within these subjects, political science honors students would have to become familiar with: "representative primary materials; prescribed books that may be considered classics; and representative secondary sources." Under "Structure and Function of Government in the United States," for example, primary materials included: the Constitution, typical Acts of Congress (e.g., the National Budget Act), House and Senate Rules, and significant court cases (e.g., Marbury v. Madison, Dartmouth College Case.) Prescribed books included: Tocqueville's *Démocratie en Amérique*, and Bryce's *American Commonwealth*. Secondary sources included textbooks on American government such as those of Beard, Bromage, Johnson, Munro, Myers, Ogg and Ray, Patterson, and Young.[49]

In combination, the proposals in Appendix B of the Virginia Plan and the sample program outlines were convincing to the Virginia faculty. By early 1937 the honors tutorial recommendations of the Committee on Honors Courses, which had first submitted its Virginia Plan in 1935, "were accepted with slight change by the Committee on Academic Legislation, were approved by the Faculty of the College without a dissenting vote and were endorsed by President Newcomb."[50] Gooch's honors tutorial scheme—Appendix B of the Virginia Plan—had been approved for the 1937–38 academic session. Thus unlike the honors great books part of the Virginia Plan submitted by Buchanan, the honors tutorial program part of the Plan met with "better success" in Charlottesville.[51]

Putting the Honors Program in Place

In February 1937 Gooch, having ended his hiatus from the chairmanship of the Committee on Honors Courses, received a letter from Newcomb stating: "I think the time has come when we should appoint the Committee on Degrees with Honors, because I believe that this Committee should organize this Spring and decide on those Schools which are prepared and willing to offer a set program of studies for Degrees with Honors beginning next session."[52] The new Committee on Degrees with Honors thus officially replaced the original

Committee on Honors Courses which had created the Virginia Plan.[53] The new committee membership remained the same as the old one, except that two new members, James Southall Wilson of the English Department and W. Harrison Faulkner of the Germanic Languages Department, took the places of Barr and Buchanan who had left the previous summer for the University of Chicago.

The new Committee on Degrees with Honors subsequently invited any school, that is, department, to submit a proposed program. Those programs had to conform to the new honors regulations in the 1937–1938 *Virginia Record*. Each department also had to give the assurance that every honors candidate would "be under the direct supervision of a member of the faculty of the School who, in his capacity as Supervisor, will meet regularly with the candidate at least once a week for at least one hour" for the student's tutorial.[54]

At first most Schools, though in favor of the program, declined to participate due to lack of time and personnel. Initially, for example, the School of English stated that while "the English Faculty is in favor of the Honors Plan passed by the Academic Faculty," it was not prepared to offer honors work, but that it hoped that it would be able to do so once it had personnel "adequate to give Honors courses under favorable conditions." Other Schools were ready to move ahead. In the spring of 1937 the Philosophy Department submitted, not only an outline of the proposed program of study as Gooch had done for Political Science, but its complete program procedures, albeit tentative ones, in its *Program for Degrees with Honors in Philosophy*. "In defining the aim," stated the document, "we take our start from Jefferson's statement of the goal of education as embodied in this institution. Namely, to exert a salutary and permanent influence on the *virtue, freedom,* and *happiness* of those to be educated." Thus, the objective of the program was defined extrinsically, "with respect to the subject matter to be undertaken and mastered by the student," and intrinsically, "with respect to the student's own internal development over the period of Honors work."[55]

In the course of taking the philosophy honors program students needed to demonstrate a comprehensive knowledge of the history of philosophy, take the course in Logic and Metaphysics, and undertake some work outside of philosophy. As for readings in the program, the department cited, "the list in the Appendix [A] of the original [Virginia Plan] report of the Honors Committee as illustrative of the materials we should employ." In specific, mention was made of works by Plato, Aristotle, Augustine, Aquinas, Dante, Kepler, Spinoza, Kant, Hilbert, and Whitehead. Additionally, plans for tutorial guidance were proposed:

(1) Each candidate will be assigned to a member of the staff, and such member will serve as the candidate's chief tutor, with regular weekly meetings.

(2) It will be the duty of the chief tutor to provide the opportunity for special tutorial meetings of the candidate with other members of the staff.
(3) The selection of the chief tutor and arrangements for special tutoring opportunity must depend in part upon the needs and interests of the individual candidate.[56]

The Philosophy honors program was approved by the new Committee on Degrees with Honors. English too found its way clear to offer a program. The few upperclassmen invited to participate were the very brightest students. In the early years of the program they numbered at most three or four in a department, and sometimes only three or four in the entire College of Arts and Sciences.[57] Honors students generally met weekly with their departmental tutors to review their weekly papers or, in the case of the sciences, their research, to discuss their readings—which were often but not exclusively great books relevant to their discipline—and during their fourth year, to work on their senior theses. At the end of their fourth year, honors students took both written and oral exams that were graded by faculty members other than their tutors and eventually by external examiners from other colleges and universities. The examiners, not the respective departments, would then recommend to the Committee on Degrees with Honors whether a student should graduate with highest honors, high honors, honors, or merely pass—as though the student had been a regular departmental major. Altogether, four schools graduated a total of six honors students in the first cohort of Virginia Plan honors students in the spring of 1939: two in philosophy, two in English, and one each in Physics and Political Science.[58]

A Unique and Unknown Program

By the end of the 1930s the Virginia faculty had tabled the underclassmen great books part of the Virginia Plan for lack of funds but implemented the upperclassmen honors program part of the Plan. In the process, the University of Virginia had created an undergraduate program that was unique in American public higher education. As will be discussed in Chapter 5, while other colleges such as Swarthmore had honors seminar programs and, as already noted, the University of Virginia had had its own "Special Honors" program, the new honors program that came out of the Virginia Plan was different from all others. Only the Virginia Plan honors program had the combination of one-on-one "Oxbridge"-style tutoring, not group tutoring seminars as was done at other institutions, and full exemption from class attendance for honors students. As a result, "At the time of its inception no other state university in America offered any such program."[59]

The historical literature on this point is wanting. For example, in stating that the Honors Program at the University of Virginia started in 1937, Virginius Dabney is only partially correct.[60] It is true that the Honors Program proposed in the Virginia Plan, which exists to the current day, was adopted in 1937. However, Special Honors at Virginia had been in existence since 1924. J. Winfree Smith's history of the St. John's Program in its formative years, *A Search for the Liberal College*, correctly noted that the current Honors Program at Virginia, proposed in the Virginia Plan, was a reform of the existing program in Special Honors. But Smith, who earned his B.A. as well as an M.A. in History and a Ph.D. in Philosophy at Virginia, devoted only two paragraphs to the honors tutorial scheme, and failed to mention that the resulting program was unique in American public higher education. To be fair, Smith's subject was not Virginia, it was St. John's. Yet considering that, as a result of the Virginia Plan—which also provided the basis for the St. John's "New Program" curriculum—the University of Virginia developed what was the sole one-on-one "Oxbridge"-style tutorial system in the country, it seems a significant historical oversight. Other literature makes no reference to Virginia's program at all.

Conclusion

Because the great books scheme was not adopted in 1936 when Barr and Buchanan were in Charlottesville, their accounts of the effort describe the Virginia Plan as a failure, as far as the University of Virginia was concerned. On the other hand, because the tutorial part of the plan was adopted in 1937 by the faculty senate, Gooch and later administrators at the university regarded the 1930s history of the Virginia Plan as a partial success. It was noted earlier that Barr thought that Newcomb was "an awful choice" for president. It is telling that Gooch, perhaps reflecting his appraisal of the results of the Virginia Plan and his partiality to the honors tutorial scheme, said of Newcomb, "on the whole, I think he was the best president we ever had."[61]

The honors tutorial program was in effect for the 1937–38 academic year. Of the new program, Dabney recorded that:

> President Newcomb explained that the "more favored students, during the latter half of their four-year course, shall be enabled to pursue their studies in their chosen field of concentration on a firmer basis and a higher plane than the less gifted." He added that these honor students would be afforded "unlimited opportunity, under proper guidance, to master thoroughly their specially chosen subjects," and they would be "at liberty . . . to claim exemption from course requirements." Final comprehensive examinations for a degree with honors "will demand a rigid compliance with particularly exacting standards of scholarship."[62]

But World War II soon intervened and life at the University was profoundly disrupted. Questions about the best way to produce liberally educated students were put on hold. The war years, and many changes, would pass before renewed efforts were made to implement the Virginia Plan great books scheme at Virginia.

CHAPTER 4

Developments at Virginia, Chicago, and St. John's

> "On with the opera maxima."
> —Scott Buchanan

The University of Virginia

Despair in the Old Dominion

"You can't do the thing at Virginia . . . and you know it. . . ." Adler wrote from Chicago to Buchanan not long after the Virginia Plan had been submitted and President Newcomb had been unable, or perhaps unwilling, to raise the necessary funds to implement the great books honors scheme for underclassmen.[1] Buchanan had been clinging to the hope that Newcomb might yet secure the funds for the great books scheme outlined in Appendix A of the Virginia Plan. He wrote Adler: "Supposing something happens, we may have some excitement about that."[2] However, as directly stated by Adler, those hopes were unlikely to be realized. Buchanan and Barr were faced with the question of what, if anything, to do next. As Buchanan put it, he and Barr found themselves in a difficult situation: the "anomaly of serious conservatives in exile."[3]

Curricular developments in Charlottesville and Hyde Park were intertwined in the mid-1930s and the "liberal artists" at both universities were in close communication. In fact, around the time that the Virginia Plan was submitted to Newcomb by the Gooch Committee on Honors Courses in November 1935, Adler proposed to Hutchins that Barr should be named the Dean of the College at Chicago. As Adler wrote to Buchanan, he proposed Barr for three reasons: "(1) [Barr] is sound about college education, as sound as anyone can be; (2) [Barr] has guts of the kind [Hutchins] needs to put over the really radical program we have all been talking about; and (3) [Barr] is a man of character, a gentleman, and not a politician."[4] Adler also proposed that Buchanan should be named a professor in the College at Chicago. Just as Adler stated to Buchanan that the Virginia Plan—meaning just Buchanan's great books scheme in this case—would not be adopted at Virginia, so too Adler said, ". . . you may not be able to do it here [at Chicago], but the chance with Winkie as Dean and you and I and Arthur [Rubin] as professors in the College is pretty great."[5] Although Barr, Buchanan, and Adler were all enthusiastic about the prospect, Hutchins did not extend any formal offers to Barr or Buchanan—that would have to wait until 1936 and the plans for a new Committee on the Liberal Arts at Chicago. In the meantime, Barr and Buchanan faced the task of trying to implement the Virginia Plan at the University of Virginia.

When it became obvious that the great books scheme was facing serious difficulty—that funds would not be forthcoming—Buchanan became increasingly despairing. He wrote Adler that he was "completely washed up" at Virginia and "completely washed up on academic philosophy."[6] Barr's own recollections support the case that Buchanan was quite unhappy. Barr recalled: "[Buchanan] had sort of had it. He liked a lot of things about the University of Virginia but he didn't want to continue teaching there, and I don't think he wanted to continue teaching in a department of philosophy anywhere."[7] Unhappiness became despondency. At one point, Buchanan wrote: "I am terribly low, . . . I have simply got to leave this place; suicide is the end from all these drift of events if I don't manage to change things somehow."[8]

Fortunately for Buchanan, change was coming. Indeed, when Buchanan's scheme in the Virginia Plan for a great books program for select underclassmen was not implemented, his departure from Charlottesville for Chicago was probably inevitable. By 1936, after several years of conversations with Hutchins and Adler about a possible move to Hyde Park, Chicago had become very attractive to Buchanan. Such a move finally became possible when Buchanan and Barr were invited to come to Chicago for the 1936–37 academic year as visiting professors of the liberal arts. They would join Adler, McKeon, and others as members of Hutchins' new Committee on the Liberal Arts.[9] This committee, wrote Barr, would pool the experience of its members and construct "a practicable curriculum that would furnish the undergraduate with a truly liberal education."[10]

Barr and Buchanan Move to the University of Chicago
From the Grounds to the Quadrangles
President Hutchins had secured funds to establish the Committee on the Liberal Arts and make faculty offers after publishing *The Higher Learning in America* in the spring of 1936. Marion Rosenwald Stern, who had inherited a fortune from her father, Julius Rosenwald, was one of several wealthy benefactors moved by Hutchins' arguments in *The Higher Learning*. For the Committee on the Liberal Arts, the Board of Trustees of the University of Chicago acknowledged: "From four anonymous donors, pledges of a total contribution of $22,000 per year for a period of three years beginning July 1, 1936, for the purpose of analyzing and reformulating the content and methods of teaching in the liberal arts."[11] According to Chicago historian William McNeill, Arthur Rubin "was the impresario behind this venture." Rubin, "a man of private means and no professional occupation," had helped to secure the funds for the committee from Marion Stern.[12]

At this point, Barr recollected, "Bob [Hutchins] and his cohorts . . . attempted to form a committee . . . and they were going to try to work out some sort of curriculum. Most of them, I'm sure, had never even seen the one at Virginia, which stuck."[13] Indeed, at that time, Adler reminded Buchanan in a letter that he was still waiting for "the outline of your Virginia Honors Course."[14] Buchanan did get the Virginia Plan to Adler so that it could become part of the Committee's discussions once it started meeting the coming autumn.

In addition to Barr, the senior members of the Chicago Committee on the Liberal Arts were to be the three associates who had originally worked together at the People's Institute in New York, namely, Adler, Buchanan, and Richard McKeon who had come to Chicago from Columbia in 1934. In the meantime, Hutchins decided conveniently that the Committee would be advisory to the Dean of the Humanities Divison, who happened to be McKeon, and that McKeon would be the spokesman for the Committee.[15]

Although it had yet to meet, the nascent Committee, being independent both financially and from the regular university departmental structure, quickly drew fire from hostile faculty members who referred to it as Hutchins' "favorite project," "kitchen cabinet," and "brain trust."[16] By August 1936, two months before the committee had even had its first meeting, Hutchins wrote to the Dean of Faculties, E. T. Filbey, that: "The Committee on the Liberal Arts got off to such a bad start in public opinion last spring that I am anxious that all other handicaps to its successful operation should be removed."[17] As historian Mary Ann Dzuback puts it, "The timing of the venture, concurrent with the publication of *The Higher Learning*, made it appear to be another effort of the president to foist his own men and ideas on the division, which, of course, it was."[18]

In spite of the difficulties that had already arisen, Buchanan was enthusiastic, for it appeared that the primary obstacle to curricular reform at Virginia, namely, money, had been overcome in Hyde Park. In contrast to Charlottesville, Buchanan recalled that:

> The situation at Chicago was more favorable. President Hutchins, who had by this time published his book, *The Higher Learning in America*, had been able to raise enough money to establish a Committee on the Liberal Arts. Hutchins and Adler had led a seminar in the great books for some years. McKeon, as Dean of the Humanities, could release some of the time of his colleagues and graduate students for the work of the Committee. Stringfellow Barr and I were invited to join and bring some of our graduate students with us.[19]

Buchanan was eager to leave Virginia, but Barr had tremendous affection for his alma mater. Although the great books scheme in the Virginia Plan had not been implemented, initially Barr did not want to leave Charlottesville for Chicago: "I didn't want to go, I had an enormous and deep attachment to the university I was teaching in—my alma mater—and I'd been very happy teaching there."[20]

When the discussions concerning the Committee on the Liberal Arts were just starting in the mid-1930s, Barr believed that Hutchins and Adler probably did not understand what Buchanan saw in him. Barr proffered, "I'm guessing, but I don't quite see anything that would have made Hutchins or Adler, at that time, invite me. Later maybe. I had a rather good working relationship with both, but at that time I didn't." Likewise, Barr viewed his possible colleagues a bit askance. Of the early 1930s Barr recollected that: "[Hutchins] talked at Charlottesville once or twice, like most of the people that listened to him then, I disliked him—he seemed truculent, smart-aleck sort of, a boy wonder trying to make the world over in an instant, and I thought that didn't help him, in a way. It may have made him feel pretty skillful, which he was, damn him."[21]

In spite of his misgivings, Barr was eventually convinced by Adler and Buchanan to take a one-year leave of absence.[22] Barr and Buchanan started to make their plans for the move to Chicago, which included consideration of which graduate students to bring with them, even though they were aware that the news announcing the formation of the Committee on the Liberal Arts had not been universally well received at Chicago. Indeed, in a February 1936 letter Buchanan wrote to Adler, "Drop a line once a week to let us know that the whole CLA [Committee on the Liberal Arts] is not blown up again."[23] For his part, Barr recorded that: "I was very disappointed when Newk [Newcomb] refused to act. He said [the great books scheme] couldn't be done. Well, as a result, I went out, but the Chicago thing sounded so, kind of, messy, in just human terms: people at each other's throats, and so on, and I didn't want to spend my life in a cat house.[24]

While agreeing to go, Barr was clearly not at ease with the prospect. Writing from his interim quarters at the Colonnade Club, the University of Virginia's faculty club, Barr related to Adler that "today I moved" and "already the moving psychosis is fading." Barr had requested a confirming letter from Hutchins before requesting leave from Virginia, since, as he related to Adler, "I have a horror of misunderstandings and consequent indigence, now that I near forty."[25] Of this seeming formality, Buchanan wrote Adler that: "Leaving Virginia had seemed gay and bold, but when one comes to the final break, although only for a year, one wants to be legally secured to one's step-mother's apron strings. Tell Bob [Hutchins], if it worries him that Winkie [Barr] will get over it when we get to work, and that the Colonel must have his mint julep while he has to sit on the ancestral porch waiting for something to turn up."[26] Happily, but in retrospect, ironically, Barr wrote to Adler on the Ides of March, "it has been many years—since 1919, to be exact—since I approached a coming year with the same quality of interest and excitement I feel now."[27]

In addition to outside faculty hostility, the future members of the Committee itself were having their own difficulties. Since their days together in New York, Adler and McKeon had grown so far apart philosophically that Adler told Hutchins that a balance of power needed to be maintained on the Committee, and that "for every 'McKeonite' there be a 'Buchananite' on the staff."[28] Similarly, to Buchanan, Adler wrote: "The Dick [McKeon] problem certainly grows," but, "it certainly will not spoil next year if we are careful." Buchanan wrote back that, regarding the infighting: "I dread litigation, recrimination, and retaliation, since they should be incompetent, immaterial, and irrelevant for our enterprise. Poor Bob [Hutchins]. He must think he has a bevy of prima donnas on his hands. On with the opera maxima."[29]

By late February, 1936, Barr and Buchanan were able to advise Adler, who served as their primary Chicago contact, as to which two of their students ought to accompany them from Virginia. One was Catesby Taliaferro, who had just earned his Ph.D. in Philosophy; the other was Charles Wallis, a "brilliant" man who had just earned his B.A.[30] Also, Adler had proposed that Barr and Buchanan should help him teach his Trivium course in the Law School and the Honors Course with Hutchins. Buchanan replied they would, and presciently suggested that doing so would provide "a possible asylum from the possible catastrophes of the committee meetings" and added, "I don't mean to be ominous."[31]

Barr, in the meantime, wrote to Adler that:

> I have this a.m. [March 6, 1936] broached the year's leave to Newcomb. He regretfully accedes, but very gracefully. He expresses legitimate doubts about my ever returning should I be invited to remain; but he is definitely nice about everything. [Buchanan] saw him yesterday, with equally cordial results, as Scott may by now have stated to you."[32]

Buchanan did tell Adler within a week, adding that, "Newcombe (sic) objects only that Winkie and I should be leaving together this year when he is under fire."[33]

Barr also entertained the idea of teaching in the history department at Chicago in addition to his other obligations. To Adler he wrote:

> If there is any possibility that I can aid our joint enterprise by forming a link with the "professional" historians . . . I want it to happen. If you disagree with this diagnosis, be candid. You do, after all, know the ground, which I don't. But remember I am far less oppressed by the academic racket than, I judge, Scott [Buchanan] is, for example.[34]

Adler had already proffered that such a link might well be helpful. He thought Barr should be able to do so, "without placing too heavy a burden upon yourself. After all, next year should in some sense be a year off for you. . . ." especially since ". . . the work of the CLA . . . will be mostly play anyway and not work."[35]

Barr's recollection was that at first, teaching in the department might not have been an option: "the History Department said that if I came they wouldn't speak to me, because I was such a stinker." Because the Committee on the Liberal Arts was not officially part of any department, and because some of the members, especially the "Virginia gang," had received faculty appointments solely by Hutchins' invitation, there was a great deal of antagonism toward the committee; as Barr put it: "this was a hated group."[36] Many on the Chicago faculty believed that forming the committee was essentially Hutchins' attempt to make an end-run around the standard faculty appointment procedures. Barr believed the faculty thought Hutchins was tricking them again, and appointing his own friends, as had been done with Adler's appointment several years earlier.[37] As Barr put it, "Where the hell did Barr come from? Where did Buchanan come from? We didn't ask them here." Later in life Barr said that he agreed with the faculty. He suggested that, in the view of the Chicago faculty, "we wouldn't have come in the way we had if we'd been honest men. They were saying there is a trick going on here. And by God, I think there was a trick. I didn't like it. And I think it made [Buchanan] and me both very uncomfortable."[38]

From the faculty's point of view, a committee, which did not have the usual faculty connections, had been assembled to create a new college curriculum. Moreover, this independent committee almost certainly would not look favorably on the current curriculum offered by the faculty, and by association, perhaps take a dim view of the existing faculty itself.

Faculty concerns notwithstanding, the history department overcame its discomfort and, as Barr recollected, "later they found I was harmless and asked me to give a course." Barr "was smuggled into the history faculty" and wound up teaching historiography in the Fall Quarter of 1936.[39] Also, Barr's course would wind up adding a slight degree of legitimacy to the nascent committee, or at least one of its members, since the course was in, and approved by, the history department.

But in the spring of 1936 all still appeared up for grabs. In May Buchanan wrote a letter to Hutchins in which he stated: "From what I hear I am afraid that I am a rabbit that has jumped into the Chicago hat, and it appears that the hutch is crowded. I am sorry, but on the whole calmly excited. I hope that does not appear frivolous. If I could fully believe what I hear, I should express sincere regret. They will take me back here [at Virginia] if that would relieve the conflict. Let me know."[40]

Such a reply never came from Hutchins, and Barr and Buchanan moved to Chicago in the summer of 1936. When Barr and Buchanan left, the Virginia student humor magazine, *The Cavalier*, saw fit to comment on their departure:

> We lament the removal from the University's brain trust, even if only for a year, of Stringfellow Barr. The flaming red hair and the bright green suit of the University's best lecturer have long been a fixture of the Virginia panorama. First-year men especially have lost much. History A1 is in the hands of a new and competent teacher, but the famous lecture about temple prostitution, the caustic castigations of his classes for the uninspiring cut of their faces, the classic rages, the dislike for coeds, and, above all, the illuminating teaching will be missing. Winkie Barr's tem-

porary stay at Chicago will mean that the University has lost one year of a grand professor—and the University cannot afford it.[41]

As for Buchanan, *The Cavalier* gave the sense that the less-than-warm feeling Buchanan had for Virginia was perhaps mutual:

> As for Scott Buchanan, he has shaken the dust of Rugby Road from his heels forever. At the University of Chicago, where he will work under an educational theory similar to the "honors school" he advocated for Virginia, we wish him the best of fortune. Respected and admired by the group of earnest students that gathered about him, he was little known to the greater number of University students. And so, in the minds of most students, the obituary to the career of Scott Buchanan, philosopher and teacher, at this University will be: "His name looked well in the Catalogue."[42]

The Chicago Committee on the Liberal Arts
Debacle On the Midway

In his 1935–36 Report of the President, Robert Hutchins wrote that:

> The seven liberal arts were grammar, rhetoric, logic, arithmetic, geometry, music and astronomy. They constituted the whole of general or preprofessional education in the Middle Ages. In view of the state into which these disciplines have fallen, the vocational attitude of most students, and the ignorance and hostility of many professors, it is doubtful whether they can be adopted to contemporary conditions. The difficulties of framing a program of general education without some resort to them, however, justify the attempt.[43]

The Committee on the Liberal Arts was that attempt. According to Buchanan, the Committee was "a three-year project working out a curriculum in the Liberal Arts for the liberal college."[44] Barr, many years later and more cautiously, said the purpose was to determine, "whether there was any way of working out a genuine liberal arts curriculum at an American college." The committee members "thought that the Columbia colloquium and the People's Institute and the Virginia Plan were all highly relevant and would have been hard pressed to name anything else that was." Finally, the Committee on the Liberal Arts was an attempt to "draw on all the past experiences you could and spend plenty of time in doing what the Virginia Plan was supposed to do . . . except that certainly [Buchanan] wouldn't want that third and fourth year that Virginia settled for, that . . . Bob Gooch wanted."[45]

An organizational meeting of the Committee on the Liberal Arts was held on October 3, 1936. The senior members of the group in attendance were

Adler, Barr, Buchanan, McKeon, and Rubin. Junior members included Catesby Taliaferro and Charles Wallis of the "Virginia contingent" and three of McKeon's graduate students from Columbia.[46] The members dealt with numerous business matters. They also drew up a list of goals, noted by Adler:

1. Three year assignment: a list of a hundred books; combining the Columbia list and the Virginia list.
2. One year assignment: a shorter list of books to read. Not yet determined.
3. The communal reading of several classics, such as the *Poetics* or Russell or St. Thomas.
4. The drawing up of a list of books referred to as *necessary* by each member of the group reporting.
5. A report by each member of the group on general topics in relation to the arts, such as Buchanan on the Transcendentals and Adler on rational psychology, etc.[47]

When the committee next met for its first regular meeting, Barr recalled, "all hell broke out. And it just went to pieces." The committee members quickly discovered that they held differing ideas concerning educational philosophy, metaphysics, and how to best obtain a true liberal arts education. Adler wanted to start a Great Books curriculum that would commence by reading Aquinas. Buchanan and Barr wanted to start with Aristotle. McKeon wanted to start by examining where the liberal arts stood in the current day.[48] For his part, Barr stated that, "I was green as grass, I couldn't even follow the argument. Just terminologically I couldn't follow the argument."[49] The entire environment became charged with verbal violence and conspiracy: "You know," said Barr, "tell it to them rough, make them like it."[50] The manners of the group, or more precisely the lack thereof, "horrified" Barr: "Really an appalling display, unworthy of any institution of learning anywhere on earth and I hated it."[51]

Buchanan's recollection of the first meeting was less visceral:

The first meeting of the Committee on Liberal Arts will never be forgotten by any of those present. . . . Although there was good will and agreement on the problems set by poetry and mathematics, or the liberal arts, and in spite of many interchanges of lectures and papers, McKeon, Adler, and I, each of us, had constructed and complicated quite different universes of discourse which reached into deep matters of method and metaphysics. The three worlds separately had absorbed and accumulated the energies of our associates. They also carried within them the stresses and strains in our chaotic intellectual culture. Brought into proximity, the three worlds discharged their energies at each other. Heat and light became thunder and lightning. There was never another general meeting of the whole committee. We agreed to disagree and to pursue our separate courses.[52]

Although the participants differed in their interpretation of the difficulties experienced by the Committee on the Liberal Arts, Barr's summation is quite plausible: "there wasn't enough common intellectual experience to hold it together."[53] This, of course, had become one of the primary criticisms made by the liberal artists: that collegiate education in America did not provide its students with a common intellectual experience that allowed for common discussion. That the participants had all studied under the elective system in college and been unable to reach a common basis of discussion is perhaps the ultimate irony of the episode.

Because of the debacle, McKeon and his students determined to create a separate study group while Adler decided to pursue his own work. Barr, Buchanan, Taliaferro, and Wallis, the "Virginia contingent" as they called themselves, also formed their own group and retained the title of the Committee on the Liberal Arts. Buchanan noted that, "Our presence made McKeon, the Dean of the Humanities Division, a great deal of trouble."[54] Indeed, McKeon demanded that Hutchins make the Committee responsible to the President's Office, not the Humanities Division. This left the Virginians to fend for themselves against a faculty already hostile to Hutchins' plans to remake education at Chicago in his intellectual image.[55] The ensuing onslaught was fierce. "The University of Chicago saw red, and they almost burned our books so we couldn't read," recalled Buchanan.[56] The experience convinced Barr that he was wrong in his earlier assumption "that Virginians could outgossip any other group of people in America."[57]

Thus "failed" the second curricular reform effort that Barr and Buchanan had been instrumental in creating. As had been the case in Charlottesville with the great books scheme, the Chicago experience was a qualified failure since the work done there made future work at another institution possible. Buchanan later suggested that the inability of the Committee on the Liberal Arts to fulfill its charge might ironically, at least in retrospect, have been a useful development, for it meant that the various constituencies were able to develop their own liberal education experiments:

> Although there were sharp and clear intellectual differences that separated us, differences that cannot be expounded here, and also some differences that have always issued in what are traditionally known as "battles of the liberal arts," there were more practical difficulties in the strategy and organization of education that required separate working solutions or laboratories of experimentation. Hutchins, Adler, and McKeon had already introduced an educational ferment into the large University of Chicago. They had a strong following among the faculty and the students; also a strong opposition. They had obligations to continue. The Virginia

contingent, as Barr and I and our associates called ourselves, had brought the Virginia plan which needed a more speculative development in the ivory tower before it could undertake the problem of practice and administration. This we did in the isolation of one of the stone towers at the University during the remainder of the year.[58]

Historian William McNeill, capturing the discontent of everyone involved, summed up the Committee by stating: "they began by quarreling and ended by sulking."[59] In 1950, Reuben Frodin, then Editor of *The Journal of General Education*, and Assistant Dean of the College of the University of Chicago from 1943 until 1946, wrote that:

The presence of the committee on the liberal arts on the Chicago quadrangles caused a furor far out of proportion to the usual campus reaction when a committee tries to wrestle with an intellectual problem. Those faculty members who objected to Hutchins' educational views were joined in objection to the committee's activities by those who felt that one major revision of a curriculum (i.e., the College's) in a short span of years was enough. The group interested in continuous study and revision of the liberal arts program was, as is usual in "crisis" situations, inarticulate by comparison with the objectors.[60]

"What do we do now?"

After the committee blew apart, the Virginia group huddled and literally asked, "What do we do now?" Buchanan had resigned from Virginia, so he was stuck in Hyde Park, but Barr supposed he would return to Charlottesville once his leave of absence had concluded. For the rest of the 1936–37 academic year Buchanan suggested that they "just sit down and read great books," and so they did.[61] Barr wrote that: "the Committee on the Liberal Arts foundered on personal problems and a rump committee of five, under Buchanan's chairmanship, proceeded to read and discuss some of the books listed in the Virginia Report."[62] The reconstituted committee, reduced in size, consisted of the four Virginians and occasionally Arthur Rubin.[63] Within a week or two of the original committee's denouement, said Barr, "we went into this little five-people dream of Euclidism."[64]

Barr also noted of the rump committee that, "at this point, when [Buchanan] was forty-two and I was forty, our lives suddenly converged. And I do not believe they could have done so had it not been for Chicago and Plato and Euclid."[65] As had happened to Hutchins in his work with Adler, Barr had a conversion experience, of an intellectual kind, during his committee work with Buchanan:

Two of these works changed the course of my life: Plato's *Dialogues* and Euclid's *Elements*. I had already read a little Plato, even in the original. As a schoolboy I had of course studied geometry in a version that might fairly be termed Euclid with some of the really interesting parts omitted. The real Euclid was another dish of tea, and I became tremendously excited. Moreover, as I read or re-read the *Dialogues* and watched Buchanan lead our discussions of them I tardily got some glimmer of how really powerful the act of teaching can be when the teacher can teach dialectically. The discussion groups at Balliol, my conversations with Mieklejohn, the adult seminars I had helped Buchanan lead in Richmond, all fell into place. I was now certain that dialectic was the most powerful of all devices for moving the mind and imagination; but, alas, I felt certain also that few persons in my profession would ever recognize its value. I observed that what Buchanan displayed that seemed so unprofessorial was his extraordinary ability to listen and his apparent assumption that it is sometimes the dullest person present who raises the best question. I saw now that, aside from a disarming streak of sentiment about the [New England] town meeting, his deep sense of human equality was perhaps the same sense that led Aristotle to make the declaration that all men desire by nature to know.[66]

As for pedagogy, Barr recorded that: "The Chicago seminar convinced me that the academic lecture, even when supplemented by reciprocal opinings, was no substitute for Socratic dialectic if the undergraduate was to acquire those arts, or skills, that had once been called the liberal arts."[67]

During the 1936–37 academic year the Committee members read classics from the Virginia list and produced essays relevant to the liberal arts. Junior member Catesby Taliaferro wrote a paper titled, "Plato and the Liberal Arts: A Plea for Mathematical Logic." Charles Wallis wrote a paper titled "St. Thomas and the Liberal Arts," and translated Saint Bonaventure's "De Reductione Artium Ad Theologiam."[68] However, the most important written work to come out of the committee comprised by the Virginians was a series of essays by Buchanan.

Buchanan's Essays: Sequels to the Virginia Plan

As part of his committee work, Buchanan wrote three essays addressed to Hutchins. Under the collective title, "The Classics and the Liberal Arts," the first was titled, "Tradition and General Education," the second, "The Classics," and the third, "The Liberal Arts." Numbering forty-one pages *in toto*, these three essays are an excellent statement of Buchanan's beliefs about liberal education at that time and are, in essence, the expository sequel to the Virginia Plan. In the opening paragraph of the first essay, which follows below, Buchanan declared his intentions and explained the role of Robert Gooch's Committee on Honors Courses at Virginia in formulating a proposal for liberal education. Buchanan started:

My take-off will be from Virginia for two reasons: first, because, as you know, I got practically involved in curricular problems there, and in my attempts to persuade my colleagues of the rightness of certain directions in which solutions might be sought I persuaded myself of their validity with respect to general considerations which might be relevant anywhere. (See appended Scheme for General Honors [Virginia Plan Appendix A] for the details of the conclusions and recommendations as of 1935.) Secondly, because I have not yet been able to learn anything from the doings of the local committee on the liberal arts which helps me to improve and correct the Virginia proposals. Improvement and correction are sadly needed, as I know from my own experience in drawing the scheme up and as it is confirmed by comments by my colleagues on the Chicago Committee. On the other hand, no other comparably articulated scheme has been presented and it seems wise to push ahead with this beginning in the same hope that I had in Virginia that it would irritate and stimulate another better proposal. It should be noted that the "Scheme" is for a small group of better students as it is written and also that it is a piece of rhetorical literature addressed very particularly to the President of the University of Virginia. It will necessarily seem simple-minded and quaint to the President of the University of Chicago. I hope to make amends for some of its faults in what I am going to say in sequel.[69]

Arguing that "I should like to make as strong a case as I can for what might be called traditionalism in education," Buchanan referred Hutchins to the following sources: Whewell, *Cambridge Education*; Newman, *The Idea of a University*, *The Development of Christian Doctrine*, Part I, *The Grammar of Assent*; and Eliot, "Tradition and the Individual Talent" (an essay in *The Sacred Wood*), *After Strange Gods*, and "Modern Education and the Classics" (an essay in *Essays Ancient and Modern*).[70]

Buchanan also addressed additional issues in this first essay that are central to the liberal arts movement. Regarding the proper material for a liberal education, Buchanan stated that: "My first and most general point is that the only available medium which is adequate to the intellectual salvation (education) of the American student is the great European tradition." From this tradition, "We should find the right selection from our heritage which will convey through itself the burden of wisdom of Europe, a small number of books of intrinsic merit both in subject-matter and in form of presentation.... They should be organized in a rational narrative order; see the poor attempt in the Virginia list. These should be the canon of liberal education...."[71]

Regarding the issue of whether liberal education ought to be an elite or mass concern, Buchanan proffered the opposite stance from the one officially taken in the Virginia Plan. As Buchanan had noted earlier in the essay, the General Honors Scheme proposed at Virginia was responding specifically to Newcomb's charge that a program be created for honors students. Free of this constraint, Buchanan argued in favor of a democratic approach: "I do not think this general education should be aimed at merely the intellectual aristocracy. I doubt if that exists in this country except in the eye of the American who has not quite recovered from the patriotic fervor of the American Revolution."[72] Clearly Buchanan was demonstrating what Barr thought of as Buchanan's New England town meeting background and its emphasis on egalitarianism, a view of the world not favored in the University of Virginia's Jeffersonian conception of higher education at the time. Regarding mass versus elite liberal education, and the means to achieve that education, Buchanan made a final point:

> I doubt if there can be an American intellectual aristocracy unless the whole mass is somehow brought a little higher than it is being brought by our public education. I can think of no more effective or fit way to accomplish this preliminary task than the general reading of the classics with as much of the liberal arts as can be recovered and made effective at present. I am here following the parallel with the sacraments. They are the minimum of discipline and they are for everybody.[73]

Having established the outlines of their endeavor, Buchanan was ready in his second essay to tackle "the classics." Acknowledging that there would be those in academia who would reject his philosophy of education meant that while the easiest way to discuss the classics "would be to appeal to the words tradition and classics," because "everybody knows that a tradition of a civilized culture is constituted by its classics," such an approach would be insufficient. Referring to all of learned society, Buchanan stated that: "We are not sure what our classics are, and many of us do not think that the classics in general or some particular item or group of items are important." As a result, the foundations of his arguments had to be solid. "It will be better for us to take a longer road now so that we can fall back for reinforcements when the issues are joined out on the front lines of the academic battle."[74]

Defining the purpose of the liberal arts was critical. Buchanan suggested that: "There are some interesting equivocations in the historical usages of words in the liberal arts. For instance, at one time the name of the liberal arts was supposed to have come from *liberi*, children; at another *liber*, book; at another from *liberus*, free-man." The way Buchanan dealt with this multiplicity of meanings has a beauty to it: "Since liberal is an adjective, and adjectives may have many modes of attribution, I like to indulge my etymological appetites in thinking that liberal comes from all three, and says that liberal education makes free men out of children by means of books."[75]

Because the mode of apprehension was books—great books to be exact—the question becomes, "What is a great book?" Buchanan believed that great books met four intrinsic criteria. First, "The great books are those that have the most readers. The numerical measure is a bit shocking, but . . . it assumes that men are rational and that if a book is read by many men, it must have the stuff that properly interests the most genuine men."[76] Second, "great books are those that have the greatest number of possible interpretations."[77] Third, "Great Books raise unanswerable questions."[78] Finally, "The last intrinsic criterion is that they shall be works of fine art, as well as of liberal art. Their form of presentation must be such that they have an intrinsic truth that shines out immediately, clearly, and convincingly to the disciplined mind."[79]

Buchanan noted further that in combination, great books spoke with each other—they engaged in what Hutchins referred to as "the Great Conversation"—and "in the end or rather continually we know more truth, provided we don't forget as fast as we learn, and that depends on our intellectual capacity which in turn depends on our discipline in the arts." Accordingly, Buchanan argued one must read the classics serially:

> The general objection on the part of all regular faculty members to this program is that the books are too difficult for the student. They are making judgments on real experiences with the books, they say. That may be doubted, but their point remains until they are asked whether they have ever had students read these books in the traditional order from beginning to end. They have no experience and we who have taught honors have only a meager experience. However, a little thought about the order and its implications will suggest an answer. . . . The last helps to understand the first, as Freud helps to understand Sophocles and Sophocles to understand Freud, Euclid helps Newton as Newton helps Euclid. The principle here is that mutual implication in subject matter increases facilitation in learning at some higher ratio than compound interest.[80]

The real problem, as Buchanan saw it, was that "We are all products of a bad educational system without benefit of the classics and the arts in the integral sense that I have been outlining." The result, both outside of, and within, the original Committee on the Liberal Arts was that:

> We consequently appear to each other as heretics and sinners. I have proposed again and again that we read any hundred books together to the best of our ability; I believe there is magic in these books even for us. I have proposed that we read them with an equal balance of mathematics and language, which none of us have done. I have proposed that we work at the liberal arts beginning with mathematics, since that is the only concern in contemporary thought. These, with their counterproposals, have broken the committee into parts. We have done those things we ought not to have done, we have left undone those things we ought to have done, and there is no health in us. . . . I forget what comes next for a good Episcopalian.[81]

In the third essay, "The Liberal Arts," Buchanan argued that, via the process that the nineteenth-century American philosopher C. S. Peirce referred to as "abduction," he would endeavor to present a discourse on the liberal arts. In doing so, he noted that "I am indebted to both the people here [at Chicago] and in Virginia with whom I have worked," among others.[82] Buchanan then proceeded to present an involved discussion of the arts of the *trivium* and the *quadrivium*. Of particular importance was that the different liberal arts ebbed and flowed at different times. He noted that Richard McKeon had given a lecture in which he showed how, "the Alexandrian, the Roman, and the 13th century cultures could be distinguished intellectually by the fact that logic and rhetoric were subsidiary to grammar in Alexandria, grammar and logic were subsidiary to rhetoric in Rome, and grammar and rhetoric were subsidiary to logic in 13th century Paris. In each age the three arts had different formulations singly and relatively to each other."[83] This ebb and flow demonstrated "the continuity of the tradition and the complementary lights that one stage of development in the arts throws on the others." The ebb and flow also "parallels in an interesting way the list of classics as it changes from period to period. At one time Horace and Virgil are more important than Hesiod and Homer, Dante is more important than Thomas, Aristotle is more important than Plato, etc. and vice versa."[84]

Buchanan ended by stating the problem of liberal education and offered a proposed solution:

> The problem is this. There is no way of keeping the tradition constant with all classics and all the arts held in equal esteem or even in a constant proportional esteem with respect to one another. Not even a five foot bookshelf and an accompanying encyclopedia would accomplish this. Therefore we cannot draw up a list of books and write a syllabus for instruction for a liberal college, and suppose that it is exhaustive and exclusive for a liberal education. It seems that the practice of one of the arts necessarily eliminates any adequate practice of the others, and the appreciation of any classic in some sense distorts some others. Therefore it is important to find out what our present stage of virtue and appreciation is so that we may know what can and what can't be adequately done next. The arts can be practised only *ambulando*, not at one stroke, nor perhaps even in one generation.
>
> I suggest that we are rhetorically minded at present, but our best rhetoric is advertising, and that is not a good place to find discipline in the liberal arts. I suspect we find our highest virtues in mathematical rhetoric, that is in measurement. Mathematics is the queen of our sciences, much as we hate to admit it, and the physicist is the prime minister. Our educational cabinet should be organized around mathematical physics. But not to make the mistake of thinking that what is is right, or will be right tomorrow, we should have a fully equipped cabinet. The

mathematical physicist should be matched by a poet, and the five other liberal arts should have their equal representation; and let the argument go wherever it will.[85]

Buchanan's statement is important for in it he rejected the charge, often made by his detractors, that the "liberal artists" were solely interested in retrieving old-fashioned education and dropping it into modern education. He and his fellow travelers did want to rescue the liberal arts from their displacement, but they also wanted to adapt them to contemporary uses, as can be seen in his emphasis on mathematical physics. Tried and true methods (arts) adapted to current uses—this was their charge.

In the final analysis Buchanan left no doubt as to what he believed to be the gravity of what the Chicago Committee on the Liberal Arts, even with all its difficulties and disagreements, was attempting to undertake. Buchanan concluded:

I should like to propose a new issue, one that I believe has both scholarly and administrative strategy in it. It has to do with the reason why we have both a Trivium and a Quadrivium, why one is up when the other is down straight through European history. There is a great rift between so-called verbal and mathematical thought throughout the tradition, and there are a lot of ghosts ranged on the two sides making faces at each other. At the extremes are the pure mathematicians and the theological humanists. In between are the intellectual bastards, Leonardo holding the center. The modern scientist is in direct line of descent from the center. The mathematical logician confirms Aristotle's statement about mules, that bastards are impotent and barren. This issue goes back to Plato and the failure of the Syracusan adventure, and can be found anywhere along the line, to wit, in the Chicago Committee on the Liberal Arts. This is a real issue and a great scandal. I think something can and should be done about it. It is the task that Plato set for the Academy; it would be a grand job to set for the 20th century and the Chicago curriculum in the Classics and the Liberal Arts. Greater men than we have seen the problem and failed; we might try pyramiding.[86]

The essays thus ultimately proved to be a mission statement. The committee members had invested the full weight of academic history into their efforts. The necessary path seemed clear.

The committee members continued their reading and discussions. At the end of March, 1937, the Committee on the Liberal Arts submitted a report to Hutchins. Two drafts exist in the archives and it is instructive to consider the first draft and the changes subsequently made before its submission. The final draft follows below, with the first draft text in brackets.

REPORT TO THE PRESIDENT ON THE COMMITTEE ON THE LIBERAL ARTS
March 29 [25], 1937

This committee was organized in October, 1936, to study the liberal arts with a view to determining their usefulness in education and research. Four anonymous donors gave $23,200 [$22,000] a year for three years to support the work. The Committee was originally conceived as advisory to the Dean of the Humanities Division. As its work has developed, it has seemed wise not to limit it exclusively to the study of those subjects falling within that division. At the instance of the Dean and with the advice of the Divisional Committee on Policy, the Committee on the Liberal Arts has therefore been made advisory to the President. We understand that plans for the new appointments, if any, will in the future be reported to the Senate Committee on University Policy instead of the Committee on Policy of the Humanities Division.

The membership of the Committee at present is Scott Buchanan, Chairman; Stringfellow Barr, Arthur L. H. Rubin, Research Associate; Catesby Taliaferro, Research Assistant, and Charles Wallis, Research Assistant.

[Since the members of the Committee have had ten or fifteen years' experience in teaching the 75 or 100 great books of the western world, both in adult education and in honors courses at various universities, we have begun the re-study of these books in the effort to reconstruct their connections with one another and their mutually helpful understandings. In this task we have had recourse to the great interpretive tradition that in European history has gone by the name of the liberal arts.] We have begun with an historical study of those writers who may be supposed to have something important to say about the liberal arts. We are seeking their completest formulation from the Greeks to the present and are attempting a formulation which, we hope, may shed some light on their contemporary applications. By the end of the current year we shall have in written form our preliminary studies of the liberal arts in Plato, Aristotle, Euclid, and Kant, and perhaps one or two others. Next year we shall proceed to more recent writers.

We have no intention of considering at any time questions of organization or administration. We are concerned with subject-matter and methods of study. We have, of course, reached no conclusions of any kind. At the present stage of our investigation we are prepared to say only that the liberal arts seem capable of exploitation in contemporary education, that they are only slightly submerged under our present academic procedures, that experimental operations in the scientific laboratory best exemplify current applications of the liberal arts, and that language and mathematics may be the best introduction to the best of our modern disciplines.

We may need to add to our membership either for a few weeks or for the balance of the grant, either from the University faculty or outside it. We understand that the donors of the original funds are prepared to supply a reasonable amount of additional money for these purposes.

Because of our belief in the importance of this project the majority of us have given up our academic posts elsewhere. [We do not care to be considered as candidates for academic posts, aside from membership on the Committee, at Chicago.] We wish to devote ourselves exclusively to this project and do not wish to be diverted by teaching, administrative, or departmental obligations. [We think of the Committee as perhaps the beginning of a permanent group which might be attached to any university or college anywhere at any time, whose functions might undergo continuous development and change in view of the rapidly increasing difficulties of keeping the ends and methods of education clear and practical.]

Scott Buchanan, Chairman, Stringfellow Barr, Arthur L. H. Rubin, Catesby Taliaferro, Charles Wallis[87]

Of particular importance in the report, both in its draft and final forms, is the emphasis placed by the Committee on present-day education. The Committee was "attempting a formulation" of the liberal arts that they hoped "may shed some light on their contemporary applications." They believed that "experimental operations in the scientific laboratory best exemplify current applications of the liberal arts" and that "language and mathematics may be the best introduction to the best of our modern disciplines." Clearly, and as will be discussed later in this chapter, the charge that their work was regressive or sought to impose "medievalism" was misinformed. They wanted contemporary forms of the arts, not old ones.

Another critical point is the Committee's stated independence. Although stricken from the final draft, the original closing lines which stated that the Committee might "be attached to any university or college anywhere at any time" demonstrated that they conceived of themselves as dealing with universal issues, and were not institutionally bound. As will be seen in Chapter 5, this idea would resurface when Barr and Buchanan left St. John's on another venture in 1946.

Practical Considerations

In spite of the substantial goals in their report to Hutchins, the approaching end of the 1936–37 academic year necessitated that the members of the Committee on the Liberal Arts (the Virginia contingent had kept the original title) consider the mundane issue of how to best continue their work, if at all. Barr, for example, was faced with a choice. One option was to return to Charlottesville; he had taken only a one-year leave of absence from the University of

Virginia. However, in a complete reversal of positions from the previous year, this time it was Barr, not Buchanan, who believed he should resign from Virginia. Barr did not even want to discuss the matter: "More than anything, [studying Euclid] led me not to want to go back to talk with Newcomb."[88] But Buchanan believed Barr should return to Charlottesville, talk with Newcomb, and see if staying at Chicago was what he really wanted to do.

Barr doubted that such a conversation would be worthwhile. To Buchanan he said, "I don't think much will be gained by talking to [Newcomb]. I don't think he understands what we're concerned about. I don't think I could teach him in the little time granted to me." But Buchanan was unwavering. Barr reflected that: "I think [Buchanan's] dread was that there'd be remorse, and I'd feel: Well, why did I do that? He knew if anything [transpired] like what later was St. John's, there'd be a lot of danger in it, a lot of hardship and danger, and that I might later then say what the hell did I get in this mess for, when I had a place I loved, which was in Charlottesville, teaching."[89] Years later Barr wisely observed that, "[Buchanan] knew I was deeply involved in the University of Virginia and my holding on with one hand to it [in 1936] seemed to him to keep me from really looking at what we were going to do [in Chicago.]" As a result, after the debacle with the original Committee on the Liberal Arts, Barr believed that Buchanan was concerned that if Barr did not visit Charlottesville and see what might still be accomplished there, that Barr might "very easily think the whole thing has been a messy operation and should have been avoided. . . ." Barr recalled his conversation with Buchanan: "I'm going back and if [Newcomb] can give a cogent reason for me rejoining that faculty, I may do it. But if he starts buddying about it, starts getting soapy, I want to know that, because I don't want to waste my time."[90]

In late February 1937 Barr wrote to his mother that he would soon be in Charlottesville "to have quiet talks with Newcomb . . . and Bob Gooch and to look at things and collect my wits for a decision." Barr had determined that: "Something is at stake which I value more than my preference for living in Virginia, and I have turned out unexpectedly to be clergyman's son and grandson. But before reaching an ultimate decision, I need to talk to people down there."[91]

Barr did meet with Newcomb, and the conversation did live up to Barr's preconceptions:

> Well, Newcomb got soapy, and he said, "everyone here is very devoted to you." Well, I wasn't asking for a vote. I wasn't running for office, I didn't need a vote of confidence. I could see that my ideas on education didn't interest him or elicit any enthusiastic support, so there was no victory so far as I was concerned. . . .[92]

Barr's second option was to stay at Chicago. The Committee on the Liberal Arts was to be funded for three years, so Barr could continue pursuing his interest in their work. Moreover, Louis Gottschalk, the chairman of the history department at Chicago, wanted Barr to become a full member of the department. As noted earlier, in the spring of 1936 the department had not been very receptive toward Barr, but by the spring of 1937 they were eager to have him stay on and teach. The reason he was asked by the department to stay on, Barr later recalled, was, "to put it simply and brutally and without modesty, I lectured better than most people there and the kids liked it."[93]

The decision was not an easy one for Barr, but he decided to continue with the Committee on the Liberal Arts. The Board minutes from March 11, 1937 noted that Barr was reappointed "visiting professor of the Liberal Arts for two years from July 1, 1937, with an annual salary of $6,000."[94] Accordingly, on April 3, 1937 Barr sent a letter of resignation to Newcomb. In the letter Barr stated that he was resigning with "deepest personal regret," that he was "sacrificing a permanent connection with the one institution I love best, for a two-year appointment in one I care nothing about." Nevertheless, Barr felt he had to make the decision he did:

> My twelve years of teaching in the University [of Virginia] were the happiest of my life. But, as you know, I have for many years felt that American undergraduate education was in desperate need of drastic revision. My service on the [Gooch] committee which reported to you on a possible program of honors work convinced me there was a solution. My service this year on the Committee on the Liberal Arts here in Chicago has strengthened that conviction. . . . it is my duty to see this job through . . . . Wherever I am to work from now on, my heart will always be in my own State and at my own Alma Mater.[95]

Further insight into Barr's decision, and Newcomb's reaction to it, comes from correspondence between Barr's mother, Ida Barr, and Newcomb. Ida Barr had forwarded her son's February letter to her on to Newcomb in the desire that the President see the "very frank statement of why Winkie has left you and me."[96] Newcomb replied in part that:

> When he talked to me here I was confident of his final decision, which was not communicated to me until April. He thinks American college education is in serious need of change and believes that Buchanan and he have found the best solution. He is genuinely convinced that what he is doing in Chicago offers the largest opportunities for important service and he has persuaded himself that it is his duty to undertake the task.[97]

No sooner had the Virginia or Chicago question been resolved than a third option quite unexpectedly presented itself: to go to St. John's College in Annapolis, Maryland to overhaul the nation's third oldest school.[98] Barr had been convinced by Buchanan that something needed to be done about liberal education in America: "that part didn't take too much sweat on [Buchanan's] part because I was very discouraged about what one could do in the elective system."99 But whether St. John's was a good option compared to staying at Chicago was unclear.100

St. John's College
The Move to Annapolis

"That little college stinks," Barr once said of St. John's. The college was in poor shape: it was badly in debt, enrollment had declined, three administrations had folded in recent years, the school had even lost its accreditation.101 But the picture was not all bad. Barr recalled: "St. John's was a funny mixture. It was shocking, decaying, crooked, in a mess, demoralized, beautiful, elegant, a civilized community. People had cocktails and all these stories could be told at a cocktail party and that made life gayer. . . . A lot of the old South's rot and decay. Sort of a William Faulkner quality about a lot of it."102

The possibility of going to Annapolis had developed because an Oxford classmate of Barr and Buchanan's, Francis Miller, who was a trustee of St. John's College, had discussed both the College's problems and the work of the Committee on the Liberal Arts at Chicago with Buchanan at a meeting in Alexandria in May 1937.103 The crisis faced by the St. John's Board called for drastic measures. According to Buchanan, for the Board: "The first action was to be in terms of educational policy, second, in terms of personnel, and then and only then in terms of financial rehabilitation." Certainly thinking about the difficulties the Committee on Honors Courses at Virginia had experienced with President Newcomb, Buchanan added: "This, it should be noted, reverses the usual order of procedure in reform. Administrators will not take positions unless money is assured, and they do not embark on educational projects until they are given tenure and general approval." Yet in the unusual case of St. John's, "the Board discussed educational policy with several members of the Committee on the Liberal Arts at the University of Chicago. Having decided on their educational program they took up the question of the Presidency and the Deanship. They are only now taking up the question of finances."104

This order of priorities was demonstrated when Barr and Buchanan met with the entire Board of St. John's at the University Club in Baltimore on June 4, 1937. The liberal artists found the start of the meeting quite encouraging. The chairman of the Board's presidential search committee, Richard Cleveland, the son of Grover Cleveland and a very capable individual, played an influential role during the meeting.105 Of him, Barr recalled, "Dick [Cleveland] was a rather imaginative person. Princeton B.A., and Harvard LL.B.—and I think he thought 'God, that's an interesting idea, and in any case, they're capable of interesting ideas, they're capable of rallying an institution that supposedly deals with ideas.' "106 Buchanan also reacted positively to the Board: "We sat and explained the program that we would put in. We didn't discuss anything else until we did get that across. How much they understood, of course, was very difficult to know, but they were impressed. And I felt that somehow we had come to terms with them."[107] They had come to terms; Barr and Buchanan were offered the helm of St. John's. Taking into account the difficult situation at Chicago, and weighing the problems and possibilities in Annapolis, Barr and Buchanan decided to make the move. "It was a great relief for everybody but the donors of the money for [the Committee on the Liberal Arts at Chicago] when St. John's called the members of the Liberal Arts Committee to put its program into operation in little old Annapolis."[108]

The curriculum Barr and Buchanan proposed for St. John's may not have played as much of a role in their move to Annapolis as either of them have claimed. This is not to suggest that the curriculum, based on the Virginia Plan and refined at Chicago, was unimportant, for that is not the case. However, institutional factors played a critical role in the process. Late in life Barr stated that: "I'm too stuffy a historian to admit that St. John's called us. St. John's wanted a president, all right. They had to have one quick." It was the dire financial straits in which the college found itself, believed Barr, that resulted in their move to Maryland. Buchanan, argued Barr, believed that "history wanted us there. . . . But [Buchanan] makes it seem as if we were doing something so exciting at Chicago that somebody in Baltimore or Annapolis or both said, 'God, let's have 'em do it here.' And that's not it. A mortgage was the issue at Annapolis."[109] Clearly both curricular and institutional factors played critical roles in the adoption of the liberal arts program at St. John's.

Once Barr and Buchanan had agreed to the St. John's effort, filling the senior administrative positions was not easy. Barr and Buchanan, who had been in talks with the Board, had offered the presidency of St. John's College to Hutchins, hoping to lure him from Chicago permanently, but he declined.[110] Barr, not wanting the position, then proffered that Buchanan should be president since the academic program they planned to implement, which was based on the great books scheme in the Virginia Plan, was Buchanan's "baby." Buchanan steadfastly refused. Barr acquiesced and on July 1, 1937 Barr was appointed president. He subsequently named Buchanan as the Dean.[111] Although he refused an administrative position at the college, Hutchins did join the Board of Visitors and Governors, and in March 1938 he became its Chairman. As Buchanan put it: "President Hutchins, by becoming a member of the governing board, can at least vicariously pursue an educational policy to which he is devoted without angering the lions of academic prestige at the University of Chicago."[112]

As they had done the year before from Charlottesville, Catesby Taliaferro and Charles Wallis again followed Barr and Buchanan, this time to Annapolis. Taliaferro had been hesitant. In a July 1937 letter to Adler he wrote, "I have terrible misgivings about Annapolis, I mean about the Southern students I shall have to teach there. Going from the Middle West to Southern Maryland turns out to be a very bitter pill: a few years ago, I should never have thought of it that way."[113] Indeed, as a Virginia graduate, Taliaferro was himself a Southern student. Adler responded that while "anything outside New York looks the same to me," he thought Taliaferro should go to Annapolis: "St. John's is terribly important for all of us. It must succeed, and you must do everything you can to help it." Adler's personality conflicts with McKeon had deepened, and he saw no point in Taliaferro staying at Chicago: "Chicago is hopeless. From now on, everything will be progressively McKeonized. That's my way of saying that poison is being sprayed on the tree of knowledge."[114] Taliaferro and Wallis both decided to move to Annapolis. Fellow "liberal artists" Mortimer Adler and Mark Van Doren also became regular lecturers at the college. With all the primary actors involved, St. John's College had become the centerpiece of the liberal arts movement.

During this period correspondence between Barr and Newcomb at the University of Virginia continued. President Newcomb wrote to Barr that:

> If congratulations are in order, you have mine straight from the heart. I am, however, somewhat inclined to send you the sort of message that Dr. Blackwell sent me upon my election to the presidency of the University of Virginia. He simply said, "I welcome you to the noble band of martyrs."
>
> Seriously I hope you are going to have a splendid opportunity at St. John's to try out the plan of education in which you have been so much interested during the last year or two. You have my best wishes for high success.[115]

Barr's mother, Ida, was less enthusiastic. She confessed her concern in a letter to President Newcomb:

> I suspect you are feeling just as I am about Winkie's latest move, pleased that he has a chance to try his wings, but terribly frightened at what a big bite he has to chew! No one knows better than you do how painful it is to run a plant with no money. Besides that, it takes years to persuade the world a place of that sort has recovered even after it has done so. I have said, and shall say, not a word to discourage him, but you can guess what I feel. . . . If Winkie was taking this step from self interest I would not care so much, people have to pay for such motives, but doing it in the spirit in which he is, a fall would be such a hard one, he so firmly believes in what he is trying to do. If he fails, it will hurt much more than just not making a go of being a president. I want to thank you for your last letter, and for keeping his place open. Now, I shall pray you may get the best man in the country to fill his place. Love to you both from a very anxious mother. Affectionately, Ida Barr.[116]

Newcomb, maintaining that money was at the heart of the viability of the Virginia-inspired reforms, replied in part to Mrs. Barr that:

I trust very much that he is going to be able to have the necessary money to give his proposal a fair tryout. I am of the opinion that a small college is probably the most satisfactory place for this tryout. It seems to me to be largely a question of the money which, of course, is always to be regretted but seems in this life to be an unavoidable barrier to many of our hopes and dreams.[117]

Newcomb's comments again suggest that funding certainly played a pivotal role in the University of Virginia's decision to pass on implementing the Virginia Plan great books scheme in 1936. Yet his comments also suggest that the program may have been too radical for Virginia. Because of its challenges to the status quo, implementation at Charlottesville would have been difficult with or without the availability of funding. Newcomb appears to have believed that a smaller institution would offer fewer impediments to curricular innovation.

The St. John's "New Program"

At St. John's, Barr and Buchanan implemented the "New Program" which Mortimer Adler referred to as a "radical innovation in collegiate education."[118] Buchanan wrote that at St. John's, "the trustees allowed us to re-establish a very sick college according to the outlines of the Virginia plan."[119] Moreover:

> Our research on the history of the liberal arts has progressed apace, and now we know enough to correlate their various historical formulations with the books on which and in which they were first practiced. The St. John's program embodies our findings to date, and a major part of the teaching staff's work is the continuation of this research and the consequent revision of the list of great books.[120]

The curricular program implemented at St. John's in September 1937—commonly referred to as the "New Program"—was based "on several fundamental rediscoveries of what a liberal education is and on the pooled experience of teachers at Columbia, Chicago, Virginia, and in adult education in New York [The People's Institute]."[121] The roots of the "New Program," said Barr, were:

> as old as the liberal arts themselves. But the New Program was called new to distinguish it from the Old Program already in force at St. John's. And this Old Program was the typical elective system of departmentalized courses totted up to make a bachelor's degree. The paradox therefore continues: since the elective system was introduced by President Eliot of Harvard only a few decades ago, the Old Program was very new indeed.[122]

As a practical matter, the New Program was "a four-year, all required curriculum, based on the Virginia list of Great Books, with plenty of mathematics and science and plenty of laboratory."[123] The books were read in English translation (some of which was first done at St. John's) in the interest of speed, but all students had to take a year of Greek, Latin, French, and German, consecutively, during their four years. In addition to learning better the function of language, the foreign language study was designed to let the students "refer intelligently to the original text for doubtful meanings."[124] Classes were conducted as seminars—as discussion groups—although detailed drill was used to understand books like Euclid's *Elements*. To these were added expository lectures on the liberal arts. The Virginia Plan's emphasis on scientific and mathematical classics was reflected in the policy of requiring students to take four years of laboratory science.

In spite of Buchanan's belief that the "Oxbridge"-style program proposed by Gooch in Appendix B of the Virginia Plan was premature—that undergraduates would not be ready for it—it is instructive to consider how much of the Oxford method of education appeared in Annapolis. Some of Oxford's presence must be attributed to Barr, who was more receptive to Gooch's scheme than was Buchanan. Of the program of instruction implemented at St. John's, Barr recollected that:

> I think more than [Buchanan] and I were conscious of was borrowed from Oxford. I think it was an attitude rather than institutional arrangements. I was the one that said to [Buchanan], "For God's sake, put in the Don Rag. Because I think that it is absolutely essential that these people, when they get through a course, ought to be able to talk intelligently about it." And the Don Rag impressed me very much. The English just couldn't imagine not having a crack at it. Just asking [for] a lot of paper and reading it didn't seem to them an adequate accounting, and it took some time for us to convince the faculty and students of the necessity for real communication between them, for genuine conversation and not with a ruler in your hand and grade book in the other. That was one of my few contributions, I think, to instruction. But I thought they proved at Oxford that if you couldn't talk intelligently about what you were doing, then you weren't getting much. But the average professor then would say, "Well, how could you talk about it?" because he's dishing out information and then checking to find out if the information has stuck, is being remembered. And he didn't realize that awakening certain powers is more vital than giving you any item of information.[125]

The pedagogical initiatives required changes in how professors—"tutors" in the St. John's parlance—worked. The main faculty innovation at St. John's was that all faculty members had to become generalists able to teach in any part of the curriculum. They had to be "competent as liberal artists, regardless of what their previous academic specialty had been and regardless of what had been the subject of their Ph.D."[126]

As president, Barr also implemented significant changes in student life starting in 1938. One was that fraternities were no longer allowed to use college dormitories. Without homes the fraternities closed.[127] Barr had "great reservations about Greek-Letter fraternities" and he believed that the fraternities at St. John's "were withering." As a result he suspended their right to free campus housing in the belief that they were of no benefit to the college, and that they were in fact a detriment to the new college that they were trying to craft. Barr had been a fraternity member as a college student. He had joined Alpha Tau Omega at Tulane and moved his membership to ATO in Charlottesville when he transferred to the University of Virginia as an undergraduate. Although he did not have "any philosophy of fraternity-ism" he did believe that, at institutions at which the fraternity system was strong, not belonging to one meant that "you'd pay a penalty." At Virginia, Barr's fraternity experience had been mixed. He had several friends there, but he also believed that "the whole thing has a little bit of boarding school snobbery in it" and that "this seems to me silly stuff." [128]

The other major change in student life was Barr's decision to take St. John's out of intercollegiate athletics effective in the autumn of 1939. He stated: "Intercollegiate athletics involves scheduling games a year or two in advance without reference to the College's internal needs on the date the contest is played. It involves substituting a spectator psychosis for student participation. It meshes the College with a semi-professional system in which scores are more important than pleasure and skill."[129] Ironically, and perhaps to allay fears that the college was no longer in favor of athleticism, concurrent with this decision was the announcement that athletic scholarships would be offered to qualified students—even though intercollegiate competition was banned—and that intramural athletics would be greatly expanded.[130]

These two changes were deeply resented by the students. Yet along with the academic and pedagogical changes, they were all geared toward building a program that Barr and Buchanan believed offered a true liberal education, the purpose of which, Barr wrote, "is to free the human intellect, to render usable the intellectual powers which in varying degrees all men possess...."[131]

Friends and Foes

There was widespread interest in and debate about the "New Program" throughout the country. Numerous well-known individuals took sides as to whether or not St. John's represented an advance or a regression in collegiate education. As noted in the Introduction, Walter Lippman waxed that "In the future men will point to St. John's College and say that there was the seed-bed of the American Renaissance."[132] Similarly, in 1943 fellow "liberal artist" Mark Van Doren offered that the St. John's program:

> represents the first serious effort in contemporary America to build a single and rational curriculum suited to the needs of minds which have

work to do, and which someday should be unwilling to forgive any system of education that had required of them less discipline than this. Education is honored when it is hard, but it is most honored when it is hard and good.[133]

Critics, however, charged the New Program at St. John's was old-fashioned and reactionary. John Andrews Rice, founding president of the progressive Black Mountain College, asserted that:

> St. John's College, in Annapolis, is a vocational school, without a vocation. With a curriculum straight out of medieval Oxford, it trains its students, not for the church, as Oxford did then and not for any office in or under an oligarchy, but for something pleasantly vague: to be artists in the art of thinking, Neo-Thomist dialectitions, lawyers, without law.[134]

Indeed, Barr recorded that:

> We were called fascists because we had abolished the "freedom" of the elective system; crypto-Catholics because we all read some of the treatises of St. Thomas Aquinas . . . ; frauds because some of the books listed were not in English—they were not, until we translated them; dilettantes because clearly no reputable scholar would teach in all these "fields;" and antiquarians because, since we insisted that everyone study Greek and Latin, we must obviously scorn natural science—although St. John's was perhaps the only liberal arts college in the country that required four years of laboratory of every student.[135]

The debate did not just center on St. John's. It had originally started with the philosophies advocated by Adler and Hutchins. In December 1936 Charles Clark of the Yale Law School delivered the William Moody Lecture at the University of Chicago. In his address, titled "The Higher Learning in a Democracy," he argued that Hutchins wanted to use metaphysics to restore unity to higher learning, much as theology had provided a unifying structure in the past. Hutchins had said that, "If we can revitalize metaphysics and restore it to its place in the higher learning, we may be able to establish rational order in the modern world as well as in the universities." Unfortunately, argued Clark, "I fear this does not carry us forward to a solution. Theology offers a program of action. Metaphysics does not." Even if it did, proposed Clark, there would still be the problem of defining that metaphysics: "its content remains unclear." To the extent that Hutchins developed the idea, Clark suggested that: "[Metaphysics] remains only a symbol of an ideal, unfortunately barren, devoid of all stimulating vitality. It is identified with the highest wisdom, which in turn, is identified with knowledge of the highest principles and causes. But this is all there is of definition given us of the ultimate principle of unity upon which a university is to be built." As a result, one develops "a feeling that the keystone of the arch has been omitted."[136]

At this point Clark had arrived at a common criticism from friend and foe of Hutchins' philosophy as it was presented in *The Higher Learning in America*, namely, that Hutchins never defined his metaphysics.[137] Clark stated further that this omission, although problematic for Hutchins' argument, was a good thing. "The proper answer would seem to be not merely that it has been omitted but that there is none—there should be none." A metaphysics that served as a rationale for intellectual unity could easily be authoritarian, just as theology could be dogmatic. Although Hutchins was to be thanked for highlighting problems in higher learning, he was overzealous in his criticisms. "The worst is bad; the best is worth conserving; we should not throw out all to substitute a false medievalism in the vain hope that there lies progress." In short, argued Clark, "The development of an authoritarian attitude toward education is the one way to kill it."[138]

Clark proceeded to argue that American higher education should instead look to "the best" in the higher learning, "the experimentalism, the originality of our scholars." In doing so democratic society would "guard and cherish the intellectual independence of the universities." Ultimately, Clark concluded: "We are returning to Thomas Jefferson for many articles of belief. Let us return in closing to his statement of the aims of the University of Virginia when he said: 'This institution will be based on the illimitable freedom of the human mind, for here we are not afraid to follow truth wherever it may lead, nor to tolerate error as long as reason is left free to combat it.'"[139]

Sometimes critiques conflated, understandably but often not appropriately, what was being done by Barr and Buchanan and what was being said by Adler and Hutchins. Critic John Pilley argued that: "When [Hutchins] speaks of metaphysics as the highest of the 'sciences,' he comes near to talking the absolutist language, [but] his good sense is too great to carry him far along those lines." Hutchins' associates were not as fortunate:

> In contradistinction to President Hutchins, both Professor Adler and Dean Buchanan believe in the absolute truth of their own particular systems of metaphysics, and—quite consistently with their own thinking—regard anyone who does not accept their metaphysical conclusions as heretical. Their systems of metaphysics are in fact nothing but theologies which they find it expedient not to call by that name.
>
> Anyone who is trying to discover what the Hutchins program is in practice will be perplexed at finding that a schism already divides its two leading practitioners. Whereas Scott Buchanan's orthodoxy, which provides the educational philosophy of studies at St. John's College, is on the whole Pagan and Platonic—leading to enormous emphasis being placed on mathematics—that of Mortimer Adler, which underlies his

teaching at Chicago, is Catholic and Aristotelian. Both orthodoxies are at one in being vigorously antidemocratic, although their authors seem not to recognize this. Here, however, it is important to remember that a man who is convinced of the absoluteness of a theory of knowledge or a theory of value, however little it may be capable of substantiation, may quite sincerely denounce all other values as "error." There is no reason to suppose that the Judges of the Inquisition were anything but sincere even in the sixteenth century when the verbal basis of medieval philosophy was becoming so generally recognized.[140]

Pilley concluded that: "Today there are many who advocate a return to the conditions of the Middle Ages. Though their arguments are various we must be on guard against them all."[141]

Unfortunately for the educational debate, there were simplistic and sometimes puerile statements all around. *The New Leader* couched the debate as: "John Dewey versus Robert Hutchins—proponents of opposite educational concepts. The Old Man represents progressive ideas. The Young Man retreats into medievalism."[142] Conversely, an educational traditionalist, Francis Donnelly, argued that an article by Malcom MacLean, a progressive, used easy and "opprobrious terminology," referring to Hutchins as "very medieval" and "a facist (sic) dictator." Donnelly continued that after berating Hutchins,

> Believe it or not, here is Professor MacLean's curriculum for unifying education: "Science principles for weather, automobiles, radio, television, next war and diseases; social principles of the Supreme Court, crime, money, population trends; esthetic principles of streamlined planes and trains, lampshades and clothing." This curriculum is to prepare the student "to find a job, to sell bonds, write radio script, teach children—to help solve the conflict between the A.F. of L. and the C.I.O.—to choose a girl to marry, bring up children, support a church, vote effectively, pick the best doctor for ills and evaluate motion pictures." How the nondescript curriculum is to effect all these happy results we are not told. The Professor has a trusting faith in the experimental psychologists and their "diagnostic research projects" and in a complete study of "contemporary society." "Then and only then" can we formulate our educational policy.[143]

Such easy attacks, made by those in favor of and those against the liberal arts movement, tended to obscure more substantial discussions.

One such discussion was attempted in 1944. In an exchange with Alexander Meiklejohn, John Dewey stated that "we are now being told that a genuinely liberal education would require return to the models, patterns, and standards that were laid down in Greece some twenty-five hundred years ago and renewed and put into practice in the best age of feudal medievalism six and seven centuries ago."[144] Dewey continued that:

> The notion that language, linguistic skills and studies can be used of the same ends and by the same methods under contemporary conditions as in Greek, Alexandrian, or medieval times is as absurd in principle as it would be injurious in practice were it adopted.... The idea that an adequate education of any kind can be obtained by means of a miscellaneous assortment of a hundred books, more or less, is laughable when viewed practically.... It marks a departure from what is sound in the Greek view of knowledge as a product of intelligence exercised at first hand. It marks reversion to the medieval view of dependence upon the final authority of what others have found out—or supposed they had found out—and without the historical grounds that gave reason to the scholars of the Middle Ages.
>
> The reactionary movement is dangerous (or would be if it made serious headway) because it ignores and in effect denies the principle of experimental inquiry and firsthand observation that is the lifeblood of the entire advance made in the sciences—an advance so marvelous that the progress in knowledge made in uncounted previous millenniums is almost nothing in comparison.[145]

Alexander Meiklejohn, in *A Reply to John Dewey*, argued that Dewey misunderstood the reformers' intentions:

> Does the study of the past imply that we intend to imitate it? That was certainly not true in the Experimental College. It is not true in St. John's College. Both those institutions have engaged in the attempt to cultivate, in the minds of teachers and pupils, the processes of critical intelligence. They study Homer, Plato, Euclid, Aquinas, Newton, Shakespeare, Darwin, Marx, Veblen, Freud, not because these great minds were right but in order to find out how right, and wrong, they were, in order to find out what "right" and "wrong" are. One does not, for example, study Ptolemy because he is "superior" to Copernicus. One studies him in the belief that a prior understanding of Ptolemy may contribute to a better understanding of Copernicus. And, that being true, I can find no basis whatsoever for the assertion that the study of the past implies the acceptance of the standards of the past as superior to our own.[146]

Meiklejohn continued by arguing that studying the great authors did not lead to nor imply dogmatism:

> When St. John's turns to Homer and Plato to find a beginning for its study of the humanities, to Euclid and Archimedes to find a beginning

for its study of the sciences and technologies, it is not looking to those writers for "the last words" on those subjects. It is looking for "first words." Its entire scheme of education is built upon the basic postulate that, from the time of the Greeks until the present, the knowledge and wisdom of men have been growing, that, with many losses as well as gains, they are still growing. And the intention of the curriculum is that the student shall follow that growth in order that he may be better equipped to play his part in the intellectual and moral activities of his own time and country.

As he follows the sequence of ideas the pupil will be confronted, not with one "static" set of dogmatic beliefs, but with all the fundamental conflicts that run through our culture. He will find Protagoras at war with Plato, Kant at war with Hume, Rousseau at war with Locke, Veblen at war with Adam Smith. And he must try to understand both sides of these controversies. He is asked, first of all, not to believe, but to think, as a precondition of justifiable belief. How that program could commit St. John's to the acceptance from the past of "fixed" and "static" ideas, I do not know. Such acceptance would seem to me more nearly a contradiction of the program than a deduction from it.[147]

To Dewey's concerns about the important role of science in contemporary society, Meiklejohn replied that St. John's students took: "(1) four years of required mathematics, (2) four years of required laboratory practice, (3) four years of required reading of the masters of scientific discovery (approximately one-half of the great-books assignment)."[148]

The arguments against St. John's were enjoined by philosopher Sidney Hook, who, having flipped the argument, proposed that the liberal artists had an incorrect understanding of progressive educational philosophy. "On the college level," said Hook, "progressive education takes its point of departure not only from the objective needs and capacities of different individuals but from the declared aims of a liberal education. It attempts to discover through *intelligent guidance* what course of study will best enable this particular student to achieve the most of what a liberal education strives to impart to all students." Some subjects as a result will be essential. Unfortunately, and similar to Hutchins with metaphysics, Hook failed to elaborate on his arguments. In terms of pedagogy, however, Hook did offer that:

> Differences in the needs, background and capacities of those who are at all educable point not to the necessity of a tailor-made curriculum in the early years of college but to the wisdom of adopting different techniques of instruction, specialized assignments, and projects of graded difficulty to students of different powers. [Progressive education] avoids holding them all to one dead level of uniformity, low or high, easy or hard.[149]

Hook also argued that contemporary American collegiate education had been misrepresented by the liberal artists:

> The defects of the elective system in current education have long been recognized. But the steps that have been taken to remedy them have not. Partisans of the St. John's curriculum write as if the elective system in our colleges is the result of progressive education, as if any prescription is incompatible with its philosophy, and as if all colleges operate with an unrestricted elective system with no common core of required studies.[150]

Hook rightly argued that the elective system was introduced before progressive education made any headway. He also stated that: "Most liberal arts colleges that reflect the philosophy of progressive education require almost a solid two years of prescription in certain fields of knowledge...."[151]

Other arguments made by Hook, however, were misrepresentations. Of "the spokesmen for St. John's" Hook stated that: "All of them are firmly convinced that the classic tradition should constitute the substance of college studies because it is a great storehouse of truths which provide answers to the perennial problems of human life and destiny." Truths and answers are in fact not what the leaders of St. John's claimed to provide, but rather an understanding of what humanity has thought about these ideas—an important distinction. Likewise, Hook stated that: "In effect, what Messrs. Barr, Buchanan, and Hutchins are saying is that the social problems of Graeco-Roman, medieval, Renaissance and post-Renaissance culture—out of which many of the great classics were born—are worth studying but not the social problems of the twentieth century."[152] Again, Hook is incorrect in this assertion. One of the goals of the liberal arts movement as construed by Buchanan and Barr was to reconstruct the liberal arts in order to have a tool with which to understand the contemporary world. In an imaginary conversation that Barr created for a lecture he gave at an association convention in 1939, an antagonist refers to the St. John's Program as "archaism:"

> [Antagonist:] Why spend four years reading the Greeks, when modern writers have said the same things in up-to-date form? [Barr:] We read the Greeks only in the freshman year. The juniors are reading Voltaire, Locke, Kepler, and writers of that period. Next year their list will include William James, Freud, Flaubert, and Karl Marx.[153]

In their minds, at least, Barr and Buchanan wanted to reconstruct the liberal arts for modern application, not return to some past period of history.

To the argument that the great books should not be the centerpiece of a curriculum, Barr replied: "A classic, unlike a college textbook, can be understood at many levels, as witness the experience all of us have had with Shakespeare or with Plato."[154] Indeed Barr argued that "those who have taught the great books have found them more 'contemporary,' more relevant to this year's experience in short, than three-year-old textbooks are."[155] Moreover:

> the greatest books have generally been written in the light of other great books, frequently to confute those others. Each civilization tends to produce a constellation of these great writings, which taken together form a great conversation. One such conversation started in Greece, was carried on in the Roman Empire, continued through the Middle Ages and the Renaissance, and is still going.[156]

To the charge that the New Program was culturally limited because it did not contain great works from non-Western civilizations, Barr argued that: "On the whole, I'd stick to *our* conversation, the one that started in Greece, not because the one that started in China is no good, but because we already half understand our own and had better finish the job."[157] Buchanan added that:

> Four years is a short time for reading the books we already have on the list. If I did not think people would go on gradually studying the books these lead to I should think we were a complete fake. We are doing the first reading of the few books which will initiate us to the study of all the things we should know, including other books. I think the great books of the Orient are included in that perspective.[158]

Barr also noted that when others reviewed the St. John's book list, "you always got a kick-back from some professor" which said something to the effect of "don't fool with all that stuff, why don't you put in more of my stuff?," which Barr stated was "a good way to kill it."[159] As an example, one of Barr's colleagues at Virginia, Garrard Glenn, a professor in the Law School, wrote to Barr upon receipt of a copy of the "New Program" at St. John's that:

> This program, indeed, has restored my equanimity. . . . You really do not end with those two troublemakers, Marx and Freud, nor does your prospectus indicate that all culture reaches its climax with the two individuals in question. If I might make a suggestion, however, it is that Francis Bacon be balanced by Descartes and Montaigne. I think you and [Buchanan] slipped just a little into your Victorian background when you omitted the thought of this balance.[160]

In the final analysis it appears that spokesmen on all sides of the debates often misunderstood or misrepresented what their opponents were doing and believed. What they could agree on was the general confusion regarding liberal education. Dewey stated: "We are agreed that a genuinely liberal education is badly hampered by confusion of aims and procedures."[161] Meiklejohn too concluded that: ". . . we are dealing with a problem so difficult that men were unclear and perplexed about it long before we came on the scene and that other men will, presumably, be unclear and perplexed about it long after we are gone."[162]

Conclusion

In the early 1940s Hutchins proposed that the criticisms of the St. John's program were the result of the nature and organization of American universities: "Their faculties are the product of that educational system which ought to be changed; they have a vested interest in its maintenance. These men are all specialists. Their professional standing depends on their concentration on their specialties. Few of them have a liberal education, and few of them are interested in getting one."[163] It was for these reasons, argued Hutchins, who went even further than Newcomb, that an undertaking like the "New Program" at St. John's could only happen in unusual circumstances:

> I would say that one of the things that brought St. John's into existence was the inadequacies of Virginia and Chicago. They showed the necessity of separating from established institutions and creating a new, full-time residential enterprise. If the Virginia and Chicago efforts had not been made, the answer would always have been that the St. John's program could be incorporated into some existing institution.[164]

As will be seen, Hutchins' insight may well have been true in terms of existing institutions, but creating new ones *sui generis* was not easy either. St. John's particular situation—an existing college desperately in need of being made over—would be, in retrospect, the most fertile ground for bringing the ideals of the liberal arts movement to realization. What Barr and Buchanan accomplished in Annapolis was quite significant. Forty years later, eminent historian Frederick Rudolph called their program "a most remarkable feat" that was "almost outrageous in its audacity," and he concluded that: "St. John's not only paid respect to the intellectual heritage of the modern world and built a community around a shared discussion of the problems and questions that have confronted man because he was man; St. John's may also have been the first, and only, intellectual community in the history of American education."[165]

CHAPTER 5

Great Plans, Modest Accomplishments

"If satisfactory arrangements can be made"
—Colgate Darden

Honors Programs and General Education Reform

Frank Aydelotte, Swarthmore, and Virginia

In his 1944 book, *Breaking the Academic Lockstep*, Frank Aydelotte, the Director of the Institute for Advanced Study in Princeton, noted that:

> An introductory honors course . . . was proposed to the President of the University of Virginia by a committee in 1935, but was never acted upon by the faculty. It was intended to provide during the first two years, by the use of a selected list of the greatest classics from Greek times down to the present, a broad liberal education for a small group of the best students. These students would then be expected during their last two years to follow the honors program now in use at Virginia, with some modifications and improvements as desirable.[1]

Although some of his facts were wrong, Aydelotte believed that Virginia had tremendous potential, particularly if it instituted the full Virginia Plan. He proffered that: "If the faculty of the University of Virginia build upon the foundations which have been so well laid the result will be an outstanding example of the possibility of the adaptation of the honors idea to the conditions of a state university."[2]

Why was Aydelotte such a booster of the Virginia Plan? Like Barr, Buchanan, and Gooch, Aydelotte had been a Rhodes Scholar. At Oxford he had observed "the intellectually stimulating practice of separating honors students from pass students." Later, as the president of Swarthmore College in Pennsylvania, Aydelotte, with $4 million from the General Education Board, made the college the first to inaugurate an honors program and have it endure. The honors program started in 1922 at Swarthmore was not the first attempt at such a program. Harvard, Yale, Princeton, Columbia, and other institutions had all tried various honors programs before World War I, but "these early programs were denied the necessary commitment and resources" to make them work. These attempts, however meager, had nevertheless as historian Frederick Rudolph put it, "provided a clear challenge to the idea of the undergraduate college as a democracy of equals."[3]

In Aydelotte's conception of it, the honors idea was based on the belief that abler students need a more "severe course of instruction." When compared to the regular course of instruction, the work for honors students "must be different; it must not only be harder but must also offer more freedom and responsibility, more scope for the development of intellectual independence and initiative." Without such a regimen, argued Aydelotte:

> The academic system as ordinarily administered is for [the] better and more ambitious students a kind of lock step: it holds them back, wastes their time, and blunts their interest by subjecting them to a slow moving routine which they do not need. It causes, furthermore, the atrophy of the qualities of independence and initiative in more gifted individuals by furnishing too little opportunity for their exercise.[4]

Aydelotte was also arguing specifically that his own time, 1944, was of critical importance to higher education since liberal education had been pushed aside by the training and vocational demands of wartime and the preceding Depression. In short, "If our liberal education is to meet the needs of the postwar world we must clarify its aims and improve its quality."[5] Because this was the case, argued Aydelotte, "we must break the lock step of the course and hour system if we are to give our students of varying levels of ability a training which will develop adequately the powers of each." In order to accomplish this, American institutions of higher learning had to look to the "Anglo-Saxon" model rather than the continental model, because "the English universities have long ago faced and solved this problem" by setting up a system whereby one receives either a pass degree or an honors degree.[6]

Inaugurated under Aydelotte, the Swarthmore honors program for upperclassmen, like those that followed it, relied on the English tradition of giving the better students far greater freedom in their academic work, under the guidance of a tutor, and requiring written and oral examinations at the end of the senior year. This pattern, argued Aydelotte, removed the better American student from the standard American academic requirements which "are too much concerned with processes, assuming that if the student goes through the motions, he will get an education."[7]

Much of the Swarthmore program was replicated at other institutions and, as seen earlier, at Virginia starting in 1937. Honors work during the last two undergraduate years at Swarthmore was divided into four parts which corresponded to the four semesters allotted, and was conducted seminar style. Attendance at regular courses during this time was entirely voluntary. No examinations were conducted until the end of the senior or fourth year when honors students had to complete written and oral final comprehensive exams, conducted by outside examiners.[8] In the seminars carried out over the two years, work was divided into weekly topics. During the two-hour weekly seminar meetings the students and the tutor discussed their common readings for that week. Student papers, each on a different aspect of the week's topic, were also read and discussed.[9]

One significant difference between the Swarthmore and Virginia conceptions of honors work was group versus individual tutoring. Regarding the use of seminars over individual tutorials, Aydellotte wrote that:

> Our faculty decided for several reasons that honors instruction could more feasibly be given at Swarthmore in seminars than in individual tutorials. For one thing, the American professor knows how to conduct a seminar and he has not ordinarily had experience in the fine art of individual tutorial work. Furthermore, the informal discussions in the seminar we have found enormously stimulating to the students concerned. The seminar, in addition, is a convenient means of training young members of the Faculty to conduct Honors work, and it tends to some extent to protect the student against a poor tutor.[10]

This mode of instruction was a significant pedagogical difference from the practice at Virginia, where the individual tutorial was favored. Because Swarthmore conducted honors instruction in seminar form, that is, four or five students per tutor, students as a rule did not have individual instruction. Each seminar was also conducted in a "field," as opposed to a department. Students at Swarthmore generally selected a primary subject that was complemented by one or two additional subjects. According to Aydelotte, common combinations included: "English Literature, English History, and Philosophy; Economics, History, and Political Science; Mathematics, Astronomy, and Physics; [and] Physiology, Zoology, and Chemistry."[11]

Honors students at Virginia, by contrast, usually had individual instruction within a single department. This did not mean that students could not study subjects outside of their department. Students were admitted to honors work in more than one department, but all the relevant departments had to recommend, and the Committee on Honors Courses had to approve, such a course of study.[12] This meant that honors work at Virginia was conducted within a departmental structure, not a "field" structure as at Swarthmore.

As for pedagogy, the one-on-one mode of tutorial instruction was favored at Virginia because it was thought to be the most effective, but this mode was not exclusive. Writing in 1960, the chairman of the Committee on Honors Courses, David Yalden-Thomson of the Philosophy Department, offered the following:

> A plausible criticism . . . is that in some, or all, subjects something can be accomplished in seminars which cannot be achieved either in tutorials or lectures, namely, the benefits of directed discussions among intelligent students. To a limited extent there is some seminar work, for some tutors in some Departments, e.g., Economics, Political Science, and Philosophy occasionally take two, three, or four tutorial students at the same time in order to promote exchanges of ideas. . . .

While acknowledging the possible strengths of seminar instruction, Yalden-Thomson argued that there were advantages to individual tutorial instruction as well:

> All who have experience of tutoring or of being tutored are aware of the way in which individual Honors students vary in their responses to working jointly with other Honors students, whether in tutorials or seminars. Some students welcome, say, a joint tutorial with one other student of similar intellectual capacities, while others object to such a procedure.[13]

In short, the Honors Program at Virginia was set up so that benefits could be derived from both forms of instruction.

Virginia's honors program drew praise from Aydelotte as seen below in his summary comments. In particular, his synopsis gives an excellent overview of how Virginia's honors system worked in 1944, seven years after its inception.

> It is difficult for large institutions to experiment, to follow any but well-trodden paths, and particularly difficult to persuade state legislators to appropriate funds for a program of this type, limited to the few, when they find it hard enough to supply the needs of the many. Under these circumstances it is all the more creditable that honors plans are in operation in a number of our stronger state institutions and that two at least, Virginia and Ohio, have taken positions of leadership in the movement. The admirable program at the University of Virginia . . . replaces entirely the course and hour system in the Junior and Senior years. . . .
>
> The University [of Virginia] is one of the oldest and most conservative of our state institutions and not one of the richest. These facts make it all the more remarkable that Virginia should have developed an honors plan which, while it does not affect all departments (or schools, as they are called in Jefferson's phrase) and reaches as yet only a small proportion of the student body, is nevertheless thoroughgoing and well conceived. There is a regulation which permits groups of two or more schools or departments to combine to formulate an honors program, but this has not as yet been acted on in practice. On the other hand, the word "subject" is broadly used and may embrace the field of more than one school or department. Thus, an honors program sponsored by one department may involve a request by the department to a professor in another to give the student concerned tutorial instruction. . . .
>
> Virginia has made the conditions for entering honors work extremely severe, seeking quality rather than numbers. The chairman of the honors committee studies the records of the students in their second year in the University to determine the high-standing men. Those interested in

honors work are invited to an informal interview with the chairman and on the twofold basis of academic record and personal qualifications, honors students are chosen.

A plan of study for the Junior and Senior years is made out by the major department in consultation with the student and this plan must receive the approval of the faculty committee on degrees with honors. Once accepted the plan becomes both the basis for the student's work and a guide for setting his final comprehensive examination. There is some difference between departments as to the scope of honors work. The method of teaching is usually by individual tutorials, although here also procedure varies. Final examinations are set by outside examiners or by members of the Virginia faculty who have had no part in teaching the student who is being examined. They include both written papers and an oral.

All degrees with honors must be recommended to the faculty by the honors committee. Some member of the committee follows closely the examination of each student, the reports of the examiners in all departments are considered, and after careful discussion degrees are recommended. The plan seems to have been admirably thought out in all its details. It is carefully administered by the Committee on Degrees with Honors rather than by departments, and its prospects of success are all the brighter for the fact that the number of students in the early years has been small so that every problem and every difficulty could receive individual attention.[14]

While Virginia's honors program had been in place from 1937 and throughout the war, Aydelotte's commentary indicates that Virginia's role in the liberal arts movement had resulted in the University attracting national attention as educators began to investigate curricular models for the post-war era.

This attention was significant because a second wave of general education reform followed World War II. Just as war had precipitated the first "revival" and a quest for social integration after World War I, so too the second revival was spurred on by war and the perceived need to strengthen Western democratic values against communism.[15] Particularly noteworthy at that time was the 1945 Harvard report *General Education in a Free Society*, known as the "Red Book." It won praise for articulating the importance and goals of general education, and it also provided considered reflection on the various proposals regarding general education made up to that time. It did not, however, provide a compelling program to provide an "over-all logic, some strong, not easily broken frame" for general education and it was ultimately rejected at Harvard, though it served as a model at other institutions.[16] Ultimately no national consensus emerged during this second period of general education reform, save that some amount of it was deemed desirable to counter communism and undesirable aspects of curricular atomization, vocationalism, and professionalism.[17] The revival was slowed by the technocratic concerns raised by *Sputnik* and eventually halted by the student movement of the late 1960s with its calls for relevance and rejection of prescriptions of all kinds.

The University of Virginia

Curriculum Committees Without End

Just as Aydelotte believed that a thorough-going examination of liberal education was necessary if it were to fulfill its vital role in the post-war era, so too the faculty and administration of the University of Virginia believed that wartime necessitated a reconsideration of liberal education at Mr. Jefferson's University. One statement on the curriculum at that time, probably written by President Newcomb, claimed, "in these days of War, when so much emphasis must be rightly given to education for the development and use of technical skills, there is widespread fear among many leaders in the field of liberal education that in the postwar world the cause of liberal education may suffer greatly." In order to preserve liberal learning "the Arts and Sciences must indeed find a common meeting-ground in the colleges of the future." As for the arts:

> Truth, Goodness, and Beauty, constituting the cultural core of the Greek tradition and representing the ideas toward which the spiritual development of western civilization has tended for twenty-five centuries, inspired and ennobled by the social gospel of nineteen hundred years of Christian influence, will always have a firm and lasting place in any program of liberal education. Without such ideals to inspire and lead man on, civilization would lose its impetus and man his dream of noble living. Such ideals have given us the finest that man has to treasure in the world of art, music, painting, sculpture, and great literature. No program of education can afford to neglect them. They form the basis of the art of living in its truest sense. To foster them in our halls of learning is to foster the Arts—the humanistic core or tradition.[18]

At the same time, and in harmony with the place that Buchanan argued for mathematics and the sciences in the Virginia Plan, this Virginia curriculum statement also argued the necessity of mathematics and science:

> Those who preserve the humanistic tradition must not forget that there are others who labor wisely and long to discover and preserve the instrumentalities that make our civilization possible. Technical achievement is just as much a part of our American tradition as is the humanistic lore that wise men have bequeathed to us. He is not liberally educated who champions one tradition and neglects the other. Liberal education, in

bringing the Arts and Sciences together in fact as well as in theory, will become a finer, richer type of education.... The Arts and Sciences must become one in purpose and spirit for the enrichment of mankind.[19]

In response, during the 1940s the University established no fewer than seven different committees to consider the institution's curriculum. In addition to seemingly constant self-evaluation, these committees also solicited material from other institutions that were making changes, including Chicago's plans from 1931 and 1942, the 1945 Harvard *Redbook*, Columbia's plans in 1946, and Princeton's in 1947.

In December 1943 the faculty of the College of Arts and Sciences authorized a Special Committee on Curriculum "to consider and report to it desirable changes in the curriculum of the College, its methods of instruction, and its requirements for graduation." The committee undertook its task during the following year and in January 1945 it recommended that each student should take a year-long course in "Oral and Written Expression," pass a proficiency exam in elementary mathematics, demonstrate proficiency in a foreign language, and take at least one course in each of the following areas: the exact sciences, the natural sciences, history, the social studies, literature, the fine arts, music, speech and drama, and philosophy.[20]

In the interim, the University's Post-War College Committee, with Dean of the College Ivey F. Lewis serving as chairman, also issued a report that emphasized the special importance of liberal education. The committee asserted in its August 1944 report that a liberal education:

> ... is the very kind of education which enables one most effectively to adjust himself to the demands of change. This it does by giving him the capacity for adjustment to his environment. Liberal education so enriches one's mind that he is not dependent upon Hollywood or Radio City or the swank Country Club for relief from boredom. It seeks to give its beneficiary the capacity for adjustment to whatever circumstances may surround him rather than to train him for the performance of some specific task which he may never be called on to perform or which may be rendered obsolete and useless by scientific invention or technological advancement.[21]

While recognizing that the construction of a new curriculum "has been the subject of study by another committee," the post-war committee suggested that "the scope and content of the first two years of college work be more coherently defined than has been done in the past and that a central core of subject matter considered as the necessary equipment of all educated persons should be prescribed for the first two years."[22]

This course of reasoning followed the same logic used in the Virginia Plan, that is, that the underclass years be spent in a prescribed course of study, although now the recommendation was that all students should follow this regimen. The Virginia Plan's philosophy is seen even more strongly in the postwar committee's judgment that "the reorganized liberal arts subjects shall in the future, as in the past, constitute the essential core of the college curriculum and that the chief aim of the college should be to develop a well planned, carefully articulated liberal arts course of study."[23]

A third report was generated by the standing Committee on Academic Legislation in September 1944, several months before the report by the Special Committee on the Curriculum, and one month after the release of the report of the Post-War Committee. To the degree requirements for the B.A., which had been revised in 1935, the Committee recommended that designated courses in each of the following be added: English and American literature; history; and economics, political science, or sociology.[24] This recommendation was rejected by the faculty and a new group, the "Balz Committee," was established to consider curriculum issues further. Under Albert Balz, chairman of the Philosophy department and a supporter of the Virginia Plan honors program established in 1937, this subsequent committee took a different tack. It made two assumptions: "a) that students who have had the advantages of excellent training in secondary schools should not be held back by their less fortunate comrades and b) that all students must possess a knowledge of certain fundamental subjects before being admitted to courses in which such knowledge is taken for granted." Through a proposed system of advanced standing determined by examinations that placed students in "precandidacy" and "candidacy" statuses, students of different preparations and abilities could proceed through their undergraduate education at different rates and at different levels. In spite of the proposed variability, "the faculty was to have much greater control than heretofore over the election of courses by all students since the committee felt that eighteen-year-old boys can scarcely arrange a well-integrated program for themselves." The Balz Committee report was submitted to the Committee on Academic Legislation, which approved it, but it too was subsequently rejected by the faculty.[25]

Somehow the faculty, unsatisfactorily it would turn out, determined to revise the B.A. requirements in 1945. Compared to the 1935 curriculum, the new one was more prescribed. The required number of English credit hours was doubled. A year-long required course in history was added. The other requirements remained the same, except that Greek and Latin were no longer required.[26]

No sooner were these changes made than additional curricular revisions were considered. Two new committees, perhaps chastened by the experiences of the previous ones, strove to find a balance in their recommendations between too much prescription and electivism. The new Curriculum Committee on Requirements did not propose to abolish the elective system, but was "convinced of the wisdom of exerting considerable control over the student's election of courses." As a result, the Committee members suggested that their recommendations did not "establish some radically new conception" of bachelor's education.[27]

A more vigorous statement for finding a middle ground came out of yet another group, "The Committee of Ten," which argued in 1946 that liberal education had been displaced by "an uncoordinated hybrid" that threatened "the extinction of liberal education." The Committee observed that:

> many have proposed abandoning the liberal courses entirely; some have insisted on over-specialization in one field and have thus neglected liberal studies. The result of such proposals would give greater emphasis to the specialist who, more often than not, tends to have little knowledge of problems beyond his field, or to have little interest in them. At any rate, such a specialist is apt to view the rest of the world chiefly in the light of his own specialty.[28]

Although concerned about overspecialization, this Committee also rejected the traditional liberal arts philosophy:

> Others who look critically at modern education move in an opposite direction. They seek to return to the strictest academic orthodoxy, to revert to the historical seven-fold principles of liberal education. Coming from the period of decline of the Roman Empire, these were not originally intended to suggest those ideas of freedom from ignorance and prejudice which is the usual implication of liberal education today. Instead they suggested the accomplishments which befitted a "free man"— free in the sense of being a member of the privileged aristocracy rather than of being a slave. And although this original conception has been greatly broadened, its influence can still be felt among those who seem to believe that liberal education is merely designed to impart certain intellectual graces for their own sake. Such a point of view seems to us as sterile as the modern formless and over-specialized education is unbalanced and misleading.[29]

The Committee of Ten thus recommended a required curriculum that consisted of English, methods of critical analysis, economics, government, science, art, mathematics, history, foreign language, English and American literature, and what the committee members referred to as a "Fourth Year Tie-Up Course" which, in the tradition of the old moral philosophy course of the eighteenth and early nineteenth centuries, would provide "an opportunity to seek answers to some of the broader questions raised during [the student's] four years of study." This course, in a modern twist, would also "afford the student the chance to exchange views and information with those concentrating in other fields." As to method, the committee suggested that greater attention needed to be paid to life outside the classroom; that although the underclass years were the most important, all four years of college should be given over to liberal learning, not specialization; and finally that instruction should as much as possible be done in small groups.[30]

These further recommendations came to naught. But that did not mean that the current curriculum, just revised in 1945, was considered acceptable. In his 1947 Annual Report, for example, Virginia's new President, Colgate Darden, noted that:

> Study of the curriculum best adapted to give a broad but sound training for the responsibilities of citizenship has continued without interruption for some years.... Within the framework of a program for liberal education a number of new courses have been added. It is interesting to note that the historical approach to mastery of a subject, so strongly urged by President Conant of Harvard, has been adopted in the Schools of Astronomy, Biology, History, and Psychology. The School of Philosophy has always used this approach.[31]

The upshot of all these considerations was the faculty's determination that a more capacious approach to the study of liberal education reform was necessary. Accordingly, "The Liberal Arts Committee" was formed in 1947 by a "weary" faculty.[32] Unlike the previous committees, mercifully the Liberal Arts Committee was relieved of the responsibility of suggesting specific curricular revisions. The Committee instead saw its charge as "the stimulation of interest in basic principles and fundamental policy" for the college curriculum. Along these lines, rather than issue a formal plan, the Committee decided to issue a bulletin "to keep before the Faculty one of the most important problems that faces the College today," that is, "the problem of liberal education."[33]

Over the next four years the Liberal Arts Committee provided periodic bulletins which related information the members felt would be useful to the broader faculty's consideration of liberal education. Examinations of liberal education reforms at numerous institutions were offered, including Dartmouth, Yale, Washington & Lee, Princeton, Wisconsin, Buffalo, Harvard, Amherst, and others. Summaries were then published and distributed since "it should be of value to consider what others are thinking and doing."[34] Additionally, student-faculty relations were reviewed. General observations were also offered as to the objectives and methods of liberal education. In the end, the Committee argued of liberal education at Virginia that "first we must decide which, if any, of the stated objectives of liberal education are to be ours. Then, we must decide how much we are willing to discommode ourselves to achieve these. Then, and only then, will we be in a position to start juggling semester-hours."[35] At this point, however, events associated with St. John's and the "liberal artists" again entered the Virginia story; consequently consideration now turns to events in Annapolis before continuing with the developments in Charlottesville.

Liberal Arts, Incorporated

As noted earlier, World War II had shifted the focus away from liberal education reforms for a few years as the necessities of more specialized training to support the Allied effort became paramount. The war's approaching conclusion prompted renewed consideration throughout academia of what best constituted a proper undergraduate education. Barr and Buchanan believed that their new program at St. John's College, which was based on the great books part of the Virginia Plan, was the answer—although they were increasingly convinced that Annapolis was an inauspicious location for the program. Throughout the war St. John's had been wrangling with the United States Navy which had tried, and almost succeeded, in claiming the St. John's campus for expansion of the Naval Academy. Because of the experience, Barr and Buchanan became convinced that the future of their great books program would never be safe in Annapolis, despite the fact that the end of the war in 1945 drastically diminished the legitimacy of the Navy's claim.[36]

Then in 1946 a pledge from philanthropist Paul Mellon's Old Dominion Foundation provided a chance to safeguard the program. In his autobiography, *Reflections in a Silver Spoon*, Mellon recorded that in 1940 he had read an article by Walter Lippmann praising St. John's. He drove from his family estate, "Oak Spring," in Upperville, Virginia, to Annapolis to meet with Barr and offer financial support for the program.[37] Mellon was so intrigued, however, that he decided to enroll, even though he was fourteen years older than the incoming freshmen. In a letter to a friend at that time Mellon stated:

> I have been interested in many general aspects of education ever since my own undergraduate days at Yale and at Cambridge. About a year ago I learned of the St. John's College program, and was immediately impressed by its soundness. I felt that it might be the answer as a much-needed departure from the usual higher educational forms and methods in this country. In the meantime, after several visits to the College in Annapolis and several interesting conversations with the men responsible for the new program in the College, plus a thorough study of the curriculum itself, I decided that I would like to see the experiment actually in operation, from day to day. I believe in it enough to want to become a part of it, rather than read about it or hear about it, second hand....[38]

Mellon's decision to enroll reflected the argument of the liberal artists that first-hand exposure was the best—why read what someone else has said when you can read the original—or, in this case, why hear about the program when you can take it yourself? Mellon stuck with the program, which gave him difficulty (especially mathematics), for about six months before registering for the draft and serving in World War II.

The war ended in the summer of 1945 and in 1946 Mellon wrote to Barr that:

Ever since last June I have been interested in setting up an initial endowment for the St. John's Program. I have been deterred from action by doubts as to whether St. John's College could keep its campus. I have felt that if it could not, it might be more in the interest of American education to find a stronger institutional vehicle to develop the educational program which you initiated at St. John's.

I am therefore placing at the disposal of the Old Dominion Foundation securities currently producing an income of $125,000 per annum, which may be used for the purpose of developing the type of education now carried on at St. John's College for other similar purposes. I am instructing the Trustees of the Foundation that they may rely on your personal judgment as to whether St. John's can be expected to preserve the campus or whether some other college you may designate will better carry out my intention and thereby become the beneficiary of these funds.[39]

Later Mellon agreed to contribute a total of $4.5 million to endow a great books program, either at St. John's or at another institution.[40] Mellon had been wary of the Navy's ultimate intentions. Barr recalled that upon suggesting to Mellon that he, Barr, "get a statement by the Navy that they don't want [St. John's]" Mellon replied: "Winkie, the next Congress could change it. There's no way you can get it with a stick."[41] Barr later recalled that "I was finding it difficult to get financial support, because everybody thought the ax was going to drop—no time to give money to a college when it may disappear." As a result, "I thought we ought to try and find some other place."[42]

Because of their reservations regarding Annapolis, Barr and Buchanan—through a corporation set up with Hutchins, Adler, Van Doren, and others called Liberal Arts, Incorporated—determined instead to use the Mellon money to establish a new liberal arts institution like St. John's at the former Hanna estate in Stockbridge, Massachusetts. As Hutchins wryly wrote to Alexander Meiklejohn in October 1946, "Winkie [Barr] and Scott [Buchanan] are coming here next week and we are going to found a new university. We will keep you informed."[43] The Hanna property, it was originally thought, had enough existing buildings and unoccupied land to accommodate the immediate and future needs of the new institution. The new college was to be nondenominational and have a maximum of about 300 students and a faculty of thirty.[44] By this time Barr, Buchanan, and probably Mellon, were convinced that the future of their program would never be safe in Annapolis, in spite of the fact that, in a letter written in June 1946, James V. Forrestal, Secretary of the Navy, had stated that a decision by the House Naval Affairs Committee made it possible "for the college to pursue its plans with assurance that it will be secure on its historic site for the foreseeable future."[45] Barr recalled "I thought it was stupid to think there will be [St. John's in] Annapolis [given] the Navy's preference. . . . Life is too short to be threatened for the rest of it, and we had all our hands full, and I think it would have made a great deal of sense to have moved up there [to Stockbridge]."[46]

Stockbridge also made sense to Barr because Buchanan had over the past year been loosening his ties to St. John's and Barr knew Buchanan would eventually leave the college. Winfree Smith argued that Buchanan's increasing withdrawal from St. John's was manifest by Buchanan's assumption of adult education duties in Washington D.C. in 1945 and his year-long leave of absence from the College effective June 1946. This change in Buchanan's attentions meant that Barr, who earnestly wanted Buchanan's help with their educational endeavors, knew that their work could not continue in Annapolis. Because of the battle with the Navy and Buchanan's increasing withdrawal from his deanship, Barr decided in his capacity as advisor to the Old Dominion Foundation to use the Mellon money to support the Stockbridge endeavor instead of St. John's.

Although Hutchins, Adler, and Van Doren all "helped sponsor the effort" to create Liberal Arts, Incorporated in November 1946, none of them would leave their respective positions to join Barr and Buchanan in Massachusetts.[47] Indeed, neither would McKeon or Meiklejohn, nor would any of the faculty or board members of St. John's. To all of these individuals the prospects for the Massachusetts endeavor looked bleak.[48] Only a few years earlier in 1937 St. John's had seemed doomed to failure—Hutchins had advised Barr and Buchanan not to take up the struggling college. But the St. John's risks looked mild compared to the Stockbridge proposal; that "college" did not even exist. It was highly unlikely that Hutchins, the President, McKeon, a Dean, and Adler, a full professor, would have been willing to resign from the University of Chicago, one of the most prestigious institutions in the country, to pursue such a risky venture; and in the end they did not. Buchanan wrote that everyone they had counted on had let them down. Further he and Barr believed that while nobody wanted to commit to the Stockbridge project each person they had tried to involve thought "it would be a fine thing for someone else to do."[49]

Adding to their Massachusetts woes, Barr and Buchanan, through Liberal Arts, Incorporated—and in what Buchanan later referred to as "a fit of personal generosity"—had agreed that St. John's would receive $150,000 for the period between January 1947 and July 1948 from the Mellon endowment, thereby reducing significantly the annual money available for Stockbridge, which was to open in September 1948.[50] They had also broadened their plans to have not only a new liberal arts college in Stockbridge but also a graduate school, "devoted to the search for the unity of knowledge and wisdom, which would continually discover and revise what all men should know," and an adult education program, "which would continue the liberal arts for the rest of the student's life."[51] In addition to staffing problems, the expanded plans made the funding question of critical importance. The Mellon gift would have thrown significant operating money to St. John's, but it became clear that it was entirely insufficient to establish a new college in Massachusetts. Also, Mellon had wanted to endow the program at St. John's or at a college like it, not create a new university, and thus in the end he was unwilling to support the Stockbridge venture. The lack of funds, and the unwillingness of friends, faculty, or board members to join Barr and Buchanan because the venture appeared too risky, combined with Mellon's ultimate refusal to support the effort, resulted in the demise of the Stockbridge endeavor in August 1947.

In spite of this outcome, Paul Mellon's interest in the St. John's Program proved essential to its long-term vitality. Rejecting the "dynastic" desire of his father, Andrew W. Mellon, that he have a career with the Mellon Bank, Paul Mellon instead became a life-long philanthropist who distributed personally and through foundations, over six hundred million dollars. From 1941 until 1969, when it became part of the Andrew W. Mellon Foundation, Paul Mellon's Old Dominion Foundation—named for the Commonwealth of Virginia—dispersed grants to the arts, education, conservation and preservation, psychiatry and religion, science, and a few general charities, such as the Red Cross. Old Dominion's grants, which totaled over eighty-six million dollars, were, as Mellon put it, "not intended to be full and continuing support for its recipients, but rather to encourage new ventures when they were most in need of assistance."[52]

Substantial assistance was provided to St. John's by the Old Dominion Foundation during the 1940s, 50s, and 60s to help underwrite the College's substantial deficit and allow it to build an endowment capable of offsetting the annual deficits. At the same time, perhaps because of the funding problems in Annapolis, Mellon and Old Dominion had "misgivings" about St. John's plans in the late 1950s to open a second campus in Santa Fe, New Mexico. Mellon's same reluctance to start a college from scratch had appeared in the Stockbridge venture. Nevertheless, Mellon was very generous toward St. John's. He and the Old Dominion Foundation eventually contributed in excess of twelve million dollars to St. John's in the form of campaign support, building funds, general support, pledged support, and endowment.[53] Yet Mellon was also cautious, as shown by his unwillingness to support the Stockbridge college or, as will be seen, to turn over the four and a half million dollars in endowment to Liberal Arts, Incorporated after Barr and Buchanan left St. John's in 1947.

Barr, Darden, and Mellon

Although the overly ambitious Stockbridge endeavor was crumbling in early 1947, Mellon was nevertheless deeply interested in supporting the creation of a St. John's type program at the University of Virginia. Mellon's estate was located in Virginia and he had a strong desire to support the Commonwealth, including its educational institutions, with his philanthropy. Coincidentally, Colgate Darden, the new president of the University, wanted badly to improve the quality of the education offered at Charlottesville. During the spring of 1947, the same time that the Stockbridge endeavor was foundering, Darden and Bob Gooch had made promising overtures to Barr and Mellon regarding the possibility of furnishing "the St. John's type of education" at the University of Virginia.[54] As an advisor to Mellon's Old Dominion Foundation and president of Liberal Arts, Incorporated, Barr once again cast his eyes toward Charlottesville.

How all of these developments came together, and their outcome, is a complicated and perhaps forever incomplete story, but much of what transpired can be ascertained by piecing together the extant evidence. As noted earlier, throughout the 1940s multiple committees at Virginia had considered the nature of the challenges that would confront the university in the years following the war. The committees at Virginia believed that liberal arts education was critical and yet lacking at Virginia; indeed, according to Ivey F. Lewis who was the Dean of the College and the chairman of the Committee on the Post-War College, the committee members "spent more time on this problem than on all the rest of the questions we discussed."[55] The extent of their efforts is revealed by the fact that these committees actively solicited information from numerous institutions, including Columbia, Chicago, Harvard, Yale, Princeton, and Swarthmore, on the general education reforms made at those institutions.

Many at the university were also keen on Barr's work at St. John's. In fact, when John Newcomb had announced that he would step down from Virginia's presidency in 1946, Stringfellow Barr had been one of the leading candidates for the position. Of the four men nominated for president by Harry Clemons, the University Librarian, two were Stringfellow Barr and Robert Gooch. Similarly, Robert Gooch's nomination letter stated that the next president of the University needed the following characteristics: "(1) genuine scholarly interests and attainments; (2) educational leadership; (3) institutional loyalty; (4) administrative capacity. I know of no one who possesses this combination in the same degree as President F. S. Barr, St. John's College...." In a letter to Dean Lewis, Allan Gwathmey of the Chemistry Department stated that Colgate Darden was his first choice: "He is a man of vision, and able administrator, the recognized leader in the state, and one who has an appreciation of the overall problems in Virginia." But Barr was Gwathmey's second choice:

> F. Stringfellow Barr is unquestionably one of the great and acknowledged leaders of education in America. It is unnecessary to dwell on his background and his personal charm. He has a passionate love for the University of Virginia, although the University has often failed to appreciate him. In my opinion, the criticism often offered that he is too radical and too fiery is absurd. He is more than a man with just a pet theory of undergraduate education. I feel that he would, and should, insist on the opportunity to experiment in education, but there would not be the

slightest chance of him disrupting the University in an undignified manner on behalf of some special theory of education. I am sure that Barr would accept the position only if a strong personal appeal were made to him to accept the leadership of education in Virginia, and if he were allowed the opportunity to experiment with academic units within the University. I should most certainly welcome such experiments.[56]

Robert Gooch, "a true scholar, gentleman, and athlete" and also "a profound student of modern education" was Gwathmey's third choice.[57] In the end former governor Colgate Darden, both despite and because of his connections with the state house in Richmond, was determined the favorite of the faculty and the choice of the Board of Visitors, but these letters show that Barr was definitely held in high esteem at the University in 1946. Some of this interest reflected the pressing need to improve the academic quality of the university.

The Virginia Option

One possible way to spur this improvement developed in April 1947. On the 25th of that month Buchanan and Barr met with Mellon and other officers of the Old Dominion Foundation in Washington D.C. to discuss the difficulties facing the Stockbridge endeavor. At that meeting Barr made it known that their old colleague from Virginia, Bob Gooch, wanted to use the upcoming change in administration in Charlottesville to bring the great books program to the University of Virginia, where it had first been conceived. Buchanan had strongly advised Barr to authorize Gooch to take up the matter with incoming president Colgate Darden. As Buchanan put it in a May letter to Meiklejohn, "Bob Gooch, a member of the Committee at the University which made the first formulation of the program, a very influential fellow there where no influence is at all strong, has talked to Darden and he is very much interested in getting Winkie to bring the program there."[58]

Barr noted that Mellon seized on this possibility "with great avidity" and within days Barr and Gooch met with Mellon at Upperville to discuss the Virginia option. Gooch claimed Darden was enthusiastic. Mellon was likewise enthusiastic about the possibility, so much so that all other options were postponed until the Virginia option could be explored. On May 7, 1947, Barr, Buchanan, Darden, and Gooch met in New York to discuss the possibilities. Barr found Darden to be "boyishly enthusiastic" about both the St. John's program and of it serving "as a possible means of awakening the University from its long lethargy."[59]

Several weeks later, Barr sent a politically astute, if perhaps somewhat disingenuous, letter to Darden in which he stated his interest "on my part in your warm invitation to Scott Buchanan and me to bring the St. John's Program to the University." Barr continued: "I was so interested in the subject of our conference when I last saw you that I think I failed to tell you how confidently I look forward to your administration of the affairs of the University—regardless of whether it should seem wise for us to join forces. So much that is good and that is important for Virginia and for the rest of the Country could happen at the University but has not yet happened."[60]

In spite of his letter to Darden, however, Barr came away from their meeting unconvinced that Virginia was the best option for several reasons. One was his continuing concern, as had been the case with president Newcomb in 1937, that enthusiasm in Charlottesville was as much about Barr and Buchanan as it was about the great books program. Barr confided to Alexander Meiklejohn that Darden and Gooch were "I fear equally enthusiastic about getting Scott and me 'home' again."[61] Barr was also unsure that Darden would provide the necessary leadership to allow the program to thrive at Virginia. Fresh from government and new to academia, Darden, as had been the case with Newcomb in 1936, might not do what was necessary to implement and safeguard the program. Barr did not want mere possibilities in Charlottesville—they had had those before—he wanted assurances. In Annapolis the threat had been an acquisitive Navy. In Charlottesville Barr believed that lack of presidential leadership might ultimately be a fatal problem. Barr was also probably unnerved by Mellon's interest in the University of Virginia because he—Barr—still wanted to work out the program in Stockbridge. Because of these concerns Barr determined that, "after careful reflection I considered Charlottesville too soft to recommend."[62]

Barr's Proposals to Mellon

Barr wrote to Mellon in May 1947 to relay his concerns about Virginia and to let him know that he would not recommend the university as the beneficiary of Mellon's gift. The timing of the letter is critical in understanding Barr's reasoning. In mid-May 1947 the Stockbridge project was still alive, although in serious trouble. In spite of the difficulties in attracting faculty and in securing sufficient funds for the endeavor, to Barr and Buchanan the Stockbridge option still seemed the most likely to be free of the type of difficulties that ostensibly drove them from Annapolis, and deterred them from returning to Charlottesville. Stockbridge would be entirely their own operation; Barr and Buchanan would call all the shots. They would control the purse strings on the $4.5 million gift from Mellon—$500,000 of which had already been used to buy the Stockbridge property. They would have no interference from external or internal constituencies. Unlike in Annapolis, there would be no Navy, and there would be no leadership problems or existing faculty with which to haggle, as Barr feared could be the case in Charlottesville. At Stockbridge the program of liberal arts education would be entirely of their own design. It was also ambitious with its tripartite organization of undergraduate college, graduate school, and adult education in the liberal arts.

The lack of sufficient funds, especially building funds, for Stockbridge was a real problem, but also a known one. By contrast the nature of the relationship between Barr and Darden and their respective organizations (Liberal Arts, Incorporated and the University of Virginia) was ambiguous. As Buchanan wrote to Meiklejohn at that time, "the amorphous nature of the University of Virginia is the puzzle we have to solve...."[63] What form would "the St. John's type of education" take at Virginia? Who would make those decisions? Who would control the money for the venture? Would it be supported by the university, or beleaguered, or even subsumed? Unknown but nevertheless possible problems at Charlottesville were certainly to be avoided if possible. Clearly Barr and Buchanan wanted the freedom and the responsibility, and perhaps the power and possible prestige, embodied in the Stockbridge proposal. Stockbridge was a grand plan, and it was theirs alone. Choosing to go join forces with Darden at the University of Virginia must have seemed like a distant second-best. Also, Barr loved his alma mater, but he knew Buchanan was unlikely to want to return to Charlottesville long-term. Thus in mid-May 1947, Barr was still trying to make their plans for Stockbridge come to fruition.

But Barr also knew that Stockbridge was in trouble, and doomed if Mellon withdrew his support for it. With all of these considerations in mind, a beleaguered Barr submitted three recommendations to Mellon, "(1) lying low a bit until the skies cleared in terms of personnel and perhaps of building costs, (2) going ahead immediately at Stockbridge providing [Mellon] could put up a building fund or (3) calling it all off." Barr also stated that if calling off the Stockbridge plans seemed the wisest course of action, and if the Old Dominion Foundation wanted to make the gift to Virginia in spite of Barr's reluctance, that "[Buchanan] and [Barr] were willing to go there at least for a bit and do what could be done."[64]

At this point Barr and Mellon found themselves with opposing views of how best to precede. Barr recorded that Mellon "did not understand my doubts about Charlottesville" and "made clear to me his doubts about Stockbridge." Mellon proposed another meeting for the two of them and Buchanan in Washington D.C. on June 9th. Mellon made it clear at their meeting that he would not put up any additional money for a building fund or anything else. Yet Mellon was willing to consider, as Barr put it, "releasing a portion of his gift to remodel and equip what we already possess at Stockbridge."[65]

In spite of Mellon's accommodation, the officers of the Old Dominion Foundation were not willing to put any further funds toward Stockbridge. As early as April the foundation officers had been unwilling to follow Barr's recommendations to do so. As Buchanan summarized the situation: "Even [Mellon] could not trump them with his donor's will."[66] Mellon consequently wrote to Barr that he believed that further action in Stockbridge was impossible and, as Barr saw it, "it was either Virginia or nothing." At yet another meeting in Washington D.C. on July 2nd, "[Mellon] opened the discussion by repeating this ultimatum, although in a very friendly fashion."[67]

With Mellon having determined that the Stockbridge project was finished, the board members of Liberal Arts, Incorporated capitulated and decided to develop proposals that would involve the University of Virginia and thus satisfy Mellon's and Old Dominion's desire for an institutional mooring, and yet also preserve as much autonomy and control for Liberal Arts, Incorporated as possible. After all, $4 million was a large amount of money and Barr, Buchanan, and the other board members of Liberal Arts were not eager to pass it on to others at Virginia or elsewhere who might not have the same understanding of, or commitment to, their type of liberal arts education. President Newcomb's inability to secure funding, it will be recalled, was ostensibly what had scuttled the plan to implement the underclassman great books scheme part of the Virginia Plan at Virginia in 1936. With the Mellon millions tantalizingly close to their hands, Barr and Buchanan were not about to jeopardize their plans. Stockbridge might have been dead, but since Mellon was so interested in Virginia, they endeavored to find a solution in Charlottesville.

Liberal Arts' Proposals for Virginia

On July 17, 1947, Adler, Barr, Buchanan, Hutchins, and Van Doren met in New York "and agreed that Barr and Hutchins should seek authorization of Paul Mellon to make alternative proposals to Colgate Darden. . . ." Darden's original proposal to Liberal Arts, Incorporated had been to have them fund a St. John's type of education at Virginia. As Barr had indicated earlier to Mellon, this plan was problematic because it was apparently conceived by Darden as more supplementary than revolutionary in nature. Darden wanted to add such a program to Virginia's offerings, not make over the college of the University of Virginia in St. John's image. Darden's initial proposal would have subsumed the liberal arts project; it would have been a means, and not an end, at Virginia. Moreover perhaps the greatest appeal of the Stockbridge project had been its autonomy. Barr and Buchanan, in their view at least, would have been free to do what they wanted in Massachusetts, and that included making their brand of liberal arts education the end—the goal—of their institution at Stockbridge. When the Liberal Arts board members met in New York that July day they sought to preserve that independence in any potential Charlottesville plans.

Out of their deliberations came two proposals. One was to establish "a completely autonomous college at the University [of Virginia] with [Mellon's $4 million] gift as endowment." The second proposal was to "give three fourths of the gift to the University of Virginia for the restricted purpose of teaching the St. John's Program there and giving the remaining fourth of the gift to Liberal Arts, Inc."[68] The first proposal was relatively straightforward compared to the second one. In the first, the college was not to be part of the University of Virginia, but rather related to it. The St. John's program would operate in University of Virginia buildings with the Liberal Arts, Incorporated directors as trustees. The second proposal to use $3 million for the new college and direct the remaining $1 million to Liberal Arts, Incorporated was more complicated. Three million would go to Darden "to work out the project in Charlottesville with [Barr]." The other million would go "*with no strings attached*, to Liberal Arts, Incorporated, to spend at their discretion in the Berkshires or elsewhere 'to promote the St. John's type of education.'" Barr noted in a letter to Meiklejohn that this option "would obviously include lending me support at the University of Virginia" and that "I would be willing to tackle Virginia if I knew I could count on Liberal Arts, Incorporated, to help me do the things the Charlottesville red tape may prevent my doing."[69] This letter shows Barr's continuing concern that his endeavors might be hampered at Virginia and he wanted to make sure that they would not be.

Armed with these two new proposals, Hutchins and Barr met with Mellon on July 21, 1947 in New York. Mellon was "interested by both but not very clear on the purposes of Liberal Arts, Incorporated, and hence not clear on the uses to which it would put a million dollars in the event that only three million went to Charlottesville." Because the purpose of Liberal Arts, Incorporated remained unclear, and consequently because the trustees of the Old Dominion Foundation, and Mellon, were unlikely to approve directing $1 million of the $4 million endowment to Liberal Arts, "Mellon stated that he thought it would help a great deal if [Barr] could provide [Mellon] with a statement of the purposes of Liberal Arts, Incorporated. . . ." Barr recorded that "I undertook to attempt such a statement." However, his attempt must not have been persuasive. Mellon immediately telephoned Donald Shepard, a lawyer and trustee of the Old Dominion Foundation, to discuss the two proposals and while "Shepard warmly approved $4,000,000 at Charlottesville [he] shivered at subtracting from the gift $1,000,000 for Liberal Arts, Incorporated."[70]

In retrospect, such reluctance was probably warranted as there is no definitive record of what Liberal Arts, Incorporated planned to do with the $1 million. Probably some would have been earmarked for Barr at Virginia. Yet in his letter of July 23, 1947 to the Non-Resident Board Members of Liberal Arts, Incorporated, Barr noted that, while Mellon was conferring with Shepard by phone, "I delivered to Mellon *pro forma* the written project for Stockbridge showing estimates by reputable builders for remodeling the Hanna place . . . at a total cost of $668,000, including $200,000 for equipment."[71] Apparently the members of Liberal Arts, Incorporated still hoped to save Stockbridge, even as they were developing proposals for Charlottesville. Regardless, it appears that what Barr, Buchanan, and the other members of Liberal Arts really wanted was to keep as much control over the money as possible. Control of the money determined who controlled the outcome of events, and because of their earlier experiences in Charlottesville and Annapolis, Barr and Buchanan certainly wanted to avoid situations in which money and events were beyond their control.

The other players in this tripartite power struggle, that is, Mellon and Old Dominion, and Darden and the University of Virginia, likewise knew that with the money went the power to determine the course of events. They were not any more willing than Barr, Buchanan, and Liberal Arts, Incorporated to give up that control until they were certain that their desired outcomes would be achieved. The members of Liberal Arts were unable to give them those assurances. As a result, the discussions between all parties remained difficult.

In the meantime, since he was interested in both of Liberal Arts' proposals for Charlottesville, Mellon did not want to wait for Old Dominon's unlikely approval of Liberal Arts' second proposal before moving ahead. While there would have to be further discussions with the Old Dominion Foundation regarding the second proposal, Mellon and the trustees of Old Dominion liked Liberal Arts' first proposal to direct all $4 million to the proposed new college at the University of Virginia. As Barr related to the Liberal Arts board members, "Mellon urged that Darden be offered the alternatives involving Charlottesville."[72]

Barr, Darden, and the Charlottesville Proposals

Within a week, Barr and Hutchins met with Darden and Gooch in Washington, D.C. to discuss the two proposals for Charlottesville. Reflecting the collaboration that had existed between them since the creation of the Virginia Plan Committee in 1934, Barr recorded that Gooch "has been chiefly instrumental throughout in urging the Virginia solution" to Liberal Arts' search for an institutional mooring for their liberal arts program. Barr and Hutchins laid out their two proposals. Regarding the first proposal for an "autonomous college at the University with [Mellon's $4 million] gift as endowment," Darden "stated that the University would welcome the new college and he would do all in his power to facilitate its coming." Barr recorded further that:

> [Darden] is prepared to purchase a 175 acre tract contiguous to the university property for $150,000 and lease it to the new college. Although it includes considerably fewer buildings than our Stockbridge property, [Darden] is confident it could immediately house 60 students and he is prepared to have the college use University [of Virginia] facilities, including the library, classrooms and laboratories, athletics, medical service, etc.[73]

Particularly appealing to Barr and Hutchins was that this solution, if it transpired, would eliminate the vexing "building problem," the lack of adequate classroom and dormitory space that, along with inadequate funds and an inability to recruit adequate staff, had hamstrung the Stockbridge proposal.

Darden was less happy with Liberal Arts' second proposal "of giving three-fourths of the gift to the University of Virginia for the restricted purpose of teaching the St. John's Program there and giving the remaining fourth of the gift to Liberal Arts, Inc." Darden believed that the second proposal was a "half-hearted and timid solution" that might well create an "ambiguous relation" between Liberal Arts, Incorporated, and the University of Virginia. Instead, Darden "suggested, as an alternative to placing a fourth of Mr. Mellon's gift in the hands of Liberal Arts, Incorporated, with a view to tempering the bureaucratic impediments of a large university, the possibility of indicating in the terms of the gift that one-fourth of the income was to be paid only on the warrant of the Director of the 'required curriculum' in the present Department of Arts and Sciences in the University."[74] This solution was Darden's compromise attempt to remove Liberal Arts, Incorporated, from the picture, but still afford Barr, who was most likely to be the "Director of the 'required curriculum,'" a fair amount of discretion over the Mellon funds. This comment also suggests that Liberal Arts, Incorporated now hoped to use the $1 million as insurance for their program, at least vis-a-vis the University of Virginia.

The meeting apparently produced cautious optimism in all parties, and Barr agreed to visit Charlottesville to inspect the contiguous property that Darden had offered for the new college. Before Barr's visit, Darden also mentioned a second piece of property "closer to the center of the University which would be available legally only if the new college surrendered autonomy." Such a solution was probably unpalatable to Barr, but the first property sounded like a compromise with which all interested parties might be able to live.

Barr's Visit to Charlottesville

Although the prospects for Charlottesville appeared promising, Barr was most disappointed with his visit on August 3, 1947. According to Barr, the University's position had changed enough to make the prospect of a new college in Charlottesville impossible for all practical purposes. He wrote:

> I have inspected the property contiguous to the University of Virginia. . . . Unhappily Mr. Darden revised his position on very important points and the property we inspected is wholly inadequate to our purpose. Mr. Darden is no longer able to purchase the 175 acre tract and lease it to a new college, nor would it house the 60 students he thought it would house, nor is it within a mile of the university library; it is almost three miles from the library; nor is he sticking by his offer of University facilities with the sole exception of the library.[75]

Why Darden changed his positions regarding the proposals is a matter of speculation. It is possible that he or others at the University decided that an autonomous yet "contiguous" college at Virginia was an idea potentially fraught with problems. Upon further reflection and perhaps conversations with other University officials who may have been more familiar with the likely reaction of the faculty or the Board of Visitors to the idea of a contiguous college at the University of Virginia, Darden probably determined that the proposals were untenable. Also, in spite of the Mellon endowment, the funding for the project may well have been considered a possible problem. The funds available had not been considered adequate for the Stockbridge venture. Some of the parties involved may have felt likewise about the new Charlottesville college, in spite of the proposed relationship with the University. The questions regarding the nature of the University's legal relationship with the new college could well have been an additional issue that defied easy agreement. Whatever the ultimate reason or reasons, it is clear that Darden decided to pull back from his earlier offers toward the proposed college.

Darden's reversal probably did not make a difference since, regardless of reciprocal arrangements, Barr believed that both pieces of property were completely inadequate.[76] Even if Darden had preserved the earlier proposed reciprocal benefits for the new college, it was clear that the Charlottesville properties did not do away with Liberal Arts' "building problem." Indeed, the second smaller piece of property did not have any buildings on it at all when Barr visited.[77]

It is also possible, the building problem notwithstanding, that Barr determined that the proposals would not work. Barr wrote:

> My net impression of the trip is that, although Mr. Darden would like to see something like the St. John's Program taught at Charlottesville, he does not know enough about the Program or even about the University (he has just switched from a political career to academic life) to make any solution immediately possible.[78]

Barr's concerns about Darden's appreciation of their liberal arts program and his willingness to fight for it, first expressed in May to Mellon, had not been assuaged.

Barr Ends the Liberal Arts' Virginia Initiatives

Because of his continuing concerns and what he felt was backpedaling by the University on issues that resulted in insurmountable obstacles, Barr ultimately determined that the multi-million dollar proposal for a new liberal arts college in Charlottesville should be abandoned. He and Darden apparently had subsequent discussions about the project before Barr finalized his decision, and it seems that Darden believed that something could be worked out. But in the end Barr could not support the venture, and, as Mellon's official advisor to the Old Dominion Foundation, it was ultimately Barr's decision to make. To Darden he wrote, "After the careful consideration you advised, I sent the letter"— referring presumably to a letter to Old Dominion which relayed his decision not to designate the University of Virginia as the institution to receive the Mellon endowment. Barr added, "I am as certain as one can be in such matters that I acted wisely. I am advised that, as a result, the gift reverts to the general funds of the Foundation."[79]

Concurrent with his decision to not designate the University of Virginia as the institution for the Mellon endowment, Barr decided that "I do not think that I as advisor to the Old Dominion Foundation am in any position to secure stable support from Old Dominion to Liberal Arts, Incorporated, or to any other body" because of "the fact that the Trustees of Old Dominion disagree with my judgment." In order to meet "our moral obligation to St. John's," Barr made a final recommendation that the Old Dominion Foundation make the promised gift of $150,000 to St. John's by July 1, 1948. Barr then resigned as advisor to the Old Dominion Foundation, "thereby terminating the whole four million dollars episode."[80]

With the advantage of hindsight it is quite incredible that all involved parties were so intransigent that no use was found for Mellon's munificent gift. While starting a new college was probably overly ambitious, there is no doubt that St. John's needed the endowment. Also, with World War II over, and with the assurances from Secretary Forrestal, it seems St. John's was relatively safe in its native location. The University of Virginia, too, was a reputable institution with demonstrated interest in the type of education Mellon was interested in supporting. To the extent that money was the impediment to implementing Buchanan's great books scheme in the Virginia Plan at Virginia in 1936, Mellon's gift would have been tremendously useful in Charlottesville.

In the end, rightly or wrongly, none of the actors in this debacle were willing to risk a compromise. Perhaps because of the large amount of money involved none of the relevant individuals were truly willing to surrender control over that money. The Old Dominion Foundation, which held the Mellon endowment, was ultimately unwilling to act upon Barr's recommendations to support a new college in Massachusetts, even though Mellon had appointed Barr as the official advisor to the Old Dominion Foundation in the spring of 1946. The cause of Liberal Arts Incorporated was severely hurt when none of the non-resident board members (Adler, Hutchins, Meiklejohn, and Van Doren) were willing to join the effort on a full-time basis. At Virginia Darden could not find a way to bring the program and the millions to Charlottesville, in spite of Mellon's expressed desire that he do so. Lastly, Barr and Buchanan had effectively taken an all or nothing stand—and they wound up with nothing. In the process they deprived both St. John's and Virginia of the possibility of much needed support, and they deprived themselves of having an opportunity to strengthen their version of liberal education. Although such an opportunity at St. John's or Virginia would perhaps not have been of the magnitude they hoped, for neither institution ever countenanced the expansive liberal arts undergraduate, graduate, and adult education programs envisioned for Stockbridge, it arguably would have been better for their philosophy of education than not to have had at least some implementation with Mellon's millions. In what became a high stakes game of control, all the players discussed compromise, but were ultimately unwilling to accommodate each other. As a result, everyone lost.

This is not to suggest that nothing was achieved but rather that not as much was achieved as might have been had the individuals involved been able to work out their differences. The outcome of the Mellon episode is similar to that of the Committee on the Liberal Arts at Chicago in the sense that all the actors were intransigent enough that, in spite of an apparently shared goal, they were unwilling or unable to effect a solution. Principles and pride may have been saved in these similar outcomes, but the overall cause of the liberal arts movement undoubtedly suffered from the inability of the participants to make these endeavors succeed. As will be seen, further developments in the liberal arts movement did evolve at Virginia in the 1950s. Also, much came out of the 1936 Chicago debacle. Indeed, the related establishment of the New Program at St. John's in 1937 would, in hindsight, become Barr and Buchanan's greatest institutional achievement. Nevertheless, years later, in reflecting on the decision to leave St. John's and the aborted attempt to establish a new liberal arts college (and reversing what he said in his 1947 letter to Darden), Barr stated, "I don't claim for a second I made a wise choice."[81]

Once the Old Dominion episode was over, one-year-old Liberal Arts, Incorporated was left in the lurch since all funds reverted to the Old Dominion Foundation. Without the Mellon endowment the self-described "educational and charitable corporation" was destitute. In August 1947 Barr issued a statement on behalf of Liberal Arts, Incorporated which stated, in part, that:

> The trustees of the Old Dominion Foundation have felt it was unwise to authorize invasion of principal, for fear that the remaining endowment would be insufficient to accomplish the purpose of the gift. They also felt that in the circumstances it would be wiser to place endowment with an existing institution capable of housing the educational project which Old Dominion was prepared to endow.
>
> On their side, the Directors of Liberal Arts, Incorporated, have encountered serious and time-consuming difficulties in assembling promptly a staff competent to handle the curriculum envisaged, because of numerous personal commitments springing from war and post-war conditions.[82]

Accordingly, and "after carefully weighing these obstacles," the Directors of Liberal Arts, Incorporated—Adler, Barr, Buchanan, Hutchins, Meiklejohn, and Van Doren—decided to liquidate their corporation.[83]

The University of Virginia
"If Satisfactory Arrangements Can Be Made"
In the same letter to Darden in which he stated that he would not designate the University of Virginia as the institution to receive the Mellon endowment,

Barr acknowledged that in doing so, he was consequently putting an end to Liberal Arts, Incorporated, and thus to his employment as well. Surprisingly, Barr then noted that "of the things I might do, your suggestion that I return to the University interests me the most." Apparently, Barr and Darden, who were friends and had been classmates at Virginia before World War I, had discussed the possibility of Barr returning to the University, even if the Mellon money did not come with him.

It was clear to Barr that the University of Virginia was now his best option. Of course, Barr did not say this. Instead he wrote to Darden, not insincerely, that the principal reason he wanted to return to Charlottesville was Darden's desire "to do something about undergraduate education and the chance that I might be useful to such an effort." Barr stated further, and somewhat incredibly considering what had just transpired between him and the University, that, "I would have no fear that we would fail to find sufficient funds as plans developed. In my experience, though lumps of money cannot be counted on to cause good planning, good educational planning does draw the necessary money."[84]

That Darden in particular was still interested in having Barr in Charlottesville after the Mellon debacle seems somewhat amazing; why is a matter of speculation. Darden was a gentleman and he may have felt some obligation to help Barr who, by his own decision, was now unemployed. Barr was also a respected, albeit controversial, nationally known educator who represented a cutting edge philosophy of liberal arts education. This philosophy was one with which Darden had some sympathy, especially to the degree that it might help him achieve his goal of improving the academic quality and standing of the University of Virginia. A more pragmatic possibility, alluded to in Barr's letter, is that Darden hoped Barr's presence at the University might mean Mellon money for Virginia in the future. After all, Darden knew that Barr and Mellon were friends and that Barr, as the president of Liberal Arts, Incorporated, had been charged by Mellon with the responsibility to determine where Mellon's money should go. Such potential might reappear in the future. In short, to Darden, Barr probably represented potential which would be maximized by his presence at the University.

Darden graciously replied to Barr that he "should like very much to see you return to the University if satisfactory arrangements can be made." Satisfactory arrangements would, it turned out, be difficult to achieve over the next three years. Initially Darden suggested that Barr return to the School of History, where he used to teach. Barr replied that History would be a good place for him, but that "if it were a few months earlier, I should urge the creation of a School in the College" since this would be the best way "to adapt to the needs of the University whatever of my experience at Annapolis may prove assimilable. . . ." What Barr was suggesting was essentially Buchanan's great books scheme in the Virginia Plan—a college in the college. However, Barr acknowledged that "it is presumably too late to do that before the session opens. The next best would be to make sure my teaching is the running of a seminar or seminars on the Great Books, not lecturing in a specialized subject matter."[85] Barr did not want to lecture on "history," rather, he wanted to conduct the sort of great books seminars first outlined in the Virginia Plan.

At the same time that he was discussing his possible return to Charlottesville with Darden, Barr was also trying to secure a grant to take a year off to write the second half of a history of modern Europe.[86] Barr enlisted help from Hutchins to whom he wrote:

> I like the looks of things at Virginia, not for a four-million-dollar splurge but for some quiet and possibly fruitful work. I am pretty confident something will come of it. Darden is heading in the right direction but badly needs guidance.... Please note that I am not depressed by the outcome of Stockbridge, that I am deeply interested by Charlottesville, but that I think I ought to have a year's writing first if it can be achieved.[87]

In a separate letter to Chicago magnate Marshall Field, Barr indicated his belief that the proposed work at Virginia would be valuable, and he was hopeful that the great books scheme in the Virginia Plan was a possibility: "If I go Charlottesville this fall, it will be only for the purpose of teaching—although I have some hope that in two or three years Colgate Darden and I can get a 'School' or even a 'College within the College' going."[88]

Ultimately Barr did get a grant to take the year off. Darden wished him well, probably aware that with a twelve-month grant, Barr would again be looking for employment in the not distant future. He would soon have another chance to get Barr to the University. Six months later, in January 1948, a round of discussions between Barr and Darden recommenced. Barr stated he still wished to return to the University: "In terms of personal, selfish desire, I would rather be teaching some seminars on the great books, at the university, than doing anything else I can think of, or being anywhere else I can think of. But personal desires are tricky foundations for mature men to build good plans on. I want above all to be useful, preferably to the cause of liberal education."[89]

Because he did not, and would not, want any administrative duties, Barr related to Darden that he was "therefore selfishly without regret that 'the new college' blew up—although I tried to bring it off." This was a problematic assertion considering that, in the end, Barr was ultimately the one who had ended the new college project at Virginia. Nevertheless, Barr stated that he still wanted to return to the university and eventually submit some educational plans for Darden's consideration. These plans, said Barr, would be "worth a 'fight'—if by then you haven't had all the academic fights you want!"[90] Darden replied that he wanted Barr to "return to your ancient anchorage" and that he fell in "wholeheartedly with [Barr's] thought of coming up in a year or two with some good plans...."[91]

Barr's Globalist Interests Further Delay His Return

It appeared that Barr would finally return to the University of Virginia for the 1948–1949 session. At the end of June 1948 Darden offered Barr a two year visiting professorship in the Schools of History, Economics, and Political Science.[92] Specifically Darden proposed that Barr teach a new course approved by the faculty senate but which lacked an instructor. Entitled "The Development of American Political Thought and Institutions," the course was designed to stress "the great ideas which have influenced American development." As Darden saw it, one of the university's needs would be met, and Barr would be able to inaugurate a course with a heavy emphasis on the great books.

Darden's proposal, however, was not appealing to Barr who wrote to Darden that the proposal seemed "a less good beginning than the beginning you and I planned here [in New York this spring]."[93] Moreover, not only was Barr not interested in teaching the course, he would not be coming to the University at all that fall. Instead he had signed on as the president of the Foundation for World Government in New York. Darden was naturally surprised by Barr's response. Darden wrote, "I felt that only the courses were to be determined by subsequent conferences and that you were all set to come to the University in September" but, concluded Darden, "no damage has been done."[94]

To understand Barr's decision and the later political reactions of others to him in the 1950s it is necessary to briefly explore his involvement with some of the "globalist" movements that appeared in the wake of World War II. At the same time he was writing to Darden about returning to Charlottesville he was also writing about the rise of the Cold War. To Darden he wrote, "I think much is at stake: the insiders I most respect are unanimous in their diagnosis that we are heading straight for World War Three and that what will be left, even of the victor, will be a chemical mixture of anarchy and communism."[95]

But Barr's concerns had led him to do more than write; indeed, Barr had become increasingly involved with the World Government movement. After the war, Barr and his colleagues engaged in several world government endeavors. In a sense, these undertakings were a high watermark for the "liberal artists" in terms of their aspirations and their presumptions. They had moved from trying to reform American colleges and universities to trying to establish new governance frameworks for the world. Although their motivations were varied and multiple, Barr's involvement stemmed both from his close association with the liberal artists assembled at Chicago in 1936 and from his belief that the United Nations was in danger of suffering the same fate as the League of Nations.

In 1946, as he was preparing to leave Annapolis, Barr, along with Adler, Buchanan, Hutchins, and others became members of the Committee to Frame a World Constitution. Shuttling between Chicago and New York, this group fancied itself similar to America's Founding Fathers as it crafted a new document for governing the affairs of humanity in the second half of the twentieth century. Careful minutes of the proceedings were kept out of a sense of being involved in an endeavor of historical proportions. When the first copy of the constitution came out, however, it was generally greeted with dismissal, and in some cases, hostility. The *Chicago Tribune* referred to the committee as "one of a rash of militant globalist organizations" which "would supplant the United Nations, abolish the United States and all other countries as nations, and govern, tax and regulate the world's people, with power to seize and manage private property. . . ."[96] Given the growing conservatism in America after the war, it is not surprising that the document and its committee were not well-received by the general public. The constitution, and the committee, quickly became an historical footnote.

Nevertheless, by 1948 Barr had become involved with the world federalist movement and within several months he had been "sucked in" to the degree that Barr related to Darden that he could not accept a position at the University of Virginia.[97] Having been "persuaded to drop U.Va." by other world federalists to work full time on the cause, Barr wrote that, "In 1948 I postponed returning to college teaching and started the Foundation for World Government, whose major concern became the economic development of the unindustrialized countries."[98] He remained president of the foundation, primarily a grant-making organization, until it was dissolved in the mid-1950s due to lack of funds, and presumably a lack of interest.[99] In spite of promising beginnings Barr's project failed to capture significant interest, drew hostility, and ultimately became marginal.

Virginia Makes Changes that Echo the Virginia Plan
During Barr's continuing absence, the University of Virginia moved ahead with plans to reform undergraduate education on Grounds. In his 1949 annual report President Darden wrote that a core curriculum at Virginia needed "serious consideration in the near future."[100] Then in 1950 Darden announced that, with the assistance of the Committee on College Policy (the successor to the Post-War College Committee), the College of Arts and Sciences would be divided into Lower and Upper Divisions, "corresponding roughly to the two-year periods of required courses and free electives."[101]

The Lower Division encompassed the underclass years while the Upper Division consisted of the upperclass years. While relatively little was changed for upperclassmen, significant changes were instituted for the underclassmen. Darden wrote that "the Lower Division has been founded on the principle that a student's academic work is his primary reason for being in a University, and that therefore his studies are the central factor of his life here."[102] Accordingly, new living and social arrangements were established in the form of a house system and a new student center, Newcomb Hall, was to be constructed. The new living arrangements were regarded as particularly important. Of the underclassman, Darden wrote that "his House will accommodate a group of 140 students; these are less his playmates than his fellows in a real academic sense. Lounges and playing fields are there, but so are House libraries and reading rooms, and so are House counselors."[103] These changes represented the collective consensus of the committees that studied undergraduate education at Virginia throughout the 1940s, yet at their core they reflected much of the 1935 Virginia Plan. The decision to split the academic work of the college into underclass and upperclass years, with special housing for underclassmen, even the special libraries, was largely the same pattern proposed for underclassmen in the Virginia Plan, except that, in its 1950 incarnation, all students, not just honors students, would participate.

The parallels with the Virginia Plan were not a coincidence. Throughout the later 1940s Darden, Barr, and Gooch had been in close contact concerning educational reforms at Virginia. It is inconceivable that the Virginia Plan proposals did not enter their discussions, particularly since the upperclassman honors program in the Virginia Plan, championed by Gooch, had been in place since 1937. Also, by 1950 Darden and other top administrators were well informed of the Virginia Plan and its educational prescriptions, if they had not been previously aware of them, because of a memorandum from Ivey F. Lewis, Dean of the College and Chairman of the Committee on College Policy.

In this memorandum Lewis, in words remarkably similar to those written by Barr, Buchanan, and Gooch in 1935, stated that "the type of elective system introduced by President Eliot of Harvard University"—as distinct apparently from the type introduced by Thomas Jefferson at the University of Virginia fifty years before Eliot—had created "profound dissatisfaction in this country with some features of the liberal arts college program." Lewis continued:

> Now, in my opinion, and in the opinion of many, but not all, of my colleagues, it is impossible, except by the grace of God and the resiliency of young American manhood, to give a young man the sort of education he needs to face life with the terrific urgencies that the present generation will have to meet, if we fail to give him the anchor of his tradition.[104]

That anchor could be provided, but it would mean implementing the full philosophy enunciated in the Virginia Plan. There was, argued Lewis, "hope of fundamental improvement along two lines, both of which use the same technique of acquainting the students in small tutorial classes with the great classics of our western civilization from the Greeks to the present time." Lewis suggested that the work of Aydelotte and Barr represented the most promising paths for education at Virginia:

> The first of these promising avenues of approach really stemmed out of Oxford University and has as its major spokesman Frank Aydelotte,

formerly President of Swarthmore College, now Director of the Institute of Higher Studies located in Princeton, New Jersey. The second is the experiment, so interesting and so promising, worked out and tried by one of our own alumni, Stringfellow Barr, at St. John's College. The Honors Work of Aydelotte and the Great Books Program of St. John's are so much alike in their basic philosophy and aims that either could be adapted to our situation at Virginia.

Lewis then summarized the history of the Virginia Plan at Virginia from 1934 to 1950:

> The actual approach here has been toward the Honors program. In 1934 Mr. Newcomb appointed a committee of Stringfellow Barr, Arthur F. Benton, Scott Buchanan, Robert K. Gooch and John J. Luck to study the situation at the University of Virginia and propose some plan by which at least some of the better students could be more truly educated for citizenship than by the prevailing methods. This committee offered two programs, one, (Plan A), to cover all four years[105] and the other, (Plan B), to institute Honors work as a substitute for the Major Subject in the last two years of a student's residence. Plan A appealed to Mr. Newcomb, but for lack of money was not pushed. To be successful, such a plan requires top flight teachers and a stern limitation of enrollment to a maximum of 20 students per section. Failure to reach this objective was followed by Messrs. Barr and Buchanan setting up the St. John's program in 1937.
>
> Plan B had better success. It was duly inaugurated in 1937 by voluntary efforts of some professors beyond the line of normal duty. I have talked with students who elected Honors work, and am convinced from their experience that such work, of tutorial and seminar character, has values lacking in the usual course work.
>
> The faculty, always a conservative body, agreed readily to delegate to the Honors Committee, (Mr. Gooch, Chairman), the authority necessary for the administration of Honors courses. I have heard no expression of criticism from professors, and believe the faculty would desire to develop further the type of instruction given in "Honors" or "Great Books" courses.
>
> ... The subject of this memorandum has received long and careful consideration at the University of Virginia since 1934. A plan worked out by a special committee was approved by the faculty and has been in successful operation since 1937. The University of Virginia is in my judgment fully prepared to make a great contribution to American college education in general, as well as to is own students, by showing that in a State University, with all its pressures of numbers, a genuine and

practical training in the liberal arts can be provided and successfully administered, and a type of training offered that will better fit our graduates for the stern test of life in their generation.[106]

This memorandum is most important for it demonstrates that in 1950 the administration was well aware of the Virginia Plan and still quite interested in seeing its overall philosophy, if not all of its particulars, enacted. It also gives a sense of how Darden's administration conceived of the history of the Virginia Plan at Virginia. The failure to enact Plan A—Buchanan's great books underclassman scheme which proposed an honors college within the regular College of Arts and Sciences—was attributed entirely to a lack of funds. No mention was made, for example, of the objection voiced in 1936 that such a plan might relegate the regular students and their faculty to second-class status. It could be that Lewis thought this unimportant, particularly since the Lower Division was for all students, and not divided into regular and elite sections. It is also possible that the memorandum gave Darden reason to try once again to bring Stringfellow Barr back to the University of Virginia.

Barr's Proposal to Return to Charlottesville

Although still working full-time as the president of the Foundation for World Government, Barr renewed his official correspondence with Gooch and Darden early in 1950. Darden replied that "I want to talk to you about our common project here" and that "I am anxious to see you return to the University." At the same time, Darden noted that to do so he, Darden, would "have to raise funds privately since the General Assembly cut substantially our requests for the coming biennium."[107] Although they met at the University Club in New York to discuss their plans, Barr soon wrote, "... now it is nearly May. Meanwhile, I gather an appointment might be fiscally awkward for you anyhow. Why not postpone for a year?"[108] Once again, Barr's return to Charlottesville was put off for another academic year.

Finally, in the autumn of 1950, Darden, perhaps having learned from the previous years that it would be best to start planning early, asked Barr once more to come to Charlottesville "to discuss our plans for next year."[109] Having taken the Southerner down from New York, Barr stayed at the Colonnade Club for two nights before Thanksgiving and met with President Darden and Dean Lewis.[110] Darden and Barr agreed that Barr would submit a memorandum to Darden outlining his proposal for the coming year.

What Barr submitted was essentially Appendix A—the underclassman great books scheme—of the 1935 Virginia Plan. In his memorandum to Darden, Barr stated that "undergraduate education is the weak spot in the University of Virginia." He maintained that the University had two moral responsibilities: "It not only owes its undergraduates more than it is giving them; it also owes its sister universities whatever guidance and leadership it has the courage and wisdom to supply." After discussing how leadership had to come from the administration—Barr's perennial concern about Darden—since most faculty members were the product of the very educational system which needed correction, Barr stated that enlightened faculty members would rally to reform, but "any sweeping reform is out of the question." He cautioned that gradual steps should be pursued. But he also hinted at his ultimate hope. "Instead of trying to catch up with Harvard," Barr wanted the University of Virginia to "seize the leadership of college education in America."[111]

Barr proposed three main steps which apparently he believed were not "sweeping." First, Darden should establish a committee of faculty members committed to reform. Second, the Board of Visitors should establish a School of General Studies within the Academic Department. This new School of General Studies would design courses, and not survey courses, that would ground a student in "the Western tradition, which created America and the modern world." Also, initially the School might "have to confine its instruction to only a small portion of the undergraduate student body." Also, in establishing this School of General Studies, Barr advised that the Board of Visitors should declare that "confronted with the same problem that elicited the Harvard Report on General Education in 1945, it was determined to create conditions under which the faculty might reasonably hope to solve that problem." Such a statement, argued Barr, "would provide a useful and needed warning to academic saboteurs."[112]

Third, once the School of General Studies was established, a Professor of General Studies (obviously Barr himself), should be appointed and should present courses for the School. Aware of the difficulties the person in this position might encounter, Barr requested that if selected for the position he wanted the title of Visiting Professor so that he "could resign in two years without embarrassment." In this position Barr would suggest starting with two reading courses, "on an elective basis, meeting once a week in the evening for two and a half hours of round-table discussion." The first course would be "The Western Tradition I." Readings would come from Greek, Roman, and Medieval works, "representing many 'fields' of human thought." The second course, "The Western Tradition II," would utilize readings from the Renaissance to the present.[113]

Looking forward, Barr suggested that Western Tradition I be a prerequisite for Western Tradition II, and that the first course be restricted to students in the Lower Division; that certain courses be required concurrently or as prerequisites; that students in the courses have common residence facilities; and that special lectures, open to the public, be arranged for the enrolled students.

The greatest obstacle to his proposals, as Barr saw it, would be the lack of qualified faculty to teach in courses such as these. Material means were a lesser concern: "Money can be found if something genuine happens." Finally, Barr concluded that the memorandum should remain confidential—"in enterprises like this one, tact would appear to be the oil without which all machines grow hot and jam—even faculties." In closing, Barr offered Darden "one last word, based on hard-won experience. If the undergraduate college is indeed the weak spot in the University's instruction, then the program outlined here deserves first priority on your own thought and attention. If it receives less than that, I predict failure."[114]

The similarities of Barr's 1950 proposal to those of the 1935 Virginia Plan are striking; indeed, it is obvious that Barr's memorandum to Darden is of a piece with Plan A of the Virginia Plan. Barr's contention that the mess in which higher education found itself would best be remedied with seminars on the great books of the Western tradition, a limited enrollment of underclassmen, prerequisite or concurrent courses, special lectures, and common facilities could all be found in Buchanan's underclassman scheme in the Virginia Plan.

Darden's Reaction and Decision

Much like Newcomb had reacted to the original Virginia Plan when it was presented in 1935, Darden likewise stated to Dean Lewis of Barr's memorandum that "I do not find myself in accord with his sweeping condemnation of college work, but I have no doubt of the value of the courses which he suggests, and I should like so much to have him give them."[115] Lewis replied:

> Yes, the condemnation is too sweeping, but that is the way of God's Angry Men. . . . However, there is much in what Winkie says. The increasing compartmentalization of knowledge, so essential for the training of specialists at the research and graduate level, has sifted down into the colleges and . . . has broken up the field into unrelated special disciplines. In this process any sort of unifying and guiding aim has been lost. In my opinion the only broad field in which unity can be found lies in what Winkie calls the Western Tradition. . . . A School of General Studies would be the obvious first step in what would probably develop into a bitter controversy in the faculty. The insecure, the timid, the lazy, the narrow, the small minded would line up with the men who glorify research and honestly believe the extension of knowledge to be the primary duty of a university. . . .

Lewis proffered that, regardless of the duties of a university, the proper function of a college was to teach young people to think and that Barr's proposal was a step in the right direction.

> In short I think Winkie is fundamentally right, but so free from the current climate of educational opinion that the installation of courses in the Western Tradition must be regarded as the opening skirmish in a long

and hard campaign. I would like to be in the thick of this fight because of my conviction that the proposal charts the direction in which we must ultimately move.[116]

Darden decided to move forward, and consequently Barr decided to move back to Charlottesville. What followed is the final chapter of the Virginia Plan at the University of Virginia.

CHAPTER 6

The Virginia Plan at Virginia

"The University probably needs transfiguration"
—Scott Buchanan

The University of Virginia

Barr Returns to Charlottesville

Stringfellow Barr returned to the University of Virginia in 1951. His old friend Scott Buchanan wrote, "I am glad you are back in Charlottesville since . . . the University probably needs transfiguration. . . ."[1] Barr had a two-year appointment as a Visiting Professor in the Political Science Department, of which Barr's other old friend, Robert Gooch, was the chairman. Barr's primary responsibility at the University was to teach a two-year course crafted out of a mix of Darden's 1948 and Barr's 1950 proposals. Titled Political Science 73–74, "Origin and Development of American Political Thought and Institutions," the course description was as follows: "Reading and seminar discussion of the great political classics of the Western tradition including *The United States Constitution, The Federalist Papers,* and selected works of Plato, Aristotle, Locke, Calhoun, de Tocqueville, and Bryce."[2] The course, in spite of its departmental mooring, was concerned with more than political science, indeed, it was largely an introductory great books seminar. As at St. John's, the first book read was Euclid's *Elements.*[3] The second year of the course, titled Political Science 75–76, The Western Political Tradition, offered "Reading and Seminar discussion of great political classics, including selected works of Plato, Plutarch, Cicero, Dante, and Montesquieu."[4]

Barr quickly regained the immense popularity he had enjoyed as a professor in the history department in the 1920s and 1930s. Barr was interesting and prominent, both academically and sartorially. In a community awash in sport coats from Brooks Brothers and J. Press, Barr liked to wear flamboyant suits in green or white.[5] He gave lectures on liberal education and made presentations to the larger university community, including the 1952 address to entering students on "The University and the Honor System."[6] Barr's great books seminars were so popular among the students that they were soon oversubscribed. The first class in 1951 consisted of fifteen to twenty students and met in a conference room on the top floor of Alderman Library from 7:30 until 9:30 in the evening. Staige Blackford, a student in the class, recalled that "he had never taken anything like it." The class was conducted seminar style, just like at St. John's. As a teacher Barr was "ebullient." He would throw out questions to provoke a response. Barr even brought in Buchanan to teach Plato. At the end of the year, the final exam was conducted Oxford style: there was no written test, only an oral exam with Barr. After the final, Barr held a cocktail party for the students.[7]

In 1952 Barr's class was held in New Cabell Hall. The fifteen or so students and Barr sat around a rectangular table with additional chairs around the walls. Again the final was a one-on-one oral examination. Referring to him as "rumpled, tweedy, and academic," one student in the class, Pete Anderson, noted that Barr was very engaging, that he "teased conversation out of people, thereby provoking discussion."[8] Another student in the class, Chauncey Olinger, noted that "we learned for the first time that with great or even very good books there were not so much 'right answers' to the questions raised but various interpretations of what the author meant. Suddenly, in that seminar, we had become adults intellectually."[9] Olinger suggests that Barr was "perhaps the most interesting character to bestride the University of Virginia in the twentieth century."[10]

The student reaction to Barr, however, was not universally positive. One student, John Marshall, thought Barr was a "pompous ass" who could be very condescending and did not treat everyone in his seminar equally, but instead had his favorites.[11] Certainly Barr was no shrinking violet. Olinger recorded that, "When a student made a response that strongly suggested that he had not read the assigned book, Barr courteously invited him to cite the page in the text to which he had reference."[12]

Barr was also "a controversial figure" outside of the classroom. Although his great books course "was highly esteemed," he "aroused passions" because of his liberal politics.[13] Barr feared that he would suffer political criticism from other faculty members and claimed that "there were two or three people who were sort of faithfully McCarthyite hounds." Particularly upsetting to Barr was that "others didn't tell them to sit down." People would say "they would rather not get mixed up in that, you know . . . this so disgusted me."[14] "I was having a good time teaching but I was horrified beyond belief that anybody that dared talk about me and Jefferson would think that they weren't McCarthyites."[15] As a result, Barr later recalled, "by the end of the first year I knew I didn't want to be there permanently because, as I put it to one of my oldest friends there, unfortunately, when I go to my seminar . . . I have to pass under . . . a marble slab and on it was a quotation from Thomas Jefferson, well, the gist of it was, it may cost you something to tell the truth but tell it anyway, but I can't remember the exact quotation. It's a swell remark."[16]

In addition to teaching great books seminars, the other understanding related to Barr's return to Charlottesville was that the University would consider implementing a great books curriculum for all underclassmen modeled on the St. John's program. Barr had understood that President Darden would appoint him chairman of a curriculum review committee charged with revising the undergraduate curriculum at Virginia.[17] However, upon arrival in Charlottesville, Barr discovered that he was not on a committee at all. Why is unclear. Perhaps, as had been the case with the aborted Mellon initiative, Darden had promised Barr more than he could deliver. Or perhaps Darden believed that Barr would have been a liability to any proposal associated with him. Whatever the reason, Barr's public role in reform at Virginia was limited.

In spite of the Liberal Arts, Incorporated debacle, Paul Mellon remained interested in Barr and the University of Virginia. In the Spring of 1952, Mellon gave the University of Virginia one of the first edition sets of the fifty-four volume *Great Books of the Western World*, which was edited by Robert Hutchins and Mortimer Adler and published by Encyclopedia Britannica.[18] Mellon probably also paid Barr's salary during the two years that he was teaching at Virginia.[19] Mellon's continuing support of the great books seminars at Virginia was certainly in keeping with his educational and philanthropic philosophies. This is demonstrated by the explanatory notes for a philanthropic organizational chart drawn up in 1957 and signed by Paul Mellon which indicated that the Old Dominion Foundation was interested in pursuing "grants in Virginia." The chart also listed "strengthen University of Virginia" as one of the Virginia projects and noted that an Advisory Board to the foundation for Virginia projects should include Colgate Darden.[20]

Barr's Departure and its Meaning

As noted above, Barr's popularity with the students did not always carry over to other university community members, especially some faculty. Barr was an acerbic critic. His educational arguments remained remarkably consistent as he continued to bash away at the lack of liberal education in academia. Following one lecture he gave several years later in College Park, Maryland, for example, Barr noted: "Spoke extemporaneously. Somewhat abusively, about contemporary historiography. Prepared for hisses. Loud applause. Probably each applaudant applied my remarks to his seating neighbors, not himself."[21]

Barr was outspoken about more than higher education, however. Always cantankerous and politically liberal, Barr made enemies among the conservative Virginia faculty. Being an outspoken critic of McCarthyism made Barr anomalous in the early fifties. As a result of his beliefs and past actions, some faculty on the conservative Grounds of the University of Virginia verbally attacked him as a dangerous radical. A particularly vitriolic antagonist was David McCord Wright, a member of the Economics department who attacked Barr "for his economic and political views."[22] This perception was certainly abetted by the fact that Barr brought the Foundation for World Government from New York City to Charlottesville when he accepted his faculty appointment in 1951 and that he continued to work as the part-time president of the Foundation during his time at the university. These conditions made for a very uncomfortable situation for Barr. He recounted that one colleague at Virginia had "been on the local radio and said practically all the faculty were pro-Communists or Socialists or something wicked."[23] Barr stated that "when this McCarthy stuff started I knew I didn't want to stay."[24] Because of the political feelings against him his contract was not renewed. In an October 1954 letter to a colleague at Williams College, Barr wrote:

> ... my two year appointment as Visiting Professor of Political Science (actually made so that I could, if possible, inoculate my alma mater with some Great Books Seminars) expired in June 1953; and, although the inoculation worked, faculty bickering led the president not to invite me to rejoin the faculty permanently. On the whole, I think that may have been just as well, both for the institution and for me.[25]

It is instructive to consider the reasons for Barr's departure from the University of Virginia for it was generally Barr's politics that were suspect, not his curricular philosophy. Barr had returned to Virginia as a Visiting Professor, ostensibly for two years. As those two years were drawing to a close, as Barr stated in a 1975 interview, "There was pressure on the president because I had a coterie of alumni—I had rather large classes in history—a coterie of alumni who swore by me and I think President Darden may have asked me to stay in order to pacify them. I don't think he wanted me to stay—and I rewarded him: I said I didn't want to stay."[26] There was also pressure on Darden from Barr's detractors. "The McCarthy stuff was getting rougher and rougher and the president, who was an ex-congressman, was delighted when I said I thought I'd had all I wanted, because he was under pressure from the nitwits he had—not numerous but bothersome—and I was supposed to be highly dangerous."[27]

Political discomfort may not have been the sole source of Barr's unhappiness in Charlottesville, however. Some of Barr's acquaintances have suggested that, in addition to the repressive political atmosphere, Barr was also disenchanted with the way the University was changing during that time. Years later Barr stated: "it seemed to me that [the University of Virginia] was taking over all the worst of American education, and then still giving itself airs, as if they all agreed with Jefferson."[28] Barr may well have been referring both to the politics and the administrative direction he found on Grounds. One of Barr's former students in the 1930s who became a life-long friend, Charles E. Moran, believed Barr was frustrated by the University in the 1950s. Barr had vision, but was also fiery and controversial and this created problems for him. Moran believed Barr suffered from a "lack of fulfillment" during his return to the University.[29]

Another acquaintance, Raymond Bice (who became the University Historian after Moran) claimed that Barr liked to think of the University as an Ivy League school. In the early 1950s, Virginia was still fairly small with a total enrollment of about 3000 students. However, like many institutions, the University was growing rapidly after the war and Barr, suggested Bice, may well have believed that Virginia was getting too large because large numbers of students were incompatible with the type of educational program that Barr believed should be pursued at Virginia.[30] A 1950s student in Barr's seminar, Pete Anderson, likewise believed that Barr did not find the changes at Virginia in the 1950s to his liking.[31] This contention is borne out by Barr's own comments. Referring to the university in the early 1970s, Barr remarked: "Now it seems to me, it's more of the same. . . . What is it, seven thousand students or some? It's a hell of a mess. And I don't see many ideas . . . I could name a dozen 'multiversities,' that it multi-ish resembles. No, I'm afraid I'd be very unhappy there now . . . if I were still teaching."[32]

It seems likely that Barr was highly ambivalent about the University of Virginia by the time he departed in the summer of 1953. The McCarthyite presence at Virginia was disturbing to him. Of the McCarthyites Barr stated: "the idea of a community in the university Thomas Jefferson had founded, talking the way they were talking, just made me ill. I wanted to get out." Yet Barr loved the University: "I was devoted to that place. The town is beautiful . . . and Jefferson had left his print. It had a quality I haven't seen on any other campus."[33]

This ambivalence is perhaps best reflected in his edited comments in a 1975 interview. Speaking of his departure from Charlottesville in 1953 Barr stated that "I would have left at the end of two years . . . unless they'd begged me to stay, and I wouldn't have stayed." However, when Barr edited the interview transcript he crossed out "and I wouldn't have stayed."[34] Thus Barr's final word on the subject was that he would have left at the end of the two years—perhaps.

Barr was not begged to stay. A 1957 letter to Mrs. Barr from a friend in Charlottesville reveals the feelings that the Barrs must have felt from this rebuke: "Another head has fallen into the bucket at the University! This time it was in the English Dept. MacAleer has bit the dust and all because MacAleer is one of the few people connected with this Univ. who can speak the English language. . . . Why oh why does this University always cut its own throat?"[35]

When it became known that Barr would not be staying at the University, one of the students in his Political Science 73–74 class, Chauncey Olinger, drafted a letter to be signed by willing students in Barr's classes. The letter read as follows:

> As you know, the Board of Visitors has not invited Mr. Barr to return next year to continue with the kind of instruction we have had for the last semester. Thus, as it now stands, the two courses will not be taught at the University next year. We believe that this kind of instruction should be available to the students of the University on both the first and second year class level, again next year.
>
> We have found in this course a rational and intelligent attempt to understand the world in which we live, through the dialectical investigation of government, ethics, mathematics, religion, and other aspects of human existence. The books we have read have been important landmarks in human thought, making it possible for the student to partici-

pate in the struggle of ideas, which has so greatly shaped men's lives. This dialectical discussion method has not been a boring and dogmatic recitation of notes, but rather a dynamic give-and-take, in which each man has been able to develop his rational faculties, to express his own ideas, and to learn new ideas.

Believing for these reasons, that this kind of course has far more to offer than the usual courses, it is requested that those students of Mr. Barr's classes, who are interested in the continuance of such courses, list their names, addresses, and phone numbers below. A meeting of those who sign will be arranged in the near future to determine how effective group support for the continuance of these courses may be developed.[36]

After obtaining the support of his fellow students, Olinger submitted a petition to the Department of Political Science, the Faculty Senate, and the administration of the University of Virginia. The petition, which was signed by thirty-eight students in the classes, read:

We request the Department of Political Science, the Faculty Senate, and the Administration of the University of Virginia to continue Political Science 73–74 and 75–76.

As students in these seminars we have found both the approach and content unusually rewarding. Through dialectical investigation we have attempted to understand the basic principles of government. Fundamental books on political problems have been analyzed in give-and-take discussion. We find the expression, criticism, and exchange of ideas an invaluable method of learning.

For these reasons, we think that it would be profitable to continue these courses.[37]

The petition was favorably received by several members of the faculty, including Robert Gooch, the chairman of the School of Political Science, who asked that the petition be addressed solely "to him alone to expedite handling and guidance of the petition in accomplishing its purpose." In a May 1953 letter to Olinger, Gooch wrote:

This is just a word to acknowledge the petition which you have handed me, requesting the continuance, if possible, of the courses Political Science 73–74 and Political Science 75–76.

May I say in my personal capacity that I am greatly heartened by this action on the part of you and your fellow students? That some of you should desire to continue an intellectual experience which you have found exceptionally rewarding is both reasonable and intelligent; that all of you desire to see this experience available for other students is as inspiring as it is unusual.

I should like to add that I was much impressed by your suggestion in conversation concerning my initial comment that compliance with your petition might involve insuperable budgetary problems. Your belief that certain members of the College Faculty might voluntarily participate in continuing the opportunities you recommend struck me as sound and promising. On the basis of many years of experience with the Degree with Honors, I am convinced that the most fruitful reward a student possesses of genuine intellectual curiosity can have here results from the willingness on the part of certain members of the College Faculty to render available to such students, time, assistance, and sympathy far beyond the demands of an already onerous schedule.

I am sure you and your fellow petitioners will be glad to learn that a committee, of which I am pleased to have been asked to be a member, has been set up on the invitation of the Lower Division of the College, with a view to establishing seminars similar to those you have found so valuable. I am of the opinion that such a scheme promises very real advantages over continuation of the seminars in the Department of Political Science. Mr. Jack Dalton is chairman of the committee. I am handing on to him your petition.[38]

This petition aided in the establishment of the Lower Division Seminars which grew out of some of the broader post-war curricular reforms discussed in the previous chapter. It is to this further development that this study now turns.

Continuing Curricular Proposals at Virginia

The time of Barr's tenure as a visiting professor—the autumn of 1951 through the spring of 1953—was a period of continued curricular proposals at the University of Virginia. Although reviews had been conducted since the war years, the nature of the proposals during Barr's time was much closer to that found in the 1935 Virginia Plan. While Barr kept a low profile during his return to Charlottesville, Barr's friends were deeply involved in curricular reform efforts during this time, and it seems highly probable that Barr's views were represented by Gooch and others. All involved may have decided that Barr could be more effective behind the scenes. The nature of the reforms proposed during Barr's two-year tenure certainly suggests that Barr had a hand in their conception.

One proposal came from the Committee on Degrees with Honors. From its creation by President Newcomb in 1934, Robert Gooch had served as the chairman of the Committee on Honors Courses which had authored the Virginia Plan. He remained chairman of this committee, which was reconstituted as the Committee on Degrees with Honors, after Plan B in the Virginia Plan—

the Honors Program for upperclassmen—was implemented by the faculty in 1937. Gooch remained closely involved with the attempts to implement the remaining part of the Virginia Plan—the great books program for underclassmen—during the next two decades. Gooch was likewise involved in the 1947 negotiations between the University, Paul Mellon, and Liberal Arts, Incorporated to establish a great books college affiliated with the University. He was also instrumental in the discussions between President Darden, Dean Lewis, and Stringfellow Barr that ultimately resulted in Barr's return to Charlottesville in 1951.

The great books part of the Virginia Plan for underclassmen had, of course, not been adopted at Virginia in 1936. Starting in the autumn of 1951 Barr's courses—Political Science 73–74 and 75–76—were the first to introduce general great books courses into the first and second year curriculum. However, Gooch and his committee decided that the Honors Program would be a good way to expand the role of the great books in the upperclass years—beyond what was already done by the existing Honors Program. It will be recalled that the Honors Program established in 1937 was departmentally based. Although Gooch's Committee on Degrees with Honors served an oversight function by approving departmental honors program proposals, the content of the programs was ultimately determined by the participating departments. The departmental programs often relied heavily on great books to comprise their honors readings, but they also chose those books that were closest to the relevant discipline. In early 1952, with Gooch still serving as chairman, the Committee on Degrees with Honors put forward a proposal which stated that, "During the course of around 20 years, and even after the establishment of the 'departmental' Honors Degree, the Committee have (sic) studied the question of General Honors." Now, the Committee was ready to present to the faculty of the College "a proposal for a program of General Honors work, to be available to qualified students in their third and fourth sessions [i.e., years]."[39]

This new program in General Honors was to be offered in addition to the "departmental" honors program. It was to be overseen by a General Honors Staff that would be "analogous to . . . the staff of a School—English, say, or Chemistry, or Political Science—that may offer an Honors Degree Program." The new General Honors Staff would act like a regular department or, adhering to Jefferson's terminology, "School." As had been the case since 1937: "The staff of the School has the responsibility of organizing and proposing a program that, if approved by the Honors Degree Committee, is carried out by the School concerned." Gooch's Committee now proposed that: "In a similar manner, it is assumed, the responsibility for organizing a General Honors program will rest with a General Honors Staff, and the program it proposes must have the approval of the Honors Degree Committee as the agent of the Academic Faculty." In other words, Gooch's committee—the Committee on Degrees with Honors—was proposing that a new school, directed by a General Honors

Staff, be established. This new school would subsequently propose a general honors program to be approved by Gooch's Committee on Degrees with Honors. Additionally, "The Committee will, of course, gladly make available to the General Honors Staff, if established, its accumulations of materials representing some 20 years of the Committee's history."[40]

This rather cozy arrangement was furthered by the Committee's statement that "an opportunity has arisen for the University to make application for a substantial grant from a Foundation for such development of our Honors work. The Committee also have (sic) reason to believe that this application for funds has a good chance for favorable action by the Directors of the Foundation."[41] The Foundation was never named, but it is likely, given its stated goals and association with Gooch and others, that it was Paul Mellon's Old Dominion Foundation.

The Committee members then presented a specimen plan for the B.A. with General Honors that they believed would "enable the exceptionally able student to escape from what President Aydelotte had called 'the academic lockstep.'"

> The plan proposes the reading, analysis, interpretation, and critical discussion of books universally regarded as of enduring value and of books, recent and current, regarded as exceptionally representative of the basic issues of the twentieth century. . . . Moreover, the plan envisages the study of the natural and social sciences, with special laboratory exercises in the natural sciences and experience in what might be called "laboratory work" in the social sciences.
>
> The plan places emphasis on discussion and the excitation of varying individual capacities, rather than upon lectures. It proposes small classes, ranging from ten to twenty students and using all pedagogic devices, whether those of the scientist or of Socratic discussion. The plan calls for its own special faculty, composed of scholars who manifest a nice balance between the arts and the sciences, between the values of living affairs and the abstract thought of the mathematician.[42]

More specifically, the program would employ tutorials, seminars, lectures, and natural science laboratories. Each student would have a language tutorial three hours a week to help the student understand "the language arts." Each student would have a mathematics and logic tutorial for three hours a week that would emphasize "classical and recent mathematical work." Additionally, for two hours a day two days a week, and with two instructors, students would engage in reading seminars. Similar to the seminar led by Hutchins and Adler at Chicago, and Barr's courses at Virginia, this seminar would focus on "the cultural tradition of Western Europe and its developments beyond the geographical limits that the expression suggests. Moreover, and in an amelioration of earlier proposals, because "this tradition cannot be objectively viewed without a basis of comparison . . . the General Honors staff would plan to introduce the student to some other culture outside our own tradition." For three hours a week each student would have a natural science and a social science tutorial and laboratory. Finally, there would be a one-hour required lecture each week "to be given by visitors and by members of the University faculty with a discussion period afterwards."[43]

Although Gooch's Committee on Degrees with Honors apparently believed that their plan provided the best of both of the schemes in the Virginia Plan since it utilized both seminars and tutorials, great books and honors work, others did not see it this way. Archibald Shepperson, a professor of English, replied that he disliked the elevation of logic proposed by the plan. Done for its own sake, such elevation would, he argued, place logic in "utopian seclusion, untrammeled by contact with the world of things as they are." Doing so would tend "toward the neo-medievalism which has had, in my view, such a deplorable effect upon the literature and thought of our time." The bulk of Shepperson's objections however, were not based on the course of study.[44]

Shepperson wrote that "the General Honors Staff would be far too important and potentially influential a group not to be required to operate under the Faculty's direct control." Also, establishing a General Honors School, "would foster, however inadvertently, jealousies and antagonisms inherent in the very nature of the situation." Both non-honors students and faculty, implicitly relegated to second-class status, would "chafe" under the proposed arrangement. Also, Shepperson understandably disliked the anonymity of the foundation interested in supporting the general honors initiative. Because of this, the foundation's "policies and reputation cannot be known." More important, Shepperson was concerned about the personnel who might be employed to support the proposed program:

> If, for example, men of the type of President Meiklejohn, formerly of Amherst, and Chancellor Hutchins, formerly of Chicago, should be appointed, with or without pressure from the foundation, I should be opposed to any plan, however good, that might be suggested. My reason is that such men, as far as I can judge, have succeeded far better in antagonizing those with whom they attempted to work than in effecting such educational reforms as they have undertaken, however meritorious these may or may not have been.[45]

Another English professor, Fredson Bowers, also argued against the General Honors plan. He too proposed that the plan was a bad idea on several accounts. First, the plan was unbalanced "in its emphasis upon Philosophy and its allied subject of Mathematics, together with Natural Sciences. I do not believe that the study of the Great Books . . . substitutes for a student's elective-course study in such cultural subjects as History, Music, Art, and Literature." Bowers also suggested that some professors, namely those whose fields were well-represented in the proposal, would naturally be more partial to the proposal. Likewise, the converse was also true. "I do think it is worth pointing out that the General course can naturally be viewed with more professional enthusiasm by some than by others." Bowers added that the proposal might well be coming at undergraduate education backwards:

> We are in a period in which standard academic routine is being re-examined, and the latest panacea is General Education, a concept with which I have some sympathy.... Nevertheless, I suspect that the soundest way of improving education is from the bottom up, as Harvard and Princeton are trying to do. The emphasis there is on giving all students as early as possible a very broad background and only gradually leading them in towards a deeper and more specific study of limited areas.... So far as I can see, the General Honors proposal approaches the problem from a completely opposite point of view, substituting General Study as the apex of the pyramid instead of its base.[46]

Bowers had, however, more than just curricular concerns that were wrapped up in professional ones. The foundation grant might be a problem for, although it might get the General Honors program started, he doubted that the foundation would endow it. As a result the program would eventually become an enormous financial liability for the University. He also objected to "the idea of a college within a college" because it would promote discord among the students and among the faculty. Also, "The General Honors course, with its segregation and its experimentalism, divorces itself from normal academic processes rather than builds upon the foundation of what we have."[47] Of course, this "divorce" was a primary reason why the Committee proposed the plan in the first place. He concluded by arguing "with all the force of my experience and convictions against the proposed plan for special classes and supervised work in General Honors administered to a segregated group of students by a segregated and autonomous staff, whose educational policies and theories are almost inevitably going to clash with those of the general faculty."[48]

The most significant response came from a group of professors who, like Gooch, were involved with the existing "departmental" honors program that had been established in 1937 by the Virginia Plan. In a letter addressed to Gooch, these seven professors stated the following:

> In terms of your committee's circular to members of the faculty, we would like to respond with one suggestion in regard to the plan for a General Honors Degree. It is that a General Honors program be introduced for suitable students in their first and second year of study, to be followed by two years of "Departmental Honors."
>
> Our grounds for this proposal are: (1) the character of the present program of required studies in the first two years, being primarily concerned with the average student, is not such as to produce the maximum

of intellectual development among the best students; (2) the primary aim of education at universities is to teach students to think and intellectual discipline and skill cannot be acquired without concentration in one field for a period of two years or more. Hence we think that whereas a suitable General Honors Program would be most helpful for able students in their first two years in the College, no "general" program should be introduced for the third and fourth years.[49]

This suggestion was essentially what the Virginia Plan had recommended "as an integral whole" in 1935: general honors work for the best students in the first two years followed by departmental honors work in the last two years. As will be seen, it also set the stage for the next curricular proposal.

Because the General Honors plan included modern works, social science, and study of non-western culture, in addition to the more traditional liberal arts material, it avoided many of the criticisms of the St. John's program. Yet, because of faculty resistance, the committee's proposal of General Honors in the liberal arts for select upperclassmen was not accepted. The Honors Program established by the Virginia Plan remained exclusively departmentally based as it had been since 1937.

Toward the Full Virginia Plan

Of those seven professors who, in remarkable agreement with the Virginia Plan, suggested to Gooch that general honors work ought to be conducted in the first two years of College, two would become particularly important in the future of honors work at Virginia in the post-Barr era. One was David Yalden-Thomson who became the chairman of the Committee on Degrees with Honors after Gooch stepped down from the position. The other was Marcus Mallett, a fellow professor of philosophy with Yalden-Thomson, and also the Associate Dean of the Lower Division.

It will be recalled from the previous chapter that President Darden split the College into Lower and Upper Divisions in 1950. This split, which divided the underclassmen from the upperclassmen, was intended to promote greater academic excellence among the Virginia undergraduates. In particular, the Lower Division was designed to do so via common living quarters (the new McCormick Road dormitories), resident faculty advisors, structured events and intramurals, and significant course prescriptions during the first two years.

The Lower Division Committee, appointed by Darden in May 1950, consisted of five men charged with developing the policies for the Lower Division.[50] As Mallet put it in 1951, "The [Lower Division] Committee interprets [its] purpose as the creation of a pattern of collegiate life in which intellectual interest and academic achievement are central, but which will also be conducive to an early general maturing of the younger student."[51] With these goals in mind, the Lower Division Committee instituted a series of meetings for first and second year students "designed to acquaint the student with the various fields of learning offered by the University" and to "provide an opportunity for students to hear some of the outstanding professors speak on topics of general interest to persons seeking an education." The first meeting, held on the evening of October 27, 1951, featured Stringfellow Barr, who spoke on "The Meaning of Liberal Education."[52]

Although the creation of the Lower Division represented some movement toward the goals expressed in Buchanan's scheme in the Virginia Plan—including greater faculty-student contact, regular lectures, and common living arrangements for underclassmen—they were also for all underclassmen. This aspect was in line with Barr and Buchanan's later belief that liberal education was for all students, not just honors students. While Barr and Buchanan may have always believed that was the case, the Virginia Plan was nevertheless directed at elite students. The Virginia Plan's specific call for liberal arts education for elite first and second year students that was grounded in the great books was renewed in the spring of 1953. Barr's friend Marcus Mallett, acting on the advice he and others had given Robert Gooch in their response to the General Honors plan, proposed "a special Lower Division program for well prepared and able students." It will be recalled that in his 1950 memorandum to Darden, Barr, reiterating Buchanan's great books scheme in the Virginia Plan, had proposed the establishment of a School of General Studies with two great books courses in "The Western Tradition" for select underclassmen. Barr did teach two great books courses in the Political Science Department during the 1951–52 and 1952–53 academic years, but his other proposals got no further. Mallett proposed to build on the foundations laid by Barr:

> The plan would be to request the Academic Faculty, through the Committee on Academic Legislation, to allow the Lower Division to experiment next year with a group of from fifteen to twenty carefully selected students. These students would be assigned to a specific section, which would not be open to other students, in each of their courses. The understanding would be that the instructors of these special sections would be allowed great freedom in the type and amount of material to be covered. The experimental group would take, in the first year, Mathematics 1–2, English 1–2, a foreign language, and Chemistry 1–2. In addition, they would take a new course, tentatively entitled "Lower Division Seminar I." The proposed Lower Division Seminar would be a discussion group, under the "dual leader" plan, and the material would be certain selected classics of western civilization. It is intended as a continuation of the sort of thing that professor Stringfellow Barr has been doing in Political Science 73–74, but more generalized.[53]

Mallett believed that this program, over time, would allow the University of Virginia to develop "an integrated Liberal Arts program for the experimental group."[54]

As for administrative structure, the Committee on the Lower Division "felt strongly that the Lower Division Seminar should not be under the jurisdiction of any one department in the College." This position was essentially the same as the one proposed in Buchanan's 1935 Virginia Plan underclassmen scheme which proposed a college within the college for elite students, and in Gooch's 1952 proposal for General Honors for elite upperclassmen. Because Gooch's 1952 proposal had foundered in part on the plan to establish a new General Honors Staff that was to be analogous to that of other existing departments, Mallett's proposal, backed by the Lower Division Committee, sought to avoid similar difficulties by keeping the proposed elite program within the bounds of the Committee's purview. Mallett wrote:

> Since this would be a radical departure from tradition, the Lower Division Committee decided to appoint a Committee on Lower Division Seminars under whose auspices the seminars would be offered. It was decided to ask Mr. Jack Dalton to be chairman of this committee, and to ask Mr. Gooch, Mr. Weedon, and Mr. Mallett to serve as the other members. The Committee's function would be to prepare a syllabus for the seminars, and submit it to the faculty via the Committee on Academic Legislation.[55]

In addition to avoiding the same administrative pitfall that had contributed to the rejection of Gooch's General Honors proposal, the Committee on the Lower Division had the additional advantage of strong student support for the idea of the seminars, as manifested by Chauncey Olinger's petition which was discussed earlier in this chapter :

> In view of the fact that the proposal for this special program was partially occasioned by a petition from students requesting that the Political Science Seminars be continued, the Committee would also propose to the Committee on the Lower Division Seminars that a "Lower Division Seminar II" be offered next year as a substitute for Political Science 75–76. Other than this, the Committee did not feel that it should, at this time, discuss the extension of the special program into a second year. However, it is definitely envisaged, if the Faculty will allow this experiment, that it will become a two-year program.[56]

Whether the Faculty would allow this experiment, and in essence adopt the underclassmen idea first proposed by Buchanan in the 1935 Virginia Plan, was determined at a faculty meeting on May 26, 1953. Those opposed to Barr, Gooch, and their like-minded colleagues had defeated Gooch's General Honors proposal a year earlier and now they likewise arrayed to defeat Mallett's proposal. It will be recalled that Barr's most vocal detractor had been David McCord Wright. It is thus not surprising that Wright made a vigorous attack on the Lower Division Special Program which proposed to continue Barr's courses. Although he could not be at the meeting, Wright submitted a letter to the faculty to present his views:

> On the agenda for this evening I see the announcement of two new courses, the "Lower Division Seminars" 1–2 & 3–4 entitled the Liberal Arts Tradition, designed to deal with concepts of history and tragedy, mathematics and the sciences, politics and society, and poetry and philosophy. Everybody here, I am sure, knows how deeply interested I have been in this sort of work and you will recall that Professors Hart, Moffatt, myself and several others formed an ad hoc committee about seven years ago [1947] to draw up general curricula of this type. From our work came the seminar in "American Political Thought and Institutions," which now appears to be defunct.[57]

Wright continued that he did not wish to seem opposed to the courses, because he was in favor of the subject matter—they would "implement" some of his "deepest interests"—yet he was unable to go along with the proposal and his reason related "to fundamental principles and not to persons or personalities." He believed that the proposed scheme could not guarantee that a "sufficient variety" of viewpoints would be provided. Without such safeguards, the course might become, as they "have become in many universities, mere superficial indoctrination centers."[58]

Another absent safeguard was any regular departmental oversight. As for the concepts taught, Wright wanted to know "whose concepts?" With history, would the course emphasize "Oswald Spengler, Henry or Brooks Adams, Karl Marx or Joe McCarthy?" In addition to this important consideration, the courses had been constructed by "an *ad hoc*, and apparently self-constituted, committee...." As a result, Wright stated:

> I feel that the present course should not be adopted unless a definite committee of a considerably wider range of opinion than the one indicated here be placed in charge of the seminars and the selection of the speakers. I say this not to narrow the range of speakers or to exclude any particular individual. I have never opposed individuals. I have opposed the principle of closed indoctrination. Let each point of view have a hearing but let none of them dominate. Is not this the liberal arts tradition?[59]

Wright then suggested that the seminars be placed, as had been done with the "American Thought" course, under the auspices of several departments, including his own. In the absence of this type of oversight, the university would suffer. Wright concluded:

If the cause of the liberal arts fails at this University, and I devoutly hope it will not fail, will it not be because of mistaken zeal? Because a few men, with an enthusiasm in itself wholly commendable, have unfortunately confused the study of, let us say arts in general, with their theory of art, of history with their theory of history, of government with their theory of government. . . . Nobody, gentlemen, that I know of wants to stop any of you from saying your say and presenting your views. But many of us do profoundly distrust establishing so broad a course as this without a guarantee that it shall not be dominated by any one view.[60]

Overall, Wright's letter makes clear that, like Archibald Shepperson in the General Honors debate, he was opposed to the people who had crafted the Lower Division proposal to the degree that he, as Shepperson had put it, would "be opposed to any plan, however good, that might be suggested."[61] Wright stated his objections related "to fundamental principles and not to persons or personalities," yet this statement was shown to be compromised when he concluded that in proposing the special program "a few men" had "confused" liberal arts education with their own theories.

Wright's other concerns about representation and administrative structure were certainly regarded as legitimate by some, but in the end his argument did not carry the day; the Lower Division Special Program was approved. There were four Lower Division Seminars offered during the mid-1950s; they were listed in the course catalog as follows:

Lower Division Seminar 1–2: The Liberal Arts Tradition, I. Messrs. Constantine, Dalton, Gooch, Gwathmey, Mallett and Weedon. Six semester-hours. *Open to first year men.* Reading and seminar discussion of selected classics of Western civilization. The first semester is concerned with concepts of history and tragedy; the second with mathematics and the natural sciences.

Lower Division Seminar 3–4: The Liberal Arts Tradition, II. Messrs. Constantine, Dalton, Gooch, Gwathmey, Mallett and Weedon. Six semester-hours. *Prerequisite: Lower Division Seminar 1–2.* Reading and seminar discussion of Western civilization. The first semester is concerned with ethics, politics, and society; the second with poetry and philosophy.[62]

It had taken eighteen years and some modifications, but starting in 1953 the complete Virginia Plan, first proposed in 1935, could now be taken by honors students at the University of Virginia. Gooch's "departmental" honors tutorial program for upperclassmen, outlined as the second scheme in the Virginia Plan, had been in operation since 1937. Buchanan's great books scheme for underclassmen, outlined as the first scheme in the Virginia Plan, had been modified somewhat, but essentially the gifted students in the Lower Division

Special Program would follow the ideas proposed by Buchanan: selective seminars, use of the great books, even common social occasions. The great books seminars for underclassmen and the honors program for upperclassmen, originally "recommended as an integral whole" in the Virginia Plan, finally existed together at the University of Virginia.

The Virginia Plan: Peak and Decline
The Special Program and the Lower Division Seminars

The Lower Division Special Program for the best incoming students was in operation for the start of the 1953–54 school year. The top five percent of the entering class was invited to participate in this elite program and fifteen students accepted the offer. They were enrolled in special advanced sections of mathematics, English, chemistry, and in the lower division liberal arts seminar. They also had to complete a foreign language course of their choice; this one course was not included in the special program. In the autumn of 1954 these same fifteen students took the second-year lower division liberal arts seminar together, although their other classes were not exclusive. As was envisioned in the Virginia Plan, these elite students were also brought together for social occasions, although no common living arrangements were ever implemented save that all first year students were housed in the new McCormick Road dormitories.[63]

While the Virginia Plan had presented the under- and upperclassmen schemes as an integral whole, in practice there was not an automatic link between the two programs. Some professors, including Gooch, thought that there was a strong connection. Others, such as Mallett and Yalden-Thomson, the directors of the under- and upperclassmen honors programs respectively, tended to be more partial to their own programs. As a result, there was no presumption that all of the students who took the special honors program as underclassmen would take the honors tutorial program as upperclassmen. Similarly, a student did not have to take the special program to be accepted into the tutorial program. Of the fifteen students who started in the special program in the fall of 1953 approximately one-third enrolled in various departmental honors programs for their last two years of college.[64]

One of these students was George Thomas. After completing the special program, he enrolled in the Honors Program in Philosophy. Thomas later became a professor of philosophy at Virginia, and eventually the chairman of the committee which oversaw the Honors Program at the University. Thomas argued that there was a connection between the two programs in the sense that the two were complimentary—just as the Virginia Plan had intended. Thomas stated that in the Lower Division Special Program the great books were presented, not as a sacred corpus of wisdom to be passed on, but rather as a methodological tool. According to Thomas the books taught one how to think, not what to think. One learned how to weigh arguments, how to critique them, and how to justify them. To Thomas the great books were the best texts for this education and as a result, they were highly useful for students who continued in the departmental honors program as upperclassmen.[65]

Full implementation of the Virginia Plan, however, was short lived. After two years the Lower Division Special Program was discontinued and the seminars, formerly titled the "Lower Division Seminars," were renamed the "Liberal Arts Seminars," the title they retained through the 1960s. Why the special program was discontinued is a matter of speculation. It had been proposed as an educational experiment. For the faculty, the existence of special elite sections of the required courses was undoubtedly a burden. Another likely reason is that the eligible students did not like having all selective classes. An early 1950s "Report on Meeting with First-Year Men of Top Academic Standing" noted that, "there was unanimous agreement against 'elite' sections for advanced students—all felt that a very important aspect of their experience here would be cut off if they were in any way segregated." What does not appear to be a reason for discontinuation of the special program was a dissatisfaction with the "liberal arts tradition" seminars. The top students expressed "unanimous and enthusiastic agreement that the great lack in the first-year program is the fact that there exists no opportunities for small seminar discussions which cut across departmental lines."[66] The special program had established elite sections, which the students had said they did not want; but the seminars did meet the students' stated desire for interdepartmental seminars, which the liberal arts seminars definitely were.

Although the Lower Division Special Program was dropped, the renamed Liberal Arts Seminars were still geared toward the best students. Most superior students took them anyway, even though they were not required. Indeed, Raymond Bice argued that if one wanted to be an honors student as an upperclassman, it was often presumed that one had taken the Lower Division/Liberal Arts Seminars as an underclassman.[67]

The mid-1950s marked the high point of the liberal arts movement at the University of Virginia. Although Buchanan's college within the college was never set up, the 1935 Virginia Plan had been largely enacted. First the honors tutorial program for elite upperclassmen—Part B of the Virginia Plan—had been adopted in 1937. Then the great books seminars and the special program for elite underclassmen—Part A of the Virginia Plan—had been implemented in 1953. Although the special program was abandoned after two years, the core of the special program, that is, the Lower Division seminars, were retained and expanded as the Liberal Arts Seminars.

The Liberal Arts Seminars

Robert Gooch taught in the Liberal Arts Seminars for more than ten years. His syllabi for his seminar included Buchanan's opening section from the Virginia Plan which quoted Aristotle on the ends and means of education, which listed the seven liberal arts, and which described the reasons for studying the great books. Buchanan's passage also described how the course had "been devised to bring whatever is known of the European tradition of liberal education to bear on the education of the best minds in the University of Virginia." Although the Lower Division Special Program had lapsed after only two years, the seminars were still regarded as being for the best students, so the Virginia Plan text written by Buchanan was still appropriate for Gooch's syllabi. Students also received Gooch's essay on "The Meaning of a Liberal Arts Education" in which Gooch stated that real learning required real work, but that real work did not guarantee understanding: "The hope of the serious entering student therefore involves an act of faith. If he deserves the name of student he is capable of this faith."[68]

The four liberal arts seminars, one for each of the four underclass semesters, met twice a week to discuss the weekly readings. Of the seminars, the College Catalog stated that: "Some of the principal writings in the liberal arts tradition of Western civilization are read and discussed by small groups. The purpose is to develop ability to analyze and relate the basic ideas implicit in these writings." The first two seminars, collectively titled "The Liberal Arts Tradition I," were open to first-year men. Seminar 1 was "concerned with concepts of history and tragedy;" Seminar 2 "with mathematics and the natural sciences." By the 1960–1961 academic year, some of the principal works read in these seminars were:

> Liberal Arts Seminar 1: Homer, *Illiad, Odyssey*; Herodotus, *The Histories*; Thucydides, *The Peloponnesian War*; Aeschylus, *Prometheus Bound*; Sophocles, *Antigone, Oedipus the King, Oedipus at Colonus*; Euripides, *The Bacchae, The Trojan Women*; Aristophanes, *The Clouds, Lysistrata*; Plato, *Apology, Crito, Meno, Phaedo*; Aristotle, *The Poetics*; Euclid, *The Elements, book 1*.
>
> Liberal Arts Seminar 2: Euclid, *The Elements, book 5*; Lucretius, *On The Nature of Things*; Galileo, *Two New Sciences*; Newton, *Principia, selections*; Lavoisier, *Elements of Chemistry, book 1*; LaPlace, *Essay on Probabilities*; Harvey, *Motion of the Heart and Blood*; Darwin, *Origin of the Species*; Poincaré, *Science and Hypothesis, Science and Method*; Dedekind, *Essays on Theory of Numbers*; Einstein, *Relativity, The Special and General Theory*; Hilbert & Cohn-Vossen, *Geometry and the Imagination*.[69]

The next two Seminars, 3 and 4, collectively titled "The Liberal Arts Tradition II," had Seminars 1 and 2 as prerequisites. Seminar 3 was "concerned with ethics and politics"; Seminar 4 with "literature and philosophy." Some of the principal works read in these seminars were:

> Liberal Arts Seminar 3: Plato, *The Republic*; Aristotle, *Nicomachean Ethics*; Cicero, *The Offices*; Aquinas, political writings (selections); Dante,

The Divine Comedy: Inferno; Rabelais, *Gargantua and Pantagruel;* Machiavelli, *The Prince;* Calvin, *Institutes of the Christian Religion (selections);* Montaigne: *Essays (selections);* Hobbes, *Leviathan (selections);* Locke, *Second Treatise on Civil Government;* Hume: *Of The Original Contract;* Rousseau, *The Social Contract;* Smith, *The Wealth of Nations (selections); The Declaration of Independence* and *The Constitution of the United States;* Marx, *Capital, The Communist Manifesto (selections).*

Liberal Arts Seminar 4: The Bible, *The Books of Job and Isaiah;* Plato, *Phaedrus, Symposium;* Virgil, *The Aeneid;* Augustine, *The Confessions;* Bonaventura, *The Mind's Road to God;* Aquinas, *Of The Teacher;* Dante, *The Divine Comedy: Purgatorio;* Descartes, *Discourse on Method;* Marlowe, *Tragical History of Dr. Faustus;* Goethe, *Faust, Part I;* Milton, *Paradise Lost;* Volatire, *Candide;* Hume: *Dialogues Concerning Natural Religion;* Kant, *Fundamental Principles of the Metaphysics of Morals;* Melville, *Billy Budd;* Tolstoy, *War and Peace;* Kierkegaard: *Fear and Trembling;* Eliot, *The Waste Land;* Stravinsky, *The Poetics of Music;* Auden, *Christmas Oratorio.*[70]

Students also had weekly writing assignments. One year, for example, the question on Lucretius was: "Does Lucretius' attitude toward death (pp. 133–138) have emotional as well as rational appeal? Discuss this aspect and compare with the Judaic-Christian attitude."[71] For Lavoisier: "Galileo and Newton are often referred to as the founders of modern science, Lavoisier as the founder of modern chemistry. How might Lavoisier have been influenced by Galileo and Newton? How might Galileo and Newton and therefore Lavoisier, have been influenced by Socrates?"[72] Finally, an Einstein question was: " 'God is deep but He is not malicious' is the translation of the motto Einstein placed over the mantle of a faculty meeting room at Princeton. Please discuss."[73]

The writing assignments for each week were also changed each year. The following, for example, were the writing assignments given in Liberal Arts Seminar 2 between 1954 and 1958 on Harvey:

1954: Poincaré in Chapter IX of his *Science and Hypothesis* affirms that "Experiment is the sole source of truth. It alone can teach us something new; it alone can give us certainty." Apply this affirmation to Harvey's *The Motion of the Heart and Blood.*
1955: With what degree of precision does Harvey appear to employ "demonstration," "argument," "proof"?
1956: Comment on the attitudes of Galileo and Harvey toward Aristotle.
1957: In Chapter XIV, Harvey sums up his idea of the circulation of the blood: "It has been shown by *reason* and *experiment* that blood by the beat of the ventricles . . ." What significance do you attach to clinical observation in this argument?

1958: A current biographer of Harvey, Chauvais, states that "Harvey's method was based on experiment only, . . . experiment with no *a priori* postulate accepted as certain or even probable." Discuss.[74]

The semester concluded with a written comprehensive examination. Finally, the liberal arts program maintained some of the social comraderie advocated in the Virginia Plan by hosting a dinner in the Rotunda at the end of the year for the faculty and students in the program.[75]

Its work accomplished, the Lower Division Committee was dissolved in 1955. A new Department of Liberal Arts was created to oversee the liberal arts seminars. This "department" was really more of an interdepartmental program than a traditional department. Marcus Mallett served as the chairman of the Liberal Arts Department and he was "a salubrious influence on his students."[76] By the 1959–1960 academic year, these seminars were so popular that sixteen faculty members were teaching in them.[77] The seminars were also expanded; Liberal Arts Seminars 5 and 6 were introduced for the 1960–1961 academic year. Titled "The Liberal Arts Tradition III," these seminars were "concerned with irrationality and infinity in literature, mathematics, philosophy, psychology, science and theology."[78] Finally, in a distinct departure from earlier practice, in the early 1960s the seminars were made available to all undergraduates, not just the better underclassmen. The belief that liberal education was important for all students, and not just the better ones, had finally become manifest in Virginia's Liberal Arts Seminars.

While this departmental independence was deemed desirable during the 1950s by its promoters, it ultimately proved detrimental to the great books program in the 1960s. As faculty time became increasingly expensive some departments refused to release their faculty for seminar teaching because they wanted the full earning power of their faculty to be devoted to their home department. Because each seminar needed two faculty members, this trend created a real faculty shortage for the seminars. Increasingly, faculty who wished to participate had to do so gratis.[79] Faculty availability might have been resolved, but there was another change of equal if not greater threat to the liberal arts seminars: a lack of student interest in the great books themselves.

The student protests of the later 1960s and early 1970s had prompted a series of actions and reactions in the curriculum. Calls for socially "relevant" education—"education capable of providing leverage against society's most immediate pressing needs"—resulted in the elimination of many curricular requirements. Additional room for practical and frankly political considerations usually came at the expense of liberal education, which was often pejoratively branded as "elitist." The Carnegie Council study of educational reforms made between 1967 and 1974 concluded that:

major curricular change [during those years] was seldom accompanied by extended faculty consideration of the larger aims of collegiate education or judgments about what knowledge was most worth having. All too frequently, rather, changes were framed by the exigencies of the moment and by immediate political expediency.[80]

The historical synthesis of Julie Reuben introduced in Chapter 1 suggests that such an outcome is not surprising given the lack of agreed-upon standards by which to judge competing claims. This lack of consensus arose, not just from differing philosophies of education, but also from the structure of universities. Put simply, schools were no longer cohesive communities of scholars, but instead groups of sets of scholars. Universities, in the words of Clark Kerr, had become "multiversities."[81] The lack of cohesion in the curriculum reflected the lack of cohesion in the university overall.

Like schools around the nation, Virginia underwent exceptional change in that turbulent era. The university's gentlemanly character, and many of the interests that had sustained it, receded. Although the liberal arts seminars remained in a transformed state as "university seminars," they lost entirely their great books focus, becoming, instead, seminars on vogue interests. For the 1969–1970 academic year the most popular seminars included: "races, ghettos, and revolutions," "radicalism in politics," "the study of the future processes of social, economic, and political change," "the nature and meaning of revolution," "psychiatry, morality, and the law," "law and civil disobedience," and "nonsense: its meaning and effect."[82] These changes left Mallett, still in charge of the seminars, a bitter man.[83] The great books seminars, first proposed in the 1935 Virginia Plan, and first offered by Stringfellow Barr in 1951, had, by 1970, disappeared from Grounds.

The Honors Program Revisited: 1960

The other part of the Virginia Plan—the honors tutorial program—fared better, but not without its own challenges. In 1960 David Yalden-Thomson, who had replaced Robert Gooch as the chairman of the Committee on Honors Courses, replied to a memorandum from mathematics professor and Dean of the College, William Duren. Duren wanted to eliminate the honors program. He believed that the program was elitist; that it was inefficient with its one to one student-faculty ratio; and that its pedagogical method was too often incompatible with the laboratory sciences.[84] Additional criticisms were that the program had too few participating students and departments—some faculty felt "shut out of the fraternity"—and that the admission standards to honors work were too low.[85]

In his reply, Yalden-Thomson proceeded methodically to answer these criticisms. Regarding cost, the sole pecuniary charge to the University was the cost of bringing external examiners to Charlottesville for a day to conduct the Final Oral Examination. Otherwise the University provided no added staff, added salary, or reduced teaching load to the departments and faculty who worked in the Honors Program. Yalden-Thomson noted one significant expense: "the energies and time of those who have been tutoring. To undertake tutorial work in addition to a regular teaching load is of course to reduce the time and effort which a scholar might be devoting to research instead."

As to the criticism, made by Duren, that the program was a "failure," Yalden-Thomson replied that small numbers did not in and of themselves indicate success or failure. It was noted that there were forty students in the program, spread across eight departments, at that time. More pointedly, given the lack of administrative support from the University, "it might appear remarkable . . . that any Honors work was being done at all."

The criticism that Honors work was better suited to some subjects than others had a more ambiguous answer. While some in the sciences had made this claim, Yalden-Thomson noted that individual or seminar honors work was being successfully conducted in laboratory sciences at Cambridge and Swarthmore. Thus, "wherever intrinsic excellence of education is the *desideratum*, there Honors work is appropriate."

As for the complaint that certain departments were excluded from participation in the Honors Program, Yalden-Thomson noted that the program was completely voluntary—students and departments could participate, or not, as they wished. Moreover, up to that point the Committee on Honors Programs had never rejected a department's program. The program, save a few key points like the total absence of class requirements, had been relatively loosely defined.

Finally, regarding the criticism that student admission standards were too low, Yalden-Thomson pointed to the low number of participants and to the fact that departmental faculty members determined which students would be admitted to the program. If students were not honors material, why would faculty members agree to tutor them on their own time?

Looking forward, Yalden-Thomson and the Committee on Honors Degrees argued against the temptation to "hybridize" the program by adding course requirements to the last two years of college for honors students. The committee had serious objections to this proposal, arguing, as Gooch had done in 1934–35, that the two systems were incompatible and attempting to combine honors work and course work for credit, as had happened at other institutions, would "corrupt and probably destroy" the honors work. Yalden-Thomson argued that although "work corresponding roughly to the Liberal Arts Seminars in this College" and in "Great Books" courses was often termed "honors work," the Honors Degree at the University of Virginia should be limited to upper-class work designed "to prepare a student for a set of final examinations at the end of two years of directed study." This final point was thought to be critical: "The end—the purpose—of honors work is preparation for a Final Honors examination. Tutoring is not more than a means to that end. This is also the explanation of the genesis of this method of teaching, namely, that it was thought to be the most effective means of preparing a student in the field in which he was to be examined."[86]

Yalden-Thomson closed by noting that Dean Duren had requested that the Honors Program adapt in ways to make it "more convenient" to account for students in the registration system. Yalden-Thomson replied that it was "parodical" to suggest that "an educational system of the University should be changed for the greater convenience of administrators." Instead he proposed that the Honors Program should be encouraged. After all, noted Yalden-Thomson, Dr. Aydelotte, former Director of the Institute for Advanced Studies, had "described [the program] as 'well conceived' and 'an outstanding example of the adaptation of the honors idea to the conditions of a state university.'"[87]

The Echols Scholars Program

Only a few months later, Dean Duren revived Marcus Mallett's ideas manifest in the Lower Division Special Program. Acknowledging that "a special honors-type program was needed to take effect when the student enters College," in May 1960 Duren announced that the University would be instituting the Echols Scholars Program, named for the late Professor William H. Echols.[88] The program was remarkably similar to Mallett's 1953 Lower Division Special Program. Using Aydelotte's language, it was stated that the Echols Scholars Program was designed to free the better student "from the standard 'lock step.'" Although Echols Scholars were eventually relieved of course prescriptions, in 1960 all first-year students had several requirements: "At the present time the five first-year courses consist of: English 1–2, Mathematics 1–2, Language, Science, Elective (usually Liberal Arts Seminar 1–2 for students with high ability)." To open up one more elective for the Echols Scholar so that he might "anticipate his specialization" or "invest it in his general education," the faculty was asked, and they agreed, to drop the English 1 and Math 1 requirements. This permitted Echols Scholars to take: "Math 2 and English 2, Language, Science, Elective, Elective (Liberal Arts Seminar will be strongly advised.)" In line with Mallett's special program of seven years earlier, departments were asked to support the Echols experiment "by providing special sections or such adaptations of their normal offerings as they judge appropriate."[89]

The curricular similarities to the special program were mirrored by other similarities. The first group of Echols Scholars was elite, numbering just thirty-five. The new program also achieved the goal of common living arrangements for elite students first expressed by Buchanan in 1935. The students lived together in Echols House, one of the new residential facilities.[90] In summary, the current day Echols Program, with its complete electivism, does not resemble the structure outlined by Buchanan. However, most of the ideas embodied in the original Echols Program were rooted in the underclassmen scheme of the Virginia Plan, even though it was an indirect, not a direct, result of the Plan.

The Honors Program Revisited: 1968

By 1968 the Honors Program at Virginia was again under pressure. Francis Hart, chairman of the Committee on Special Programs (CSP), which had replaced the Committee on Honors Degrees, wrote another defense. Drawing on the work of fellow committee members and on "the testimony of such authorities as Messrs. Gooch, Yalden-Thomson, and Mallett," Hart proposed to respond to new conditions. They were: "(1) the expansion of the program during the past few years; (2) the evidence of growing interest among non-participating departments; (3) the desire of some participating departments to carry on their own programs regardless of CSP policies and guidelines."[91]

The program had grown. Whereas there were thirty-two students enrolled in the Honors Program in 1960–61, there were eighty-seven enrolled in 1967–68. In spite of rising numbers, the CSP stated that the Honors program "must in fact and not just in pretense be a single, flexibly uniform one, supervised effectually by the College faculty through its elected CSP." In order for a uniform system to exist, the CSP believed that the Honors Program had to be more flexible. The most significant change, one to which Gooch and Yalden-Thomson had always been fundamentally opposed, was the decision to permit up to one half of an honors student's time to be devoted to required course work, providing all of this work would be tested in the Final Honors Examinations. Of course, departments could still allow less or no course work. A second change was that, while external examiners were to continue to be used for the Finals, departments, because they had worked with honors students, could inform the examiners of the student's preparation.[92] A third change was to list honors work and rough hour equivalents, although no grades, on the honors students' transcripts. Finally, with shades of Gooch's unsuccessful 1952 proposal for a General Honors Program, the CSP noted "the regrettable failure so far to create interdepartmental honors programs." The CSP concluded that "if the College Honors Program is ever to approach its full potential, it must include provision for interdisciplinary and college-wide Honors activities."[93]

Although the CSP suggested that "Honors work, where departmental conditions and CSP policies permit, seems likely to expand considerably," exactly the opposite happened over the next dozen years. Between 1968 and 1981, the number of participating departments slipped from eleven to three, and from eighty-seven students to fifteen.[94] The decline came about largely for perennial reasons. Some professors did not believe in the honors approach, arguing, as

Buchanan had in the 1930s, that undergraduates were not ready to be studying a subject at such an intensive level and that such work belonged instead at the graduate level. Classics professor emeritus Arthur Stocker noted that this was the objection that kept the Classics Department from ever offering an honors program.[95] In its 1968 report, the CSP had acknowledged that: "The Honors candidate does develop critical independence at the expense of breadth; his relative inexposure to predigested knowledge or interpretation may cause temporary difficulty or cause him to 'test' poorly" on the GRE.[96]

There were other administrative reasons for the decline of the Honors Program. Faculty who taught in the Honors Program invested a great deal of time, yet received no course credit from the University. Moreover, it was the sole method by which a student could earn a degree with honors at the University.[97] Departments, especially those that did not believe that the Honors Program worked well in their discipline, nevertheless wanted a way to recognize their best students. When the University adopted the option of awarding degrees with distinction, most departments dropped the Honors Program and its more demanding obligations.[98] The new Distinguished Majors Program featured both college and departmental requirements. Distinguished majors students had to have a minimum 3.4 G.P.A., they had to write a senior thesis, and they had to take advanced courses. The individual departments determined their own requirements for a student to graduate with highest distinction, high distinction, distinction, or pass.[99] Thus, while there were pedagogical objections to the honors program, such as the belief that it was too intensive too early in a student's academic career, and that it was not applicable to certain disciplines, the majority of the objections were often based on personal and institutional factors: too time-intensive, no credit, no pay, exclusive, and so on.

According to Glenn Kessler, philosophy professor and Chairman of the College Honors Program in the early 1980s, the program had suffered largely because of the college faculty: "It's a vicious circle. The departments aren't interested in joining or in promoting the program because there's no student interest. And there's no student interest because they're not made aware of it."[100] The Economics Department dropped the Honors Program in the early 1980s because, according to Economics Honors Program chairman John Pettengill, "There's no one on the faculty interested in taking over the program."[101] This left just Government and Philosophy, the two departments that had always had the strongest honors programs and which had been a part of the program since its start in the 1937–1938 academic year. Both programs held celebrations on Grounds for their Fiftieth Anniversaries in 1988, and these two remaining departments, with strong student and alumni approval, have maintained vital Honors Programs to the current day.[102] At the beginning of the twenty-first century they are all that officially remain of the Virginia Plan at the University of Virginia.

Conclusion
An Unfinished Story

"*The consequences have been a radical reform of teaching and learning in a small province of the modern academy.*"
—Scott Buchanan

The Virginia Plan, the Liberal Arts Movement, and Their Influence

Looking back in 1967, Stringfellow Barr stated that "the awful thing is that liberal education has been so punk in my lifetime."[1] Perhaps. His hope that higher education would turn away from the elective system and embrace his and others' prescriptive great books model has had marginal effect by some measures. The elective system unquestionably remains the dominant curricular mode in American higher education. Required courses and distribution requirements temper electivism, but those institutions, such as St. John's, that strongly limit electivism are noteworthy because of their rarity. The "great books," too, are a minority curricular presence. Indeed, since the late 1960s, the very concept of a Western canon has been under assault.

Yet by other measures the Virginia Plan and the liberal arts movement have been remarkably influential. The Virginia Plan, which effected a groundbreaking expansion of the great books corpus by adding scientific and mathematical classics to the literary and historical canon, helped make the reading of primary sources both acceptable and desirable. In *The Opening of the American Mind* Lawrence Levine notes the remarkable fact that when Charles Eliot became the president of Harvard in 1869 the College had one history professor, Henry Torrey, who "was responsible for ancient, medieval, and modern history and American constitutional history, all of which he taught out of textbooks."[2] The nineteenth-century notion that the classics should be the preserve of the scholar, and that the textbook should be the primary pedagogical instrument for teaching students, was discredited by the liberal arts movement.

The results of this change were profound. Historians John Brubacher and Willis Rudy note that the effort to have students "rely on books rather than lectures . . . encouraged them to go to the library with syllabus or bibliography in hand to examine numerous sources, many of them original." Brubacher and Rudy also note that "colleges unwilling to adopt the 'Great Books' program of St. John's nevertheless welcomed a wider reading of classic authors within the frame of reference of their own campuses." A related result of the liberal arts movement, taken for granted in the second half of the twentieth century but unheard of in the nineteenth, was the enhanced importance of the college library with its move "to establish open bookshelves, increase the space allocated to reserve books, and multiply the number of duplicates."[3]

The liberal arts movement also contributed to the effort to make sure that the Germanic lecture model was supplemented with the English tutorial and seminar models. Similarly, honors instruction, which began in the 1920s at Swarthmore and advanced at Virginia, grew during the period of the liberal arts movement, especially after World War II when "large-scale promotion of honors programs occurred." In particular, "momentum came from the formation of the Inter-University Council on the Superior Student and the newsletter it published as a clearinghouse on honors programs in hundreds of colleges over the country."[4]

Ironically, the "culture wars" of the later twentieth century have demonstrated the tenacity of both the honors and the great books approaches to higher education. Twenty years after Barr's remark about liberal education Chicago professor Allan Bloom, arguing that the best way to remedy academia's aridity and political correctness was through "the good old Great Books approach," would re-invigorate a national discussion regarding the best means of liberally educating America's students.[5] The particulars change with time, but the central issues of what to teach—and why—remain as pertinent today as when the Virginia Plan was drafted in 1935. The argument of the Virginia Plan for a curriculum centered on the great books and honors work has remained a vital and contentious part of the larger debates concerning college curricula for more than sixty years, having neither remade academia in its image, nor faded as a footnote in the history of American higher education. Instead the ideas in the Virginia Plan have endured.

Correcting the Historiography

This study has endeavored to correct the incomplete place accorded the University of Virginia and its 1935 Virginia Plan in the liberal arts movement. Clearly the University of Virginia, as noted at the time by Walter Lippmann and Frank Aydelotte, was central to the liberal arts movement. This study has also corrected the often inaccurate portrayal of the Virginia Plan.

As seen throughout the book, many historical accounts neglect entirely Virginia's role in the movement. Brubacher and Rudy's statement that the great books program was, "spawned at Columbia, encouraged at Chicago, and actually put into operation at St. John's College in Maryland" for example, was noted in the Introduction.[6] Likewise, historian Bruce Kimball, discussing the rise of honors programs, notes that "Wells, Franklin and Marshall, Colgate, Reed, Southwestern at Memphis—followed the example of Swarthmore in instituting honors courses, tutorials, seminars, and comprehensive or general examinations."[7] Virginia's honors program is completely ignored by Kimball, even though the progenitor of the honors program, Swarthmore president Frank Aydelotte, argued in 1944 that Virginia had "taken [a] position of leadership in the movement."[8]

Even accounts which do recognize Virginia's role, such as the one by J. Winfree Smith described in Chapter 3, do so only in a propaedeutic way. Indeed, even the most conscientious histories, such as the one by Amy Kass, have failed to appreciate the work and results at Virginia that followed the Liberal Arts, Incorporated debacle of 1947. Her assertion that "the last effort to institutionalize the ideas underlying the [Liberal Arts] Movement was made in the late 1940s" has been shown to be incorrect.[9] As shown in Chapter 6, the curricular experiments and courses implemented at Virginia in the 1950s were a significant part of the movement, albeit not enduring ones.

Also, Kass and others who have treated the great books part of the liberal arts movement have largely ignored the place of honors tutorial work in the philosophy of the movement. Part of the significance of the Virginia Plan was that it combined both great books seminar work and honors tutorial work. The other formative institutions in the liberal arts movement, namely, Columbia, Chicago, and St. John's did not seek to the same degree to merge these two types of instruction. They all had great books seminars and elements of the Oxbridge system, but not one-on-one honors work with capstone Final Examinations. The material studied, the skills developed, and the discipline acquired in the honors program, liberal by their very nature, all suggest that a more capacious definition of the liberal arts movement is required. The liberal arts movement was more than the great books movement; it also included the Oxbridge pedagogy of tutorials and final honors examinations.

Broadening the Argument

This study has shown that the responses to and results of the liberal arts movement were varied and more complex than as presented in the conventional historiography. When educational historian Frederick Rudolph stated that "a return to ancient Greece and Rome was not an idea that recommended itself to most educators and observers," he misapprehended events in two ways.[10] First, those who objected to the curriculum itself, such as John Dewey and Sidney Hook, usually charged that the liberal artists were neo-medievalists, not classicists. Second, many of the objections had little if anything to do with the curricula proposed. Indeed, in 1946 when consideration of the underclassmen great books part of the Virginia Plan was renewed by Robert Gooch, Dean of the College Ivey Lewis, and others at Virginia who believed that the time was right to finally implement the rest of the Virginia Plan, Lewis wrote, "I have heard no expression of criticism from professors, and believe the faculty would desire to develop further the type of instruction given in 'Honors' or 'Great Books' courses."[11]

While educational philosophy did play a role in some objections to the Virginia Plan and the larger liberal arts movement, there was often a combination of personal and institutional factors that played equally into the outcomes resulting from the Plan and the movement. Resistance to the liberal artists themselves was a significant factor in objections to the proposed curricular changes. It will be recalled that Archibald Shepperson and David McCord Wright at Virginia both came to the point where, as Shepperson put it, "I should be opposed to any plan, however good, that might be suggested" as long as the liberal artists supported it.[12]

Other objections had to do with organization. Fredson Bowers at the University of Virginia, although against Robert Gooch's 1952 General Honors proposal, stated that he had "some sympathy" with the concept of general education, but he believed, in that case, that such education should come in the first two years of college, not the last two.[13] Additionally, some objections had to do with pedagogy. Philosophy professor Arthur Stocker noted that certain faculty members believed that the Honors Program introduced concentration too soon, before enough breadth had been acquired. Faculty jealousy also mixed with the pedagogical objections. The non-elite students, and the faculty who taught them, would potentially suffer second class status if the Virginia Plan proposals were adopted.[14]

In addition to actual objections, other important institutional factors, such as funding, played a significant role in the final decisions to adopt or reject curricular proposals put forth by the liberal artists. The strongest example, of course, is the fate of Scott Buchanan's Virginia Plan great books scheme for Virginia underclassmen in 1936, which ostensibly foundered because President Newcomb could not afford to pay for it.

In summary, and in an expansion of the existing literature, the archival evidence demonstrates that philosophical, personal, and institutional factors all contributed significantly to the history of the Virginia Plan specifically, and the liberal arts movement more generally.

The Typicality of Virginia's Experience

For many years, the great books Liberal Arts Seminars and the tutorial Honors Program that developed at Virginia both retained the elitist philosophy put forth in the Virginia Plan in 1935. While Hutchins at Chicago and Barr and Buchanan at St. John's argued stridently that liberal education, derived through the study of great books, was an essential education for all, the manifestations of the Virginia Plan, as they were implemented at Virginia, were never so intended. The great books program for underclassmen had been proposed as a "college within a college" for honors students and the tutorial program for upperclassmen was likewise designed for a select few. Aydelotte, in his discussion of honors work, stated that some objected to honors work because "such a system is not democratic." He stated that:

> All students who enter the College, it is argued, have a right to the same training; it is unfair to select out a few and to give them advantages which

are denied to others. Such an objection seems to me to imply a desire, not for intellectual democracy, but for intellectual communism. The fact that all men are equal before the law does not mean that they are equal in Greek or Mathematics. . . . Equality of opportunity is all that a university can be expected to provide: The responsibility for measuring up to that opportunity or failing to do so must rest upon the individual.[15]

Virginia's position on the education of its best students has likewise been elite in this sense.

In the Introduction to this study it was proffered that the University of Virginia was more representative of higher education's response to the liberal arts movement than that of the other formative institutions because Virginia's reaction to the movement was more modest than that of Chicago, Columbia, or St. John's. In short, Virginia did not radically alter its undergraduate course of study for all students. Its honors work was strictly for elite students. In this sense the University of Virginia was typical of institutions of higher education in the relative modesty of its actual curricular changes. Like Virginia, most American colleges and universities continued to base their undergraduate instruction on a mix of prescription and election in subjects divided into departmental divisions.

On the other hand, Virginia was rather atypical relative to the other formative institutions of the liberal arts movement in its adherence to an elite "honors" model of liberal education. Indeed, along with the other formative institutions, additional schools had been making democratizing adjustments for all students for years. Princeton, for example, began requiring a thesis of all seniors in 1925. Yale soon made the same requirement, thereby, as Rudolph put it, "generalizing and democratizing a practice that in its origins had been intended for the most able and the most motivated."[16] This practice of making more modest but universal changes was fairly common. Ironically then, Virginia's role, because of its elitism, also made it rather atypical compared to other colleges and universities.

Contemporary Virginia and the "Jeffersonian Curriculum"
In an introductory brochure, the philosophy faculty claim that:

Graduation from the Honors program in Philosophy will give one an intellectual experience as close to that achieved by Rhodes Scholars at Oxford University as is possible in the United States. Indeed, it is likely that no other college in the United States offers a tutorial program that fully duplicates the Oxford tutorial system.

For the few students who study in the program today, the results are presumably as superb as those self-reported by the alumni at the Fiftieth Reunion of the program in 1988. It is nevertheless remarkable that more than sixty years after the original Virginia Plan was conceived—with all the promise it possessed both as understood by contemporaneous commentators, and during a brief period in the 1950s when it was fully implemented at Virginia—that today the Plan's manifestations at Virginia are so few. The non-departmental great books seminars are gone, and of the many departments that offered tutorial work, only Philosophy and Government and Foreign Affairs still adhere to the original vision of the Virginia Plan.

These changes notwithstanding, the issue of what constitutes the best undergraduate liberal education is a perennial one. As its senior class gift, the University of Virginia Class of 1998 decided to donate money to promote a "Jeffersonian curriculum," which it claimed was to be modeled on the Virginia Plan of 1935. Even more striking is that this gift designation was chosen over the other final possibility, the promotion of a diversity initiative. The actors do change, but in many ways the issues do not. After several years, what will come of the Jeffersonian curriculum initiative remains uncertain. If it remains merely an idea not fully adopted by the University, then it will join a long list of well-intentioned but ultimately sidelined efforts at curricular innovation at Virginia. On the other hand, if adopted it may mean that path-breaking developments from both the nineteenth and the twentieth centuries will figure in a unique way in the curriculum at the University of Virginia in the twenty-first century.

An Unfinished Story

Recalling a conversation held with Hutchins in 1937, Barr stated that Hutchins feared Barr and Buchanan might well fail in their attempt to establish their program at St. John's. Barr recalled, "[Hutchins] thought I might fall on my nose. And so did I. The other thing I thought was, if we succeed, it will spread like wildfire. . . . And I was wrong on both counts. I did not fail and it did not spread."[17]

The philosophy embodied in the liberal arts movement will probably never completely triumph or fail. Rather, as has been the case since the 1930s, its influence will wax and wane for multiple reasons: philosophical, pedagogical, personal, and institutional. What is certain is that the liberal arts movement has fostered a continuing legacy, one which has been most significant in American colleges and universities. In spite of their detractors, the great books, honors programs, and especially the liberal arts are widely promoted throughout the nation. Created in large part by the Virginia Plan, the final outcome of the liberal arts movement has been, and remains, an unfinished story, but its importance in higher education is undeniable.

Sources

Interviews

Anderson, Samuel A. (Pete) II , Architect for the University, University of Virginia. Interview by author, May 12, 1999, Charlottesville, VA.
Bice, Raymond C., Professor of Psychology Emeritus, and University Historian, University of Virginia. Interview by author, May 10, 1999, Charlottesville, VA.
Blackford, Staige D., Editor, *Virginia Quarterly Review*, University of Virginia. Interview by author, June 7, 1999, Charlottesville, VA.
Hyman, Sidney, Senior Fellow, Great Books Foundation, Chicago, IL. Interview by author, August 24, 2001, Chicago, IL.
Marshall, John, Professor of Philosophy, University of Virginia. Interview by author, June 9, 1999, Charlottesville, VA.
Moran, Charles E., University Historian Emeritus, University of Virginia. Interview by author, June 3, 1999, Charlottesville, VA.
Nelson, Charles A., Editor and Visitor Emeritus, St. John's College. Interview by author, August 28, 1999, Croton-on-Hudson, NY.
Olinger, Chauncey G., Jr., Investment broker and Columbia University oral historian. Telephone interview by author, June 7, 1999, New York, NY; and, Interview by author, August 28, 1999, Riverdale, NY.
Poe, L. Harvey, Jr., Lawyer and St. John's College Tutor Emeritus. Interview by author, April 19, 2000, Washington, D. C.
Ryan, Alan, Warden, New College, Oxford University. Interview by author, March 22, 2000, Charlottesville, VA.
Stocker, Arthur F., Classics Professor Emeritus, University of Virginia. Interview by author, June 3, 1999, Charlottesville, VA.
Thomas, George B., Professor of Philosophy, University of Virginia. Interview by author, June 18, 1999, Charlottesville, VA.

Archival Collections

Alderman Library, University of Virginia, Charlottesville, VA

Stringfellow Barr Papers
Robert Gooch Papers
Colgate Darden Papers
John Newcomb Papers
University Archives

University Archives Record Groups:
2/1/2.491 II Report of the Committee on Honors Courses; Barr—Newcomb correspondence
2/1/2.491 III Barr—Newcomb correspondence; 1937 Committee on Honors
2/1/2.551 I President's Papers (1946)
2/1/2.551 II President's Papers (1947)
2/1/2.552 President's Papers (1948)
2/1/2.561 President's Papers (1949)
2/1/2.562 Committee on the Liberal Arts; Ivey Lewis Papers
2/1/2.591 Honors Courses debates
19/2/6.781 Bulletins of the Liberal Arts Committee
19/2/7 (4903a) Faculty Committee on the College
19/3/4.541 (4903) University Senate; Committee on the Reorganization of the College
20/18/1.771 Committee on the Future of the University (1972)

20/29 1935 Curriculum Revision
20/59 Committee on the Liberal Arts
20/61 (7986) Committee on the Lower Division
21/60.811 Robert Gooch
21/60.821 Robert Gooch
21/17 Stringfellow Barr (empty)
26/9 Colgate Darden—Oral History Interview (n.d.)
26/11 Stringfellow Barr—Oral History Interview (1972)
26/13 Robert Gooch—Oral History Interview (1973)
5547d Robert Gooch Papers
7690 Virginius Dabney Papers
8053 Stringfellow Barr Papers

Greenfield Library, St. John's College, Annapolis, MD

Stringfellow Barr Papers
Collection includes the following transcripts of interviews with Barr:
March 14, 1968 by Frank Kelly, Center for the Study of Democratic Institutions, 45 pages
September 12, 1972 by Douglas Tanner, University of Virginia Oral History, 32 pages
June 29, 1975 by Francis Mason, 82 pages
July 6, 1975 by Charles and Mary Wiseman, 75 pages
July 13, 1975 by Allan Hoffman, 78 pages
July 27, 1975 by Francis Mason and Howard Baldwin, 57 pages
August 3, 1975 by Allan Hoffman, 104 pages
August 24, 1975 by Allan Hoffman, 80 pages
October 5, 1975 by Francis Mason and Allan Hoffman, 55 pages
October 12, 1975 by Harris Wofford and Stephen Benedict, 137 pages
November 22, 1975 by David Rea and Allan Hoffman, 155 pages

Maryland State Archives, Annapolis, MD

Stringfellow Barr Papers—St. John's College. Series No. T1404
Collection includes the following transcript of an interview with Barr:
1972 by Chauncey G. Olinger, Jr., 122 pages

Regenstein Library, University of Chicago, Chicago, IL

Board of Trustees Minutes
Mortimer J. Adler Papers
President's Papers 1925–1945
President's Papers 1940–1963
Robert M. Hutchins Papers and Addenda

Wisconsin Historical Society Archives, Madison, WI

Alexander Meiklejohn Papers
Collection includes Barr, Hutchins, Education, and Universities and Colleges, as subjects

Introduction

1. Walter Lippman, "The St. John's Program," reprinted from "Today and Tomorrow," *New York Herald Tribune*, December 27, 1938. Alexander Meiklejohn Papers, Box 57, Folder 4, Wisconsin Historical Society Archives, Madison, WI.
2. The liberal arts movement will be defined more fully later in this introduction. Some of the best examples of dialectical reasoning, that is, using logic to discern truth from error, especially in matters of opinion, can be found in the Socratic dialogues. Socrates' questioning of the slave boy in the *Meno* is perhaps the most famous.
3. David Denby, *Great Books: My Adventures with Homer, Rousseau, Woolf, and Other Indestructible Writers of the Western World* (New York: Touchstone, 1996), pp. 11, 19.
4. Justus Buchler, "Reconstruction in the Liberal Arts," in *History of Columbia College on Morningside Heights*, edited by Dwight Miner (New York: Columbia Press, 1954); Daniel Bell, *The Reforming of General Education* (New York: Columbia University Press, 1966); Lionel Trilling, "Some Notes for an Autobiographical Lecture," in *The Last Decade: Essays and Reviews, 1965–75* (New York: Harcourt Brace Jovanovich, 1979); Gerald Graff, *Professing Literature: An Institutional History* (Chicago: University of Chicago Press, 1987; pp. 132–136); Timothy Cross, *An Oasis of Order: The Core Curriculum at Columbia College* (New York: Office of the Dean, Columbia College, 1995); John Van Doren, "The Beginnings of the Great Books Movement at Columbia," *Columbia: the Magazine of Columbia University*, Winter 2001, 26; Carl Hovde, "What Columbia College is Known For," *Columbia: the Magazine of Columbia University*, Winter 2001, 32.
5. Michael R. Harris, *Five Counterrevolutionists in Higher Education* (Corvallis: Oregon State University Press, 1970); Robert M. Hutchins, *Great Books: The Foundation of a Liberal Education* (New York: Simon and Schuster, 1954); Mortimer Adler, *Philosopher At Large: An Intellectual Autobiography* (New York: Macmillan Publishing Co., 1977), and *A Second Look in the Rearview Mirror: Further Autobiographical Reflections of a Philosopher at Large* (New York: MacMillan Publishing Co., 1992); Harry Ashemore, *Unseasonable Truths: The Life of Robert Maynard Hutchins* (Boston: Little, Brown and Company, 1989); Milton Mayer, *Robert Maynard Hutchins: A Memoir* (Berkeley: University of California Press, 1993); William H. McNeill, *Hutchins' University: A Memoir of the University of Chicago, 1929–1950* (Chicago: University of Chicago Press, 1991); Mary Ann Dzuback, *Robert M. Hutchins: Portrait of an Educator* (Chicago: University of Chicago Press, 1991); F. Champion Ward, ed. *The Idea and Practice of General Education: An Account of the College of the University of Chicago* (Chicago: University of Chicago Press, 1950, 1992).
6. Harris Wofford, Jr., ed. *Embers of The World: Conversations with Scott Buchanan* (Santa Barbara: The Center for the Study of Democratic Institutions, 1969); Charles A. Nelson, *Scott Buchanan: A Centennial Appreciation of His Life and Work* (Annapolis: St. John's College Press, 1995), and *Stringfellow Barr: A Centennial Appreciation of His Life and Work* (Annapolis: St. John's College Press, 1997), and "The Barr/Buchanan Connection" (Annapolis: St. John's College, 1997, unpublished); Richard E. Miller, *As If Learning Mattered: Reforming Higher Education* (Ithaca: Cornell University Press, 1998); J. Winfree Smith, *A Search for the Liberal College: The Beginning of the St. John's Program* (Annapolis: St. John's College Press, 1983).
7. Bruce Kimball, *Orators and Philosophers: A History of the Idea of Liberal Education* (New York: The College Board, 1995), p. 3.
8. John S. Brubacher and Willis Rudy, *Higher Education in Transition: A History of American Colleges and Universities*, 4th ed. (New Brunswick, N.J.: Transaction, 1997), p. 274.
9. Frank Aydelotte, *Breaking the Academic Lockstep: The Development of Honors Work in American Colleges and Universities* (New York: Harper & Bros., 1944), pp. 91–92.

10. "New College to be Founded in Berkshires," *Pittsfield (Mass.) Berkshire Evening Eagle*, December 9, 1946, 1–2. Meiklejohn Papers, Box 57, Folder 4, Wisconsin Historical Society Archives, Madison, WI.
11. "Report of the Committee on Honors Courses to the President of the University." RG 2/1/2.491 II. Box 13, 1934–36 Honors Courses—Reports of the Committee. Special Collections, Alderman Library, University of Virginia, Charlottesville, VA. The omission of the honors scheme is perhaps indicative of Buchanan's, and to a lesser degree Barr's, bias toward the great books scheme in the Virginia Plan. Interestingly, Barr's copy of the Virginia Plan, now located at the Maryland State Archives in Annapolis, does not contain Appendix B.
12. See J. Winfree Smith, *A Search for the Liberal College: The Beginning of the St. John's Program* (Annapolis: St. John's College Press, 1983), pp. 18–19.
13. Amy Apfel Kass, *Radical Conservatives for Liberal Education* (Ph.D. diss., Johns Hopkins University, 1973; [Ann Arbor: University Microfilms, 1973]), p. 134.
14. Frederick Rudolph, *The American College and University: A History* (New York: A. Knopf, 1962; reprint, Athens, GA: University of Georgia Press, 1990), p. 480. (page citation is to the reprint edition.)
15. Richard Miller, *As If Learning Mattered: Reforming Higher Education* (Ithaca: Cornell University Press, 1998), p. 25.
16. "Report of the Committee on Honors Courses," Special Collections, University of Virginia.
17. Laurence Veysey, *The Emergence of the American University* (Chicago: University of Chicago Press, 1965), p. 338 n. 236.
18. Kass, *Radical Conservatives*, p. 1, abstract.
19. Mark Van Doren, *Liberal Education* (New York: Henry Holt and Co., 1943), p. 72.
20. Ibid., p. 81.
21. Mortimer Adler, "What is Liberal Education?" (http://www.realuofc.org/libed/adler/wle.html) Adler noted that "nowadays, of course" to the seven traditional liberal arts "we would add many more sciences, natural and social. This is just what has been done in the various modern attempts to renew liberal education."
22. Kass, *Radical Conservatives*, p. 1, abstract.
23. For example, Allan Bloom's call, made in his best-selling 1987 jeremiad *The Closing of the American Mind*, for a return to the great books results in part from his experience in the "Hutchins College" at the University of Chicago in the 1950s. His proposal was not part of the movement, which had faded several decades earlier, but rather a call for a revival, in part, of the philosophy of the movement.
24. Ernest L. Boyer and Arthur S. Levine, *A Quest for Common Learning: The Aims of General Education* (Princeton: The Carnegie Foundation for the Advancement of Teaching, 1981), pp. 2–3. Because the terms "general education" and "liberal education" were and are often used synonymously, both in the past and in the current day, some further elaboration may prove instructive. Boyer and Levine argue that general education is a twentieth-century term for the first component of liberal education, under which may be included skills (the "discipline" of the classical *trivium*) and knowledge (the "furniture" of the classical *quadrivium*). It represents the interdependent "breadth" component of a liberal education. The elective and specialized (major) parts of the curriculum are the second and third independent components of a liberal education. Additionally, some suggest that the extra-curriculum is a fourth component of a liberal education. Boyer and Levine thus suggest that liberal education, at least as often understood at the end of the twentieth century, consists of these three or four components and exists only when they are combined. While this definition may be of current value, it is not applicable to the period of the liberal arts movement. (See Boyer and Levine, *A Quest for Common Learning*, pp. 18, 32.)
25. Bell, *The Reforming of General Education*, p. 282.
26. Ibid., p. 152.
27. Christopher Lucas, *American Higher Education: A History* (New York: St. Martin's Griffin, 1994), p. 252.
28. Brubacher and Rudy, *Higher Education in Transition*, p. 272.
29. Boyer and Levine, *A Quest for Common Learning*, p. 15.
30. Ibid., p. 9.
31. Kimball, *Orators and Philosophers*, p. 212.
32. Edward J. Power, *Educational Philosophy: A History from the Ancient World to Modern America* (New York: Garland, 1996), p. 26. Of Quintilian's list, Power writes that: "Only the

best authors were on it, and those recognized for their transparency of expression were preferred. Livy was better than Sallust; Cicero was in a class all by himself."
33. Earlier great books lists had been assembled by Sir John Lubbock for the Workers' and Mechanics' Institutes in England in the 1880s (Kass, *Radical Conservatives*, pp. 20–21) and by Columbia English Literature professor George Edward Woodberry, who was Erskine's professor when Erskine was a graduate student at Columbia. (Chuncey G. Olinger, Jr., "The Origins of the Honors Program at the University of Virginia," uncompleted draft of remarks prepared for the reunion of Honors in Philosophy alumni, the University of Virginia, September 23–25, 1988, p. 2.)
34. Hutchins, *Great Books*, pp. 4–5.
35. Ibid., p. 20.
36. Robert M. Hutchins, *The Higher Learning in America* (New Haven: Yale University Press, 1936, revised ed. New Brunswick, NJ: Transaction, 1995), p. 78.
37. The history of the tutorial system at Oxford and Cambridge is long and multi-faceted. Although no definitive history on the system exists, descriptions of it can be found in the multi-volume set, *The History of the University of Oxford* (Oxford: Clarendon Press, 1997.) Alan Ryan, Warden of New College, Oxford, noted that the current form of the tutorial came into view by the 1880s. In its current conception, all university students have a tutor with whom they meet, often after dinner, in groups of two or three to present short papers which are then critically discussed. Topics assigned (e.g., "discuss Kant's *Prolegomena*") are usually quite broad. This differs from the form of tutorial common throughout the first three-quarters of the nineteenth century when tutorials were more akin to recitations, i.e., to read a book and then recite passages back orally. (Author's interview with Alan Ryan, Warden, New College, Oxford, March 22, 2000, Charlottesville, VA.)
38. Stringfellow Barr, transcript of interview with Chauncey G. Olinger, Jr., 1972, p. 10., courtesy of Chauncey Olinger.

Chapter 1

1. Bruce Kimball, *Orators & Philosophers: A History of the Idea of Liberal Education* (New York: The College Board, 1995), p. 2.
2. Frederick Rudolph, *Curriculum: A History of the American Undergraduate Course of Study Since 1636* (San Francisco: Jossey-Bass, 1977), p. 10.
3. The term "trivium," referring to the three language arts, was first used during the Carolingian Renaissance among the English scholar Alcuin's (730–804) circle of scholars at Charlemagne's palace school in Aachen, of which Alcuin was the master. The term "quadrivium" was first coined by Boethius (480–524), a minister to the Ostrogoth king in Italy, to refer to the four mathematical disciplines. Kimball, *Orators and Philosophers*, pp. 47–51. As the seven *artes liberales*, these terms do not necessarily have the same meanings as current parlance would suggest. The Trivium consists of: 1. Grammar: the art and science of concrete things as they are used in the mediums of expression; 2. Rhetoric: the art and science of applying such notations to things both concrete and abstract for practical and theoretical ends; and, 3. Logic: the art and science of discovering and applying abstract forms. The Quadrivium consists of: 1. and 2. Arithmetic and Geometry: the mathematical arts and sciences that correspond to grammar in the Trivium; 3. Music: the art and science that deals with applied mathematics in all the natural sciences; and, 4. Astronomy: the art and science that deals with proportions, propositions, and proofs, including mathematical logic. J. Winfree Smith, *A Search for the Liberal College: The Beginning of the St. John's Program* (Annapolis, MD: St. John's College Press, 1983), p. 18.
4. Rudolph, *Curriculum*, pp. 30–31.
5. Julie Reuben, *The Making of the Modern University: Intellectual Transformation and the Marginalization of Morality* (Chicago: University of Chicago Press, 1996), p. 23.
6. Rudolph, *Curriculum*, p. 39.
7. Ibid., p. 14.
8. Christopher Lucas, *American Higher Education: A History* (New York: St. Martin's Griffin, 1994), pp. 109–110.
9. Rudolph, *Curriculum*, pp. 112–113.

208 • Notes to Pages 19–27

10. *The Yale Report of 1828*, reprinted in the *ASHE Reader on the History of Higher Education*, eds. Lester F. Goodchild and Harold S. Wechsler (Needham Heights, MA: Ginn Press, 1989), p. 172.
11. Ibid., p. 173.
12. Lucas, *American Higher Education*, p. 134.
13. Reuben, *Making of the Modern University*, p. 25.
14. Thomas Jefferson Wertenbaker, *Princeton, 1746–1896* (Princeton, Princeton University Press, 1946), p. 235.
15. Caroline Winterer, "The Humanist Revolution in America, 1820–1860: Classical Antiquity in the Colleges," *History of Higher Education Annual* 18 (1998): 111–129.
16. Ibid.
17. Christie Farnham, *The Education of The Southern Belle: Higher Education and Student Socialization in the Antebellum South* (New York: New York University Press, 1994), pp. 16, 25–27, 38. Regional formulations of women's education in the Antebellum era, including the prevalence of collegiate education and the accepted societal roles for women, are a matter of debate. In addition to Farnham, see Barbara Solomon, *In the Company of Educated Women: A History of Women and Higher Education in America* (New Haven: Yale University Press, 1985), pp. 14–42.
18. John Brubacher and Willis Rudy, *Higher Education in Transition: A History of American Colleges and Universities*, 4th ed. (New Brunswick, NJ: Transaction Publishers, 1997), p. 42.
19. Frederick Rudolph, *The American College and University: A History* (New York: A. Knopf, 1962; reprint, Athens, GA: University of Georgia Press, 1990), p. 290.
20. Charles W. Eliot, quoted in Hugh Hawkins, *Between Harvard and America: The Educational Leadership of Charles W. Eliot* (New York: Oxford University Press, 1972), p. 92.
21. Ibid., p. 93.
22. Rudolph, *American College and University*, pp. 290–295. Eliot wrote that: "The elective system is, in the first place, an outcome of the Protestant reformation. In the next place, it is an outcome of political liberty." (As quoted in Hawkins, *Between Harvard and America*, p. 94.)
23. See Wertenbaker, *Princeton*, pp. 304–307, and Hawkins, *Between Harvard and America*, pp. 95–105, for more on the debate between McCosh and Eliot.
24. Laurence Veysey, *The Emergence of the American University* (Chicago: University of Chicago Press, 1965), pp. 55–56.
25. Lucas, *American Higher Education*, p. 170.
26. Eliot took exception to this convention too, arguing that *in loco parentis* was "an ancient fiction which ought no longer to deceive anybody." Charles Eliot, as quoted in Hawkins, *Between Harvard and America*, p. 111.
27. George Marsden, *The Soul of the American University: From Protestant Establishment to Established Nonbelief* (New York: Oxford University Press, 1994), p. 201.
28. James McCosh, as quoted in Marsden, *Soul of the American University*, p. 201.
29. Rudolph, *American College and University*, p. 460.
30. For a thorough examination of Washington, DuBois, and their philosophies of education, see Louis R. Harlan, *Booker T. Washington: The Wizard of Tuskegee, 1901–1915* (New York: Oxford University Press, 1983), and David Levering Lewis, *W. E. B. DuBois: Biography of A Race, 1868–1919* (New York: Henry Holt and Co., 1993).
31. See James Anderson, *The Education of Blacks in the South, 1860–1935* (Chapel Hill: University of North Carolina Press, 1988).
32. See Solomon, *In the Company of Educated Women*.
33. Lucas, *American Higher Education*, pp. 210–213.
34. Brubacher and Rudy, *Higher Education in Transition*, pp. 266–267.
35. Veysey, *Emergence*, p. 191; Lucas, *American Higher Education*, pp. 210–213.
36. For more on Lowell and how his views on liberal culture were manifest, see Marcia Graham Synott *The Half-Opened Door: Discrimination at Harvard, Yale, and Princeton, 1900–1970* (Westport, CT: Greenwood Press, 1979); on West, see Wertenbaker, *Princeton*; and on Woodberry, see Rudolph, *Curriculum*, p. 189.
37. Rudolph, *Curriculum*, p. 189.
38. Ibid.
39. Ibid., p. 240.
40. Ibid., p. 189.

41. Veysey noted that while many proponents of liberal culture used this phrase, others spoke of "culture," "general culture," or of "liberal education." (Veysey, *Emergence*, p. 180.)
42. Rudolph, *American College and University*, p. 454.
43. Ernest L. Boyer and Arthur Levine argued that there have been three general education revivals during the twentieth century: one after World War I, a second after World War II, and a contemporaneous one. (Ernest L. Boyer and Arthur Levine, *A Quest for Common Learning: The Aims of General Education*, Princeton: The Carnegie Foundation for the Advancement of Teaching, 1981.)
44. Rudolph, *Curriculum*, p. 247.
45. Boyer and Levine, *A Quest for Common Learning*, p. 15.
46. Ibid., p. 12.
47. Rudolph, *Curriculum*, pp. 237–238.
48. Reuben, *Making of the Modern University*, p. 255.
49. Ibid., p. 7.
50. Ibid., pp. 264–265.
51. Ibid., pp. 268–269. As elaboration, Reuben writes: "Universities never renounced their traditional moral aims. Educators continued to believe that universities should prepare their students to live 'properly' and contribute to the betterment of society. Contemporary interest in multicultural education indicates that this is still an important imperative in universities today. But universities no longer have a basis from which to judge moral claims. The Protestant synthesis that provided moral guidance up until the late nineteenth century did not survive the adoption of modern standards of scholarship or increased cultural diversity. Despite the hopes of its early advocates, scientific inquiry never produced authoritative intellectual standards for determining what it means to live 'properly' or how to identify what constitutes social 'betterment.' Without a means of adjudicating moral claims, contemporary debates about what college students should learn seem to be reduced to 'politics'" (p. 269). The dilemma Reuben describes is almost certainly aggravated by the widespread adoption of a "postmodern" synthesis, particularly in the humanities, that, ironically, had become the disciplinary refuge of moral reflection in the later twentieth century. This postmodern synthesis denies the very legitimacy of a basis for the evaluation of moral claims. The result, of course, is a potentially pernicious radical relativism that renders the still espoused moral aims of the university not only impossible to achieve, but also illegitimate. While there are many books on post-modernism, one view informed by the liberal arts movement is found in *Rediscovering Values: Coming to Terms with Postmodernism* (Armonk, NY: M. E. Sharpe, 1997) by Hugh Mercer Curtler, an alumnus of St. John's College.
52. Justus Buchler, quoted in Daniel Bell, *The Reforming of General Education* (New York: Columbia University Press, 1966), p. 21.
53. Bell, *The Reforming of General Education*, p. 21.
54. Nine colleges were founded in English America before the Revolution: Harvard College, 1636; the College of William and Mary, 1693; the Collegiate School at New Haven, 1701, renamed Yale College; the College of Philadelphia, 1740, renamed the University of Pennsylvania; the College of New Jersey, 1746, renamed Princeton University; King's College, 1754, renamed Columbia University; the College of Rhode Island, 1764, renamed Brown University; Queen's College, 1766, renamed Rutgers College; and Dartmouth College, 1769. (Lester Goodchild, "The History of American Higher Education: An Overview and a Commentary," in the *ASHE Reader on The History of Higher Education*, eds. Lester F. Goodchild and Harold S. Wechsler [Needham Heights, MA: Ginn Press, 1989].)
55. John W. Burgess, quoted in Bell, *The Reforming of General Education*, p. 16.
56. As a guide, Erskine used the list drawn up by Sir John Lubbock for use in the Workers' and Mechanics' Institutes in England in the 1880s. (Amy Apfel Kass, *Radical Conservatives for Liberal Education* (Ph.D. Diss., Johns Hopkins University, 1973 [Ann Arbor: University Microfilms, 1973], p. 20.) Erskine's list included the following: Homer, Herodotus, Thucydides, Aeschylus, Sophocles, Euripides, Aristophanes, selections from Greek Art, Plato, Aristotle, Lucretius, Vergil, Horace, Plutarch, Marcus Aurelius, St. Augustine, *The Song of Roland*, *The Nibelungenlied*, St. Thomas Aquinas, Dante, Bacon, Descartes, Hobbes, Milton, Molière, Locke, Montesquieu, Voltaire, Rousseau, Gibbon, Adam Smith, Kant, Goethe, American State Papers (Declaration of Independence, Constitution of the United States, The Federalist Papers), Victor Hugo, Hegel, Sir Charles Lyell, Balzac, Thomas Malthus,

210 • Notes to Pages 30–33

Jeremy Bentham, Pasteur, Karl Marx, Tolstoy, Dostoyevsky, Nietzsche, William James, Galileo, Grotius, Montaigne, Shakespeare, Cervantes, John Stuart Mill, and Darwin. (See Hugh Morehead, *The History of the Great Books Movement*, 2 vols. [unpublished doctoral dissertation, Department of Education, University of Chicago, 1964], p. 690; and Kass, *Radical Conservatives*, p. 21.)

57. Kass, *Radical Conservatives*, p. 19.
58. Bell, *The Reforming of General Education*, pp. 13–14.
59. Just as Mortimer Adler would take Erskine's course as an undergraduate at Columbia, so too would future fellow "liberal artist" Scott Buchanan be an undergraduate at Amherst during Meiklejohn's tenure. On another point, this interdisciplinary experience at Amherst, and the success of "Contemporary Civilization" at Columbia, encouraged Meiklejohn to establish an interdisciplinary two-year "experimental college" at the University of Wisconsin:

> In the first year of its two-year program [Meiklejohn] proposed that students devote the whole year to a study of an ancient civilization such as the Greek or the Roman. To penetrate the spirit of such a culture as that of the Greeks it would be necessary to come at it from all sides—its poetry, its drama, its philosophy, its politics, and its economy—but none except in relation to all the rest. In the second year Meiklejohn proposed taking up a modern, most likely American, civilization in the same manner. The main aim would not be so much to gain information, although that was important, as to develop a philosophical habit of mind in grasping the over-all significance of the way the various parts of a culture interact. This promising innovation lasted a few years and then folded its tent, not for want of merit, but for want of students, who were actively discouraged from electing it by a midwestern philistinism emanating not only from politicians but even faculty. (Brubacher and Rudy, *Higher Education in Transition*, pp. 272–273.)

For more on the experimental college see Alexander Meiklejohn, *The Experimental College* (New York: Harper & Row, 1932), and *Freedom and the College* (Englewood Cliffs, N.J.: Prentice Hall, 1923).

60. Brubacher and Rudy, *Higher Education in Transition*, p. 272.
61. Kass, *Radical Conservatives*, p. 19, n. 22.
62. Mark Van Doren, *The Autobiography of Mark Van Doren* (New York: Harcourt, Brace, and Co., 1958), p. 131.
63. Brubacher and Rudy, *Higher Education in Transition*, p. 275.
64. The original Literature Humanities reading list for 1937–38 is as follows. Fall Semester: Homer, *Iliad*; Herodotus, *The Persian Wars*; Thucydides, *The History of the Peloponnesian War*; Aeschylus, *Oresteia*; Sophocles, *Oedipus the King; Antigone*; Euripides, *Electra; Iphigenia in Taurus*; Aristophanes, *The Frogs, Plutus*; Plato, *Ion, Apology, Republic*; Aristotle, *The Poetics, The Ethics*; Lucretius, *On the Nature of Things*; Aurelius, *Meditations*; Virgil, *Aeneid*; Augustine, *Confessions*. Spring Semester: Dante, *Inferno*; Machiavelli, *The Prince*; Rabelais, *Gargantua and Pantagruel*; Montaigne, *Essays*; Shakespeare, *Henry IV, Parts 1 and 2*; Cervantes, *Don Quixote*; Milton, *Paradise Lost*; Spinoza, *Ethics*; Molière, *Tartuffe, The Misanthrope, The Physician in Spite of Himself*; Swift, *Gulliver's Travels*; Fielding, *Tom Jones*; Rousseau, *Confessions*; Voltaire, *Candide*; Goethe, *Faust, Part 1*. (David Denby, *Great Books* [New York: Touchstone, 1996], pp. 465–466.)
65. Bell, *The Reforming of General Education*, pp. 21–22.
66. Boyer and Levine, *A Quest for Common Learning*, pp. 10–11.
67. In *Higher Education in Transition*, Brubacher and Rudy make a similar oversight to which, as stated in the introduction, this study serves as a corrective. They state that "... the 'Great Books' curriculum [was] spawned at Columbia, encouraged at Chicago, and actually put in operation at St. John's College in Annapolis." (p. 274) Like Boyer and Levine, Brubacher and Rudy missed the formative role of Virginia in the creating the great books curriculum.
68. Bell, *The Reforming of General Education*, p. 26.
69. Robert Streeter, *One in Spirit: A Retrospective View of the University of Chicago on the Occasion of its Centennial* (Chicago: University of Chicago Publications Office, 1991), pp. 35–36. The "Latin issue" was a problem at the University from its inception. Upon reviewing plans for the opening ceremonies in 1892, Geologist Thomas Chamberlin wrote to Harper:

> In addition to the general objections, the singing of the Latin hymn is especially distasteful to some of us, because of the regrettable attitude of some of the advocates of

Latin toward the free development of the science courses. To some of us Latin has come, as a result of this, to stand for much the same thing in the scholarly world that Romanism does in the ecclesiastical world, and this is likely to grow in intensity as long as the existing intolerant attitude is maintained and its ill effects continue to be felt. The introduction, therefore, of a special feature that specifically commemorates the attitude of the old scholasticism, from whose tyrannies we are not yet escaped, is especially distasteful in a general assembly.... (p. 36.)

70. Ibid., p. 35.
71. Ibid., pp. 83–84.
72. These reforms were remarkably similar to the early practices at the University of Virginia where "a student completed the course [of study] as fast, or as slowly, as he was able" and where one could graduate only after passing general examinations. (Brubacher and Rudy, *Higher Education in Transition*, p. 102.)
73. Harry S. Ashmore, *Unseasonable Truths: The Life of Robert Maynard Hutchins* (Boston: Little, Brown, and Co., 1989), p. 33.
74. Robert Maynard Hutchins, *The Higher Learning in America* (New Haven: Yale University Press, 1936; revised ed., New Brunswick: Transaction, 1995), p. 33.
75. Ashmore, *Unseasonable Truths*, p. 92.
76. William H. McNeill, *Hutchins' University: A Memoir of the University of Chicago, 1929–1950* (Chicago: University of Chicago Press, 1991), p. 34.
77. Bertrand Russell, *A History of Western Philosophy* (New York: Simon & Schuster, 1945), p. 478.
78. Edward Peters, *Europe and the Middle Ages* (Englewood Cliffs, N.J.: Prentice-Hall, 1983), p. 222.
79. Russell, *History of Western Philosophy*, pp. 461–462.
80. Peters, *Europe and the Middle Ages*, p. 221.
81. Ibid., p., 223.
82. Russell noted, for example, that there are five proofs given for the existence of God in the *Summa*. One of them is the argument of the unmoved mover. Russell summarizes Aquinas's proof as follows: "There are things which are only moved, and other things which both move and are moved. Whatever is moved is moved by something, and, since an endless regress is impossible, we must arrive somewhere at something which moves without being moved. This unmoved mover is God." (Russell, *History of Western Philosophy*, p. 455.)
83. Russell, *History of Western Philosophy*, p. 452.
84. McNeill, *Hutchins' University*, p. 37.
85. Ibid.
86. Ibid., p. 36.
87. Ashmore, *Unseasonable Truths*, p. 147.
88. Ibid., p. 93.
89. Ibid., p. 98.
90. Rockefeller's original intention was to ensure a Baptist educational presence in the burgeoning city of Chicago. When the original University of Chicago, established in 1856 on property donated by Stephen A. Douglas from his South Side estate "Oakenwald" went bankrupt in 1886, Chicago was left without a Baptist college. This absence was highlighted by the existence of Northwestern, which had been founded by the Methodists, and Lake Forest College, which had been founded by the Presbyterians. (*The University and the City: A Centennial View of the University of Chicago* (Chicago: The University of Chicago Library, 1992), pp. 2–3.)
91. Kass, *Radical Conservatives*, pp. 122–123. A similar course, with similar results, was later instituted at the University of Chicago School of Law.
92. Hutchins, *Higher Learning*, p. 79.
93. One can derive a sense of what the course might have been like, at least in terms of content, by perusing, if not actually undertaking, the Reading Plan presented in: Mortimer Adler and Peter Wolff, *A General Introduction to the Great Books and to a Liberal Education* (Chicago: Encyclopaedia Britannica, Inc., 1959). After a preface by Robert Hutchins, the book contains information on fifteen selected readings, guides to the readings, and self-testing questions.
94. Author's interview with Sidney Hyman, Senior Fellow, Great Books Foundation, August 24, 2001, Chicago, IL.

95. Mary Ann Dzuback, *Robert M. Hutchins: Portrait of an Educator* (Chicago: University of Chicago Press, 1991), pp. 101–104.
96. Streeter, *One in Spirit*, p. 97.
97. The course grew rather famous. Outside observers such as Orson Wells, Lillian Gish, and Gertrude Stein came to the Midway to see the course in action. Details can be found in Morehead, *The History of the Great Books Movement*.
98. Rudolph, *Curriculum*, pp. 236–237.

Chapter 2

1. Thomas Jefferson, "Bill for the More General Diffusion of Knowledge [1779]," in John S. Patton, *Jefferson, Cabell and the University of Virginia*, (New York: Neale Publishing Co., 1906), p. 13. At the time, even public education was a radical notion, not to mention electivism. Patton writes that: "The planter who had Madeira in his cellar almost certainly had a tutor in his library for the intellectual behoof of his children; or he sent his sons to Princeton or to the universities of the mother country. The offspring of less fortunate folk grew up in an atmosphere in which Madeira, the clergy, and the pedagogue were little known." (p. 9.)
2. Thomas Jefferson to Joseph Priestly [18 January 1800], in Patton, *Jefferson, Cabell and the University of Virginia*, p. 16.
3. For analysis of Jefferson's designs, the subsequent reality of student life, and their relation to notions of "aristocracy" at the University during the antebellum period see Jennings L. Wagoner, Jr., "Honor and Dishonor at Mr. Jefferson's University: The Antebellum Years," *History of Education Quarterly*, vol. 26, 1986, pp. 155–179.
4. Thomas Jefferson to George Ticknor [16 July 1823], in Philip Alexander Bruce, *History of the University of Virginia, 1819–1919* (New York: The MacMillan Co., 1920), Vol I., pp. 331–332.
5. John S. Brubacher and Willis Rudy, *Higher Education in Transition: A History of American Colleges and Universities*, 4th ed. (New Brunswick: Transaction Publishers, 1997), p. 462, n. 6.
6. Ibid., p. 101.
7. Ibid., p. 462, n. 6.
8. Bruce, *History*, Vol I., p. 332. Bruce wrote that "The adoption of the degrees of master of arts and bachelor of arts was not in harmony with the principle upon which his [Jefferson's] university was built, in its theory at least, and was a distinctly regrettable, though perhaps, for practical reasons, an unavoidable departure from its fundamental character."
9. See Frederick Rudolph, *The American College and University: A History* (New York: A. Knopf, 1962; reprint, Athens, GA: University of Georgia Press, 1990), pp. 124–128 (page citation is to the reprint edition), and Hugh Hawkins, *Between Harvard and America: The Educational Leadership of Charles W. Eliot* (New York: Oxford University Press, 1972), p. 82.
10. Bruce, *History*, Vol I., p. 331. Bruce adds that "Rogers had been an instructor in that college at one time and could, therefore, write authoritatively on this subject."
11. Ibid., pp. 322–323.
12. Thomas Jefferson to W. B. Giles, December 1825, quoted in Bruce, *History*, Vol. I., p. 334.
13. Henry Shepherd quoted in Lawrence Levine, *The Opening of the American Mind: Canons, Culture, and History* (Boston: Beacon Press, 1996), p. 77.
14. Joseph A. Soares, *The Decline of Privilege: The Modernization of Oxford University* (Stanford: Stanford University Press, 1999), p. 16. Soares also noted that:
    > Oxford from the turn of the century to the interwar period was a loose federation of colleges where scions of the upper classes, with public school backgrounds, pursued gentlemanly studies in the humanities when they were not playing cricket or boating. It would be safe to assume that more dons knew about Aristotle's ethics than about James Clerk Maxwell's electromagnetic theory of light. (p. 267.)
15. Stringfellow Barr, transcript of interview with Chauncey G. Olinger, Jr., 1972, p. 8., courtesy of Chauncey Olinger; and Robert Gooch, transcript of interview with Robert Light, Charlottesville, VA., March 15, 1973. RG 26/13, Folder: Gooch, Robert Kent, p. 1ff. Virginia Oral History Project, Special Collections, Alderman Library, University of Virginia, Charlottesville, VA.
16. Virginius Dabney, *Mr. Jefferson's University: A History* (Charlottesville: University of Virginia Press, 1981), p. 454.

17. Buchanan's time at the People's Institute, an outgrowth of Cooper Union, is well documented in Mortimer J. Adler, *Philosopher at Large: An Intellectual Autobiography* (New York: Macmillan, 1977) and Amy Apfel Kass, *Radical Conservatives for Liberal Education*, (Ph.D. diss., Johns Hopkins University, 1973 [Ann Arbor: University Microfilms, 1973]). A brief account by Buchanan himself can be found in the eighteen-page "New Introduction" to the 1962 Lippincott reprint of Buchanan's 1929 *Poetry and Mathematics*. Buchanan wrote that:

> The occasion of a new edition of this particular book offers an opportunity for the writer to say in a new introduction how the idea of it originally occurred and what some of its consequences have been. After the book was written the idea was recognized by one of the more learned readers [Richard McKeon] to be the idea of the seven liberal arts. The consequences have been a radical reform of teaching and learning in a small province of the modern academy.

(Scott Buchanan, *Poetry and Mathematics*, [John Day Co., 1929; reprint, Philadelphia: J. B. Lippincott Co., 1962], pp. 11ff.)

18. Since its founding by Charles Sprague Smith, a professor of comparative literature at Columbia University, the People's Institute had, as Buchanan put it,

> had a rather remarkable career in American popular education. As the earlier Lyceum and Chautauqua had brought itinerant scientific and literary teachers to urban and rural centers of population, so the People's Institute had brought in people from distant places and traditions to hear lectures twice a week on literature, politics, economics, and society in a free open assembly. From the start there had been questions and discussion from the floor following each lecture, and these exercises had brought sharp and sometimes learned criticism and dialectic to bear upon the lectures....

(Scott Buchanan, *Poetry and Mathematics*, [John Day Co., 1929; reprint, Philadelphia: J. B. Lippincott Co., 1962], p. 11.)

19. Scott Buchanan, *Poetry and Mathematics* (John Day Co., 1929; reprint, Philadelphia: J. B. Lippincott Co., 1962), pp. 11ff.
20. Ibid.
21. Ibid.
22. Ibid. In the 1970s Stringfellow Barr noted that "theology, law, and medicine were, from [Buchanan's] point of view, a very peculiar triad. They were your relation to God, your relation to your neighbor, and your relation to the material environment," respectively. (Stringfellow Barr, Transcript of interview with Chauncey G. Olinger, Jr., 1972, p. 4. Courtesy of Chauncey Olinger.)
23. Ibid.
24. Charles A. Nelson, *Scott Buchanan: A Centennial Appreciation of His Life and Work: 1895–1968* (Annapolis: St. John's College Press, 1995), p. v. Buchanan's first three courses at Virginia as an associate professor were: "Philosophical Criticism: A study of problems arising from the interactions and conflicts of scientific, aesthetic, and moral interests"; "The Platonic Tradition in Philosophy: A study of the intellectual crises in history when Platonism has been a deciding factor; the rise of Christian theology; the beginning of modern science; recent developments in mathematics and physics"; and "Aesthetics: A critique of art and art criticism." (*University of Virginia Record*, Catalogue Number 1929–1930, Announcements 1930–1931, p. 233.)
25. J. Winfree Smith, *A Search for the Liberal College: The Beginning of the St. John's Program* (Annapolis, MD: St. John's College Press, 1983), p. 131, n. 12. "Barr received the nickname, 'Winkie,' when he was a very small boy because of his fascination with a nursery rhyme that used to be repeated to him by his maternal grandfather, the Reverend Frank Stringfellow, an Episcopal priest, who, as a scout for General Robert E. Lee during the Civil War, had had many extraordinary adventures. The rhyme went:

> Hokey, pokey, winkie, wunk
> Chubberly, cummery, chummerly, chunk.
> Hangery, wangery, chingery, changery,
> King of the Cannibal Islands."

26. Stringfellow Barr, transcript of interview with Chauncey G. Olinger, Jr., 1972, p. 110. Incidentally, Barr's father, William Alexander Barr, "who had the reputation of being an

214 • Notes to Pages 48–50

eloquent man in the pulpit," gave the sermon at the exercises held for the University of Virginia's Centennial Celebration in 1919 (pp. 113, 118).

27. At the time of World War I, the requirements for the B.A. degree at Virginia were as follows: Group Electives:
    I. Languages, 18 Semester Hours. (Two required, but 12 hours must be in Latin or Greek)
    II. Mathematical Sciences, 12 Semester Hours. (Math and Astronomy included, but 6 hours must be in Math)
    III. Natural Sciences, 24 Semester Hours. (Two Sciences must be offered)
    IV. Social Sciences, 12 Semester Hours. (History, Economics, and Government included)
    V. English, 12 Semester Hours. (Biblical Literature and Public Speaking included but 6 hours must be in English)

    To these 96 semester hours were added 30 semester hours in electives-at-large (free electives), of which 18 hours must be in one of the above groups. Additionally, of these 18 hours, one "C" course (100 to 199 level) must be included. Of the electives-at-large, 6 hours may also be in physical education. Total required semester hours for the B.A. is 126. Students pursuing the B.S. were permitted substitution of a foreign language for the compulsory Latin or Greek of the B.A. Program.
    (Bulletin of the Liberal Arts Committee, Vol. I., No. 1., 15 April 1947, RG 19/2/6.781, Special Collections, University of Virginia.)

28. After a year at Tulane University, Barr took the following courses (with grades) for his bachelor's degree:
    1913–14: Latin A1, 79, Mathematics B1, 79, Greek A2, 75, Eng. Literature B2, 81, Philosophy B1, 81; 1914–15: Latin B2, 75, Greek B1, 79, Zoology B1, 87, Philosophy B3, 86, English C1, 88; 1915–16: Geology B1, 93, English B1, 93, English B2, 97, Pol. Science B1, 90, Economics B1, 88.
    For his master's degree, Barr took the following courses:
    1916–17: Philosophy C1, satisfactory, Eng. Literature C1, 90, Economics C1, 82, English D2, 95.
    (University of Virginia transcript, Series 2, Box 14, Folder 22. Stringfellow Barr Papers, Greenfield Library, St. John's College, Annapolis, MD.)

29. Stringfellow Barr, transcript of interview with Francis Mason, June 29, 1975, p. 60. Stringfellow Barr Papers, Special Collections, St. John's College.

30. Transcript Authentication and Raven Society Certificate, Series 2, Box 14, Folders 20, 11. Stringfellow Barr Papers, Special Collections, St. John's College. The Raven Society is the University of Virginia's oldest honor society.

31. Barr, transcript of interview with Francis Mason, June 29, 1975, p. 63.

32. Letter from Stringfellow Barr to President E. A. Alderman, February 26, 1924, Series 2, Box 29, Folder 57. Stringfellow Barr Papers, Special Collections, St. John's College.

33. Barr, transcript of interview with Francis Mason, June 29, 1975, p. 61. Barr's first courses as an assistant professor were: "History B1: General History, Ancient and Medieval" and "History B2: Modern European History." (*University of Virginia Record*, Catalogue Number 1924–1925, Announcements 1925–1926, p. 158.)

34. Stringfellow Barr, transcript of interview with Charles and Mary Wiseman, July 6, 1975, p. 37. Stringfellow Barr Papers, Special Collections, St. John's College.

35. Barr, transcript of interview with Chauncey G. Olinger, Jr., 1972, p. 100; and, *Encyclopedia Americana*, International Edition, 1996, Vol. 3, p. 264, and, *Britannica Perspectives*, Vol. 1, 1968, p. 62; Stringfellow Barr Papers, Special Collections, University of Virginia.

36. Charles A. Nelson, *Stringfellow Barr: A Centennial Appreciation of His Life and Work: 1897–1982* (Annapolis: St. John's College Press, 1997), p. 1.

37. Author's interview with Charles E. Moran, University Historian Emeritus, University of Virginia, Charlottesville, VA, June 3, 1999.

38. Author's interview with Samuel A. (Pete) Anderson, II, Architect for the University, University of Virginia, Charlottesville, VA, May 12, 1999.

39. Author's interview with Charles E. Moran, Charlottesville, VA, June 3, 1999.

40. Author's interview with Staige D. Blackford, Editor, *Virginia Quarterly Review*, University of Virginia, Charlottesville, VA, June 7, 1999.

41. Dabney, *Mr. Jefferson's University*, p. 579.

42. J. Winfree Smith as quoted in Nelson, *Scott Buchanan*, p. 66.
43. Author's interview with L. Harvey Poe, Jr., St. John's College Tutor Emeritus, Washington D.C., April 19, 2000. Buchanan's Metaphysics course was described in the *Virginia Record* as: "A study of the elements of the speculative science of metaphysics and special consideration of the bases and scopes of the rational and empirical sciences and of the doctrinal positions of Aristotle, Spinoza, and Bradley." Buchanan also led reading courses on Plato, Aristotle, and Aquinas. (*University of Virginia Record*, Catalogue Number 1934–1935, Announcements 1935–1936, p. 242.)
44. Clipping from *College Topics*, May 12, 1922, in the Robert Gooch Papers, RG 21/60.821, Box 11, Special Collections, University of Virginia.
45. The new requirements for the B.A. degree adopted in 1922 were as follows:
    Required Subjects:
    I. Foreign Languages, 18 Semester Hours. (Two required, but 12 hours must be in Latin or Greek)
    II. Mathematics, 6 Semester Hours.
    III. Natural Sciences, 12 Semester Hours.
    IV. English, 12 Semester Hours. (Biblical Literature and Public Speaking included, but 6 hours must be in English)
    V. Social Sciences, 6 Semester Hours. (History, Economics, and Government included)
    VI. Philosophy, 6 Semester Hours. (Logic, Ethics, and Psychology included)
    VII. Physical Education, 6 Semester Hours.
    To these 66 semester hours were added 24 hours of Major Electives which must be taken from one of the following groups:
    I. Language, Literature, Fine Arts, and Music
    II. Social and Philosophical Sciences
    III. Mathematical and Natural Sciences
    One "C" course must be included. Additionally, 36 electives-at-large were required, for a grand total of 126 semester hours for the B.A. degree.
    Between 1922 and 1936 the requirement in Social Science was increased to 12 semester hours. Sociology was added to the Social Science group and 6 semester hours in history were required. The History of Philosophy replaced Logic and Ethics in the Philosophy group.
    (Bulletin of the Liberal Arts Committee, Vol. I., No. 1., April 15, 1947, RG 19/2/6.781, Special Collections, University of Virginia)
46. Robert Gooch as quoted in Dabney, *Mr. Jefferson's University*, p. 579.
47. Author's interview with Charles E. Moran, Charlottesville, VA, June 3, 1999.
48. The 1933 yearbook, *Corks and Curls*, lists four recipients of the Bachelors of Science with Final Honors and three recipients of the Bachelors of Arts with Final Honors. (*Corks and Curls*, 1933, p. 94. Alderman Library, University of Virginia.) The Final Honors system eventually received greater elaboration. The 1933 *Record*, for example, stated that:
    > Final honors are conferred on the basis of a final comprehensive examination, both oral and written, on some field of knowledge, and not for the work done in any or all of the regular courses required for a baccalaureate degree. Honors work involves wide and independent reading for two years, under the general direction of the professors of an academic school. It does not require regular attendance upon lectures or the passing of any tests or examinations, except the final examination, though consultations and reports may be required. Its aim is the development of a capacity for scholarly work in a field of knowledge, rather than a mastery of required details of subject matter. ("Degrees With Honors," *University of Virginia Record*, Catalogue 1932–1933, Announcements 1933–1934, pp. 264–65.)
49. Stringfellow Barr, transcript of interview with Francis Mason and Allan Hoffman, October 5, 1975, pp. 48–49. Stringfellow Barr Papers, Special Collections, St. John's College. Of Spengler's deterministic view of history, Barr later stated: "It's hazardous stuff. I mean, intellectually, very hazardous stuff when you start mucking the cycles and start showing the wheel of history. It's so easily made a cult, I think.... They say now this is coming for the following reasons."
50. Buchanan, *Poetry and Mathematics*, p. 22.

51. Harris Wofford, Jr., ed. *Embers of The World: Conversations with Scott Buchanan* (Santa Barbara: The Center for the Study of Democratic Institutions, 1969), p. 86.
52. Author's interview with L. Harvey Poe, Jr., Washington D.C., April 19, 2000. Poe later served as a tenured tutor and Assistant Dean at St. John's College. More on Poe's experiences with Barr and Buchanan can be found in Nelson, *Stringfellow Barr*, pp. 170–172. Although Barr would leave the University of Virginia for the University of Chicago in the summer of 1936, it is clear that his teaching style and content were changing by that time. In addition to his survey course, Barr was also going to teach a course on "Greek and Roman Historians" and another course on the "Civilization of the Greeks and Romans." (*University of Virginia Record*, Catalogue Number 1935–1936, Announcements 1936–1937, p. 241.)
53. Stringfellow Barr, Transcript of interview with Allan Hoffman, July 13, 1975, p. 6. Stringfellow Barr Papers, Special Collections, St. John's College. The honors program to which Barr was referring was the University's "Special Honors" program.
54. Letter from John L. Newcomb to Robert K. Gooch, September 15, 1934. RG 2/1/2.491 II, Box 13, Folder: 1934–36 Honors Courses—Reports of Committee. Special Collections, University of Virginia.
55. Letter from Otis Peabody Smith, *Life Magazine*, to President John Newcomb, June 2, 1937. RG 2/1/2.491 II, Box 2, Folder "1937–38: General Records, Articles on UVa, President's Office." Special Collections, University of Virginia.
56. *Life Magazine*, June 7, 1937. RG 2/1/2.491 II, Box 2, Folder "1937–38: General Records, Articles on UVa, President's Office." Special Collections, University of Virginia. N.B. "F.F.V." means "First Families of Virginia." President Newcomb had been sent an advance copy of the text of the *Life* article for his perusal. In a telegram to Henry Luce, the Editor of *Life*, Newcomb replied that:

> I have just seen an advance copy of your caption to the pictures of the University of Virginia which will appear in the next issue of *Life*. I most emphatically protest against erroneous statements reflecting upon the University's standing as an institution of higher education. The obvious injustice that your article will do to our educational standards and to the habits of our students will be realized by all who know the University but others may be grossly misled by the inaccuracies contained therein. I am sure you do not desire to be unjust to us and I sincerely hope that there is yet time for you to correct the errors in your captions.

A telegraph reply from a Daniel Longwell at *Life* dated June 3, 1937 reads: "I am sorry but Life's color section is already printed. But Life's editors will be glad to have you expand your protest into specific corrections that we can print in our letters to the editors column."
57. Dabney, *Mr. Jefferson's University*, pp. 153–154.
58. As will be discussed in Chapter 5, such concerns also motivated the election of Colgate Darden as Newcomb's successor in 1946.
59. Stringfellow Barr, "Jefferson's University," *The Commonwealth, The Magazine of Virginia Business*, February 1935. Stringfellow Barr Papers, 2/1/10, Special Collections, St. John's College.
60. Frank Aydellotte, *Breaking the Academic Lockstep: The Development of Honors Work in American Colleges and Universities* (New York: Harper & Brothers, 1944), p. 91.
61. The new curriculum, replacing the one that had been in effect since 1922, was as follows:
    Required Courses:
    I. English, 6 Semester Hours.
    II. Foreign Languages, 12–24 Semester Hours.* (Second-year college course in each of two languages, one of which must be Greek or Latin)
    III. Mathematics, 6 Semester Hours.
    IV. Natural Science, 12 Semester Hours.
    V. Physical Education, 0 Semester Hours (2 years required)
    To these 36 to 48 semester hours of required courses are added 30 to 42 required hours in a field of concentration, of which 18–30 are in the major and 12–24 are in related subjects. Free electives are to complete a total of 120 semester hours for the B.A. degree. Additionally, one must pass a final comprehensive examination.
    * Between 1936 and the beginning of World War II, the requirement of Greek or Latin was dropped, and it became permissible to substitute a third-year course in one foreign language for a second-year course in each of two.

(*The Bulletin of the Liberal Arts Committee*, Vol. I, No. I, April 15, 1947. RG 19/2/6.781 Folder: "Bulletin of the Liberal Arts Committee, 4/15/47—9/18/50." Special Collections, University of Virginia.)

These changes were designed to improve the education of all students. The Dean of the College, George Ferguson, explained the rationale behind the new arrangement by noting:

It is hoped that the new requirements will insure a reasonably thorough mastery of at least one important field of knowledge, that they will bring about an acquaintance with the traditional liberal arts and sciences and that they will allow a proper measure of freedom in the pursuit of individual interests. It is also hoped that they will tend to de-emphasize the idea that a degree is made up of an accumulation of fragmentary and quickly forgotten credit-hours, and will encourage a more comprehensive and permanent mastery of subjects as wholes.

(George Ferguson, "New Degree Requirements At The University of Virginia," 10 August 1935, RG 20/29, Box 11, Special Collections, University of Virginia. Additional commentary can be found in Dabney, *Mr. Jefferson's University*, p. 169.)

62. Buchanan, *Poetry and Mathematics*, p. 22.
63. J. L. Brierly and H. V. Hodson, "Literae Humaniores," in the *Handbook to the University of Oxford, 1962* (London, Oxford University Press, 1962), pp. 149–150, as quoted in Daniel Bell, *The Reforming of General Education* (New York: Columbia University Press, 1966), p. 286. Bell added the following footnote:

In effect, "Greats" is a combined school of classical history and philosophy. A knowledge of both Greek and Latin is required and the First Public Examination, at the end of the second year, includes translation from Latin and Greek into English and the rendering of passages of English prose (verse is optional) into Latin or Greek in the style of the classical authors or orators. The school covers three centuries of Greek history and a somewhat longer period of Roman history, ending with the death of the Emperor Trajan in 117 A.D. The study of philosophy is based on Plato's *Republic* and Aristotle's *Ethics*, to which is added modern philosophy from Descartes.

One always risks claiming too much for a single educational program as the formative reason for an intellectual elite. A simple sociological point must be remembered: that the better students take "Greats." As Mr. Brierly and Mr. Hodson write: "Much of the deserved fame of *Literae Humaniores* at Oxford is due to the fact that for over a century a veritable *elite* from the best schools in England has prepared itself for classical scholarship and proceeded to Oxford after intensive competitive examination. The students and teachers in this Honour School of *Literae Humaniores* have been, and probably still remain, the most naturally gifted and the most severely disciplined elements in the University, and to a greater or lesser degree the rest of us are a little bit afraid of them. It is probably true to say that no single definite curriculum of study in any one university in modern times has produced so many famous men in public life, in learning and letters."

This adulation notwithstanding, there were those who thought "Greats" could be improved. In an article draft written in the 1960s, Barr noted that the great medical scholar Sir William Osler, the president of the British Classical Association, delivered an address in which he "lamented that the Oxford School of *Literae Humaniores*, commonly referred to as 'Greats,' should not include in the 'humanities' such [mathematical and scientific] works as those of Hippocrates and Galen, of Theophrastus, of Archimedes, of Aristarchus." Given the curriculum they helped formulate in the Virginia Plan, Barr and Buchanan would no doubt have agreed with Osler. (Barr, handwritten draft of article for *The Center Magazine*, 8053h, Box 4, Stringfellow Barr Papers, Special Collections, University of Virginia.)

64. Aydelotte, *Breaking the Academic Lockstep*, pp. 23–24.
65. Aydelotte noted, for example, that: "The final examinations for the degree in *Literae Humaniores* include the great periods of ancient history and philosophy with appropriate modern comment. . . . The requirement for success is twofold: exact knowledge of certain set books and topics, coupled with capacity to deal in broad generalities with a wide range of historical and literary material." (Aydelotte, *Breaking the Academic Lockstep*, p. 23.)
66. Adler, *Philosopher at Large*, p. 87. Actually, it appears that the "Greats" courses were more elite than Adler gave credit. Joseph Soares noted that: "Dons directed their most brilliant

218 • Notes to Pages 56–59

undergraduates toward *literae humaniores* as the best place to receive an education suitable for politics and administration on the world stage." (Soares, *The Decline of Privilege*, p. 36.)

67. Buchanan, *Poetry and Mathematics*, pp. 22–23.

68. In spite of their friendship, Barr wrote that he did not solicit Buchanan's appointment at the University of Virginia in 1929. The chairman of the philosophy department, Albert Balz, knowing that Barr knew Buchanan, asked Barr for his thoughts. Barr replied:

> ... I said to Balz, this man who was inquiring of me, "He is quite difficult. I think he's worth it but a lot of people wouldn't." But I don't think that anybody with any intelligence and certainly not Scott, would want me to say, "oh, he's just a peach of a guy." Because I knew he'd make life kind of hellish for all of 'em—fruitfully, I would predict. Well, when he came, they—I think it was not only that by now they were convinced he had a mind, but that he also had a kind of charm—until the blow fell—that is, until he started asking really embarrassing Socratic questions. So they took him on and were apparently damned glad of it.

(Stringfellow Barr, transcript of interview with Charles and Mary Wiseman, July 6, 1975, Stringfellow Barr Papers, Special Collections, St. John's College.)

69. Wofford, *Embers of the World*, pp. 89–90.

70. In writing an article on Buchanan in 1968, Barr recorded that, more than twenty years after Buchanan had left Virginia, "... a young Californian, who was about to move to Virginia, asked Buchanan how to behave. 'Always remember you are in a foreign country,' he said. It was what Buchanan himself had done for seven years." (Stringfellow Barr, handwritten draft of article for *The Center Magazine*, 8053h, Box 4, Stringfellow Barr Papers, Special Collections, University of Virginia.)

71. Buchanan, *Poetry and Mathematics*, pp. 23–24. The "*ad hoc* Honors Course" to which Buchanan referred was the University's Special Honors program established in 1924. It is necessary to make an important point of clarification about a chronological problem in some of Buchanan's recollections. President Alderman died in April of 1931 and subsequently John Lloyd Newcomb was named Acting President. After more than two years of this arrangement, Newcomb officially became President on October 6, 1933. In spite of Buchanan's recollections to the contrary, it appears that, at most, Alderman only prompted formal review of the regular college curriculum, which as noted earlier in this chapter, was eventually revised in 1935. The review of honors work at the university may well have been discussed by Alderman, but as will be seen, it was Newcomb who, in September 1934, commenced the formal committee review of honors work that resulted in the Virginia Plan.

72. Letter from Scott Buchanan to Mortimer Adler, October 17, 1929, as quoted in Smith, *Search for a Liberal College*, p. 13.

73. Letter from Scott Buchanan to Robert Hutchins, February 21, 1930, R. M. Hutchins Papers Addenda, 19/3. Special Collections, Regenstein Library, University of Chicago, Chicago, IL.

74. Ibid.

75. Letter from Scott Buchanan to Robert Hutchins, March 22, 1930, R. M. Hutchins Papers Addenda, 19/3, Special Collections, University of Chicago.

76. Buchanan, *Poetry and Mathematics*, p. 22.

77. Letter from Scott Buchanan to Robert Hutchins, March 22, 1930, R. M. Hutchins Papers Addenda, 19/3, Special Collections, University of Chicago.

78. Ibid. In accepting a later invitation to spend Thanksgiving in Charlottesville with the Buchanans, Hutchins wrote: "Please make no arrangements beyond Barr in both spellings." (Letter from Hutchins to Buchanan, November 19, 1932, Hutchins Papers Addenda, Box 19, Folder 2, Special Collections, University of Chicago.)

79. Smith, *Search for a Liberal College*, p. 13.

80. Buchanan, *Poetry and Mathematics*, p. 12.

81. Buchanan to Adler, Adler Files, as quoted in Smith, *Search for a Liberal College*, p. 15.

82. Adler, *Philosopher at Large*, p. 116. Adler noted that: "In the early thirties, Scott Buchanan organized a series of theology lectures at the University of Virginia. When he invited me to give a number of them on especially difficult topics, such as the angelic hierarchy, or the resurrection of the body at the end of the world, I studied parts of the *Summa* that I might never have ventured into in pursuit of philosophical truth." (Adler, *Philosopher at Large*, p. 305.)

83. Ibid., p. 140. Mark Van Doren and Richard McKeon came out from Columbia University the following year to perform the same role.

84. Buchanan, *Poetry and Mathematics*, p. 26.
85. Barr, draft for *The Center Magazine*. Barr also noted that throughout this time Buchanan remained "thoroughly Oxonian. He never bustled or engaged in busy-work. Since he never stopped thinking, even while jesting, he lacked the average academic's motive for convincing himself that he is not idling."
86. Many years later Barr recalled this period:
    > . . . when Alderman died, the Richmond Times . . . . *Richmond Times Dispatch*, I guess, came out and said the two most likely successors were John Lloyd Newcomb and Stringfellow Barr. Well, I was only . . . . about thirty, I guess . . . . thirty-two, I suppose . . . . and never . . . . and not hungry for that job. But I was of course terribly flattered. . . .
    > . . . Newcomb succeeded him. And . . . . Newk was a nice guy, but he hadn't the slightest idea what it was all about. He was . . . . even though he was Dean of Engineering . . . . a very practical guy. But he had no liberal education that I know about really. And I was devoted to him, but I thought it was kind of an awful choice, but I don't know who the hell they could have gotten, really. Thank God I wasn't asked, because I probably would have found it difficult to decline, because of my feverish affection for the institution.

    (Stringfellow Barr, transcript of interview with Douglas Tanner, Kingston, N.J., September 12, 1972, p. 18. Accession no. RG 26/11, Folder: Barr, F. Stringfellow, Oral History, Special Collections. University of Virginia.)
87. Dabney, *Mr. Jefferson's University*, pp. 136–140. Newcomb was well regarded by the university community. In 1933 Newcomb became the first faculty member ever to receive the prestigious Raven Award from the Raven Society.
88. Letter from Buchanan to Adler, March 1934, as quoted in Smith, *Search for a Liberal College*, p. 15.
89. Ibid.
90. Barr, transcript of interview with Douglas Tanner, September 12, 1972, p. 18. Barr also remarked that "I think Bob [Gooch] probably chose the committee members." (Stringfellow Barr, transcript of interview with Allan Hoffman, August 3, 1975, p. 42. Stringfellow Barr Papers, Special Collections, St. John's College.)
91. Barr noted that: ". . . Bob Gooch, who was a former Rhodes Scholar and knew Scott [Buchanan]—never understood him very well but knew him and had known me when we were undergraduates—recognized that the elective system was pretty sick, there as elsewhere, and that there ought to be some kind of honors work—there ought to be something that every student didn't have to do but that was more worth doing than what the others did." (Stringfellow Barr, transcript of interview with Allan Hoffman, August 3, 1975, p. 42.)
92. Letter from John Newcomb to Robert Gooch, September 15, 1934, RG 2/1/2.491 II, Box 13, Folder: 1934–36: Honors Courses—Reports of Committee. Special Collections, University of Virginia.
93. Handwritten note from Robert Gooch to John Newcomb, September 18, 1934, RG 2/1/2.491 II, Box 13, Folder: 1934–36: Honors Courses—Reports of Committee. Special Collections, University of Virginia. In addition to Barr, Buchanan, and Gooch, the other committee members were chemistry professor Arthur F. Benton, mathematics professor John Jennings Luck, and Dean of the College George O. Ferguson, ex officio.
94. Barr, transcript of interview with Tanner, September 12, 1972, pp. 18–19.
95. Scott Buchanan, "A Scheme for a Course in General Honors," RG 2/1/2.491 II, Box 13, Special Collections, University of Virginia.
96. Stringfellow Barr, transcript of interview with Francis Mason and Allan Hoffman, October 5, 1975, p. 53. That Barr would have thought Gooch's political sensitivities "unfortunate" is corroborated by student recollections of them. Samuel (Pete) Anderson recalled that: "Barr played the role of dissident—a free thinking liberal; Gooch was much more buttoned-up." Author's interview with Samuel A. (Pete) Anderson, II, May 12, 1999, Charlottesville, VA.
97. Stringfellow Barr, transcript of interview with Francis Mason and Allan Hoffman, October 5, 1975, p. 53.
98. Robert Gooch, "Final Honors," handwritten statement, n.d. [1934–1935]. RG 2/1/2.491 II, Box 13, Special Collections, University of Virginia.

99. Smith, *Search for the Liberal College*, p. 17. Barr recollected further: "... I think Bob [Gooch] would have settled gladly for a transplant of Oxford. That is, trying to do some reading and some decent writing. And I think Bob rather quailed before Scott's Chicago-New York-Columbia-Adlerian stuff. And then he saw that I was interested and I think he himself got a little interested. But he, I'm sure, for his money what happened fruitfully was that some provisions were made for honors work in a field, in history or whatever you were "reading," as Oxford would put it. Bobby fell for Oxford very hard and it was probably almost snobbery, it seems to me, and I was fond of him but in this area he was limited—he had a very workable, good mind—but I don't think he ever got Scott's point." (Stringfellow Barr, transcript of interview with Allan Hoffman, August 3, 1975, p. 43.)
100. Barr, transcript of interview with Tanner, September 12, 1972, p. 21.
101. In his 1983 history, *A Search for the Liberal College*, University of Virginia graduate and St. John's tutor J. Winfree Smith argues that:
> When one considers that [Buchanan's plan] was to read in two years almost as many books as St. John's undergraduates now read in four years, and to read in their entirety books many of which are now read at St. John's only in part, and that the list contained Thomas Aquinas' *Summa Theologiae*, Part I, Newton's *Principia*, Kant's *Critique of Pure Reason*, Hegel's *Phenomenology*, Maxwell's *Treatise on Electricity and Magnetism*, etc., one sees the impossibility of the task. But the plan had not been put to the severe test of practice as it was to be later at St. John's. (Smith, *Search for the Liberal College*, p. 17.)
102. Scott Buchanan, "Supplement to A Scheme For A Course in General Honors," RG 2/1/2.491 II, Box 13, Special Collections, University of Virginia.
103. Stringfellow Barr, transcript of interview with Francis Mason and Allan Hoffman, October 5, 1975, p. 53. Based on her interview with Barr in November, 1970, in Kingston, New Jersey, Amy Kass wrote the following:
> At first, Stringfellow Barr was a severe critic of Buchanan's proposal.... Buchanan suggested a curriculum based on the great books and the liberal arts. Barr viewed this emphasis as some kind of patent medicine. However, after a great deal of teasing from Buchanan, he began making the collateral reading for his history courses some of the classics in the field. "For instance, if they were doing undergraduate ancient history, I would let them read Plutarch instead of something somebody had written about ancient Greece," Barr later recalled, "and I noticed Scott was right—that if you had discussions on the basis of Plutarch or Herodotus or Thucydides, something happened to the discussion that I had never seen before. These authors got under their hides."... As a result of this experience, Barr supported Buchanan's proposal and later joined Buchanan at the University of Chicago. (Amy Apfel Kass, *Radical Conservatives for Liberal Education*, unpublished Ph.D. Diss. Johns Hopkins University, 1973, p. 130, n. 33.)
104. "Committee on Honors Courses: Tentative Suggestions to Serve as a Possible Basis of Discussion," RG 2/1/2.491 II, Box 13, Special Collections, University of Virginia.
105. Ibid.
106. Ibid.
107. Ibid.
108. Stringfellow Barr, "Tentative Protocol Submitted to the Higher Contracting Powers," RG 2/1/2.491 II, Box 13, Special Collections, University of Virginia.
109. Ibid.
110. Ibid.
111. Barr, transcript of interview with Tanner, September 12, 1972, pp. 18–19. N.B. The monikers "Virginia Report" and "Virginia Plan" were used interchangeably by its authors. They were the same thing and in the interest of clarity this book uses exclusively the moniker "Virginia Plan." It is also important to note that, as will be explained, the Virginia Plan actually proposed two complimentary plans or schemes to be used in tandem: one plan for underclassmen and one plan for upperclassmen.

Chapter 3

1. Of the Virginia Plan great books scheme for the first two years, Barr later stated that: "It was a rather important device, ... this was the first adumbration; the second one was [Buchanan's] Supplement to the [1937 St. John's] Bulletin, which was out before there were

any people doing it … and then the full-blooded [1938 St. John's] Catalog came out when some were doing it." (Stringfellow Barr, transcript of interview with Chauncey G. Olinger, Jr., 1972, p. 14. Courtesy of Chauncey Olinger.)

2. Stringfellow Barr, handwritten draft of article for *The Center Magazine*, p. 14, 8053h, Box 4, Stringfellow Barr Papers, Special Collections, Alderman Library, University of Virginia, Charlottesville, VA.
3. Stringfellow Barr, transcript of interview with Chauncey G. Olinger, Jr., 1972, pp. 10, 11.
4. "Report of the Committee on Honors Courses to the President of the University," RG 2/1/2.491 II, Box 13, Folder: Honors Courses, 1934–36, Special Collections, University of Virginia.
5. Stringfellow Barr, Transcript of interview with Chauncey G. Olinger, Jr., 1972, pp. 13–16.
6. Smith rightly argued that the Virginia Plan was "a combination of the views of Buchanan and Gooch …" (J. Winfree Smith, *A Search for the Liberal College: The Beginning of the St. John's Program* [Annapolis: St. John's College Press, 1983], p. 17.)
7. Scott Buchanan, *Poetry and Mathematics* (John Day Co., 1929; reprint, Philadelphia: J. B. Lippincott Co., 1962), pp. 26–27.
8. Stringfellow Barr, transcript of interview with Douglas Tanner, Kingston, N.J., September 12, 1972, Accession no. RG 26/11, Folder: Barr, F. Stringfellow, p. 19. Virginia Oral History Project, Special Collections, University of Virginia. When asked to compare undergraduate education at Virginia and Oxford Barr replied:

    … the easiest way to state it in the case of examinations was that in America we examine the student to see if there's something he doesn't know, and at Oxford you examine the student to find out if there's anything he does know, and can state cogently and interestingly and maturely. So they give you terribly wide leeway on choice of subjects, because they're not trying to find corners of ignorance, they're trying to find out, "Have you any intellectual life of your own … that you're able to report on?" And this seems to me to be a big gain. (Barr, transcript of interview with Tanner, p. 8).

9. It is telling that the copy of the Virginia Plan that Barr had with him at St. John's, now in the Maryland State Archives, contained the introduction and Appendix A (the great books plan), but not Appendix B (the honors tutorial plan). (Stringfellow Barr Papers, deck 2, range 72, section 9, box 41, Maryland State Archives, Annapolis, MD.) At the same time, as will be seen in the discussion of St. John's in Chapter 4, there were elements of an Oxford education which Barr believed were essential, and which he insisted be a part of the St. John's curriculum, such as the Don Rag.
10. Amy Apfel Kass, *Radical Conservatives for Liberal Education,*" (Ph.D. Diss., Johns Hopkins University, 1973; [Ann Arbor: University Microfilms, 1973]), p. 1.
11. Ibid., p. 135.
12. Buchanan, *Poetry and Mathematics,* pp. 26–27. Although Barr, Buchanan, Hutchins, and Adler all came to believe that a liberal education was the best education for all college students, the Virginia conception of specific work in the liberal arts was always of an elite nature. A 1935 article written by Barr concurrent with the committee meetings that resulted in the Virginia Plan conveyed this elite understanding.

    … Mr. Jefferson has gone down in history as the great democrat; but every intelligent reader of a good biography of this man will recognize in him, in his tastes, in his restraints, in his sense of *noblesse oblige,* an aristocrat to the fingertips.

    The fact is that Mr. Jefferson fought strenuously against special privilege, the privilege of Hamilton's "rich and well-born." He fought for equality of opportunity. But he did *not* fight—as modern "democrats" have too often fought—for mediocrity. This will account for his own description of Jeffersonian democracy as an aristocracy of virtue and talent. He wanted character and intelligence, not birth or wealth to be the social differential. And he therefore explicitly planned a public school system and a university whose special responsibility would be to develop, for the benefit of the entire community, those potential leaders whose characters and talents seemed most worthy of development. It is this sort of democracy that has given the University of Virginia its curiously aristocratic tinge and it is this sort of democracy that attracts to the University young men from many states.

    (Stringfellow Barr, "Jefferson's University," *The Commonwealth: The Magazine of Virginia Business,* February 1935. Stringfellow Barr Papers, Section 2, Box 1, Folder 10, Special Collections, St. John's College.)

13. Virginius Dabney, *Mr. Jefferson's University: A History* (Charlottesville: University of Virginia Press, 1981), p. 170.
14. Ibid., p. 171.
15. Barr, transcript of interview with Tanner, September 12, 1972, p. 21.
16. "A Scheme for A Course in General Honors," RG 2/1/2.491 II, Box 13, Special Collections, University of Virginia.
17. Ibid.
18. Ibid. "The Original Jeffersonian Curriculum" submitted by Buchanan and the other committee members read as follows: "I. Languages (ancient): Latin, Greek, Hebrew; II. Languages (modern): French, Spanish, Italian, German, Anglo-Saxon; III. Mathematics (pure): Algebra, Fluxions, Geometry (elementary, transcendental), Architecture (military, naval); IV. Physico-Mathematics: Mechanics, Statics, Dynamics, Pneumatics, Acoustics, Optics, Astronomy, Geography; V. Physics or Natural Philosophy: Chemistry, Mineralogy; VI. Botany, Zoology; VII. Anatomy, Medicine; VIII. Government: Political Economy, Law of Nature, Law of Nations, History; IX. Law (municipal); X. Ideology: General Grammar, Ethics, Rhetoric, *Belles Lettres*, and Fine Arts."
19. Ibid.
20. Ibid.
21. Scott Buchanan, "Supplement to A Scheme For A Course in General Honors," RG 2/1/2.491 II, Box 13, Special Collections, University of Virginia.
22. Ibid.
23. Ibid.
24. Ibid.
25. Ibid.
26. Anonymous typewritten comments on the Committee on Honors' Virginia Plan. RG 2/1/2.491 II, Box 13, Special Collections, University of Virginia. As noted earlier, the committee members were willing to dispense with the term "honors" and instead institute a "President's List" as a sort of honor roll.
27. Barr, transcript of interview with Tanner, September 12, 1972, pp. 23–24.
28. Anonymous typewritten comments on the Committee on Honors' Virginia Plan. RG 2/1/2.491 II, Box 13, Special Collections, University of Virginia.
29. Dabney, *Mr. Jefferson's University*, p. 141.
30. "Annual Report of the Bursar," *University of Virginia Record*, various years.
31. Buchanan, *Poetry and Mathematics*, p. 27. Similar to the Buchanan recollection noted earlier in this chapter, the chronological sequence in this account of events is impossible. By the time that Newcomb appointed a Committee on Honors Courses—"the Gooch Committee"—in September 1934, Newcomb had been the president, not the acting president, for almost a year. When the committee presented the Virginia Plan to him in November 1935 he had been president for more than two years. The passage of almost thirty years seems to have blurred Buchanan's memory on some of these details, but chronology aside, Buchanan's other recollections square with other evidence. For example, Buchanan does suggest that Newcomb did not want to overreach his relatively new authority by undertaking such a radical departure from the status quo. This certainly agrees with Virginius Dabney's assessment of Newcomb that was discussed earlier in this chapter.
32. Barr, transcript of interview with Tanner, September 12, 1972, pp. 19–20. Just before the start of the Depression, Philip Francis DuPont, who as a student had been dismissed in 1900 for "persistent neglect of duty," bequeathed a trust fund of $6,000,000 to the university. (Dabney, *Mr. Jefferson's University*, p. 84). Presumably Barr is referring to members of Philip DuPont's family.
33. Stringfellow Barr, transcript of interview with Chauncey G. Olinger, Jr., 1972, pp. 16–17.
34. Letter from John L. Newcomb to Frederick P. Keppel, President, Carnegie Foundation, November 19, 1935. RG 2/1/2.491 II, Special Collections, University of Virginia.
35. Telegram from Frederick Keppel to John Newcomb, November 22, 1935, RG 2/1/2.491 II, Special Collections, University of Virginia.
36. Barr, transcript of interview with Tanner, September 12, 1972, p. 32.
37. Letter to John Luck from John Newcomb, March 7, 1936, RG 2/1/2.49 II, Box 13, Special Collections, University of Virginia.

Notes to Pages 94–99 • **223**

38. John J. Luck, Temporary Chairman, to the Committee on Academic Legislation, "Report of the Committee on Honors Courses to the President of the University," n.d. [1936]. RG 2/1/2.491 II. Box 13, 1934–36 Honors Courses—Reports of the Committee. Special Collections, University of Virginia. Comment 3, which was added to the existing comments 1 and 2, read: "The Dean of the College should not authorize any School to offer honors work unless the teaching load of such School shall have been sufficiently diminished to permit of adequate tutorial guidance."
39. As will also be seen in Chapter 6, this distinction was regarded as absolutely critical to later defenders of the upperclassman honors tutorial program.
40. The Committee on Honors Courses was replaced by the Committee on Special Programs in the 1960s which, by the late 1990s, no longer maintained any oversight function of the honors program.
41. Anonymous written statement submitted to Dean George O. Ferguson concerning degrees with honors, author unknown, undated [1936], pp. 1–2. RG 2/1/2.491 II, Box 13, Special Collections, University of Virginia.
42. Typewritten statement submitted to Dean George O. Ferguson concerning degrees with honors, undated [1936], pp. 1ff. RG 2/1/2.491 II, Box 13, Special Collections, University of Virginia.
43. Typewritten statement by Allan T. Gwathmey, no date [1936]. RG 2/1/2.491 II, Box 13, Special Collections, University of Virginia. Gwathmey's objection to an honors student graduating with any particular honors would be raised again by other faculty members in the 1960s and 70s.
44. In spite of this provision for possible coursework, in practice the advice of the Committee on Honors Courses seems to have been to exempt honors students from course requirements. Indeed, by 1960, students in the Honors Program were "forbidden to take courses for credit." Memo to the Committee on Academic Legislation and the Committee on Academic Policy from David C. Yalden-Thomson, Chairman, Committee on Honors Courses, February, 1960. Accession No. 5547-d, "Gooch" box, Folder 1958–62. Special Collections, University of Virginia.
45. Typewritten manuscript from the "President's Committee on Honors Courses in the University of Virginia," pp. 1–2. RG 2/1/2.491 II, Box 13, Special Collections, University of Virginia.
46. It is interesting to note that, of the seventeen departments that eventually offered honors work, these two departments were the first, in the fall of 1936 and the spring of 1937, respectively, to submit departmental honors program outlines for faculty consideration. Moreover, by 2000, they were the sole departments that continued to offer honors programs.
47. Handwritten note from R. K. Gooch, October 8, 1936, RG 2/1/2.491 II, Box 13, Special Collections, University of Virginia.
48. *Candidates for Final Honors Programme of Studies in Political Science*, by R. K. Gooch, October 1936, RG 2/1/2.491 II, Box 13, Special Collections, University of Virginia.
49. Ibid.
50. Memo from David C. Yalden-Thomson, Chairman, Committee on Honors Courses, to the Committee on Academic Legislation and the Committee on Academic Policy, February 1960, p. 1. 5547-d, Box: "Gooch," Special Collections, University of Virginia.
51. Memo from Ivey F. Lewis to President Colgate Darden, n.d. [1950], RG 2/1/2.562, Box 15, Special Collections, Alderman Library.
52. Letter from John Newcomb to Robert Gooch, February 20, 1937, RG 2/1/2.491 III, Box 7, Special Collections, University of Virginia.
53. In spite of this official name change, the monikers "Committee on Honors Courses," "Committee on Degrees with Honors" and the abbreviated, "Committee on Honors" were all used interchangeably at Virginia from this time on.
54. Letter from Robert Gooch to the Academic Schools, April 28, 1937, RG 2/1/2.491 III, Box 7, Special Collections, University of Virginia.
55. *Program for Degrees with Honors in Philosophy*, by W. S. Weedon, L. M. Hammond, and others, 1937. (Courtesy of Norman Cohen Coliver, Esq. and Chauncey L. Olinger, Jr.)
56. Ibid.
57. By the 1960s, the honors program enrolled between 32 and 87 students per year and awarded between 7 and 38 degrees with honors per year. ("The College Honors Program at

the University of Virginia, 1968," Francis R. Hart, Chairman, Committee on Special Programs, May 1968. Courtesy of Chauncey G. Olinger, Jr. and Professor John Marshall.)
58. "1939 University of Virginia Graduating Exercises" Program, June 12, 1939, p. 12. (Courtesy of Norman Cohen Coliver, Esq. and Professor John Marshall.)
59. Memo to the Committee on Academic Legislation and the Committee on Academic Policy from David C. Yalden-Thomson, Chairman, Committee on Honors Courses, February, 1960. Accession No. 5547-d, "Gooch" box, Folder 1958–62. Special Collections, University of Virginia. In the memo Yalden-Thomson wrote that:
> The present program of Honors work in the College was started on the initiative of President Newcomb in the 1930s. President Newcomb considered that, under the program for the regular B.A. degree, not enough was being done for the more gifted student. The committee which studied this matter, under the Chairmanship of Professor R. K. Gooch, recommended a new program of study leading to the B.A. degree with Honors. These recommendations were accepted with slight change by the Committee on Academic Legislation, were approved by the faculty of the College without a dissenting vote and were endorsed by President Newcomb. Thus was instituted the Honors Program presently administered by the Committee on Honors Courses. At the time of its inception no other state university in America offered any such program. (p. 1.)

This archival evidence does say "state university," so it is unclear if there were similar programs at private institutions. Although it cannot be disproved, there is no evidence or mention in the documentation that such a purely "Oxbridge" program existed elsewhere. Chauncey Olinger, a 1955 graduate of the UVa philosophy honors program, along with John Marshall and George Thomas, both chairmen emeriti of the honors program in philosophy at Virginia, all believe the current honors program in philosophy to be the sole tutorial honors program of its kind in the United States. Regardless of its possibly continuing unique status, the tutorial honors program at Virginia was, according to this archival documentation and personal interviews, the first in American public higher education.
60. See Dabney, *Mr. Jefferson's University*, p. 468.
61. Dabney, *Mr. Jefferson's University*, p. 270. Gooch also stated that: "[Newcomb] probably would have [had] a much better time and much more time to think about various academic policies and so on if he hadn't been so much restricted by this terrific disadvantage of being President during the Depression and during the war." (Robert Gooch, transcript of interview with Robert Light, Charlottesville, VA., March 15, 1973. RG 26/13, Folder: Gooch, Robert Kent, p. 1ff. Virginia Oral History Project, Special Collections, University of Virginia.)
62. Ibid., p. 170.

Chapter 4

1. Letter from Mortimer Adler to Scott Buchanan, [1935], Buchanan Files, Houghton Library, Harvard University, as quoted in J. Winfree Smith, *A Search for the Liberal College: The Beginning of the St. John's Program* (Annapolis: St. John's College Press, 1983), p. 19.
2. Letter from Scott Buchanan to Mortimer Adler, [1935], Buchanan Files, Houghton Library, Harvard University, as quoted in Smith, *A Search for the Liberal College*, p. 19.
3. Ibid.
4. Letter from Adler to Buchanan, [1935], as quoted in J. Winfree Smith, *A Search for the Liberal College*, p. 19.
5. Ibid. In regard to Adler's comments, "Arthur" is Arthur Rubin, whom Adler had met when he was an undergraduate and Rubin a doctoral student in the Psychology Department at Columbia. (A *bon vivant*, Rubin introduced Adler "to vintage wine accompanied by sliced apples, ripe cheese, and dry crackers.") Mortimer Adler, *Philosopher at Large: An Intellectual Autobiography* (New York: Macmillan, 1977), pp. 53–54.
6. Letter from Buchanan to Adler, [1935 or 1936], as quoted in Smith, *A Search for the Liberal College*, p. 19.
7. Stringfellow Barr, transcript of interview with Allan Hoffman, July 13, 1975, p. 4. Stringfellow Barr Papers, Special Collections, Greenfield Library, St. John's College, Annapolis, MD.
8. Letter from Buchanan to Adler, [1935 or 1936], as quoted in Smith, *A Search for the Liberal College*, p. 19.

Notes to Pages 102–104 • **225**

9. Mary Ann Dzuback, *Robert M. Hutchins: Portrait of an Educator* (Chicago: University of Chicago Press, 1991), p. 127.
10. Stringfellow Barr, "The St. John's Program," n.d. [1938], p.1. Stringfellow Barr Papers, Special Collections, Alderman Library, University of Virginia, Charlottesville, VA.
11. Board of Trustees Minutes, University of Chicago, 26:31, March 12, 1936, Special Collections, Regenstein Library, University of Chicago, Chicago, IL.
12. McNeill notes that, "An associate of Adler and McKeon at Columbia, Rubin was a man whose thrust after a single, saving truth made Adler seem almost like a middle-of-the-road moderate." William H. McNeill, *Hutchins' University: A Memoir of the University of Chicago, 1929–1950* (Chicago: University of Chicago Press, 1991), p. 70.
13. Stringfellow Barr, transcript of interview with Douglas Tanner, Kingston, N.J., September 12, 1972, p. 21. Accession no. RG 26/11, Folder: Barr, F. Stringfellow, Oral History, Special Collections, University of Virginia.
14. Letter from Mortimer Adler to Scott Buchanan, February 29, 1936, Mortimer Adler Papers, Box 27, Folder 5, Special Collections, University of Chicago.
15. Amy Apfel Kass, *Radical Conservatives for Liberal Education* (Unpublished Ph.D. Diss., Johns Hopkins University, 1973), p. 142.
16. Kass, *Radical Conservatives*, p. 144. For additional information on the Committee on the Liberal Arts, see: Dzuback, *Robert M. Hutchins*, pp. 127–128; Kass, *Radical Conservatives*, pp. 142–152; McNeill, *Hutchins' University*, pp. 70–71; and Smith, *Search for the Liberal College*, pp. 19–21.
17. Memorandum from Robert Hutchins to E. T. Filbey, dated August 24, 1936, Robert M. Hutchins Papers, 51/2, Special Collections, University of Chicago. Hutchins continued: "The committee should work continuously at the University on the problem it was created to study. Their efforts will be greatly facilitated and they will seem to the faculty to be much better established if they have adequate quarters."
18. Dzuback, *Robert M. Hutchins*, p. 127.
19. Scott Buchanan, *Poetry and Mathematics* (John Day Co., 1929; reprint, Philadelphia: J. B. Lippincott Co., 1962), p. 27. (page citation is to the reprint edition).
20. Harris Wofford, Jr., ed. *Embers of The World: Conversations with Scott Buchanan* (Santa Barbara: The Center for the Study of Democratic Institutions, 1969), pp. 86–87.
21. Stringfellow Barr, transcript of interview with Charles and Mary Wiseman, July 6, 1975, p. 41. Stringfellow Barr Papers, Special Collections, St. John's College.
22. Wofford, *Embers of The World*, pp. 86–87. Of the decision to leave Virginia for Chicago, Barr recounted that:

    Finally, I decided that I didn't want to go. I remember a conversation—Mortimer Adler was there. Scott and he twisted my wrist for about two hours, and finally Mortimer said, "I've got a question. You say you're interested in history and want to teach history and you don't want to go to the University of Chicago and don't feel philosophically fitted for the task that we want to undertake, and we are philosophers and you aren't. Just answer one question and I'll let you alone." It was more than one question—Scott had some too—but it came to this: "Which do you care most about, history or truth?" I knew what he meant, and said, "The truth, of course." And then I said, "Oh, go to hell! I'll come, I guess. But I'm only going on a year's leave." This disgusted Scott, and he said, "Now don't put your foot in the water that way. You're not going to find out what the water's like unless you dive." And I said, "Well, I'm not going to find out what the water's like then, because I'm going to put my foot in."

    On another occasion Barr stated that: "I went to Chicago expecting to stay there at least for three years, probably, although I accepted only for a year. . . ." In making the move, Barr's salary increased from $4500 to $6000. When he later accepted the presidency of St. John's his salary was increased to $7500. (Barr, transcript of interview with Chauncey Olinger, 1972, p. 54. Courtesy of Chauncey G. Olinger, Jr.).
23. Letter from Scott Buchanan to Mortimer Adler, February 26, 1936, Mortimer Adler Papers, Box 27, Folder 5, Special Collections, University of Chicago.
24. Barr, transcript of interview with Tanner, September 12, 1972, p. 21.
25. Letter from Stringfellow Barr to Mortimer Adler, March 15, 1936, Mortimer Adler Papers, Box 27, Folder 5, Special Collections, University of Chicago.

26. Letter from Scott Buchanan to Mortimer Adler, March 13, 1936, Mortimer Adler Papers, Box 27, Folder 5, Special Collections, University of Chicago.
27. Letter from Barr to Adler, March 15, 1936.
28. Letter from Mortimer Adler to Scott Buchanan, February 29, 1936, Mortimer Adler Papers, Box 27, Folder 5, Special Collections, University of Chicago.
29. Letter from Buchanan to Adler, March 13, 1936.
30. Letter from Scott Buchanan to Mortimer Adler, February 26, 1936, Mortimer Adler Papers, Box 27, Folder 5, Special Collections, University of Chicago. This letter contains a full description of the five students considered by Barr and Buchanan.
31. Ibid.
32. Letter from Stringfellow Barr to Mortimer Adler, March 6, 1936, Mortimer Adler Papers, Box 27, Folder 5, Special Collections, University of Chicago.
33. Letter from Buchanan to Adler, March 13, 1936.
34. Letter from Barr to Adler, March 15, 1936.
35. Letter from Mortimer Adler to Stringfellow Barr, March 12, 1936, Mortimer Adler Papers, Box 27, Folder 5, Special Collections, University of Chicago.
36. Barr, transcript of interview with Allan Hoffman, August 3, 1975, p. 44. Stringfellow Barr Papers, Special Collections, St. John's College.
37. Initially Hutchins had tried to appoint Adler to the Philosophy Department by presidential proclamation. When the department refused the appointment, Hutchins, with the approval of the Dean of the Law School, appointed Adler to the Law School faculty as a professor of philosophy of law. With this appointment, Adler taught, not only in the Law School, but also in the college. Many of the college faculty regarded this maneuver as Hutchins' attempt to circumvent the faculty's usual role in decisions regarding appointments and it made the faculty suspicious of Hutchins. See William McNeill, *Hutchins' University: A Memoir of the University of Chicago, 1929–1950*. Chicago: University of Chicago Press, 1991.
38. Barr, transcript of interview with Allan Hoffman, August 3, 1975, p. 46.
39. Barr, transcript of interview with Allan Hoffman, July 13, 1975, p. 6. The syllabus for Barr's historiography class, History 201, notes four required readings. The first three were the main works by Herodotus, Bede, and Gibbon. In addition to being required "to exhibit a reasonable familiarity with the factual content" of these readings, students were expected to criticize, "the methods of these three historians in the light of *Introduction to the Study of History*," by Ch. V. Langlois and Ch. Seignobos, trans. by G. G. Berry (New York: Henry Holt and Company, 1898), which according to Barr, was "perhaps the best known manual on modern historical methodology." "Syllabus for History 201, University of Chicago, Fall Quarter, 1936" Stringfellow Barr Papers, Section 2, Box 30, Folder 18, Special Collections, St. John's College.
40. Letter from Scott Buchanan to Robert Hutchins, May 25, 1936, Mortimer Adler Papers, Box 27, Folder 5, Special Collections, University of Chicago.
41. *The Cavalier*, September 1936, Stringfellow Barr Papers, Section 2, Box 4, Folder 23, p. 8. Special Collections, St. John's College.
42. Ibid.
43. Hutchins, "Report of the President, 1935–36" (unpublished, University of Chicago, 1937), pp. 21–22, as quoted in Harry S. Ashmore, *Unseasonable Truths: The Life of Robert Maynard Hutchins* (Boston: Little, Brown and Company, 1989), p. 137.
44. Scott Buchanan, "A Crisis in Liberal Education" (Annapolis: Capital-Gazette Press, n.d. [1938]; reprinted from the *Amherst Graduates' Quarterly*, February 1938, Vol. XXVII, No. 2, pp. 106–118), p. 13. Robert M. Hutchins Papers Addenda, Box 19, Folder 2, Special Collections, University of Chicago.
45. Barr, transcript of interview with Chauncey Olinger, 1972, pp. 42–43.
46. Committee on the Liberal Arts, "Minutes. October 3, 1936," p. 1. Mortimer Adler Papers 57, UC1, Special Collections, University of Chicago. Other members, who apparently never played much, if any, role in the committee meetings are listed in Kass, *Radical Conservatives*, p. 143ff and in Adler, *Philosopher at Large*, p. 174.
47. "The Work of the Inner Committee," Mortimer J. Adler Papers, Box 57, Folder: "Virginia Plan," Special Collections, University of Chicago.
48. See Kass, *Radical Conservatives*, pp. 146–151, for a detailed account of the members' competing philosophies.

49. Barr, transcript of interview with Chauncey Olinger, 1972, p. 38.
50. Ibid., p. 33.
51. Ibid., p. 38.
52. Buchanan, *Poetry and Mathematics*, p. 27.
53. Barr, transcript of interview with Chauncey Olinger, 1972, p. 41.
54. Buchanan, "A Crisis in Liberal Education," p. 13.
55. Barr, *The St. John's Program*.
56. Buchanan, "A Crisis in Liberal Education," p. 13.
57. Ashmore, *Unseasonable Truths*, p. 138.
58. Buchanan, *Poetry and Mathematics*, p. 28.
59. McNeill, *Hutchins' University*, p. 71.
60. F. Champion Ward, ed., *The Idea and Practice of General Education: An Account of the College of the University of Chicago* (Chicago: University of Chicago Press, 1950; reprint, Chicago: University of Chicago Press, 1992), p. 58. (page citation is to the reprint edition). Frodin's "major revision" was the 1929 "New Plan" noted in Chapter 1.
61. Barr, transcript of interview with Allan Hoffman, July 13, 1975, p. 7.
62. Barr, handwritten draft of article for *The Center Magazine*, p. 14, 8053h, Box 4, Stringfellow Barr Papers, Special Collections, University of Virginia.
63. Barr once remarked that Rubin didn't do the reading, so he wasn't really part of their group.
64. Barr, transcript of interview with Allan Hoffman, July 13, 1975, p. 14.
65. Barr, draft for *The Center Magazine*, p. 16.
66. Ibid., p.15. On a separate occasion Barr noted that: "Aristotle annoys me. I think he's got a sharp mind but he annoys me by—there's a certain aridity about him, after [reading] Plato. You feel like saying, 'Oh come on, did you ever smell a flower? Life is better than you are painting it.' But Plato seems to me just terrific." (Barr, transcript of interview with Charles and Mary Wiseman, July 6, 1975, p. 56.)
67. Ibid.
68. Catesby Taliaferro and Charles Wallis, unpublished papers. President's Papers, 1925–1945, Box 51, Folder 2, Special Collections, University of Chicago.
69. Essays from Scott Buchanan to Robert Hutchins, n.d. [1936], Number I, p. 1. Stringfellow Barr Papers, Section 2, Box 30, Folder 13, Special Collections, St. John's College.
70. Ibid., p. 2.
71. Ibid., p. 8.
72. Ibid.
73. Ibid., p. 9.
74. Essays from Scott Buchanan to Robert Hutchins, n.d. [1936], Number II, p. 1. Stringfellow Barr Papers, Section 2, Box 30, Folder 13, Special Collections, St. John's College.
75. Ibid., p. 5.
76. Ibid., p. 6. Buchanan elaborated that this criterion, "works on contemporary books as well as on ancient books, although the great contemporary book may not turn out to be great when it is as old as the ancient books are. This kind of criterion gets rid of a lot of nonsense, although it hardly gives us an easy rule to apply to books published before there were lists of best sellers, and it doesn't take account of historical accidents such as the burning of the library at Alexandria. But it serves to stop us from trying to achieve impossible angelic or divine perfection and precision in our judgments."
77. Ibid. As elaboration: "This is also shocking, particularly to those who rest their case for the liberal arts on logic and want completely ambiguous reading, writing, and arithmetic.... A really ambiguous book has no reading or interpretation at all; it is nonsense. On the other hand, a book with many interpretations has multi-dimensional-univocality; it may say many things, or the same thing in many ways, in each case gaining in artistic and intellectual power and precision. I am thinking not only of Plato, Dante, and Aesop, but also of those books that achieve great generality and therefore can be understood on all lower levels. This last point is particularly obvious in mathematical classics."
78. Ibid., p. 7. Buchanan added: "This again has a paradoxical tone about it. This does not mean that a great book merely asks questions students or professors cannot answer; many bad books try to do that. A great book answers so many questions that on the basis of those answers, questions are asked that couldn't be asked without them. I mean that, but I also mean that great books are often about matters that are really unanswerable, in short the

ultimate in thought and being. Furthermore, I should say that great books always touch these matters in more or less direct ways; they exercise the intuitive reason and the contemporary imagination."
79. Ibid. Finally: "As a work of fine art it must be a microcosm mirroring all the other books and as many things as man knows or can know. This is the hardest criterion to apply, but in relation to the others above is obvious enough to understand."
80. Ibid., pp. 12–13.
81. Ibid., p. 14.
82. Essays from Scott Buchanan to Robert Hutchins, n.d. [1936], Number III, p. 2. Stringfellow Barr Papers, Section 2, Box 30, Folder 13, Special Collections, St. John's College.
83. Ibid., p. 3.
84. Ibid., p. 12.
85. Ibid., pp. 12–13.
86. Essays from Scott Buchanan to Robert Hutchins, n.d. [1936], Number I, p. 10.
87. "Report To The President On The Committee On The Liberal Arts," March 29, 1937, President's Papers, 1925–1945, Box 51, Folder 2, Special Collections, University of Chicago.
88. Barr, transcript of interview with Allan Hoffman, July 13, 1975, p. 14.
89. Ibid., p. 10.
90. Ibid., p. 16.
91. Letter from Stringfellow Barr to his mother, Ida Barr, February 21, 1937, RG 2/1/2.491 III, Box 2, Folder: 1937–38 "B" President's Office, Special Collections, University of Virginia.
92. Barr, transcript of interview with Allan Hoffman, July 13, 1975, p. 16.
93. Barr, transcript of interview with Allan Hoffman, August 3, 1975, p. 44.
94. Board of Trustees Minutes, University of Chicago, 27: 39, March 11, 1937, Special Collections, University of Chicago.
95. Letter from Stringfellow Barr to John Newcomb, April 3, 1937, Stringfellow Barr Papers, Section 2, Box 29, Folder 56, Special Collections, St. John's College.
96. Handwritten note from Ida Barr to John Newcomb, April 15, 1937, RG 2/1/2.491 III, Box 2, Folder: 1937–38 "B" President's Office, Special Collections, University of Virginia.
97. Letter from John Newcomb to Ida Barr, April 17, 1937, RG 2/1/2.491 III, Box 2, Folder: 1937–38 "B" President's Office, Special Collections, University of Virginia.
98. To say St. John's is the nation's third oldest college, as Barr did, is debatable, although perhaps more an issue of semantics than substance. Following Harvard College and the College of William and Mary in succession, St. John's had been established as King William's School in 1696. It did not receive its collegiate charter, and the name St. John's College, however, until 1784.
99. Barr, transcript of interview with Allan Hoffman, July 13, 1975, p. 10.
100. Barr later recorded that these decisions had been highly stressful for him to make. When first presented with the idea of putting their ideas into practice at St. John's, Barr said, "I was alarmed. I had recently brought myself to resign from the Virginia faculty and, because I had strong ties with the institution and warm friendships there, I developed such a bout of psychosomatic colitis that I was hospitalized. Nevertheless, it ended by our going." (Barr, draft for *The Center Magazine*, p. 16.)
101. Barr, "The St. John's Program," p. 4. Regarding the College's debt, Barr wrote:
> From time to time the Board had asked itself questions concerning the proper function of a liberal arts college. But the most tangible answer they had received had landed them in the most trouble. In the booming 'twenties, the antiquity of the College and the colonial authenticity of Annapolis led to a confused effort to bring to life again the urbanity and poise of eighteenth-century civilization. Mr. Rockefeller was just then restoring Williamsburg, and the late Mr. Francis Garvin suggested similar glories for St. John's and for Annapolis. The College became the focus of a colonial restoration. October, 1929, fatefully intervened and left the College loaded with colonial property and with a debt under which it was still reeling in 1937.

102. Barr, transcript of interview with Chauncey G. Olinger, Jr., 1972, p. 63.
103. See Smith, *A Search for The Liberal College*, for a more extensive discussion of this period, p. 21ff.
104. Buchanan, "A Crisis in Liberal Education," p. 5.

Notes to Pages 121–124 • **229**

105. Smith, *A Search for the Liberal College*, p. 21.
106. Stringfellow Barr, transcript of interview with Allan Hoffman, August 3, 1975, p. 48.
107. Scott Buchanan, as quoted in Smith, *A Search for the Liberal College*, p. 22.
108. Buchanan, "A Crisis in Liberal Education," p. 13. Robert M. Hutchins Papers Addenda, Box 19, Folder 2, Special Collections, University of Chicago. Because of Barr and Buchanan's departure, on July 5, 1937, Hutchins named Arthur Rubin the acting chairman of the Committee on the Liberal Arts. (President's Papers, 1925–1945, Box 51, Folder 2, Special Collections, University of Chicago). By the end of the year, the Committee was dissolved "because of changes in the work and location of the personnel, [and] a foundation [The Liberal Arts Foundation] has been organized for the promotion of the work in the liberal arts which will continue the work on a different basis at Chicago and elsewhere...." (Board of Trustees Minutes, University of Chicago, 27: 280, December 9, 1937, Special Collections, University of Chicago.) The Liberal Arts Foundation, which supplied philanthropic support from Mrs. Marion R. Stern and Mrs. David M. Levy to Chicago, and anonymously to St. John's, was officially dissolved on October 17, 1942. (Robert M. Hutchins Papers Addenda, Box 85, Folder 1, Special Collections, University of Chicago).
109. Stringfellow Barr, transcript of interview with Allan Hoffman, August 3, 1975, p. 48.
110. McNeill, *Hutchins' University*, p. 71.
111. Years later Barr recalled that the two men had dickered over who should hold the administrative positions:
    > Buchanan said that I would have to be president. I scoffed at the idea and reminded him that the curriculum we had dreamed of was his baby, not mine. But, he answered, he couldn't be president: he didn't answer his mail. I retorted that this was because he believed a lot of it was not worth answering. He agreed but pointed out that his correspondents thought it was, so I would have to be president. I groaned and told him that he would have to be dean. He loudly objected, but I declined to budge.

    (Barr, draft for *The Center Magazine*, p. 16. Barr resigned from Chicago effective June 30, 1937, Buchanan effective December 31, 1937. (Board of Trustees Minutes, University of Chicago, 27:170, July 8, 1937; 28:8, January 13, 1938, Special Collections, University of Chicago).
112. Buchanan, "A Crisis in Liberal Education," p. 13.
113. Letter from R. Catesby Taliaferro to Mortimer Adler, July 5, 1937, Mortimer J. Adler Papers, Box 57, Folder: "St. John's Founding." Special Collections, University of Chicago.
114. Letter from Mortimer Adler to Catesby Taliaferro, July 21, 1937, Mortimer J. Adler Papers, Box 57, Folder: "St. John's Founding." Special Collections, University of Chicago.
115. Letter from John Newcomb to "Winkie" Barr, June 24, 1937, RG 2/1/2.491 III, Box 2, Folder: 1937–38 "B" President's Office, Special Collections, University of Virginia.
116. Handwritten letter from Ida Barr to John Newcomb, dated Tuesday [June 1937], RG 2/1/2.491 III, Box 2, Folder: 1937–38 "B" President's Office, Special Collections, University of Virginia.
117. Letter from John Newcomb to Ida Barr, June 26, 1937, RG 2/1/2.491 III, Box 2, Folder: 1937–38 "B" President's Office. Special Collections, University of Virginia.
118. Mortimer J. Adler, *A Second Look in the Rearview Mirror: Further Autobiographical Reflections of a Philosopher at Large* (New York: Macmillan Publishing Co., 1992), p. 37.
119. Buchanan, *Poetry and Mathematics*, p. 28.
120. Buchanan, "A Crisis in Liberal Education," p. 13.
121. Barr, "The St. John's Program," p. 5.
122. Ibid., p. 4.
123. Stringfellow Barr, Obituary of Scott Buchanan in *The American Oxonian*, October 1968, pp. 276–280. Stringfellow Barr Papers, Accession no. 8053h, Box 4, Special Collections, University of Virginia. Barr wrote in 1939 that the ultimate goal of a St. John's education was the following:
    > The student ought by graduation to have achieved a disciplined mind, and such an achievement implied a quickened imagination, the power to reason clearly, the capacity to apply theory in practice. In addition to being able to read, write, and reckon more skillfully and fruitfully than the American college graduate of today commonly does, in addition to being able and willing to face real prob-

lems, he should be able to recognize those eternal problems which his ancestors faced before him and which recur for every generation of human beings. Experience had taught that the best statements of those problems are the "classics" of human thought. And since the student, whether he likes it or no, will have to do his thinking and feeling in the great European tradition to which he was born, his best chance of discovering himself lay in claiming his natural heritage—the wisdom of that tradition. For that wisdom he would have to turn, not to the college textbooks which discussed it at second hand, but to the classics, the "great books," both of ancient and modern times. There in the company of great minds he would learn to deal with great problems. (Barr, "The St. John's Program," p. 12.)

124. Barr, "The St. John's Program," p. 10.
125. Barr, transcript of interview with Charles and Mary Wiseman, July 6, 1975, p. 65. Of the Don Rag at Oxford Barr recollected: ". . . they'd get you and drill the hell out of you. And they were ruthless. It was worse than being rude because if they were rude you could stand the abrasive SOBs. I don't care what you say. They were very courteous on top but obviously gunning for you and I found that it had a hell of an effect on the student body. You're on a pretty hot spot if you've been there for some months and then you walk around without knowing what it's all about." (p. 154).

To the suggestion that Oxford played an "important role" in the conception of the "New Program" at St. John's, Barr replied:

It certainly did in my case. . . . My impression is that it played a less[er] role in Scott's case. . . . For instance, I remember urging the Don Rag. I think Scott put it in because I seemed to think it important and he had no proof that it wasn't, he just didn't particularly think it was. But I think he put it in because he thought maybe I was right. He could try it. There wouldn't be any harm. And I think later was damn glad he did. (Stringfellow Barr, transcript of interview with David Rea and Allan Hoffman, November 22, 1975, p. 154. Stringfellow Barr Papers, Special Collections, St. John's College.)

At the suggestion of Barr's wife, whose father had been an Oxford don, the Oxford tradition of a "high table" in the dining hall was also implemented at St. John's. (Stringfellow Barr, transcript of interview with David Rea and Allan Hoffman, November 22, 1975, p. 154.)

126. Adler, *A Second Look in the Rearview Mirror*, p. 65.
127. Smith, *A Search for the Liberal College*, p. 45.
128. Stringfellow Barr, transcript of interview with Francis Mason, June 29, 1975, p. 57. Stringfellow Barr Papers, Special Collections, St. John's College.
129. Barr, as quoted in Smith, *A Search for the Liberal College*, p. 45.
130. Smith, *A Search for the Liberal College*, p. 45. Robert Hutchins pulled the Chicago Maroons football team, the "Monsters of the Midway," out of the Big 10 in 1939, too. (See Ronald J. Kim, *Life on the Quads: A Centennial View of the Student Experience at the University of Chicago* [Chicago: University of Chicago Library, 1992], p. 60ff). In 1951 Robert Gooch and others served on a committee at Virginia that recommended elimination of all athletic scholarships at the University and proposed abandoning intercollegiate football. The committee's recommendations were not enacted. (See Dabney, *Mr. Jefferson's University*, p. 318ff.)
131. Stringfellow Barr, *The Ends and Means of General Education*, reprinted from the Proceedings of the Fifty-third Annual Convention of the Middle States Association of Colleges and Secondary Schools, 1939, p. 10. Stringfellow Barr Papers, Special Collections, University of Virginia.
132. Walter Lippman, "The St. John's Program," reprinted from "Today and Tomorrow," *New York Herald Tribune*, December 27, 1938. Alexander Meiklejohn Papers, Box 57, Folder 4, Wisconsin Historical Society Archives, Madison, WI.
133. Mark Van Doren, *Liberal Education*. (New York: Henry Holt and Company, 1943), p. 153.
134. John Andrews Rice, "Fundamentalism and the Higher Learning," *Harper's*, May 1937, p. 266. Quoted by William Buchanan, "Educational Rebels in the Nineteen Thirties," *Journal of General Education*, 37, No. 1, 1985, pp. 3–33.
135. Stringfellow Barr, Obituary of Scott Buchanan in *The American Oxonian*, October 1968, p. 278.

136. Charles E. Clark, "The Higher Learning in a Democracy," *The International Journal of Ethics*, Vol. XLVII, No. 3, (April 1937), pp. 322–323. Mortimer J. Adler Papers, Box 77, Special Collections, University of Chicago.
137. Harry Gideonse, a critic of Hutchins at Chicago at the time that *The Higher Learning in America* was published in 1936, wrote that Hutchins had produced: "volumes in support of the thesis that there should be a unifying philosophy, [but] without specific indication of the type of unity or of philosophy...." (Harry D. Gideonse, *The Higher Learning in a Democracy: A Reply to President Hutchins' Critique of the American University* [New York: Farrer & Rhinehart, 1947], p. 3., as quoted in Bruce Kimball, *Orators & Philosophers: A History of the Idea of Liberal Education,* expanded edition [New York: The College Board, 1995], p. 279.) Winfree Smith, a more sympathetic chronicler, likewise observed that in *The Higher Learning,* "No specific metaphysics is advocated." (Smith, *A Search for the Liberal College*, p. 23).
138. Clark, "The Higher Learning in a Democracy," p. 323.
139. Ibid.
140. John Pilley, "The Liberal Arts and Progressive Education," *The Social Frontier*, Vol V., No. 44, April, 1939, p. 212. Mortimer J. Adler Papers, Box 77, Special Collections, University of Chicago.
141. Ibid., p. 216.
142. Photo caption accompanying article by Sidney Hook, "Ballyhoo at St. John's College—Education in Retreat," *The New Leader*, May 27, 1944, p. 8. Mortimer J. Adler Papers, Box 77, Special Collections, University of Chicago.
143. Francis P. Donnelly, "The Curriculum Controversy," *The Commonweal*, August 26, 1938, p. 441. Mortimer J. Adler Papers, Box 77, Special Collections, University of Chicago.
144. John Dewey, "Challenge to Liberal Thought," *Fortune*, August 1944. Mortimer J. Adler Papers, Box 77, Special Collections, University of Chicago.
145. Ibid.
146. Alexander Meiklejohn, "A Reply to John Dewey," Pamphlet, reprint from *Fortune*, January 1945. Mortimer J. Adler Papers, Box 77, Special Collections, University of Chicago.
147. Ibid.
148. Ibid. In subsequent letters to the Editors of *Fortune* in March 1945, Dewey claimed that Meiklejohn misconceived his meaning while Meiklejohn claimed Dewey had misconceived his.
149. Sidney Hook, "Ballyhoo at St. John's College—Education in Retreat," *The New Leader*, May 27, 1944, pp. 8–9. Mortimer J. Adler Papers, Box 77, Special Collections, University of Chicago.
150. Ibid.
151. Ibid.
152. Ibid.
153. Stringfellow Barr, *The Ends and Means of General Education*, p. 7.
154. Ibid., p. 11.
155. Barr, *The St. John's Program*.
156. Barr, *The Ends and Means of General Education*, p. 11.
157. Ibid.
158. Letter from Scott Buchanan to Emily Hamblen, April 27, 1940, as quoted in Smith, *A Search for the Liberal College*, p. 58.
159. Barr, transcript of interview with Chauncey Olinger, 1972, p. 46.
160. Letter to "Winkie" Barr from Garrard Glenn, "Spring Hill," Ivy Depot, VA, August 12, 1937. Stringfellow Barr Papers T1404, St. John's College 2/72/9, Box 20, Folder: Correspondence G-Gl, Maryland State Archives, Annapolis, MD.
161. John Dewey, Letter to the Editors, *Fortune*, March 1945. Mortimer J. Adler Papers, Box 77, Special Collections, University of Chicago.
162. Alexander Meiklejohn, Letter to the Editors, *Fortune*, March 1945. Mortimer J. Adler Papers, Box 77, Special Collections, University of Chicago.
163. Robert Hutchins, "Memorandum on Education," November 13, 1941, p. 5. President's Papers, 1940–1963, Box 22, Folder 5, Special Collections, University of Chicago.
164. Letter from Robert Hutchins to Barr, Buchanan, and Adler, September 8, 1944, p. 2. Robert M. Hutchins Papers Addenda, Box 11, Folder 20, Special Collections, University of Chicago.
165. Frederick Rudolph, *Curriculum: A History of the American Undergraduate Course of Study Since 1636* (San Francisco: Jossey-Bass, 1977), p. 280.

Chapter 5

1. Frank Aydelotte, *Breaking the Academic Lockstep: The Development of Honors Work in American Colleges and Universities* (New York: Harper & Bros., 1944), p. 69, n. 1.
2. Ibid. p. 92.
3. Frederick Rudolph, *Curriculum: A History of the American Undergraduate Course of Study Since 1636* (San Francisco: Jossey-Bass, 1977), pp. 230–231.
4. Ibid., p. 14.
5. Ibid., p. 7.
6. Ibid., p. 15.
7. Frank Aydelotte, "Honors Programs at Swarthmore" (Columbia University Press, *Five College Plans*, 1931) in *Readings for Liberal Education*, ed. Louis Locke, William Gibson, George Arms (New York: Rinehart & Co., 1948, 1952), pp. 45–52.
8. In 1944 Aydelotte noted that the University of Virginia employed outside examiners for the final honors examinations. However, David Yalden-Thomson, the chairman of the Virginia Committee on Honors Courses, held that outside examiners were first used at Virginia at the conclusion of the 1958–59 academic year. (Memo to the Committee on Academic Legislation and the Committee on Academic Policy from David C. Yalden-Thomson, Chairman, Committee on Honors Courses, February 1960, p. 4, n. 1. (Accession no. 5547d, Robert Gooch Papers, Folder 1958–62. Special Collections, Alderman Library, University of Virginia, Charlottesville, VA.)
9. Aydelotte, "Honors Programs at Swarthmore," pp. 45–52.
10. Ibid.
11. Ibid.
12. Yalden-Thomson, to the Committee on Academic Legislation and the Committee on Academic Policy, February 1960, p. 2.
13. Ibid., p. 6.
14. Aydelotte, *Breaking the Academic Lockstep*, pp. 91–93.
15. Ernest L. Boyer and Arthur S. Levine, *A Quest for Common Learning: The Aims of General Education* (Princeton: The Carnegie Foundation for the Advancement of Teaching, 1981), pp. 13–15.
16. Christopher Lucas, *American Higher Education: A History* (New York: St. Martin's Griffin, 1994), pp. 249–251.
17. A semantic note. Historian Christopher Lucas wrote that:
    > Interestingly, in the 1940s and 1950s, some writers attempted to introduce a sharp distinction between 'liberal' and 'general' education, the suggestion being that the former consisted of a fixed body of traditional liberal-arts disciplines, and the latter any course of study exhibiting breadth or diversity. This usage was decidedly at odds with earlier practice in the 1920s and 1930s, when the two terms were used interchangeably and almost synonymously. As always, writers harbored great expectations about what liberal-general education might accomplish, but were forever in disagreement over structure and substance (Lucas, *American Higher Education*, p. 252).
18. [President John L. Newcomb] "The Liberal Arts and Sciences Curriculum," n.d. [1946], RG 2/1/2.551, Box 8, Special Collections, University of Virginia.
19. Ibid.
20. "Report of the Special Committee on Curriculum," in a memorandum from the Office of the Dean of the College, December 29, 1944, RG 20/59 (3710), Box 11, Special Collections, University of Virginia.
21. "Report of the Post-War College Committee," August 21, 1944, RG 2/1/2.562, Box 9, Special Collections, University of Virginia, p. 5.
22. Ibid.
23. Ibid.
24. The revised 1935 curriculum is presented in Chapter 2, note 61.
25. "Summary of the Report of the Committee on Academic Legislation," and "Summary of the Report of the Balz Committee," n.d., RG 20/59 (3710), Box 11, Special Collections, University of Virginia.

26. The new college curriculum established in 1945 was as follows:
Required Courses:
English 1–2 Composition, 6 Semester Hours.
English 3–4 Literature, 6 Semester Hours.
Foreign Language, no hours listed. (A second year course in each of two foreign languages or a third year course in one.)
Mathematics 1–2, Mathematical Analysis, 6 Semester Hours.
Natural Science: Biology 1–2 or Chemistry 1–2 or Geology 1–2 or Physics 1–2, 10 -12 Semester Hours.
Social Sciences: History 17–18, 6 Semester Hours.
Physical Education: P.E. 1 and four semesters of activity courses.
To these 40 to 60 hours of required courses were added 18 to 30 required hours in the major subject and not less than 12 semester hours in related subjects for a total of 30 to 42 hours in the Major Subject. Free electives were to complete a total of 120 semester hours for the B.A. degree. Additionally, one had to pass a final comprehensive examination. ("The Bulletin of the Liberal Arts Committee," Vol. I, No. I, April 15, 1947. RG 19/2/6.781 Folder: "Bulletin of the Liberal Arts Committee, 4/15/47—9/18/50." Special Collections, University of Virginia.)
27. "Report of the Curriculum Committee on Requirements," n.d. [1946] RG 2/1/2.551 I, Box 3, Special Collections, University of Virginia.
28. "Suggested Reorganization of the College Curriculum, University of Virginia, 'Committee of Ten,'" n.d. [1946] RG 20/59 (3710) Box 11, Special Collections, University of Virginia.
29. Ibid.
30. Ibid.
31. "Report of the President of the University of Virginia to the Board of Visitors, July 1, 1946 to June 30, 1947," RG 2/1/2.551 II, Box 11, Special Collections, University of Virginia.
32. D. Clark Hyde, "The Liberal Arts Committee: Objectives and Means," n.d. [1947], RG 20/59 (3710), Box 11, Special Collections, University of Virginia.
33. "The Bulletin of the Liberal Arts Committee," Vol. I, No. 1., April 15, 1947.
34. "The Bulletin of the Liberal Arts Committee," Vol. IV, No. 5., September 18, 1950, RG 19/2/6.781, Special Collections, University of Virginia.
35. Ibid.
36. Comprehensive accounts of St. John's episode with the Navy can be found in J. Winfree Smith, *A Search for the Liberal College: The Beginning of the St. John's Program* (Annapolis, MD: St. John's College Press, 1983), pp. 67–89, and in Richard Miller, *As If Learning Mattered: Reforming Higher Education* (Ithaca: Cornell University Press, 1998), pp. 102–121.
37. Years later Barr recounted the initial meeting that he and Buchanan had with Mellon in Barr's office at St. John's: "Paul asked whether we needed any help, and the context of the remark made me think, not that he wanted to teach, but that he had certain influence and might be able to help work out the program, which interested him, clearly. My answer made it clear to him that his delicate way of saying he had rocks had missed me. I of course knew he had rocks but I didn't know he was talking about it, and [Mellon] was so embarrassed and said, 'No, I mean, could I be of any help financially?' And Scott and I burst into raucous laughter, because we did not know where the salaries were coming from on the first of the month, and it was about a week off. I told him so, so he said, 'Well, anytime you need money like that, . . . we'll fix it up.' From then on, Paul was constantly back of me." (Stringfellow Barr, transcript of interview with Douglas Tanner, Kingston, N. J., September 12, 1972, p. 32. Accession no. RG 26/11, Folder: Barr, F. Stringfellow, Oral History, Special Collections, University of Virginia.)
38. Paul Mellon, *Reflections in a Silver Spoon: A Memoir* (New York: William Morrow and Co., 1992), pp. 177–178.
39. Letter from Paul Mellon to Stringfellow Barr, April 16, 1946. Alexander Meiklejohn Papers, Box 57, Folder 4, Wisconsin Historical Society Archives.
40. Smith, *A Search for the Liberal College*, 79.
41. Stringfellow Barr, transcript of interview with Charles and Mary Wiseman, July 6, 1975, p. 69. Stringfellow Barr Papers, Special Collections, St. John's College.
42. Ibid., pp. 67–68.

43. Letter from Robert Hutchins to Alexander Meiklejohn, October 1, 1946, Meiklejohn Papers, Box 17, Folder 11.
44. "New College To Be Founded in Berkshires," *The Berkshire Evening Eagle*, Pittsfield, MA, December 9, 1946. Meiklejohn Papers, Box 57, Folder 4.
45. Letter from Secretary James Forrestal to Thomas Parran, chairman of the St. John's Board, June 8, 1946, as quoted in Smith, *A Search for the Liberal College*, p. 80.
46. Stringfellow Barr, transcript of interview with Charles and Mary Wiseman, July 6, 1975, p. 69.
47. Stringfellow Barr, Obituary of Scott Buchanan in the *American Oxonian*, October 1968, p. 279. Stringfellow Barr Papers, Accession No. 8053h, Box 4, Special Collections, University of Virginia. Hutchins' and Adler's refusal to leave Chicago had happened before. It will be recalled that Hutchins refused to give up the presidency of Chicago for the presidency of St. John's in 1937, even though the "New Program" at St. John's was closer to his own educational philosophy than what was being done at Chicago under the "New Plan" instituted in 1931. Adler also declined to move to Annapolis. Hutchins and Adler then refused to leave Chicago for the Stockbridge venture in 1946. In November 1948 Buchanan, in a letter remarkably similar in message to the one Adler had sent him at Virginia in 1936, wrote to Hutchins: "God I'd like to pull you away from Chicago: I'd still like to. You ought to be putting yourself to public service; you'd be an un-prededented (sic) solution to an unparalleled occasion. Chicago is never going to do anything but glitter with possibilities which get realized elsewhere, and you are its Cassandra. Break the curse and get out before Helen launches a thousand ships." Hutchins nevertheless remained the president of the University of Chicago until 1951 when he became an associate director of the Ford Foundation. (Letter from Scott Buchanan to Robert Hutchins, November 20, 1948, Robert M. Hutchins Papers Addenda, Box 19, Folder 2, Special Collections, University of Chicago.)
48. McKeon sent a letter to Buchanan after McKeon's visit to Annapolis to discuss the Stockbridge venture. McKeon said: "I am inclined more and more, since the visit in Annapolis, to the conclusion that if you are out of the project [at St. John's], the project as we have been talking about it for some twenty years is not feasible, and I shall not get into the new version of it [in Massachusetts] either. I am losing faith in the dialectical process: it may give another fellow a good subject matter for dialogue, but it seems to be designed for a hemlock ending." (Richard McKeon to Scott Buchanan, February 9, 1946, as quoted in Miller, *As If Education Mattered*, p. 115).
49. Letter from Scott Buchanan to Alexander Meiklejohn, May 3, 1947, Meiklejohn Papers, Box 3, Folder 1.
50. Letter from Scott Buchanan to St. John's President John Kieffer, June 8, 1948, as quoted in Smith, *A Search for the Liberal College*, p. 86; and, statement from John S. Kieffer, president of St. John's College, December 19, 1946, Robert M. Hutchins Papers Addenda, Box 85, Folder 2, Special Collections, University of Chicago.
51. Buchanan, "The Dean's Nine-Year Report," 1946, St. John's College, Meiklejohn Papers, Box 57, Folder 4.
52. Mellon, *Reflections in a Silver Spoon*, p. 358.
53. Ibid., p. 427.
54. Letter from Scott Buchanan to Alexander Meiklejohn, May 3, 1947, Meiklejohn Papers, Box 6, Folder 1.
55. Memorandum from Dean Ivey Lewis to President Colgate Darden, n.d. [1950], RG 2/1/2.562, Box 15, Special Collections, University of Virginia. Lewis wrote, "Our educational program in the liberal arts is somewhat like guiding a boy through a forest by teaching him the name of each kind of tree and not acquainting him with the forest itself."
56. Letter from Allan Gwathmey to Dean Ivey Lewis, October 23, 1946, RG 19/3/4.541, Special Collections, University of Virginia.
57. Ibid. Gwathmey also stated that, among those who should not be chosen was "anyone such as an assistant Dean from Yale, Harvard or Princeton, who has written a new book, and who has no appreciation of the background of the university or its unique opportunities for the future."
58. Letter from Scott Buchanan to Alexander Meiklejohn, May 3, 1947, Meiklejohn Papers, Box 6, Folder 1.
59. Letter from Stringfellow Barr to Alexander Meiklejohn, July 7, 1947, Meiklejohn Papers, Barr Correspondence.

Notes to Pages 151–161 • **235**

60. Letter from Stringfellow Barr to Colgate Darden, May 29, 1947, RG 2/1/2.551 II, Box 11, Special Collections, University of Virginia.
61. Letter from Stringfellow Barr to Alexander Meiklejohn, July 7, 1947, Meiklejohn Papers, Barr Correspondence. Barr also noted "I do not think, be it said to [Darden's] credit, that he was endowment-hunting."
62. Ibid.
63. Letter from Scott Buchanan to Alexander Meiklejohn, June 3, 1947, Meiklejohn Papers, Box 6, Folder 1.
64. Letter from Stringfellow Barr to Alexander Meiklejohn, July 7, 1947, Meiklejohn Papers, Barr Correspondence.
65. Ibid.
66. Letter from Scott Buchanan to Alexander Meiklejohn, May 3, 1947, Meiklejohn Papers, Box 6, Folder 1.
67. Letter from Stringfellow Barr to Alexander Meiklejohn, July 7, 1947, Meiklejohn Papers, Barr Correspondence.
68. Stringfellow Barr, Memorandum to Non Resident Liberal Arts, Incorporated Board Members, July 29, 1947. Meiklejohn Papers, "Barr Correspondence."
69. Letter from Stringfellow Barr to Alexander Meiklejohn, July 18, 1947, Meiklejohn Papers, Barr Correspondence.
70. Letter from Stringfellow Barr, Chairman, to Non-Resident Board Members of Liberal Arts Incorporated, July 23, 1947, Robert M. Hutchins Papers Addenda, Box 85, Folder 2, Special Collections, University of Chicago.
71. Ibid.
72. Ibid.
73. Barr, Memorandum to Non-Resident Liberal Arts, Inc. Board Members, July 29, 1947.
74. Ibid.
75. Stringfellow Barr, Memorandum to Non-Resident Liberal Arts, Inc. Board Members, August 7, 1947. Meiklejohn Papers, "Barr Correspondence."
76. The location of these two pieces of property is unclear, but it is possible that the larger piece was the Birdwood estate while the smaller "contiguous" property was the old golf course land on which now stand the McCormick Road dormitories, built between 1946 and 1951, and Ruffner Hall, built in the early 1970s.
77. Barr, Memorandum to Non-Resident Liberal Arts, Incorporated Board Members, August 7, 1947.
78. Ibid.
79. Letter from Stringfellow Barr to Colgate Darden, August 10, 1947, RG 2/1/2.551 II, Box 11, Special Collections, University of Virginia.
80. Letter from Stringfellow Barr to Ernest Feidler, Secretary, Old Dominion Foundation, August 5, 1947 (Meiklejohn Papers, "Barr Correspondence"); and letter from Barr to Non-Resident Board Members of Liberal Arts, Incorporated, August 7, 1947.
81. Smith, *A Search for the Liberal College*, p. 87.
82. Statement issued by Liberal Arts, Incorporated, August 18, 1947, Robert M. Hutchins Papers Addenda, Box 85, Folder 2, Special Collections, University of Chicago.
83. Ibid.
84. Letter from Stringfellow Barr to Colgate Darden, August 10, 1947, Special Collections, University of Virginia.
85. Letter from Stringfellow Barr to Colgate Darden, August 18, 1947, RG 2/1/2.551 II, Box 11, Special Collections, University of Virginia.
86. Grant letter from Stringfellow Barr to the Greenwood Foundation, August 28, 1947, R. M. Hutchins Papers Addenda, Box 11, Folder 20, Special Collections, University of Chicago. In the letter Barr asked for an expedited decision on his funding request since, "Confidentially, the president of the University of Virginia wishes me to rejoin the faculty of that institution . . . to develop there the type of education I inaugurated at St. John's."
87. Letter from Stringfellow Barr to Robert Hutchins, August 30, 1947, R. M. Hutchins Papers Addenda, Box 11, Folder 20, Special Collections, University of Chicago.
88. Letter from Stringfellow Barr to Marshall Field, August 30, 1947, Robert M. Hutchins Papers Addenda, Box 11, Folder 20, Special Collections, University of Chicago.
89. Letter from Stringfellow Barr to Colgate Darden, January 3, 1948, RG 2/1/2.552, Box 2, Special Collections, University of Virginia.

90. Ibid.
91. Letter from Colgate Darden to Stringfellow Barr, January 20, 1948, RG 2/1/2.552, Box 2, Special Collections, University of Virginia.
92. Letter from Colgate Draden to Stringfellow Barr, June 29, 1948, RG 2/1/2.552, Box 2, Special Collections, University of Virginia.
93. Letter from Stringfellow Barr to Colgate Darden, July 7, 1948, RG 2/1/2.552, Box 2, Special Collections, University of Virginia.
94. Letter from Colgate Darden to Stringfellow Barr, July 13, 1948, RG 2/1/2.552, Box 2, Special Collections, University of Virginia. Darden stated that one of his problems regarding the world government movement was that "I have never been able to see how the necessary machinery can be devised." Also, "in this [world government] venture far more than civic courage is required." (Letter from Colgate Darden to Stringfellow Barr, May 24, 1948, RG 2/1/2.552, Box 2, Special Collections, University of Virginia.)
95. Letter from Stringfellow Barr to Colgate Darden, February 2, 1948, RG 2/1/2.552, Box 2, Special Collections, University of Virginia. Darden related to Barr that "I am afraid that I am not as much of a United World Federalist as you are, although I am interested in the movement because I share your views as to the danger of war, and I am in absolute accord with you as to what would remain to victor and vanquished alike, once the shooting starts." (Letter from Colgate Darden to Stringfellow Barr, February 3, 1948, RG 2/1/2.552, Box 2, Special Collections, University of Virginia.)
96. Harry S. Ashmore, *Unseasonable Truths: The Life of Robert Maynard Hutchins* (Boston: Little, Brown, and Co., 1989), p. 276.
97. Letter from Barr to Darden, July 7, 1948.
98. Handwritten note to Robert Hutchins from Stringfellow Barr, July 9, 1948, Robert M. Hutchins Paper Adenda, Box 11, Folder 20, Special Collections, University of Chicago; and, Barr, Obituary of Scott Buchanan in *The American Oxonian*, October 1968, p. 279.
99. Barr, Obituary of Scott Buchanan in *The American Oxonian*, October 1968, p. 279. Other "liberal artists" were involved in Barr's foundation effort. Buchanan was an advisor to the foundation and Hutchins served on the board of trustees.
100. Colgate Darden, "Report of the President of the University of Virginia to the Board of Visitors: July 1, 1948–June 30, 1949," RG 2/1/2.561, Box 2, Special Collections, University of Virginia.
101. Ibid.
102. Colgate Darden, "Report of the President of the University of Virginia to the Board of Visitors: July 1, 1949–July 1, 1950," RG 2/1/2.561, Box 2, Special Collections, University of Virginia.
103. Ibid.
104. Memorandum from Lewis to Darden, n.d. [1950].
105. N. B. Lewis was wrong about Plan A being for four years. It was only for the first two—the underclass years.
106. Memorandum from Lewis to Darden, n.d. [1950].
107. Letter from Colgate Darden to Stringfellow Barr, April 13, 1950, RG 2/1/2.562, Box 4, Special Collections, University of Virginia.
108. Letter from Stringfellow Barr to Colgate Darden, April 24, 1950, RG 2/1/2.562, Box 4, Special Collections, University of Virginia.
109. Letter from Colgate Darden to Stringfellow Barr, November 1, 1950, RG 2/1/2.562, Box 4, Special Collections, University of Virginia.
110. Letter from Stringfellow Barr to Colgate Darden, November 8, 1950, RG 2/1/2.562, Box 4, Special Collections, University of Virginia.
111. "Memorandum to the President of the University of Virginia from Stringfellow Barr," n.d. [November 1950], RG 2/1/2.562, Box 4, Special Collections, University of Virginia.
112. Ibid.
113. Ibid.
114. Ibid.
115. Note from Colgate Darden to Ivey Lewis, November 25, 1950, RG 2/1/2.562, Box 10, Special Collections, University of Virginia.
116. Note from Ivey Lewis to Colgate Darden, n.d. [November 1950], RG 2/1/2.562, Box 4, Special Collections, University of Virginia.

Notes to Pages 171–174 • **237**

Chapter 6

1. Letter from Scott Buchanan to Stringfellow Barr, December 18, 1951. Stringfellow Barr Papers, Section 2, Box 7, Folder 10, Special Collections, Greenfield Library, St. John's College, Annapolis, MD.
2. *University of Virginia Record, 1952–1953*, p. 146, Alderman Library, University of Virginia, Charlottesville, VA.
3. Chauncey G. Olinger, Jr., untitled essay in *Stringfellow Barr: A Centennial Appreciation of His Life and Work*, ed. Charles A. Nelson (Annapolis: St. John's College Press, 1997), pp. 208–212.
4. *University of Virginia Record, 1953–1954*, p. 148.
5. Author's interview with Chauncey G. Olinger, Jr., Investment broker and Columbia University oral historian, August 28, 1999, Riverdale, New York.
6. Stringfellow Barr, "The University and the Honor System," An Address to Entering Students, Cabell Hall, University of Virginia, September 22, 1952, Stringfellow Barr Papers, Section 2, Box 2, Folder 19, Special Collections, St. John's College.
7. Author's interview with Staige D. Blackford, Editor, *Virginia Quarterly Review*, University of Virginia, June 7, 1999, Charlottesville, VA.
8. Author's interview with Samuel A. "Pete" Anderson, II, Architect for the University, University of Virginia, May 12, 1999, Charlottesville, VA.
9. Olinger, untitled essay in *Stringfellow Barr*, pp. 208–212.
10. Author's telephone interview with Chauncey Olinger, June 7, 1999, New York, NY.
11. Author's interview with John Marshall, Professor of Philosophy, University of Virginia, June 9, 1999, Charlottesville, VA.
12. Olinger, untitled essay in *Stringfellow Barr*, pp. 208–212.
13. Author's interview with Arthur F. Stocker, Classics Professor Emeritus, University of Virginia, June 3, 1999, Charlottesville, VA.
14. Stringfellow Barr, transcript of interview with Charles and Mary Wiseman, July 6, 1975, p. 43, Special Collections, St. John's College.
15. Ibid.
16. Ibid.
17. Author's interview with Charles A. Nelson, Editor and Visitor Emeritus, St. John's College, August 28, 1999, Croton-on-Hudson, NY.
18. "Great Books Given to Library by Mellon," *The Cavalier Daily*, May 16, 1952, Stringfellow Barr Papers, Section 2, Box 5, Folder 31, Special Collections, St. John's College.
19. Interview with Chauncey G. Olinger Jr., August 28, 1999, Riverdale, NY. According to copies of the University of Virginia budget, Barr's salary of $7,500 came from "University Funds," not "State Funds" like the other professors in the Political Science Department. This suggests that Barr's salary came from private sources, most likely Mellon. (*University of Virginia Budget, 1951–52*, p. 75., *1952–1953*, p. 77., *1953–54*, p. 78.)
20. Paul Mellon, *Reflections in a Silver Spoon: A Memoir* (New York: William Morrow & Co., 1992), p. 407.
21. Archival note, 8053, Box 9, "Engagements Accepted," Stringfellow Barr Papers, Special Collections, Alderman Library, University of Virginia, Charlottesville, VA.
22. Olinger, untitled essay in *Stringfellow Barr*, pp. 208–212. Olinger recalled: "I remember someone asking Barr in class if he belonged to any 'Communist-front' organizations and if so which, and Barr, without hesitation, replied, 'Oh, all of them.' Such cavalier remarks did little to help his standing on campus or to advance the educational program he was there to promote." Virginia was a conservative university during Barr's tenure. The Lower Division Non-Academic Activity Log for March 1952 notes that: "A resident complained that . . . the Intervarsity Christian Fellowship held a 'group discussion' in the lounge of Emmett House that . . . was pro-communistic and seditious in character." (RG 20/61, Special Collections, University of Virginia).
23. Stringfellow Barr, transcript of interview with Allan Hoffmann, August 24, 1975, pp. 48–49.
24. Stringfellow Barr, transcript of interview with Charles and Mary Wiseman, July 6, 1975, p. 46, Special Collections, St. John's College.
25. Letter from Stringfellow Barr to Frederick Schuman, October 14, 1954. Stringfellow Barr Papers, Special Collections, St. John's College.
26. Barr, transcript of interview with Charles and Mary Wiseman, July 6, 1975, p. 48.

27. Barr, transcript of interview with Allan Hoffmann, August 24, 1975, p. 48.
28. Ibid, p. 49.
29. Author's interview with Charles E. Moran, University Historian Emeritus, University of Virginia, June 3, 1999, Charlottesville, VA. As noted in Chapter 1, starting in the late 1970s Moran was the first person to serve as the University Historian at Virginia.
30. Author's interview with Raymond C. Bice, Professor of Psychology Emeritus and University Historian, University of Virginia, May 10, 1999, Charlottesville, VA.
31. Author's interview with Samuel A. "Pete" Anderson, May 12, 1999.
32. Stringfellow Barr, transcript of interview with Chauncey Olinger, 1972, p. 17. Courtesy of Chauncey G. Olinger, Jr.
33. Barr, transcript of interview with Allan Hoffmann, August 24, 1975, p. 49.
34. Barr, transcript of interview with Charles and Mary Wiseman, July 6, 1975, p. 48.
35. James Collier Marshall to Mrs. [Gladys] "Oak" Barr, November 19, 1957, Stringfellow Barr Papers, Special Collections, University of Virginia.
36. Petition to the Department of Political Science, the Faculty Senate, and the Administration of the University of Virginia, Spring 1953, courtesy of Chauncey G. Olinger, Jr. Olinger recollected that: "I went to Barr and proposed that I circulate a petition among the students in his class urging the University to arrange for him to continue teaching. Winkie told me that there was no chance that he could stay on, but, he said, what I could do if I wanted to, was to circulate a petition calling for the continuance of the course. He thought that that might have a better chance of succeeding, especially if it was not tied to himself." Olinger, untitled essay in *Stringfellow Barr*, pp. 208–212.
37. Petition to the Department of Political Science, the Faculty Senate, and the Administration of the University of Virginia, Spring 1953. Courtesy of Chauncey G. Olinger, Jr.
38. Letter from Robert Gooch to Chauncey Olinger, May 5, 1953. Courtesy of Chauncey G. Olinger, Jr.
39. Letter to the faculty from the Committee on Honors Courses, n.d., [February 1952], RG 2/1/2.591, Box 16, Special Collections, University of Virginia.
40. Ibid.
41. Ibid.
42. "Specimen Plan of a Two Years Course of Study Leading to the Bachelor of Arts with General Honors," n.d. [February 1952], RG 2/1/2.591, Box 16, Special Collections, University of Virginia.
43. Ibid.
44. Letter from Archibald B. Shepperson to the Committee on the Honors Degree, February 5, 1952, RG 2/1/2.591, Box 16, Special Collections, University of Virginia.
45. Ibid.
46. Letter from Fredson Bowers to the Committee on Degrees with Honors, February 7, 1952, RG 2/1/2.591, Box 16, Special Collections, University of Virginia.
47. Ibid.
48. Ibid.
49. Letter from Messrs. Botts, Floyd, McShane, Mallett, Tuttle, Yalden-Thomson, and Younger to Robert Gooch, Chairman, Committee on the Degrees with Honors, February 17, 1952. RG 2/1/2.591, Box 16, Special Collections, University of Virginia.
50. There were five members of the Lower Division Committee: Lewis Hammond, professor of philosophy and Assistant Dean of the Summer Session, was the Chairman; Marcus Mallett, assistant professor of philosophy and Acting Dean of the College, served as Associate Dean of the Lower Division; Raymond Bice, assistant professor of psychology, served as chairman of the Resident Advisors; George Spicer, professor of political science, and Richard Fletcher, Associate Director of Admissions, served as ex-officio members. ("Darden Appoints Policies Group," *The Cavalier Daily*, May 4, 1950).
51. Letter from Marcus Mallett to the Academic Faculty, May 23, 1951, RG 20/61 (7986), Box 1, Special Collections, University of Virginia.
52. Loose announcement flyer, n.d. [1951], RG 20/61, Special Collections, University of Virginia. The flyer noted that Barr, a "nationally known educator and visiting professor of Political Science . . . is an unusually well qualified speaker and also a very interesting one, students should make plans to hear him speak."
53. Minutes, Committee on the Lower Division, University of Virginia, March 23, 1953, RG 20/61 (7986), Box 1, Special Collections, University of Virginia.

54. Ibid.
55. Ibid.
56. Ibid.
57. Letter from David Wright to the Members of the Academic Faculty, May 26, 1953, RG 20/61 (7986), Box 1, Special Collections, University of Virginia. It will be recalled that in 1948 Darden had wanted Barr to teach this course. Darden wrote:
   Sometime ago the faculty authorized the giving of a course under the title "The Development of American Political Thought and Institutions." The announcement states that the great ideas which have influenced American development are stressed. The course is offered under the joint auspices of the Schools of History, Economics, and Political Science. The course was not given this past year due to the inability of getting the required help. It is this assignment that I should like to see you undertake. I think you will have no difficulty in making arrangements with the respective Schools for the work which you want to do. That the course is offered under the auspices of three schools would tend to give you, in my opinion, great freedom of action. (Letter from Colgate Darden to Stringfellow Barr, June 29, 1948, RG 2/1/2.552, Box 2, Special Collections, University of Virginia.)
   Barr had declined and responded that he believed this proposal to be "a less good beginning than the beginning you and I had planned [earlier]." (Letter from Stringfellow Barr to Colgate Darden, July 7, 1948, RG 2/1/2.552, Box 2, Special Collections, University of Virginia.)
58. Letter from Wright to the Members of the Academic Faculty, May 26, 1953.
59. Ibid.
60. Ibid.
61. Letter from Shepperson to the Committee on the Honors Degree, February 5, 1952.
62. *University of Virginia Record, 1956–1957*, p. 119. The Catalog entry also stated that: "The Lower Division Seminars are non-departmental in character, and hence may not be offered as part of a field of concentration. The Seminars are administered by the Committee on Lower Division Seminars which consists of all members of the instructional staff."
63. Author's interview with George B. Thomas, Professor of Philosophy, University of Virginia, June 18, 1999, Charlottesville, VA.
64. Ibid.
65. Ibid.
66. "Report on Meeting with First-Year Men of Top Academic Standing," n.d., RG 20/61 (7986), Special Collections, University of Virginia.
67. Author's interview with Raymond Bice, May 10, 1999.
68. Robert K. Gooch, "The Meaning of a Liberal Arts Education," n.d., 5547d, Robert Gooch Papers, Special Collections, University of Virginia.
69. "The Liberal Arts Seminars at the University of Virginia," n.d. [1960–61], RG 21/60.821, Special Collections, University of Virginia.
70. Ibid. The reading schedule for Liberal Arts Seminar 4 also included Shakespeare's *King Lear* and *The Tempest*. These were apparently inadvertently left off the above list.
71. "Liberal Arts Seminar 2, 1957–1958, Writing Assignment 3 (Lucretius, Books III-VI)," 1958, RG 21/60.821, Box: Gooch Papers, Special Collections, University of Virginia.
72. "Liberal Arts Seminar 2, 1957–1958, Writing Assignment 7 (Lavoisier)," 1958, RG 21/60.821, Box: Gooch Papers, Special Collections, University of Virginia.
73. "Liberal Arts Seminar 2, (Einstein)," 1957, RG 21/60.821, Box: Gooch Papers, Special Collections, University of Virginia.
74. "Liberal Arts Seminar 2, 1957–1958, Writing Assignment 11 (Harvey)," 1958, RG 21/60.821, Box: Gooch Papers, Special Collections, University of Virginia.
75. Invitation, n.d. [1960–61], RG 21/60.821, Special Collections, University of Virginia.
76. Author's interview with Arthur Stocker, June 3, 1999.
77. Olinger, untitled essay in *Stringfellow Barr*, pp. 208–212.
78. *University of Virginia Record, 1960–1961*, pp. 128–129.
79. Author's interview with George Thomas, June 18, 1999.
80. Christopher Lucas, *American Higher Education: A History* (New York: St. Martin's Griffin, 1994), pp. 262–263.
81. See Clark Kerr, *The Uses of the University* (Cambridge: Harvard University Press, 1963, 1995).

82. Virginius Dabney, *Mr. Jefferson's University: A History* (Charlottesville, University of Virginia Press, 1981), p. 451.
83. Author's interview with John Marshall, June 9, 1999.
84. Ibid.
85. Letter from William Duren to the Committee on Honors Courses, May 16, 1958, 5547d, Robert Gooch Papers, Special Collections, University of Virginia. The two-year gap between Duren's letter and Yalden-Thomson's response is explained by Duren's absence from the University during the interim.
86. Aydelotte had argued the same point in 1944:
    ... The common American organization of courses and examinations has kept the tutorial system from producing results commensurate with the expectations formed or the expense involved. Tutorial work has usually been an extra, supplementing the course and hour system, but not replacing it. For this reason neither students nor tutors have taken it seriously enough to produce the best results. The success of the student in securing a degree and in winning honors has in most colleges and universities depended upon his marks in his courses. He could neglect them only at his peril, while if he did his course work well he could neglect his tutor with impunity. In those few places where the success of the student depends entirely upon comprehensive examinations for which he prepares under the guidance of his tutor, the tutorial system has flourished; elsewhere it has been more or less halfhearted. (Frank Aydelotte, *Breaking the Academic Lockstep: The Development of Honors Work in American Colleges and Universities.* [New York: Harper & Bros., 1944], p. 114).
87. Memo from D. C. Yalden-Thomson, Chairman, Committee on Honors Courses, to the Committee on Academic Legislation and the Committee on Academic Policy, February 1960. 5547d, Robert Gooch Papers, Special Collections, University of Virginia.
88. For a more complete discussion of the Echols Scholars Program see Dabney, *Mr. Jefferson's University*, pp. 425–426.
89. William Duren, "Echols Scholars," May 18, 1960, 5547d, Robert Gooch Papers, Special Collections, University of Virginia.
90. Dabney, *Mr. Jefferson's University*, pp. 425–426.
91. Francis R. Hart, "The College Honors Program at the University of Virginia, 1968," May 1968. (Courtesy of David Yalden-Thomson and George Thomas, via John Marshall).
92. Although examiners had come from almost fifty different colleges and universities, they had come most often from the University of North Carolina and Princeton, followed by Washington and Lee, Duke, Johns Hopkins, and Columbia.
93. Hart, "The College Honors Program at the University of Virginia, 1968," May 1968.
94. Pattie Sellers, "Pragmatism Endangers Honors Program," *Cavalier Daily*, February 26, 1981.
95. Author's interview with Arthur Stocker, June 3, 1999.
96. Hart, "The College Honors Program at the University of Virginia, 1968," May 1968.
97. Author's interview with John Marshall, June 9, 1999.
98. Ibid.
99. Author's interview with George Thomas, June 18, 1999.
100. Sellers, "Pragmatism Endangers Honors Program," *Cavalier Daily*, February 26, 1981.
101. Ibid.
102. An account of these celebrations can be found in Bill Sublette, "Free to Think: Honors Tutorials Allow Independent Learning," *University of Virginia Alumni News*, January/February 1989, Vol. LXXVII, No. 3, pp. 25–27.

Conclusion

1. "Stringfellow Barr: A Rebel's View of the Young Revolutionaries," *College and University Business* 43, No. 6 (December 1967), p. 56. After leaving the University of Virginia in 1953, Barr became Professor of Humanities for ten years at Rutgers University. Then, from 1966 to 1969, he was a Fellow at the Center for the Study of Democratic Institutions in Santa Barbara which was under the leadership of Robert Hutchins. There he also rejoined Scott Buchanan who, after work for the Foundation for World Government and the Progressive Party, had become a Fellow at the Center in 1957. Buchanan died in Santa Barbara in 1968,

after which Barr retired with his wife, Gladys, to Kingston, N.J. He died in Virginia in 1982. See Charles A. Nelson, ed. *Scott Buchanan: A Centennial Appreciation of His Life and Work* (Annapolis: St. John's College Press, 1995) and *Stringfellow Barr: A Centennial Appreciation of His Life and Work* (Annapolis: St. John's College Press, 1997).
2. Lawrence Levine, *The Opening of the American Mind: Canons, Culture, and History* (Boston: Beacon Press, 1996), p. 41.
3. John Brubacher and Willis Rudy, *Higher Education in Transition: A History of American Colleges and Universities*, 4th ed. (New Brunswick, N.J.: Transaction, 1997), p. 283.
4. Ibid., p. 269.
5. Allan Bloom, *The Closing of the American Mind* (New York: Simon and Schuster, 1987), p. 344.
6. Brubacher and Rudy, *Higher Education in Transition*, p. 274.
7. Bruce Kimball, *Orators & Philosophers: A History of the Idea of Liberal Education* (New York: The College Board, 1995), p. 191.
8. Frank Aydelotte, *Breaking the Academic Lockstep: The Development of Honors Work in American Colleges and Universities* (New York: Harper & Bros., 1944), p. 91.
9. Kass did note that:
   > There have been many off-shoots and by-products of the movement throughout the American educational system. The integrated liberal arts programs on such campuses as Notre Dame in Indiana, Saint Mary's College in California, Thomas Aquinas College in California, and St. Anselm's College in Manchester, New Hampshire, are a few of the current endeavors that can be traced to this Movement. A more contemporary by-product of the Movement, however, can be seen in the large number of courses offered on many university campuses that teach their subject matters with the aid of the great books. Very few of these developments, however, have come close to the original aspiration in terms of principles, purpose, content, or scope. (Amy Apfel Kass, *Radical Conservatives for Liberal Education* [Ph.D. Diss., Johns Hopkins University, 1973; Ann Arbor: University Microfilms, 1973] p. 307, n. 21.)

   Though an enduring transformation was not achieved, the courses that were implemented at Virginia in the 1950s are an integral part of the story of the Virginia Plan and a direct manifestation of the liberal arts movement.
10. Frederick Rudolph, *The American College and University: A History* (New York: A. Knopf, 1962; reprint, Athens, GA: University of Georgia Press, 1990), p. 480. (page citation is to the reprint edition.)
11. Memorandum from Ivey F. Lewis to Colgate Darden., n.d. [1950], RG 2/1/2.562, Box 15, Special Collections, Alderman Library, University of Virginia, Charlottesville, VA.
12. Letter from Archibald B. Shepperson to the Committee on the Honors Degree, February 5, 1952, RG 2/1/2.591, Box 16, Special Collections, University of Virginia.
13. Letter from Fredson Bowers to the Committee on Degrees with Honors, February 7, 1952, RG 2/1/2.591, Box 16, Special Collections, University of Virginia.
14. Author's interview with Arthur F. Stocker, Classics Professor Emeritus, University of Virginia, June 3, 1999, Charlottesville, VA.
15. Frank Aydelotte, "Honors Programs at Swarthmore" (Columbia University Press, *Five College Plans*, 1931) in *Readings for Liberal Education*, eds. Louis Locke, William Gibson, George Arms (New York: Rinehart & Co., 1948, 1952), pp. 45–52. Aydelotte continued:
    > To hold the best back to the standards of the average in the interests of democracy means to condemn democracy to mediocrity. It has sometimes been argued that this is the inevitable consequence of the wide extension of the privilege of higher education. It is my opinion that democracy cannot afford to pay that price. If democracy meant the necessity of leveling down the best to the mediocre standard attainable by the average, then democracy would be foredoomed to failure. But true democracy means not that, but rather the development of every man to the full extent of his ability in order that the state may be provided with the trained servants who are indispensable to its success. (p. 52)
16. Frederick Rudolph, *Curriculum: A History of the American Undergraduate Course of Study Since 1636* (San Francisco: Jossey-Bass, 1977), p. 231.
17. Barr, transcript of interview with Chauncey Olinger, Kingston, N.J. 1972, pp. 102–103.

Bibliography

Adler, Mortimer J. *Philosopher At Large: An Intellectual Autobiography.* New York: Macmillan, 1977.

———. *A Second Look in the Rearview Mirror: Further Autobiographical Reflections of a Philosopher at Large.* New York: Macmillan, 1992.

Adler, Mortimer J. and Peter Wolff. *A General Introduction to the Great Books and to a Liberal Education.* Chicago: Encyclopaedia Britannica, Inc., 1959.

Alexander, Michael. *The Growth of English Education: 1348–1648.* University Park: Pennsylvania State University Press, 1990.

Anderson, James. *The Education of Blacks in the South, 1860–1935.* Chapel Hill: University of North Carolina Press, 1988.

Ashmore, Harry S. *Unseasonable Truths: The Life of Robert Maynard Hutchins.* Boston: Little, Brown and Company, 1989.

Aydelotte, Frank. *Breaking the Academic Lockstep: The Development of Honors Work in American Colleges and Universities.* New York: Harper & Bros., 1944.

———. "Honors Programs at Swarthmore." (Columbia University Press, *Five College Plans,* 1931). In *Readings for Liberal Education,* eds. Louis Locke, William Gibson, George Arms, New York: Rinehart & Co., 1948, 1952.

Barr, Stringfellow. "Scott Buchanan." *The American Oxonian,* October 1968.

———. "*The Ends and Means of General Education,*" 1939. Stringfellow Barr Papers, Special Collections, Alderman Library, University of Virginia, Charlottesville.

———. "*The St. John's Program,*" 1938. Stringfellow Barr Papers, Special Collections, Alderman Library, University of Virginia, Charlottesville.

Bell, Daniel. *The Reforming of General Education.* New York: Columbia University Press, 1966.

Bloom, Allan. *The Closing of the American Mind.* New York: Simon and Schuster, 1987.

Boyer, Ernest and Arthur Levine. *A Quest for Common Learning: The Aims of General Education.* Princeton: Princeton University Press, 1981.

Brubacher, John S. and Willis Rudy. *Higher Education in Transition: A History of American Colleges and Universities,* 4th ed. New Brunswick, NJ: Transaction, 1997.

Bruce, Philip Alexander. *History of the University of Virginia, 1819–1919.* New York: The Macmillan Co., 1920.

Buchanan, Scott. *Poetry and Mathematics.* John Day Co., 1929; reprint, Philadelphia: J. B. Lippincott Co., 1962.

Casement, William R. *The Great Canon Controversy: The Battle of the Books in Higher Education.* New Brunswick, N.J.: Transaction, 1996.

Curtler, Hugh Mercer. *Rediscovering Values: Coming to Terms with Postmodernism.* Armonk, N.Y.: M. E. Sharpe, 1997.

Dabney, Virginius. *Mr. Jefferson's University: A History.* Charlottesville: University Press of Virginia, 1981.

Denby, David. *Great Books: My Adventures with Homer, Rousseau, Woolf, and other Indestructible Writers of the Western World.* New York: Touchstone, 1996.

Duke, Alex. *Importing Oxbridge: English Residential Colleges and American Universities.* New Haven: Yale University Press, 1996.

Dzuback, Mary Ann. *Robert M. Hutchins: Portrait of an Educator.* Chicago: University of Chicago Press, 1991.

Farnham, Christie. *The Education of The Southern Belle: Higher Education and Student Socialization in the Antebellum South.* New York: New York University Press, 1994.

Goodchild, Lester. "The History of American Higher Education: An Overview and a Commentary," in the *ASHE Reader on The History of Higher Education,* eds. Lester F. Goodchild and Harold S. Wechsler. Needham Heights, MA: Ginn Press, 1989.

———., ed. and Harold S. Wechsler, ed. *The Yale Report of 1828,* reprinted in the *ASHE Reader on the History of Higher Education,* eds. Needham Heights, MA: Ginn Press, 1989.

Harlan, Louis R. *Booker T. Washington: The Wizard of Tuskegee, 1901–1915*. New York: Oxford University Press, 1983.
Harris, Michael R. *Five Counterrevolutionists in Higher Education*. Corvallis: Oregon State University Press, 1970.
Hawkins, Hugh. *Between Harvard and America: The Educational Leadership of Charles W. Eliot*. New York: Oxford University Press, 1972.
Hovde, Carl. "What Columbia College is Known For," *Columbia: the Magazine of Columbia University*, Winter 2001, 32.
Hutchins, R. M. *The Higher Learning in America*. New Haven: Yale University Press, 1936; revised ed., New Brunswick, NJ: Transaction, 1995.
_____. and Mortimer J. Adler. *The Great Ideas Today*. Chicago: Encyclopedia Britannica, various years.
Kass, Amy Apfel. "Radical Conservatives for Liberal Education," Ph.D. diss., Johns Hopkins University, 1973. Ann Arbor: University Microfilms, 1973.
Kerr, Clark. *The Uses of the University*. Cambridge: Harvard University Press, 1963, 1995.
Kimball, Bruce A. *Orators & Philosophers: A History of the Idea of Liberal Education*, expanded edition. New York: The College Board, 1995.
Kliebard, Herbert. *The Struggle for the American Curriculum: 1893–1958*, 2nd ed. New York: Routledge, 1995.
Levine, Lawrence. *The Opening of the American Mind: Canons, Culture, and History*. Boston: Beacon Press, 1996.
Lewis, David Levering. *W. E. B. DuBois: Biography of A Race, 1868–1919*. New York: Henry Holt and Co., 1993.
Lucas, Christopher J. *American Higher Education: A History*. New York: St. Martin's Griffin, 1994.
Marsden, George. *The Soul of the American University: From Protestant Establishment to Established Nonbelief*. New York: Oxford University Press, 1994.
Mayer, Milton. *Robert Maynard Hutchins: A Memoir*. Berkeley: University of California Press, 1993.
McNeill, William H. *Hutchins' University: A Memoir of the University of Chicago, 1929–1950*. Chicago: University of Chicago Press, 1991.
Meiklejohn, Alexander. *Freedom and the College*. Englewood Cliffs, N.J.: Prentice Hall, 1923.
_____. *The Experimental College*. New York: Harper & Row, 1932.
Mellon, Paul. *Reflections in a Silver Spoon: A Memoir*. New York: William Morrow and Co., 1992.
Meyer, Daniel, ed. *The University and the City: A Centennial View of the University of Chicago*. Chicago: The University of Chicago Library, 1992.
Miller, Gary E. *The Meaning of General Education: The Emergence of a Curriculum Paradigm*. New York: Teachers College Press, 1988.
Miller, Richard E. *As If Learning Mattered: Reforming Higher Education*. Ithaca: Cornell University Press, 1998.
Morehead, Hugh. "The History of the Great Books Movement." Ph.D. diss., Department of Education, University of Chicago, 1964.
Nelson, Adam R. *Education and Democracy: The Meaning of Alexander Meiklejohn, 1872–1964*. Madison: University of Wisconsin Press, 2001.
Nelson, Charles, A. *Radical Visions: Stringfellow Barr, Scott Buchanan, and Their Efforts on behalf of Education and Politics in the Twentieth Century*. Westport, CT: Bergin and Garvey, 2001.
_____., ed. *Scott Buchanan: A Centennial Appreciation of His Life and Work*. Annapolis: St. John's College Press, 1995.
_____., ed. *Stringfellow Barr: A Centennial Appreciation of His Life and Work*. Annapolis: St. John's College Press, 1997.
Olinger, Chauncey G., Jr. "The Origins of the Honors Program at the University of Virginia." Remarks prepared for the reunion of Honors in Philosophy alumni, The University of Virginia, 1988.
Orrill, Robert, ed. *The Condition of American Liberal Education/Pragmatism and a Changing Tradition*. New York: The College Board, 1995.
Patton, John S. *Jefferson, Cabell and the University of Virginia*. New York: Neale Publishing Co., 1906.
Peters, Edward. *Europe and the Middle Ages*. Englewood Cliffs, N.J.: Prentice-Hall, 1983.
Power, Edward J. *Educational Philosophy: A History from the Ancient World to Modern America*. New York: Garland, 1996.

Reuben, Julie A. *The Making of the Modern University: Intellectual Transformation and the Marginalization of Morality*. Chicago: University of Chicago Press, 1996.

Rudolph, Frederick. *Curriculum: A History of the American Undergraduate Course of Study Since 1636*. San Francisco: Jossey-Bass, 1977.

_____. *The American College and University: A History*. New York: A. Knopf, 1962; reprint, Athens, GA: University of Georgia Press, 1990.

Russell, Bertrand. *A History of Western Philosophy*. New York: Simon & Schuster, 1945.

Smith, J. Winfree. *A Search for the Liberal College: The Beginning of the St. John's Program*. Annapolis: St. John's College Press, 1983.

Soares, Joseph A. *The Decline of Privilege: The Modernization of Oxford University*. Stanford: Stanford University Press, 1999.

Solomon, Barbara M. *In the Company of Educated Women: A History of Women and Higher Education in America*. New Haven: Yale University Press, 1985.

Streeter, Robert. *One In Spirit*. Chicago: University of Chicago Publications Office, 1991.

_____. *The University and the City: A Centennial View of the University of Chicago*. Chicago: The University of Chicago Library, 1992.

Sublette, Bill. "Free To Think: Honors Tutorials Allow Independent Learning." University of Virginia Alumni News, January/February 1989.

Synott, Marcia Graham. *The Half-Opened Door: Discrimination at Harvard, Yale, and Princeton, 1900–1970*. Westport, CT: Greenwood Press, 1979.

Thomas, Russell. *The Search for a Common Learning: General Education, 1800–1960*. New York: McGraw-Hill, 1962.

University of Virginia. *University of Virginia Record*. Charlottesville: University of Virginia, various years.

University of Virginia. *University of Virginia Budget*. Charlottesville: University of Virginia, various years.

Upcraft, M. Lee and Leila V. Moore. "Evolving Theoretical Perspectives of Student Development," in *New Futures For Student Affairs: Building a Vision for Professional Leadership and Practice*. eds., Margaret J. Barr, M. Lee Upcraft, and Assocs. San Francisco: Jossey-Bass, 1990.

Van Doren, John. "The Beginnings of the Great Books Movement at Columbia," *Columbia: the Magazine of Columbia University*, Winter 2001, 26.

Van Doren, Mark. *Liberal Education*. New York: Henry Holt and Company, 1943.

_____. *The Autobiography of Mark Van Doren*. New York: Harcourt, Brace, and Co., 1958.

Veysey, Laurence. *The Emergence of the American University*. Chicago: University of Chicago Press, 1965.

Wagoner, Jennings L., Jr. "Honor and Dishonor at Mr. Jefferson's University: The Antebellum Years." *History of Education Quarterly*, vol. 26, 1986.

Ward, F. Champion, ed. *The Idea and Practice of General Education*. Chicago: University of Chicago Press, 1950, 1992.

Wertenbaker, Thomas Jefferson. *Princeton, 1746–1896*. Princeton: Princeton University Press, 1946.

Willimon, William H. and Thomas H. Naylor. *The Abandoned Generation: Rethinking Higher Education*. Grand Rapids, MI: Wm. B. Eerdmans Publishing Co., 1995.

Winterer, Caroline. "The Humanist Revolution in America,1820–1860: Classical Antiquity in the Colleges." *History of Higher Education Annual 1998*, Vol. 18., 111–129.

Wofford, Harris, Jr., ed. *Embers of The World: Conversations with Scott Buchanan*. Santa Barbara: The Center for the Study of Democratic Institutions, 1969.

Index

A

Adler, Mortimer, 2, 7, 13, 56, 173; Aquinas and, 35–36; Chicago Committee on the Liberal Arts, 108; educational philosophy of, 46–47, 52, 127, 206n. 21, 210n. 59, 221n. 12; great books and, 61; influence on Buchanan, 55, 58–59, 60, 101–102; influence on Hutchins, 35–37, 39; People's Institute and, 58, 69; Scott Buchanan and, 58–59, 60, 101–102, 122; St. John's College and, 123, 124; Stockbridge proposal and, 146–47; University of Chicago and, 61, 105–106, 108, 226n. 37, 234n. 47

Albert the Great, 35

Alderman, Edwin A., 59, 92, 218n. 71, 219n. 86; University of Virginia and, 44, 49, 53, 57

antebellum colleges, 18–20, 41–43; curriculum of, 18–20; for Blacks, 24; for women, 20–21; student life at, 21

Aquinas, Thomas, 35, 211n. 82, 220n.101

Aristotle, 35–36, 74, 89, 188; philosophies, 17

Ashemore, Harry, 2

Aydelotte, Frank: *Breaking the Academic Lockstep*, 135–37, 179; honors programs and, 4, 55, 93, 138–39, 164–65, 198–200, 217n. 65, 232n. 8, 240n. 86; Swarthmore College and, 136–37

B

B. A. degree, 18

B. S. degree, 18

Balz, Albert, 58, 142

Barr, Ida, 120, 123, 175

Barr, Stringfellow, 3, 7, 13, 213n. 25; Chicago Committee on the Liberal Arts and, 108–110, 111, 118–20; critics of, 173–74; educational philosophy of, 51–52, 126, 132; Foundation for World Government and, 162, 166, 173, 240n. 1; great books curriculum and, 39, 164–65; influences of, 51–52; Mellon and, 151–55; professorial style of, 49–51; return to University of Virginia, 171–77, 183; Scott Buchanan and, 48–49, 113, 218n. 68, 220n. 103; St. John's College and, 120–34, 148, 149, 165; Stockbridge proposal and, 146–48; the Virginia Plan and, 44–49, 54–55, 57, 60, 61, 62, 69–100, 110, 218n. 71, 220n. 1, 221n. 9; University of Chicago and, 38, 39, 98, 101, 102–107, 108, 225nn. 22; University of Virginia and, 49, 51–52, 54, 56, 118–20, 123, 149–61, 166–69, 236nn. 94. 95, 240n. 1

Bell, Daniel, 9–10, 29, 30, 31, 32–33, 37, 55

Benton, A. F., 70

Bice, Raymond, 174, 188, 238n. 50

Black Mountain College, 127

Bloom, Allan, 12

Boole, George, 58

Bourdieu, Pierre, 5

Bowers, Fredson, 180–81, 200

Boyer, Ernest, 8–11, 28, 32, 206n. 24, 209n. 43

Brubacher, John, 9–10, 26, 197, 198

Buchanan, Scott, 3, 7, 13, 240n. 1; Adler and, 55, 58–59, 60, 101–102; Barr and, 48–49, 70, 218nn. 68; Chicago Committee on the Liberal Arts and, 108–110, 111–16; competition with Gooch, 61–67; educational philosophy of, 24, 56, 126, 132, 210n. 59, 213nn. 22; great books scheme of, 61–67, 77, 78, 122, 189, 200, 220n. 103, 222n. 18, 227nn. 76, 228n. 79; honors courses at Virginia and, 61–62, 215n. 43; Hutchins and, 57–58, 111–16; Oxbridge tradition and, 125, 219n. 85; professorial style of, 50; St. John's College and, 121–34, 148, 229n. 111; Stockbridge proposal and, 146–48; the Virginia Plan and, 44–49, 53, 54–55, 57, 60, 61–67, 69–100, 122, 140, 222n. 31; University of Chicago and, 38, 98, 102–107; University of Virginia and, 56–59, 61, 70, 71, 82, 151–61, 218nn. 68

Buchler, Justus, 29

Burgess, John, 29

Burton, Ernest DeWitt, 33, 37

247

C

Cambridge: tutorial method at, 12, 83, 207n. 37
Carnegie Foundation, 92–93
Chicago Committee on the Liberal Arts (*see also* University of Chicago), 37–38, 101–105, 107–16, 119, 159; antagonism toward, 105–106, 109; Barr and, 108–110, 111, 118–20; Buchanan and, 108–110, 111–16; members of, 108–109, 117; problems of, 109–10; proposals of, 108, 121; report of, 117–18; St. John's College and, 122
Clark, Charles, 127–28
Classics, the: ancient, 63; at St. John's College, 1; curriculum, 86; liberal arts and, 75; literary, 74; modern, 55–56, 63; scientific, 74; teaching, 55–56, 71–72; Western, 2, 55–56
Clemons, Harry, 149
Cleveland, Richard, 121
College: of Charleston, 44; of William and Mary, 43
college within a college, 181–84, 200
colonial colleges, 16–18, 29, 41–43; curriculum of, 17; *in loco parentis* and, 17–18
Columbia University: Colloquium, 69, 107, 124; Contemporary Civilization course at, 30–31; core curriculum at, 2, 29, 72, 141; general education movement at, 15, 27, 29–31; General Honors courses at, 27, 29–31, 38, 45, 61; great books courses at, 2, 30–31, 45, 62; history of, 29–30; liberal arts movement at, 15, 31
Committee to Frame a World Constitution, 162–63
core courses: in Western civilization, 5, 8
curricular reform: history in United States, 13, 41, 83; liberal arts movement and, 5, 8, 23; movements, 10–11, 13, 27, 30, 39, 100, 139, 145, 177, 198, 209n. 43, 216n. 61; undergraduate, 5
curricular reform at the University of Virginia: appeal of, 52–55; committees for, 140–43; history of, 3, 15, 202, 216n. 61; liberal arts movement and, 6; obstacles to, 103, 200; President Darden and, 163–66, 172; President Newcomb and, 59–61; proposals for, 177–87; Virginia Plan and (*see* Virginia Plan)
curriculum: classical, 17, 19–20, 22, 85, 88; college, 20; core, 5, 8, 23; cultural and civic issues and, 39–40; distribution requirements, 27; elective, 21–24, 28, 30, 86, 88, 142; extra-, 28; freedom and restrictions in, 16; great books, 108; history of American, 6–7, 16–29; innovation in, 20–21; Jeffersonian, 86, 201–202, 222n. 18; lack of cohesion in, 192; liberal arts (*see* liberal arts curriculum); liberal culture and, 27; universal, 19

D

Dabney, Richard, 48–49, 83
Dabney, Virginius, 60, 99, 222n. 31
Dalton, Jack, 184
Darden, Colgate, 144, 236n. 94; a new Virginia Plan and, 166–69, 182; Barr and, 160–61, 162–63, 166–69, 172–74; Unversity of Virginia and, 148–57, 163–64
declension: fear of, 39–40, 52, 56
Denby, David, 2
Depression, the: education and, 10, 27, 91, 136
Dewey, John, 27, 129–31, 133, 199
Dobie, Armistead, 45
Donnelly, Francis, 129
DuBois, W. E. B., 24–25
Duren, William, 192, 194, 240n. 85
Dzuback, Mary Ann, 2, 103

E

Echols, William H., 194
Echols Scholars Program, 194–195
education: democratic, 16; elite, 16, 41, 83, 184, 187, 194, 201; general (*see* general education); goals of, 16, 209n. 51; liberal (*see* liberal education); of Blacks, 24–25; of women, 20–21, 24–25, 208n. 17; philosophy of, 20, 192, 199; practical/vocational, 18, 24–25, 28, 73; public, 41
elective courses: critics of, 22–23; history of, 21–24, 26; proprietorship of, 8
electivism: higher education and, 42–43, 85; issue of, 32, 42, 197, 212n. 1; philosophy of, 43
Eliot, Charles W., 22–23, 26, 42, 86, 197, 208nn. 22
English education models, 26, 198, 212n. 14
Enlightenment, 17
Erskine, John, 45; Columbia University and, 30–31, 38; General Honors course, 2, 11, 61, 210n. 59

Index • **249**

F
Faulkner, W. Harrison, 98
Ferguson, G. O., 70
Field, Marshall, 93, 160
Filbey, E. T., 103
Forrestal, James V., 146, 158
Foundation for World Government, 162, 166, 173, 240n. 1
Franklin, Benjamin, 19
fraternities, 28, 126
Frodin, Reuben, 110

G
general education, 6, 8–10, 26–28; critics of, 181; definition of, 9; reform, 9, 135–40; traditional model of, 10
general education movements: common curriculum and, 39; goals and values of, 10, 15, 27–28, 206n. 24
general/liberal education: confusion about, 9–11, 206n. 24, 232n. 17; liberal arts movement and, 10–11, 23, 71
German: higher education ideals, 21, 26; research model of education, 30, 198
Glenn, Garrard, 133
Gooch Committee (*see also* Virginia Plan), 60, 61–67, 70–100, 101, 111, 165, 178, 222n. 31; great books scheme and, 84–94, 107; on Degrees with Honors, 177–84; President's List Authority, 64–66; report on honors courses, 64–65, 69–80, 95–98
Gooch, Robert, 3, 8, 13, 119, 199; competition with Buchanan, 61–67, 219n. 91, 220n. 99; honors tutorial scheme and, 61–67, 69, 81, 125, 193, 200, 224n. 59; Liberal Arts Seminars and, 188; professorial style of, 49–50; the Virginia Plan and, 44–49, 53, 54–55, 60, 61–67, 69–100; University of Virginia and, 150–51, 166
Gottschalk, Louis, 119–20
Great Books Foundation, 38
great books movement, 38, 47, 199; philosophy of, 56, 63–66, 82–83, 113–14; unity of knowledge and, 65–66
great books program at St. John's College, 10, 98, 124–33, 145, 234n. 47; Barr and Buchanan and, 145, 159; curriculum of, 2, 4, 100, 171; traditional liberal arts and, 1; Virginia Plan and, 11, 32, 81–82, 84, 157, 164–65, 202, 221n. 9
great books program at University of Virginia, 210n. 67; Barr and, 39, 150–51, 154–56, 157–59, 160–61, 162, 164, 167–69, 171–73; Buchanan and, 160; for underclassmen, 178, 183, 187, 191; Gooch and, 150–51, 155, 164, 166; Hutchins and, 155, 161; Mellon and, 153–56, 157–59; President Darden and, 150–51, 154–57, 160–61, 162, 164, 166–68; President Newcomb and, 153; upperclassmen and, 193; Virginia Plan and, 124, 153, 163–66, 192 (*see also* Virginia Plan)
great books programs, 5, 6, 8, 12, 37, 202, 210n. 67; Columbia University, 2, 30; definition of, 11–12, 207n. 33; influence of, 197–98; St. John's College (*see* great books program at St. John's College); University of Virginia (*see* great books program at University of Virginia)
"Greats" honor revival at Oxford, 55–56
Greek Revival: college curriculum and, 20
Gwathmey, Allan T., 95–96, 149–50, 223n. 43, 234n. 57

H
Harper, William Rainey, 2, 33–34, 37
Harris, Michael, 2
Hart, Francis, 195
Harvard University: founding of, 15, 16, 20; *General Education in a Free Society,* 139; *Red Book,* the, 139, 141, 167; Report on General Education, 167
higher education: African American, 24–25; American, 99; curriculum and, 16–29; fear of declension in, 16; German, 21; great books and, 67; history of, 15; liberal arts movement and, 4; purpose and goals of, 16–18, 209n. 51; the student and, 16–29
honors: seminars, 2, 27, 136–37; students (*see* students, honors)
honors program(s), 4, 8, 85–86, 135, 198; definitions of, 12–13; general education reform and, 135–40; Swarthmore, 12, 99, 135–37; tutorials and, 13, 199; Unversity of Virginia (*see* University of Virginia)
honors program(s) at University of Virginia, 51, 53, 54, 60–61, 62–63, 66, 70, 73–83, 85, 93–100, 112, 135, 138–39, 164, 177–78, 192–94, 195–96, 198, 200–201, 218n. 71, 223n. 40, 232n. 8
Hook, Sidney, 131–32, 199

Hutchins, Robert Maynard, 2, 7, 12, 13, 27–28, 32, 173, 240n. 1; Adler and, 35–37, 39; Barr and, 101; Buchanan and, 57–59, 102, 111–16; Committee on Liberal Arts and, 37–38, 101–104, 107, 109, 111–18 (*see also* Chicago Committee on the Liberal Arts); curricular philosophy of, 37, 39; educational philosophy of, 34–35, 37, 110, 127–29, 132; St. John's College and, 122, 134; Stockbridge proposal and, 146–47; University of Chicago and, 33–34, 61, 103, 226n. 37, 234n. 47

Hyman, Sidney, 38

I

in loco parentis: colleges as, 17–18, 21, 23; decline of, 28–29

Inter-University Council on the Superior Student, 198

J

Jacksonians, 19

Jefferson's University of Virginia, 22, 41–44, 53

Jefferson, Thomas, 3, 19; educational philosophy of, 41–42, 85–86, 98, 128; Enlightenment philosophy of, 41

Jennings, John, 94

K

Kass, Amy, 4, 7, 8, 30, 82–83, 199, 220n. 103, 241n. 9

Keppel, Frederick, 92–93

Kerr, Clark, 192

Kessler, Glenn, 196

Kimball, Bruce, 3, 10–11, 16, 198

L

land-grant institutions, 21

Levine, Arthur, 8–11, 28, 32, 206n. 24, 209n. 43

Levine, Lawrence, 197

Lewis, Ivey F., 141, 149, 164–66, 168, 199

liberal artists: critics of, 35, 86–87, 116, 127–32, 199–200; curriculum reform and, 7–10; definition of, 7; liberal education and, 9, 12; philosophy of education and, 20, 47, 63

liberal arts: colleges, 19; curriculum, 6; definition of, 6, 7–8, 74, 107, 113; elective system and, 52; history of, 17; liberal arts movement and, 13; seven, 47, 86, 107, 189, 206n. 21, 207n. 3; the classics and, 75

liberal arts education: at the university, 5, 56; Blacks and, 25; traditional conceptions of, 3

liberal arts movement, 3, 129, 159, 202; curricular reform and, 5, 8–11, 134; definition of, 6, 7–8, 205n. 1, 206n. 24; general education and, 23; goals of, 28; great books and, 11, 199; higher education and, 4, 6, 112, 134; influence of, 197–98; origins and founders of, 7, 13, 26–27, 54; University of Virginia and, 6, 16, 60, 82, 139; Virginia Plan and, 82

Liberal Arts, Incorporated, 145–59; members of, 146; Stockbridge proposal and, 146–47, 153; University of Virginia and, 149, 153–61

liberal culture, 24, 26–28; elitism of, 27; philosophy of, 26; proponents of, 39

liberal education, 6, 8–10, 26; confusion about, 133, 206n. 24; definition of, 9, 74, 206n. 24; elitism of, 112–13; importance of, 141; liberal arts movement and, 13; programs, 1, 71–72; reform, 144, 145; traditions of, 16, 73–74, 112, 115–16, 129–30

Lippmann, Walter, 1, 4, 126, 145, 198

Lowell, Abbott Lawrence, 26

Lucas, Christopher, 9, 232n. 17

Luck, J. J., 70, 165

M

MacLean, Malcom, 129

Mallett, Marcus, 182–84, 187, 191, 192, 194, 238n. 50

Malone, Dumas, 49

Marsden, George, 23

Mayer, Milton, 2

McCosh, James, 22–24

McKeon, Richard, 7, 13, 38, 45–46, 58–59; educational philosophy of, 52, 69, 115; Stockbridge proposal and, 147; University of Chicago and, 102–103, 109

McNeill, William, 2, 34, 37, 102, 110

Meiklejohn, Alexander: Amherst College and, 30, 45, 48, 210n. 59; Experimental College at Wisconsin-Madison and, 8; general education reform and, 27, 129–31, 133–34; liberal arts movement and, 7, 13; Stockbridge proposal and, 147

Mellon, Andrew W., 148

Mellon, Paul, 145–46; St. John's endowment and, 146–48; Stockbridge proposal and, 146–48, 150; University of Virginia and, 149, 151–61, 173, 178–79
Middle Ages, 16–17, 28, 129
Miller, Francis, 121
Miller, Richard, 3, 5–6
Moral philosophy, 17
Moran, Charles E., 174
Morrill Acts of 1862 and 1890, 21
multiversities, 192

N
Nelson, Charles, 2, 4, 82
Newcomb, John: Barr and, 119, 123–24; curricular reform and, 59–61, 140, 177; funding for Virginia Plan and, 101, 104, 153; Gooch and, 61; the Virginia Plan and, 60, 64, 69–100, 200, 222n. 31; University of Virginia and, 6, 54, 87, 216n. 56, 219nn. 86, 224n. 59; Virginia's honors program and, 53, 113, 165

O
Old Dominion Foundation, 145–46, 148; Stockbridge proposal and, 150; University of Virginia and, 149, 151–61, 178–79
Olinger, Chauncey, 224n. 59, 238n. 36; Barr and, 175–76, 184, 237n. 22
organized athletics, 28
Oxbridge academic tradition, 82, 100, 125, 199, 217n. 63; colonial colleges and, 16; reforms of, 83, 224n. 59
Oxbridge tutorial, 55, 207n. 37; American education and, 3; honors courses and, 55, 62; St. John's and, 82; Virginia Plan and, 12, 67, 83, 100, 125, 201

P
paideia, 19, 26
Parallel and Partial Courses, 18, 20
Peirce, C. S., 115
People's Institute, 48, 213n. 17; adult seminars at, 69, 107, 124
Petengill, John, 196
Peters, Edward, 35–36
Pilley, John, 128–29
Plato, 36
Price, Governor James, 83
Princeton University, 19, 22, 135, 141, 201
Protestantism, 16–17
Puritanism, 16-17, 23, 39

Q
quadrivium: arts of, 7, 115–16, 206n. 24; curriculum, 59, 69, 75–76, 85, 88, 89; historical terminology of, 7, 17, 74, 207n. 3; seven liberal arts and, 7, 46–47, 63
Quintilian, *11*

R
Raven Society, 48
Renaissance, 17
research universities, 21
Reuben, Julie, 28, 192, 209n. 51
Rhodes Scholars, 12, 52, 55, 83
Rice, John Andrews, 127
Rockefeller, John D., 37, 211n. 90
Rogers, William B., 43
Rosenwald, Julius, 102
Rubin, Arthur, 102, 110
Rudolph, Frederick: educational philosophy of, 18; great books philosophy and, 5–6; history of American education and, 21–22, 27–28, 39, 86–87, 134, 135, 200, 201
Rudy, Willis, 9–10, 26, 197, 198
Russell, Bertrand, 35–36, 211n. 82

S
"separate spheres," 21, 25
Shepard, Donald, 154
Shepherd, Henry, 44
Shepperson, Archibald, 180, 186, 200
Smith, J. Winifree: *A Search for the Liberal College*, 4, 82, 100, 199, 220n. 101; Buchanan and, 50
Socrates, 18
Sophistes, 18
Spengler, Oswald, 51–52
Sputnik: educational concerns and, 11, 13, 140
St. John's College, 228n. 98, 229n. 123, 230n. 125; board of, 121; Buchanan and, 121–34, 145, 159, 233n. 37; critics of, 127–32, 134; curriculum of, 2, 27, 122, 132–33; great books program at (*see* great books program at St. John's College); in Santa Fe, 148; Mellon endowment for, 146–48, 158–59, 233n. 37; New Program at (*see* great books program at St. John's College); Stringfellow Barr and, 101, 120–34, 145, 159, 228nn. 100, 233n.36; student life at, 126; tutorial work at, 82
Stern, Marion Rosenwald, 102

Stockbridge proposal, the, 234n. 48; Barr and, 147, 149, 152, 155; Darden and, 148–50, 152, 155; failure of, 148–49, 150–55, 157–58; Liberal Arts, Inc. and, 148–49, 153, 155; Mellon and, 146, 148–50, 152–53, 155; Old Dominion and, 147–48, 152; origins of, 146–48; sponsors of, 147
Stocker, Arthur, 196, 200
Streeter, Robert, 38–39
student(s): counseling, 24; culture, 28–29, 126; elite, 83, 184, 187, 194, 201; honors, 62, 66, 90, 95, 99, 136–39, 181, 193, 195, 200, 223n. 44; service professionals, 28–29
Summa Theologica, 35-36
Swarthmore College (*see also* Frank Aydelotte): honors programs at, 12, 99, 135–37

T
Taliaferro, Catesby, 105, 108–109, 111; St. John's College and, 122–23
Thomas, George, 187-88
Ticknor, George, 42
traditional liberal arts, 7; undergraduate education, 1
trivium, 63; arts of, 7, 17, 46, 59, 115–16, 206n. 24; curriculum, 75, 85, 88–89; historical terminology of, 47, 74, 207n. 3
tutorial method of instruction, 2, 12, 78, 136–38; English, 12, 138; individual, 139

U
unity of knowledge, 64, 66
University of Chicago: Barr and, 38, 39, 98, 101, 102–107, 108, 225nn. 22; Board of Trustees of, 102; Buchanan and, 38, 98, 102–107; Committee on the Liberal Arts (*see* Chicago Committee on the Liberal Arts); curriculum of, 2, 33, 37, 72; general education movement at, 15, 32–39; greats books course at, 61, 62, 81; honors courses at, 27; liberal arts movement at, 15; New Plan of, 37, 103; role in liberal arts education, 2
University of Virginia: academic standing of, 54; Balz Committee, 142; Classics Department at, 196; Committee of Ten, 143; Committee on Academic Legislation, 84, 94, 97, 184, 224n. 59; Committee on College Poicy, 163; Committee on Degrees with Honors, 177–80, 182, 193, 195; Committee on Honors Courses, 44, 60–62, 64, 66, 70–100, 121, 137, 165, 177–78, 192–93, 223nn. 40, 224n. 59; Committee on Special Programs, 195–96, 223n. 40; Committee on the Lower Division, 182–86, 191; Committee on the Post-War College, 141–42, 149; curricular reform at (*see* curricular reform at the University of Virginia); Curriculum Committee on Requirements, 142; degree requirements of, 142, 163, 181, 214n. 27, 215n. 45, 223n. 44; departmental honors programs at, 181–82; Distinguished Majors Program at, 196; Echols Scholars Program, 194–95; electivism at, 42, 142, 163–64, 195; Final Honors Examinations at, 195, 215n. 48; Finances, 91; General Honors program, 178–86, 187, 195, 200; General Honors Staff, 178–80, 184; great books courses and (*see* great books programs at University of Virginia); history of, 15, 41; honors programs at (*see* honors program at University of Virginia); Jefferson's curriculum at, 41–42; Liberal Arts Committee, 144; Liberal Arts Department, 191; liberal arts movement and, 6, 188; Liberal Arts Seminars, 188–92, 193, 200; Liberal Arts, Inc. and, 149, 151–61; Lower Division Seminar program, 182–86, 187–92, 194, 238n. 50, 239n. 62; Old Dominion Foundation and, 149, 151–61, 173, 178–79; role in promoting liberal learning by, 4; School of General Studies, 167, 168; schools within, 43; seminars at, 179, 188; Special Committee on Curriculum, 141–42; the Virginia Plan and (*see* Virginia Plan); traditional liberal arts program at, 1; tutorial programs at, 179, 188, 192, 194, 200, 224n. 59; undergraduate program at, 50, 52, 54, 182, 185, 188; university seminars at, 192

V
Van Doren, Mark, 7, 13, 31, 45–46, 123; St. John's College and, 123, 126–27; Stockbridge proposal and, 147
Veysey, Laurence, 6, 23, 209n. 41
Vietnam era: third general education reform and, 11, 13
Virginia Plan of 1935 (*see also* Gooch Committee; great books program at University of Virginia): 70-80; Appendix

A of (*see* Virginia Plan, Appendix A); Appendix B of (*see* Virginia Plan, Appendix B); comprehensive exams of, 83; contents of, 73–80; crafters of, 43, 44–49, 60, 87–88; creation of, 52, 69–100; debates about, 22; drafting of, 10; elite quality of, 83, 112–13, 183, 221n. 12; faculty self-interest and, 5; failure to implement, 67, 90–93, 103, 166; financial constraints of, 90–93, 101, 153, 166; for underclassmen, 84–93, 101, 166, 183; for upperclassmen, 84, 93–100; general education and, 71; Gooch Committee (*see* Gooch Committee); great books and, 38, 61–67, 81, 83, 84–93, 110, 122, 145, 202, 220n. 1; history of, 15, 54, 164–66; Honors Degrees of, 79–80, 142; honors students of, 99; honors tutorial work and, 12, 61–67, 78, 81–83, 98–99, 137; influence of, 197–99; liberal arts movement and, 6, 26–27, 107, 197–98, 202, 241n. 10; peak and decline of, 187–96; philosophy of, 11, 142; President's List Authority, 65–66; program of instruction for, 75–79; quadrivium component of, 74, 75–77, 85, 88, 89; reception of, 69–100, 199; reforms of, 29; revised versions of, 182–96; significance of, 16; three sections of, 69; trivium component of, 74, 75, 85, 88–89
Virginia Plan, Appendix A, 4, 83, 168, 220n. 111, 221n. 9; Barr and, 3, 84, 86; Buchanan and, 3, 86, 87; funding for, 94–95, 98, 101, 165–66; provisions of, 71–72, 73–79; underclassmen and, 84–93, 181–92
Virginia Plan, Appendix B, 4, 84, 125, 165, 188, 221n. 9; Committee on Degrees with Honors and, 177–79; Gooch and, 3; provisions of, 71, 73, 79–83; upperclassmen and, 84, 93–100
vocational training, 24–25, 28, 73

W

Wallis, Charles, 105, 108–109, 111; St. John's College and, 122–23
Washington, Booker T., 24
West, Andrew Fleming, 26
Wilson, James Southall, 98
Wisconsin Idea, the, 24
Wofford, Harris, 2
Woodberry, George E., 26
World War I: first general education movement and, 10, 13, 27, 30, 39, 139, 209n. 43
World War II: globalist movements after, 162–63; second general education movement and, 10–11, 100, 139, 145, 177, 198, 209n. 43, 216n. 61
Wright, David McCord, 173, 185–86, 200, 239n. 57

Y

Yalden-Thompson, David: Committee on Degrees with Honors and, 182, 192–94, 224n. 59, 232n. 8, 240n. 85; Virginia Plan and, 137–38, 187
Yale Report of 1828, 18–20, 22, 43